ECONOMIC AND SOCIAL SURVEY OF ASIA AND THE PACIFIC 2010

SUSTAINING RECOVERY AND DYNAMISM FOR INCLUSIVE DEVELOPMENT

UNITED NATIONS
ESCAP
Economic and Social Commission for Asia and the Pacific

ECONOMIC AND SOCIAL SURVEY OF ASIA AND THE PACIFIC 2010

*Sustaining Recovery and Dynamism
for Inclusive Development*

United Nations publication
Sales No. E.10.II.F.2
Copyright © United Nations 2010
All rights reserved
Manufactured in Thailand
ISBN: 978-92-1-120592-3
ISSN: 0252-5704
ST/ESCAP/2547

FOREWORD

The Asia-Pacific region leads the process of recovery from the global financial and economic crisis and emerges as a focus of global growth and stability.

However, the recovery of the world economy at large remains fragile. This poses risks for sustained recovery in Asia as well, given its export dependence. A more balanced recovery is needed and this will require more globally concerted policy efforts.

As we embrace the emerging role of the region as a significant driver of economic growth, we should not lose sight of the challenges ahead. In parts of Asia, unemployment rates are still up and poverty remains widespread. Without addressing the poverty and climate change challenges, economic growth will prove elusive over time.

The challenges are linked. Our solutions must be, too. We must recognize our interdependence; no nation can hope to find economic security without taking into account the well-being of others. Therefore our strategies must address both global and regional imbalances, and must do so in many spheres at once: economic, social and environmental.

The United Nations will convene a Summit in September 2010 to review progress in achieving the Millennium Development Goals (MDGs). The Asia-Pacific region has made remarkable headway, which demonstrates that the MDGs are indeed achievable. But more needs to be done to scale up successes and identify and remove barriers and obstacles. Five years before the 2015 deadline, the Summit provides us with a timely opportunity to address major interconnected development challenges and to give the MDGs a final push, including in the Asia-Pacific region.

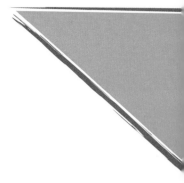

In this regard, the *2010 Economic and Social Survey of Asia and the Pacific* provides a comprehensive analysis of the challenging policy landscape and offers recommendations for the way forward. In the aftermath of the crisis, we see clear momentum for regional economic cooperation. ESCAP, as the only intergovernmental forum which brings together all the countries and territories in the Asia-Pacific region, will be playing a critical role in leading the deliberations over next steps.

As it turns out, the global crisis may give new impetus for establishing a robust regional framework for economic cooperation that will help us build more equal and sustainable economies in Asia and the Pacific. This would not only be the region's gain, but essential for the sustainable development of the world at large.

BAN Ki-moon
Secretary-General of the United Nations

April 2010

EXECUTIVE SECRETARY'S PREFACE

By early 2010, following the first global economic contraction in modern history, the contours of a V-shaped rebound were evident in the Asia-Pacific economies – assisted in large part by a number of unprecedented fiscal stimulus packages. But the rebound remains fragile and uneven, with a number of downside risks. While 2009 was a year of emergency crisis management, 2010 will be a year when economic policy making will be even more complex. Turning the rebound into a sustained recovery will mean keeping up the momentum while maintaining macroeconomic stability in the face of rising inflationary tendencies and the potential for asset bubbles.

The crisis has also drawn attention to the underlying global and regional structural imbalances built up over decades. Redressing these multiple imbalances and development gaps, and achieving a sustained recovery after the withdrawal of the fiscal stimuli, will require moving towards fairer, more balanced and sustainable patterns of development. Asia and the Pacific is unlikely to be able to return to business as usual. Instead it will increasingly have to drive its own development and create new sources of economic growth from within the region.

In this radically altered global panorama, the Asia-Pacific region is now emerging as a central participant in international economic relations. To fulfil this potential, however, it will need to implement an ambitious set of policies. The *Economic and Social Survey of Asia and the Pacific 2010* explores this complex environment and – lest the V-shaped rebound induces complacency – outlines the elements of a coherent regional policy agenda.

2009: an uneven pattern of impacts

Even at the height of this crisis, Asia and the Pacific displayed a new-found resilience. Its developing economies achieved an annual growth rate of 4.0%, making it the fastest-growing region in the world. However, almost all of this growth came from the two most populous countries: China, which grew by 8.7%, and India, by 7.2%. Indeed, excluding these fast-growing sub-continental economies, the Asia-Pacific developing economies contracted in 2009 by 0.6%.

These contrasting performances resulted from many different factors. The first concerned the extent of dependence on developed country markets. All the worst-affected countries had shares of exports to GDP that exceeded 60%, and the greater the share of these exports that were absorbed by the developed markets the greater was the economic contraction. Related to this, the countries most exposed to global trade perturbations were those, including many in East and South-East Asia, whose exports involved regional production networking arrangements – for products such as apparel, machinery, electronics, and motor vehicles. They saw their exports plummet almost twice as rapidly as in the 1997 crisis. On the other hand, countries such as Bangladesh, which exported simpler products such as low-cost garments, became more competitive and gained market share. There is also evidence that intra-regional trade has continued to expand, especially through exports to China and India.

The second factor concerned the extent of exposure to the exit of portfolio capital as investors sought to cover their losses in the western capital markets. This brought pressures on exchange rates and created financial instability as well as liquidity problems in countries that did not have adequate reserves. Although, compared with the 1997 crisis, more countries had strong foreign exchange reserves, some had to arrange bilateral swaps, as the Republic of Korea and Singapore, or seek liquidity from the IMF, as Pakistan and Sri Lanka. Nevertheless, it is by no means clear what is an optimum stock of foreign reserves since, as the crisis revealed, holding foreign reserves idle also entails both costs and risks. *Survey 2010* proposes a yardstick for gauging such vulnerabilities.

The third factor explaining the contrasting experiences was the varying capacity to respond. The countries best able to mount rapid and large counter-cyclical spending programmes were those that entered the crisis with strong macroeconomic fundamentals; in particular, stable inflationary trends, sound fiscal balances and low ratios of public debt to GDP. The massive additional fiscal spending helped reduce the impact of lower exports and the falling demand for services such as tourism, as well as reduced growth of migrant remittances. Even more important, the stimulus also afforded some protection to the vulnerable workers who had lost their jobs, typically the unskilled and very often women in the manufacturing sector and in the informal economy.

A quantitative analysis reported in *Survey 2010* shows that the stimulus packages certainly had an impact – offsetting to some extent the loss of exports. For the key economies of the region, *Survey 2010* shows that for each $1.00 lost in exports there was an average loss of $0.88 in GDP – though the figure ranged from $1.1 in Japan, to $0.4 in Malaysia and Singapore, and to $0.7 for China. If the only variable affecting GDP had been a shortfall of exports, then GDP growth in 2009 would have dropped by 7.8 percentage points. However, the actual shortfall in 2009 was only 4.2 percentage points – thanks largely to the region's fiscal stimulus packages. The forecasts also suggest that Asia and the Pacific is unlikely to see a return to pre-crisis export growth rates. In the medium term the region will need to look beyond expansionary policies and instead seek new engines to sustain the region's dynamism.

The outlook for 2010: a sharp rebound, with downside risks

The outlook for 2010 has improved significantly. The Asia-Pacific developing economies are forecast to grow by 7.0% in 2010 compared to 4.0% in 2009, led by the self-sustaining motors of China, growing at 9.5%, and India at 8.3%.

But the road ahead has a number of potential pitfalls. One concerns protectionism. Many developed countries, facing anaemic growth coupled with high unemployment, may restrict trade. This has led to prominent trade disputes that pit developed countries against large exporters from this region. Another concern is that greater liquidity in the global financial system is finding its way to Asia-Pacific emerging markets – causing exchange rates to appreciate, stoking inflationary pressures, and leading to the formation of asset bubbles. There are also echoes of the food-fuel crisis of 2007, with food prices rising again in some countries and causing special hardship for the poor.

Policy-makers are thus faced with tough balancing acts on both monetary and fiscal policy. While they will want to tighten monetary policy to restrain inflationary pressures they will need to maintain real interest rates at par with global levels – to keep their exchange rates competitive and to encourage domestic economic growth. And while they will inevitably have to move toward fiscal consolidation they will have to judge the timing and sequencing carefully if they are not to choke off economic recovery and trigger the need for further stimulus packages. Another policy consideration will be to manage portfolio capital inflows through various types of capital control. The benefits of maintaining open capital accounts, if any, are ambiguous. Instead there is a growing consensus that capital controls should be seen as important components of the policy toolkit.

As argued by the APEC leaders at their November 2009 Summit in Singapore, the advanced economies are unlikely to be able to return to 'growth as usual' or 'trade as usual'. Even if the advanced countries achieve a substantial economic recovery their demand for imports from Asia and the Pacific will not return to pre-crisis levels. This is because in order to unwind the global imbalances, many of the developed economies will need to restrain debt-fuelled consumption. The Asia-Pacific countries, for their part, will therefore need to seek new sources of growth – 'rebalancing' their economies in favour of greater domestic and regional consumption.

Survey 2010 explores different imbalances and gaps – macroeconomic, social, developmental, and ecological – and considers the potential of closing them for creating additional aggregate demand that could serve as new regional impulses for growth.

Imbalances, gaps and new sources of growth

In the past, the global imbalances have assisted the Asia-Pacific region by providing expanding markets for exports, and augmenting foreign exchange reserves. But these imbalances are not sustainable. They have resulted in growing trade and current account imbalances which the United States in particular, with its high levels of accumulated debt, will have to unwind.

There are also macroeconomic imbalances within the region – notably between the economies of East and South-East Asia and those of South Asia. In East and South-East Asia net exports have been increasing as a proportion of GDP growth while in South Asia they have been increasingly negative. In the case of East Asia this reflects a declining share of consumption in long-term growth, and in the case of South-East Asia, a declining share of fixed investment. In South Asia's case, on the other hand, the share of investment has been rising along with growing net imports.

Perhaps the most disturbing aspect of the global imbalances is the anomaly of capital flowing from Asia-Pacific developing countries to finance consumption and investment in rich countries such as the United States. This has happened largely because Asia and the Pacific lacks a well developed regional financial architecture that might have enabled the countries running current account surpluses to deploy these productively in other parts of the region.

At the same time, Asia and the Pacific has large socioeconomic and development gaps. Although the region as a whole has achieved rapid economic growth that has helped lift millions of people out of poverty it is still home to over 950 million people living under the $1.25 per day poverty line. Moreover, development has been very uneven, across subregions and between countries. This is reflected in varying patterns of progress towards the Millennium Development Goals – with South-East Asia leading the way and South Asia and the Pacific Island economies lagging behind. There are similar gaps in the levels of infrastructure development; this is evident from the composite infrastructure development scores presented in *Survey 2010*. Some economies register high scores, including: Singapore; Japan; New Zealand; Republic of Korea; Australia; Brunei Darussalam; Hong Kong, China; and Macao, China. Others still have considerable infrastructure gaps, particularly the least developed, landlocked and small island economies, such as Papua New Guinea, Nepal, Lao People's Democratic Republic, Solomon Islands, Cambodia, Bhutan, Vanuatu, and Mongolia. If the countries of the region invest in closing these socio-economic development gaps they cannot only lift levels of human development but also boost regional aggregate demand – making economic growth more inclusive and sustainable. This will demand high and sustained levels of investment that will rely on creating a new regional financial architecture that can be used to mobilize the necessary resources – from within the region and beyond.

The Asia-Pacific region also has serious ecological imbalances. These are evident, for example, in the degradation of key natural resources, such as forests and fresh water, the unsustainable use of energy, and a rapid growth of carbon emissions. Although some of these imbalances may not appear to have immediate economic consequences, they will make it much more difficult to sustain economic growth in the long term. If countries can invest in addressing these imbalances they will not only preserve the natural environment, on which so many poor people depend, but also maintain the basis for long-term growth. And in the short term they will also provide an immediate economic stimulus and thus further alleviate poverty.

In sum, therefore, as the countries of the region take steps to address macroeconomic, developmental and ecological imbalances they have an opportunity to create new motors of inclusive growth that will help them regain their economic dynamism. The region has close to one billion people living in poverty, which combined with wide development gaps, gives it considerable headroom for augmenting aggregate demand through boosting private consumption and investment. Similarly, the Asia-Pacific economies have the opportunity to develop new and greener industries and businesses based on innovations that will save energy and materials. In so doing they can provide more affordable products for the poor while maintaining growth and promoting environmental sustainability.

Survey 2010 **argues, therefore, that in the aftermath of the global economic crisis, inclusive and sustainable growth is not only desirable but also a necessary condition for regaining the region's dynamism**. It then goes on to outline a policy agenda at national and regional levels that might assist in unleashing the latent potential of domestic and regional demand to address the three imbalances in an integrated manner.

A regional policy agenda for inclusive and sustainable growth

Survey 2010 explores ways of increasing aggregate demand and supply – establishing the region on a more inclusive and sustainable path of development and boosting regional connectivity. For this purpose it proposes an agenda with five prongs. The first four may assist in expanding domestic consumption while addressing socio-economic and ecological imbalances. The fifth deals with regional consumption.

1. Strengthening social protection

If poor households can rely on systems of social protection that will automatically trigger social safety nets at times of adversity they will be able to maintain food intake and continue to use education and health services. Just as important, at normal times they will have less need to maintain precautionary savings and can use more of their income for consumption. By serving as automatic stabilizers, systems of social protection not only support households at times of crisis but also enhance opportunities for individual development.

The Asia-Pacific region now has a number of examples of ambitious social security programmes. Thailand has a universal health-care programme – formerly called the '30 baht' scheme, but now free. India has the National Rural Employment Guarantee Act (NREGA) which provides a guaranteed 100 days of employment each year to adult members of rural households and also has gender-sensitive provisions. The Philippines has the Pantawid Pamilyang Pilipino Program (4Ps), which provides conditional cash transfers to poor households for their health and educational needs. Despite these efforts, a common agenda built around social protection has been slow to emerge. Social policy institutions often remain rooted in out-dated assumptions about the household, how individuals are cared for, and its coping mechanism in times of crises. Rather than using short-term measures, interventions need to sustain a trajectory from poverty to security, as basic rights.

2. Promoting agriculture and rural development: fostering a second green revolution

In Asia and the Pacific the majority of poor people live in the rural areas and derive most of their income from agriculture – so are likely to benefit from agricultural growth. Since the 1970s such growth was based largely on the Green Revolution which helped the region achieve significant yield increases – though the high input intensity also caused well documented problems. Now, as the region aims for more balanced economic growth, it needs a second, more knowledge-intensive green revolution that combines advances in science and agricultural engineering with the region's unique traditional knowledge to make agriculture more environmentally resilient. But countries will also need to make agriculture more socially inclusive by returning ownership of land and resources to farmers, especially women, and economically empowering the poor. This will mean setting appropriate prices for key inputs and establishing institutions to help small producers achieve economies of scale in marketing and in accessing international markets. In the past, governments may have tried to achieve this through state or parastatal agencies, but in future they may choose to encourage community-based organizations and farmers' self-help groups. International partnerships and South-South cooperation can also help foster such a green revolution while also addressing concerns for food security.

3. Supporting new engines of growth: green innovations

Green Growth emphasizes environmentally sustainable consumption and production that foster low-carbon, socially inclusive development. For this purpose, countries can take an industrial policy approach – encouraging strategic collaborations between government and industry to promote investments in environmentally-friendly technologies and products. Because of market failures such investments may not be immediately profitable, so many environmentally-friendly technological innovations will initially need government support. The public support can also help develop and commercialize products that serve to raise the wellbeing of the poor and the rural areas generally by encouraging affordable and environmentally-friendly technologies such as the rural solar home electricity systems popularized by Grameen Shakti in Bangladesh. A number of Asia-Pacific countries including Japan, China, India, and the Republic of Korea are promoting such innovations as a part of their national action plans on climate change. China, for example, has become the top investor in clean energy, with investments reaching $34.6 billion in 2009, while the Republic of Korea plans to spend $84 billion over five years to develop environmentally-friendly industries and use them as engines of growth. Governments can also encourage the adoption of environmentally-sound practices and technologies through appropriate regulations and systems of incentives and taxes.

In the developing countries the introduction of these innovations can be accelerated if the developed countries that already have a range of environmentally-friendly technologies, transfer them and relax some of the provisions of intellectual property rights, and also provide some of the necessary finance – following the principle of common but differentiated responsibilities established in the United Nations Framework Convention on Climate Change.

But the developing countries can also help each other in the area of sustainable consumption and production by sharing experiences and best practices. A number of Asia-Pacific developing countries now have capabilities in a range of technologies, such as biofuels production, waste management and solar and wind power. For example, Waste Concern, an NGO in Bangladesh which has developed a system of decentralized treatment plants for managing solid waste, with ESCAP support, is promoting similar approaches in cities in Pakistan, Sri Lanka, and Viet Nam.

4. Enhancing financial inclusion

A well functioning financial system is crucial to economic growth, but this will not be enough to ensure expanded aggregate demand. If the poor are to release their pent-up demand they will need access to a more diverse and appropriate range of financial products and services. This would include savings, credit and insurance products tailored to their requirements – on more favourable terms and with less stringent demands for collateral. This has been shown to have clear benefits. Households that can take advantage of micro-finance and micro-insurance, for example, are in a much stronger position to increase their incomes – and boost their levels of nutrition and standards of education. Moreover, women in such households tend to have greater autonomy in decision making and are better able to improve the well being of their families. To date however, across most developing countries in Asia and the Pacific, financial services are used by only a small proportion of the population. The poor are typically excluded from the formal financial sector and from the services of commercial banks. Barriers exist on both the demand and supply sides. Governments will therefore need to ensure an institutional and regulatory environment that fosters an inclusive, fairer and more efficient banking system and expands and safeguards the options for the poor.

5. Evolving a regional framework for cooperative action

With some of the world's largest and fastest-growing economies, Asia and the Pacific can become an even greater economic powerhouse if it develops a more integrated regional market. But this should be on the basis of a new development paradigm that is more inclusive and sustainable.

Thus far, for historical, political and topographical reasons, the region has been better connected with Europe and North America than it has been with itself. *Survey 2010* identifies four priorities that can leverage complementarities across the region and lay the foundations for a more inclusive and sustainable path of development:

(a) Regional economic integration – The Asia-Pacific region is home to a complex network of political groupings, whose leaders in recent times have consistently envisioned the evolution of a unified economic space. The time has come to move from vision to action. For this purpose they can accelerate progress on two current overlapping proposals. The first is the East Asia Free Trade Agreement (EAFTA) which brings together the ASEAN+3 grouping. The second is the Comprehensive Economic Partnership of East Asia (CEPEA) of the East Asia Summit (EAS) whose members include those in the ASEAN+3 grouping plus Australia, India, and New Zealand (or ASEAN+6). These proposals can serve as stepping stones to an even broader, unified Asia-Pacific market and an economic community.

(b) Integrated trade and transport policies – The region has improved its highway and railway networks, but it cannot use the infrastructure effectively without the legal and regulartory bases for vehicles, goods, and people to move across borders and transit countries. Currently, many international movements are hindered by slow and costly processes, formalities and procedures. The cost of red tape is considerable and often wipes out the benefits of tariff reductions enacted over the past two decades. In future the region will need an integrated, multimodal transport system. For this purpose, it can, for example, build intermodal transfer points, also known as dry ports, where goods, containers or vehicles can be transhipped using the most efficient mode of transport – along with facilities for product grading, packaging, inspections and the processing of trade documentation. The areas surrounding dry ports can then emerge as growth poles, bringing new investment and employment opportunities to impoverished hinterlands while reducing the pressure on coastal areas. Building on its Asian Highway and Trans Asian Railway Networks, the ESCAP secretariat is now helping the region develop a network of dry ports while improving trade and transport facilitation. ESCAP, along with the ADB is collaborating with ASEAN in developing a connectivity master plan.

(c) ICT superhighways – Expanding markets and business opportunities and creating a more unified economic space will depend crucially on better intraregional ICT connectivity to reduce the digital divide and accelerate cross-border information and communication flows. One of the main tasks will be to offer greater international bandwidth – particularly for the landlocked developing countries and the Pacific island developing countries. As well as boosting economic development such connectivity can also be used to establish systems for emergency early warnings and disaster response.

(d) Regional financial architecture – The economic crisis highlighted the lack of regional response options. Most of the measures had to be taken by national governments. So far the cooperation has been largely limited to the Chiang Mai Initiative that has now been multilateralized with a reserve pool of $120 billion for meeting the temporary liquidity needs of the ASEAN+3 countries. The region now needs to further develop its financial architecture, which would include systems of intermediation between its large savings and its unmet investment needs. One option would be to create an infrastructure development fund managed by a regional institution. If this secured just 5% of the region's reserves of nearly $5 trillion it could have start-up capital of $250 billion, as well as the ability to borrow from the region's central banks. This pooling of reserves could assist the region in meeting some of its investment needs for transport, energy, water and telecommunications – estimated at more than $800 billion per annum.

Another area where regional financial architecture could make a positive contribution is in exchange rate coordination. As the economies of the region increasingly trade with each other they will need a currency management system that facilitates trade and macroeconomic stability.

If governments had access to a well endowed regional crisis response and prevention facility they would feel less need to build up large foreign exchange reserves to protect their economies against speculative attacks and liquidity crises, and could thus free up reserves for more productive investments. Enhanced regional cooperation should not, however, be regarded as an alternative to full participation in global economic relations. Rather it should be seen as a complement to it, filling in the gaps and establishing the building blocks for global multilateral cooperation.

The development of a regional financial architecture would also assist in policy coordination and in providing an Asia-Pacific perspective on various global proposals that are emerging in the G-20, the United Nations and other forums. These include, for example, an SDR-based global reserve currency, a global tax on financial transactions to moderate short-term capital flows, and international regulations for the financial sector to curb excessive risk taking.

Asia and the Pacific now has an historic opportunity for cooperation, and in recent months some of the region's major economies have started a process of deeper mutual engagement – though if they are to carry through their more ambitious plans they will need to add greater detail to general statements of intent.

Noeleen Heyzer
Under-Secretary-General of the United Nations and
Executive Secretary, United Nations Economic and
Social Commission for Asia and the Pacific

ACKNOWLEDGEMENTS

This report was prepared under the overall direction and guidance of Noeleen Heyzer, Under-Secretary-General of the United Nations and Executive Secretary of the Economic and Social Commission for Asia and the Pacific (ESCAP), and under the substantive direction of Nagesh Kumar, Chief Economist and Director of the Macroeconomic Policy and Development Division. The core team, led by Tiziana Bonapace, included Shuvojit Banerjee, Somchai Congtavinsutti, Eugene Gherman, Yejin Ha, Alberto Isgut, Nobuko Kajiura, Muhammad H. Malik, George Manzano and Amy Wong.

ESCAP staff who contributed substantively include: Amitava Mukherjee of Macroeconomic Policy and Development Division (MPDD); Aneta Nikolova and Hitomi Rankine of the Environment and Development Division; Jorge Martinez-Navarrete, Atsuko Okuda and Nokeo Ratanavong of the Information and Communications Technology and Disaster Risk Reduction Division; Yu Kanosue and Sarah Lowder of the Social Development Division; Clovis Freire, Erik Hermouet and Ilpo Survo of the Statistics Division; Yann Duval of the Trade and Investment Division; John Moon of the Transport Division; and Krishnamurthy Ramanathan, N. Srinivasan and Krishnan Srinivasaraghavan of the Asian and Pacific Centre for Transfer of Technology (APCTT).

Valuable advice, comments and inputs were received from many staff of the United Nations which include: Kee Beom Kim and Gyorgy Sziraczki of the International Labour Organisation; Pingfan Hong and Matthias Kempf of the Department of Economic and Social Affairs, United Nations, New York; and Aynul Hasan, Syed Nuruzzaman, Seung Hun Jung, Ouk Heon Song, and Marin Yari of MPDD. Iosefa Maiava, Michal Kuzawinski and David Smith of the ESCAP Pacific Operations Centre of ESCAP.

The following experts provided country reports and other inputs: Zamir Ahmed, Rajeev Malhotra, Ron Duncan, Mohammad Kordbache, Ramkishen S. Rajan, Prabir De and Prakash Shrestha.

The report benefitted from an external peer review, comments and suggestions from an eminent group of Asian policy makers, scholars and development practitioners, namely: Yilmaz Akyuz, Special Economic Advisor, South Centre, Switzerland; Mohamed Ariff, Executive Director, Malaysian Institute of Economic Research (MIER), Malaysia; Ramgopal Agarwala, Distinguished Fellow, Research and Information System for Developing Countries, India; Md. Mosharraf Hossain Bhuiyan, Additional Secretary, Economic Relations Division, Ministry of Finance, Bangladesh; Michael Busai, Acting Director/Principal Economist, Ministry of Finance and Economic Management, Vanuatu; Abdul Wassay Haqiqi, Senior Advisor to the Minister of Economy, Ministry of Economy, Afghanistan; Mohamed Imad, Assistant Executive Director, Department of National Planning, Maldives; Saman Kelegama, Executive Director, Institute of Policy Studies of Sri Lanka, Sri Lanka; Ambassador K. Kesavapany, Director, Institute of Southeast Asian Studies, Singapore; Norman Lenga, Policy Analyst, Ministry of Finance and Treasury, Solomon Islands; Ashfaque H. Khan, Dean & Professor, National University of Sciences and Technology, NUST Business School, Pakistan; Gombosuren Khandtsooj, Officer, Financial and Economic Policy Department, Mongolia; Martin Khor, Executive Director, South Centre, Switzerland; Tin Htut Oo, Director-General, Department of Agricultural Planning, Ministry of Agriculture and Irrigation, Myanmar; Pichit Patrawimolpon, Director, Office of the Governor, Bank of Thailand, Thailand; Kim Phalla, Director, Economic and Public Finance Department, Ministry of Economic and Finance, Cambodia; Prabowo, Strategic Asia (Indonesia), Indonesia; Atiur Rahman, Governor, Bangladesh Bank, Bangladesh; Reteta Rimon-Nikuata, Kiribati

High Commissioner, Fiji; João Mariano Saldanha, Senior Management Adviser for Policy Analysis and Research, Timor-Leste; Pushpa Lal Shakya, Joint Secretary of National Planning Commission, Nepal; Vo Tri Thanh, Vice President, Central Institute of Economic Management, Viet Nam; and Tandin Wangchuk, Planning Officer, Perspective Planning Division, Bhutan.

Erik Huldt and Amornrat Supornsinchai of the Macroeconomic Policy and Development Division, ESCAP provided research assistance.

Orestes Plasencia, Kim Atkinson and Chirudee Pungtrakul of the Editorial Unit of ESCAP and Peter Stalker edited the manuscript. The graphic design was created by Marie Ange Sylvain-Holmgren, and the layout and printing were provided by TR Enterprise.

Woranut Sompitayanurak, supported by Metinee Hunkosol, Anong Pattanathanes and Sutinee Yeamkitpibul of the Macroeconomic Policy and Development Division, ESCAP, proofread the manuscript and undertook all administrative processing necessary for the issuance of the publication.

Paul Risley, Mitchell Hsieh, Bentley Jenson, Thawadi Pachariyangkun and Chavalit Boonthanom of the United Nations Information Services, coordinated the launch and dissemination of the report.

CONTENTS

	Page
Foreword	iii
Executive Secretary's preface	v
Acknowledgements	xiii
Abbreviations	xxvii
Sources of quotations	xxix
Chapter 1. The beginnings of recovery and policy responses	3
Coping with vulnerability	5
Vulnerable to trade and financial exposure	5
Exposure to developed-country demand	7
Exposure to capital flows	17
Capital markets and exchange rates: renewed inflows bring instability	22
Emerging reorientation of foreign direct investment	25
Evolving impacts on jobs and income	27
Migration and remittances: bucking the pressures	31
Domestic demand and fiscal space shaping responses	33
Growth outlook for 2010	41
Recovery underway	41
Backdrop for 2010 forecast	41
Different paces of expansion	44
Downside risks persist	45
Balancing growth with stability	46
Inflation threatens from demand and supply sides	46
Asset bubbles build up	49
Avoiding premature exit	52
Sustaining Asia's dynamism	53
Chapter 2. Crisis and rebound: the differentiated impacts, policy responses and outlook at the subregional level	57
East and North-East Asia	58
Impact of the crisis	60
Policy responses	65
Outlook and policy challenges	68
North and Central Asia	69
Impact of the crisis	71
Policy responses	73
Outlook and policy challenges	77

CONTENTS *(continued)*

	Page
Oceania	78
Impact of the crisis	78
Policy responses	86
Outlook and policy challenges	88
South and South-West Asia	89
Impact of the crisis	89
Policy responses	95
Outlook and policy challenges	98
South-East Asia	100
Impact of the crisis	100
Policy responses	105
Prospects	109
Chapter 3. Multiple imbalances and development gaps as new engines of growth	115
Macroeconomic imbalances	118
Sources of imbalances	121
Socio-economic imbalances and development gaps	125
Poverty reduction: remarkable but uneven	125
Poverty-inequality-household consumption nexus	126
Poverty and multiple deprivations	129
Infrastructure and other development gaps	133
Growing ecological imbalances	136
Linkages between the three imbalances	140
Annex I	142
Annex II	143
Chapter 4. A regional policy agenda for regaining the dynamism	147
Redressing socio-economic and environmental imbalances for expanding domestic consumption	148
Strengthening social protection	148
A "Green revolution" for food security and poverty reduction	151
"Green growth": new green industries as engines of growth	154
Enhancing financial inclusiveness	158

CONTENTS *(continued)*

	Page
Expanding demand through cooperation	160
Evolving a broader framework for economic integration	161
Developing regional transportation networks and improving trade facilitation	162
Strengthening connectivity through information and communications technology (ICT)	165
Developing financial architecture for crisis prevention and narrowing the gaps	167
References and further readings	179
Statistical annex	195

BOXES

Page

1. Assessing the impact of expected downturns in export growth 35

2. Potential for economic cooperation: the Democratic People's Republic of Korea 69

3. Creating a "Eurasian Union": the Russian Federation, Kazakhstan, and Belarus 77

4. Connectivity in the Pacific 89

5. Indian National Rural Employment Guarantee Scheme 96

6. The changing direction of ASEAN trade 111

7. Sensitivity of the results to alternative methods to compute the contribution of aggregate demand components to GDP growth 123

8. Pro-poor investments in renewable energy and beyond 156

9. Connectivity for improved disaster preparedness, response and management 166

FIGURES

Page

1. World economic growth: a post-war story of rising prosperity, 1930 to 2010 4

2. The Asia-Pacific region is the fastest growing of all, 2009 and 2010 4

3. Real GDP growth, year-on-year, in selected developing and developed countries,
2008 and 2009 6

4. Spread of overnight LIBOR rates to overnight United States Federal Reserve
effective fund rates, February 2007 to January 2010 7

5. Real GDP growth of six export-oriented developing economies, by quarter,
2008 and 2009 8

6. Comparative growth performance of goods exports of major developing economies
during three crises, 1997 to 2009 9

7. Index of total United States imports and United States imports from Asian
and Pacific developing and developed economies, by quarter, 2007 to 2009 9

8. Export dependence in subregions of Asia and the Pacific, in three-year
averages, in percentage shares of GDP, 1994 to 1996 and 2005 to 2007 13

9. Net private capital flows to "emerging" Asia, 1991 to 2010 18

10. Loan-to-deposit ratios in major Asian developing economies, third quarter of 2009 19

11. Vulnerability yardstick as a percentage of foreign reserves in major
developing economies, 2008 22

12. Exchange rate movements in major developing economies, 2007 to 2009 23

13. Change in nominal effective exchange rates from peak to trough in major developing
economies during two crises, 1997 to 1998 and 2008 to 2009 24

14. Foreign reserves in six developing economies, December 2007 to December 2009 24

15. Gross inward direct investment in major developing economies, 2007 to 2009 26

16. Social expenditure as a percentage of GDP, worldwide, during most
recent year available 28

17. Labour market trends in four Asian economies, 1996 to 2008 30

18. Monthly and quarterly unemployment rates in six Asian economies,
2008 and 2009 31

FIGURES *(continued)*

Page

19. Annual growth rate in overseas workers' remittances in four developing economies, 2007/08 and 2008/09 32

20. Contributions of domestic demand, exports and imports to real GDP growth in major Asian developing economies, 2008 and 2009 34

21. Real exports of 11 major Asian economies 37

22. Interest rates in major Asian developing economies, 2008 and 2009 40

23. Economic growth rates of Asian and Pacific developing economies and world developed economies, 2003 to 2010 41

24. Average growth rates and forecasts of Asian and Pacific economies by subregion, 2003 to 2010 44

25. Consumer price inflation, year-on-year, in major Asian developing economies, 2008 and 2009 47

26. Credit growth, year-on-year, in major Asian developing economies, January 2007 to October 2009 50

27. Equity market performance in major Asian developing economies, January 2008 to December 2009 50

28. Equity market behaviour peak-to-trough during two crises, 1997 to 1998 and 2008 to 2009 51

29. Performance indices of regional emerging-market equities, 15 September 2008 to 8 January 2010 52

30. Real GDP growth of Asian and Pacific developing and world developed economies, 2003 to 2010 58

31. Map of growth deceleration among Asian and Pacific economies: Comparison of crisis-period growth with pre-crisis growth trends 59

32. Real GDP growth, year-on-year, of major East and North-East Asian economies, 2008 and 2009 61

33. Export growth, year-on-year, of major East and North-East Asian economies, 2008 and 2009 63

34. Import growth, year-on-year, of major East and North-East Asian economies, 2008 and 2009 63

FIGURES *(continued)*

Page

35. Current account balance as a percentage of GDP in major East and North-East Asian economies, 2007 to 2009 64

36. Interest rates in major East and North-East Asian economies, 2008 and 2009 66

37. Budget balance as a percentage of GDP of major East and North-East Asian economies, 2007 to 2009 67

38. Current account balance as a percentage of GDP in North and Central Asian economies, 2007 to 2009 72

39. Budget balance as a percentage of GDP in North and Central Asian economies, 2007 to 2009 75

40. Index of exchange rates movements in selected North and Central Asian economies, 2007 to 2009 76

41. Current account balances as a percentage of GDP of the countries in Oceania, 2007 to 2009 83

42. Current account balance as a percentage of GDP in South and South-West Asian economies, 2007 to 2009 94

43. Budget balance as a percentage of GDP in selected South and South-West Asian economies, 2007 to 2009 97

44. Combined share of United States and European Union purchases of merchandise exports of selected South-East Asian economies, 2006 to 2007 and 2008 101

45. Export share of electronics, machinery, motor vehicles and apparel in total exports, selected South-East Asian economies, 2006 to 2008 102

46. Budget balance as a percentage of GDP in selected South-East Asian economies, 2007 to 2009 106

47. Current account balance as a percentage of GDP in selected South-East Asian economies, 2007 to 2009 107

48. Index of exchange rate movements in selected South-East Asian economies, 2009 109

49. Trends in the real GDP of selected regions and countries 116

50. Real GDP per capita adjusted by purchasing power parity 117

51. Trade and current account balances 119

FIGURES *(continued)*

Page

52. Share of net exports of goods and services in long-term real GDP growth 120

53. Share of gross fixed investment in long-term real GDP growth 121

54. Share of consumption in long-term real GDP growth 122

55. Paths of poverty rates and GDPs per capita in selected countries 126

56. Per capita household consumption and per capita GDP in 15 Asian and Pacific developing countries 128

57. Headcount poverty and employment in the informal sector in the Asia-Pacific region 130

58. Headcount poverty and underweight children in the Asia-Pacific region 131

59. Headcount poverty and primary education survival rate in the Asia-Pacific region 131

60. Headcount poverty and access to improved sanitation in the Asia-Pacific region 132

61. Infrastructure composite scores in Asia and the Pacific, 2007 135

62. Net loss or increase in forest area between 1990 and 2005 136

63. Proportion of total renewable freshwater resources withdrawn 138

64. A schematic view of the three imbalances 141

65. FAO food price index and Brent crude oil price, January 2004 to February 2010 152

66. Asian Highway and Trans-Asian Railway Networks 162

TABLES

Page

1. Share of Asian and Pacific developing and developed economies in total United States imports, by quarter, 2007 to 2009 10

2. Trade intensity indices of Asian and Pacific economies, 2007 15

3. Intra-industry trade indices of Asian and Pacific economies, by sector, 2007 17

4. Foreign reserve adequacy, 1996 to 2009: outstanding year-end reserves position 20

5. Impact of the 2009 shortfall in exports on GDP of major Asian economies.................... 36

6. Estimated multiplier effects of aggregate demand components....................................... 38

7. Rates of economic growth and inflation of Asian and Pacific economies, in percentages, 2008 to 2010 42

8. Rate of economic growth and inflation in East and North-East Asian economies, 2008 to 2010 61

9. Rate of economic growth and inflation in North and Central Asian economies, 2008 to 2010 70

10. Trade performance of North and Central Asian economies, in percentages, 2007 to 2009 73

11. Receipts of workers' remittances in major North and Central Asian economies, 2006 to 2008 74

12. Rate of economic growth and inflation in countries in Oceania, 2008 to 2010 79

13. Recent international primary commodity prices, 2007 to 2009 84

14. Total visitor arrivals in selected Pacific island economies, in thousands of people, 2004 to 2009 85

15. Remittances inflows as a percentage of GDP in selected Pacific island economies, 2000 to 2008 86

16. Rate of economic growth and inflation in South and South-West Asian economies, 2008 to 2010 90

17. Rate of economic growth and inflation in South-East Asian economies, 2008 to 2010 101

18. Percentage changes of real GDP of major South-East Asian economies, year-on-year, 2007 to 2009 103

TABLES *(continued)*

Page

19. Import growth by ASEAN economies, by source, 2008 and 2009, in percentages 108

20. Percentage shares of imports by ASEAN economies, by source, 2004 to 2008, in percentages 108

21. Foreign exchange reserves minus gold, selected South-East Asian economies, 2009, in billions of United States dollars 110

22. ASEAN export growth, 2008 and 2009, in percentages 111

23. Percentage shares of ASEAN exporters in destination markets, in selected years 111

24. Contributions of consumption, investment and exports to GDP growth 124

25. Poverty reduction between 1990 and the mid-2000s 125

26. Inequality and household consumption growth between 1990 and the mid-2000s 127

27. Country groups on and off track for the Millennium Development Goals 134

28. Carbon dioxide emissions from selected major economies 139

29. Regional currency swings during the crisis 171

EXPLANATORY NOTES

Staff analysis in the *Survey 2010* is based on data and information available up to the end of March 2010.

The term "ESCAP region" is used in the present issue of the *Survey* to include Afghanistan; American Samoa; Armenia; Australia; Azerbaijan; Bangladesh; Bhutan; Brunei Darussalam; Cambodia; China; Cook Islands; Democratic People's Republic of Korea; Fiji; French Polynesia; Georgia; Guam; Hong Kong, China; India; Indonesia; Iran (Islamic Republic of); Japan; Kazakhstan; Kiribati; Kyrgyzstan; Lao People's Democratic Republic; Macao, China; Malaysia; Maldives; Marshall Islands; Micronesia (Federated States of); Mongolia; Myanmar; Nauru; Nepal; New Caledonia; New Zealand; Niue; Northern Mariana Islands; Pakistan; Palau; Papua New Guinea; Philippines; Republic of Korea; Russian Federation; Samoa; Singapore; Solomon Islands; Sri Lanka; Tajikistan; Thailand; Timor-Leste; Tonga; Turkey; Turkmenistan; Tuvalu; Uzbekistan; Vanuatu; and Viet Nam. The term "developing ESCAP region" excludes Australia, Japan and New Zealand. Non-regional members of ESCAP are France, the Netherlands, the United Kingdom of Great Britain and Northern Ireland and the United States of America.

The term "Central Asian countries" in this issue of the *Survey* refers to Armenia, Azerbaijan, Georgia, Kazakhstan, Kyrgyzstan, Tajikistan, Turkmenistan and Uzbekistan.

The term "East and North-East Asia" in this issue of the *Survey* refers to China; Hong Kong, China; Japan; Macao, China; Mongolia; Republic of Korea; and Russian Federation.

The designations employed and the presentation of the material in this publication do not imply the expression of any opinion whatsoever on the part of the Secretariat of the United Nations concerning the legal status of any country, territory, city or area, or of its authorities, or concerning the delimitation of its frontiers or boundaries.

Mention of firm names and commercial products does not imply the endorsement of the United Nations.

The abbreviated title *Survey* in footnotes refers to the *Economic and Social Survey of Asia and the Pacific* for the year indicated.

Many figures used in the *Survey* are on a fiscal year basis and are assigned to the calendar year which covers the major part or second half of the fiscal year.

Growth rates are on an annual basis, except where indicated otherwise.

Reference to "tons" indicates metric tons.

Values are in United States dollars unless specified otherwise.

The term "billion" signifies a thousand million. The term "trillion" signifies a million million.

In the tables, two dots (..) indicate that data are not available or are not separately reported, a dash (–) indicates that the amount is nil or negligible, and a blank indicates that the item is not applicable.

In dates, a hyphen (-) is used to signify the full period involved, including the beginning and end years, and a stroke (/) indicates a crop year, fiscal year or plan year. The fiscal years, currencies and 2010 exchange rates of the economies in the ESCAP region are listed in the following table:

Country or area in the ESCAP region	Fiscal year	Currency and abbreviation	Rate of exchange for $1 as at January 2010
Afghanistan	21 March to 20 March	afghani (Af)	48.74[a]
American Samoa	..	United States dollar ($)	1.00
Armenia	1 January to 31 December	dram	376.69
Australia	1 July to 30 June	Australian dollar ($A)	1.12
Azerbaijan	1 January to 31 December	Azeri manat (AZM)	0.80
Bangladesh	1 July to 30 June	taka (Tk)	69.20
Bhutan	1 July to 30 June	ngultrum (Nu)	46.37
Brunei Darussalam	1 January to 31 December	Brunei dollar (B$)	1.40
Cambodia	1 January to 31 December	riel (CR)	4 165.00[a]
China	1 January to 31 December	yuan renminbi (Y)	6.83
Cook Islands	1 April to 31 March	New Zealand dollar ($NZ)	1.42
Democratic People's Republic of Korea	..	won (W)	139.00
Fiji	1 January to 31 December	Fiji dollar (F$)	1.94

Country or area in the ESCAP region	Fiscal year	Currency and abbreviation	Rate of exchange for $1 as at January 2010
French Polynesia	..	French Pacific Community franc (FCFP)	85.92
Georgia	1 January to 31 December	lari (L)	1.74
Guam	1 October to 30 September	United States dollar ($)	1.00
Hong Kong, China	1 April to 31 March	Hong Kong dollar (HK$)	7.76
India	1 April to 31 March	Indian rupee (Rs)	46.37
Indonesia	1 April to 31 March	Indonesian rupiah (Rp)	3 965.00
Iran (Islamic Republic of)	21 March to 20 March	Iranian rial (Rls)	10 008.00
Japan	1 April to 31 March	yen (¥)	89.85
Kazakhstan	1 January to 31 December	tenge (T)	148.21
Kiribati	1 January to 31 December	Australian dollar ($A)	1.12
Kyrgyzstan	1 January to 31 December	som (som)	44.28
Lao People's Democratic Republic	1 October to 30 September	new kip (NK)	8 484.25[a]
Macao, China	1 July to 30 June	pataca (P)	8.01
Malaysia	1 January to 31 December	ringgit (M$)	3.41
Maldives	1 January to 31 December	rufiyaa (Rf)	12.80
Marshall Islands	1 October to 30 September	United States dollar ($)	1.00
Micronesia (Federated States of)	1 October to 30 September	United States dollar ($)	1.00
Mongolia	1 January to 31 December	tugrik (Tug)	1 442.84[a]
Myanmar	1 April to 31 March	kyat (K)	5.43[a]
Nauru	1 July to 30 June	Australian dollar ($A)	1.12
Nepal	16 July to 15 July	Nepalese rupee (NRs)	74.20
New Caledonia	..	French Pacific Community franc (FCFP)	85.92
New Zealand	1 April to 31 March	New Zealand dollar ($NZ)	1.42
Niue	1 April to 31 March	New Zealand dollar ($NZ)	1.42
Northern Mariana Islands	1 October to 30 September	United States dollar ($)	1.00
Pakistan	1 July to 30 June	Pakistan rupee (PRs)	84.73
Palau	1 October to 30 September	United States dollar ($)	1.00
Papua New Guinea	1 January to 31 December	kina (K)	2.70[a]
Philippines	1 January to 31 December	Philippine peso (P)	46.75
Republic of Korea	1 January to 31 December	won (W)	1 156.50
Russian Federation	1 January to 31 December	ruble (R)	30.43
Samoa	1 July to 30 June	tala (WS$)	2.53
Singapore	1 April to 31 March	Singapore dollar (S$)	1.40
Solomon Islands	1 January to 31 December	Solomon Islands dollar (SI$)	8.06[a]
Sri Lanka	1 January to 31 December	Sri Lanka rupee (SL Rs)	114.55
Tajikistan	1 January to 31 December	somoni	4.37
Thailand	1 October to 30 September	baht (B)	33.10
Timor-Leste	1 July to 30 June	United States dollar ($)	1.00
Tonga	1 July to 30 June	pa'anga (T$)	1.89
Turkey	1 January to 31 December	Turkish lira (LT)	1.49
Turkmenistan	1 January to 31 December	Turkmen manat (M)	2.85
Tuvalu	1 January to 31 December	Australian dollar ($A)	1.12
Uzbekistan	1 January to 31 December	som (som)	1 510.00
Vanuatu	1 January to 31 December	vatu (VT)	97.93
Viet Nam	1 January to 31 December	dong (D)	17 941.00

Note: [a] December 2009.

Sources: United Nations, *Monthly Bulletin of Statistics* website, http://unstats.un.org/unsd/mbs/app/DataSearchTable.aspx, 9 March 2010; CEIC Data Company Limited; and national sources.

ABBREVIATIONS

AADMER	ASEAN Agreement on Disaster Management and Emergency Response
ABMI	Asian Bond Market Initiative
ADB	Asian Development Bank
ADBI	Asian Development Bank Institute
AFTA	ASEAN Free Trade Agreement
APCAEM	Asian and Pacific Centre for Agricultural Engineering and Machinery
APEC	Asia-Pacific Economic Cooperation
APTA	Asia-Pacific Trade Agreement
ASEAN	Association of Southeast Asian Nations
BIMSTEC	Bay of Bengal Initiative for Multi-Sectoral Technical and Economic Cooperation
BIS	Bank for International Settlements
CAPSA	Centre for Alleviation of Poverty through Secondary Crops' Development in Asia and the Pacific
c.i.f.	cost, insurance, freight
CAREC	Central Asia Regional Economic Cooperation Corridors
CD-ROM	compact disk read-only memory
CEPEA	comprehensive economic partnership of East Asia
CMI	Chiang Mai Initiative
CNG	compressed natural gas
CPI	consumer price index
EAFTA	East Asia Free Trade Agreement
EAS	East Asia Summit
ECE	Economic Commission for Europe
EIU	Economist Intelligence Unit
ERIA	Economic Research Institute of ASEAN and East Asia
EU	European Union
EurAsEC	Eurasian Economic Community
FAO	Food and Agriculture Organization of the United Nations
FDI	foreign direct investment

ABBREVIATIONS *(continued)*

f.o.b.	free on board
FTA	Free trade area
GDP	gross domestic product
GMS	Greater Mekong Subregion
HIV	Human immunodeficiency virus
ICT	information and communication technology
ILO	International Labour Organization
IMF	International Monetary Fund
IPCC	Intergovernmental Panel on Climate Change
MDG	Millennium Development Goal
NGOs	non-governmental organizations
NREGA	National Rural Employment Guarantee Act
ODA	official development assistance
OECD	Organisation for Economic Cooperation and Development
PPP	purchasing power parity
R&D	research and development
SAARC	South Asian Association for Regional Cooperation
SARS	severe acute respiratory syndrome
SDRs	special drawing rights
TRIPs	Trade-Related Aspects of Intellectual Property Rights
UNCTAD	United Nations Conference on Trade and Development
UNDP	United Nations Development Programme
UNFCCC	United Nations Framework Convention on Climate Change
WTO	World Trade Organization

SOURCES OF QUOTATIONS

(a) Page 1: an excerpt from the message of President Hu Jintao (China) at the APEC meeting on the theme "Sustaining Growth, Connecting the Region" on 15 November 2009 (source: http://english.gov.cn/2009-11/15/content_1465068.htm).

(b) Page 55: an excerpt from the message of Prime Minister Manmohan Singh (India) at the G-20 Meeting at Pittsburgh: Plenary Session, 25 September 2009 (source: http://pmindia.nic.in/speeches.htm).

(c) Page 113: an excerpt from a speech by President Susilo Bambang Yudhoyono (Indonesia), Speech at the APEC CEO Summit, Rebuilding the Global Economy: Crisis and Opportunity, Singapore, 13 November 2009 (source: http://www.globalentrepolis.com/downloads/President SBYSpeech-CEOSummit.pdf).

(d) Page 145: an excerpt from a speech by Prime Minister Edward Natapei (Vanuatu), Speech at the Global Economic Crisis Conference, Port Vila, Vanuatu, 10-12 February 2010 (source: http://vanuatu2010.un.org.fj/pages.cfm/press-corner/speeches-statements/speech-by-hon-edward-natapei-prime-minister-of-vanuatu.html).

(e) Page 177: an excerpt from a speech by Under-Secretary-General of the United Nations and Executive Secretary of ESCAP, Noeleen Heyzer, Innovative Government: Innovation on the Road To Economic Recovery in Singapore, 3 December 2009.

(f) Back cover: an excerpt from an article by BAN Ki-moon, Secretary-General of the United Nations, *Daily News* (Egypt), 4 July 2009 (source: http://www.un.org/sgarticleFull.asp?TID=103&Type=Op-Ed).

"We should all the more get united, follow the principle of openness, cooperation and mutual benefit, strengthen coordination and work together to secure the momentum of world economic recovery and promote balanced and orderly economic growth"

Hu Jintao
President, People's Republic of China

THE BEGINNINGS OF RECOVERY AND POLICY RESPONSES

1

A year and a half after the global economic crisis hit Asian and Pacific shores, the region faces rapidly evolving challenges that underline the need for policy reforms geared to more inclusive and sustainable modes of economic growth. While the crisis did not originate here, Asian and Pacific economies have been significantly impacted because of their vulnerability to extraregional developments, primarily through trade and financial channels. This chapter reviews the differentiated impact of the crisis on countries and the challenges to recovery.

Some six decades of stable world economic growth had appeared to confirm that policymakers had mastered the art of fine-tuning countercyclical policies (figure 1). Then in 2008 financial crisis propelled a synchronized decline in world economic growth, calling into question many of the premises on which market economies had functioned since the Second World War.

Policy response at the global level was swift and unprecedented in size. Financial meltdown was averted. Emerging from the crisis, Asian and Pacific economies have shown greater resilience with faster and higher growth than have the developed world and all the other developing regions (figure 2).

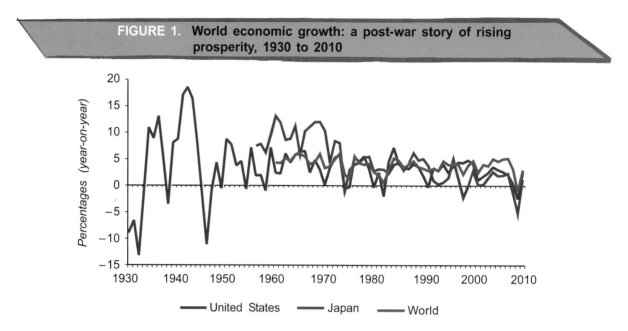

FIGURE 1. World economic growth: a post-war story of rising prosperity, 1930 to 2010

Sources: Data on United States GDP growth come from the United States Department of Commerce, Bureau of Economic Analysis, *National Income and Product Accounts Table*, available from www.bea.gov/national/nipaweb/TablePrint.asp?FirstYear =1930&LastYear=2009&Freq=Year&SelectedTable=1&ViewSeries=NO&Java=no&MaxValue=48.9&MaxChars=5&Request3 Place=N&3Place=N&FromView=YES&Legal=&Land= (accessed 26 Feb. 2010), including updates from IMF, *World Economic and Financial Surveys: World Economic Outlook Database*, Oct. 2009 ed., available from www.imf.org/external/pubs/ft/weo/ 2009/02/weodata/index.aspx (accessed 26 Feb. 2010); data on world GDP come from IMF, *International Financial Statistics*, Vol. 61, 2008 (Washington, D.C.: IMF, 2008) with updates from IMF, *World Economic Outlook Database*; data of Japan are based on data from the Economic and Social Research Institute, Cabinet Office, Government of Japan accessible at www.esri.cao.go.jp/ (accessed 26 Feb. 2010).

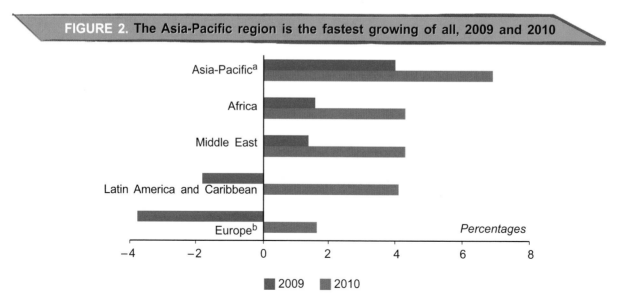

FIGURE 2. The Asia-Pacific region is the fastest growing of all, 2009 and 2010

Notes: [a] Only developing economies in the ESCAP region (excluding countries of the Commonwealth of Independent States). [b] Developed and developing member countries of the European Economic Commission.
Sources: ESCAP calculations based on data from the United Nations regional commissions.

The impact of the crisis has revealed the vulnerability of the region to external shocks – its excessive dependence on import demand generated by extraregional markets, principally the European Union and the United States of America, and exposure to financial and exchange-rate instabilities. The degree of exposure depended on demand structure in each of the economies, their fiscal space and the extent of foreign exchange reserves.

In the aftermath of the crisis, a return to "business as usual" is unlikely

---

In the aftermath of the crisis, a return to "business as usual" is unlikely, however tempting that might be with the current rebound. Debt-fuelled (both governmental and private) economies, ageing populations and a slowdown in technological innovations all point to a long period of stagnation in developed countries. The axis of growth may have shifted in a defining manner towards developing economies, with those of Asia and the Pacific particularly well placed.

The challenges and opportunities present in the altered economic balance of the world require critical policy decisions in the year ahead. While national policies remain important, the Asia-Pacific experience of the crisis has stoked recognition of the need for regional coordination in economic and financial policymaking to provide the supportive structure for growth from within the region. The region needs to adopt a new toolkit of policies while participating in creating new international financial and economic architecture.

COPING WITH VULNERABILITY

Vulnerable to trade and financial exposure

As in other parts of the world, growth in the Asia-Pacific region was severely curtailed from the fourth quarter of 2008 onwards, as exports declined with contracting consumption in developed countries. Export-dependent economies, particularly those in East and South-East Asia, suffered large reductions in growth of gross domestic product (GDP; figure 3).

The first blows of the crisis in the Asia-Pacific region fell in the financial sector from the third quarter of 2008, following the collapse of Lehman Brothers in September 2008 and the arrest in global financial flows. Capital exited Asian and Pacific asset markets as a result of risk aversion and the need for investors in developed countries to settle losses in their home markets. The initial macroeconomic effects were, however, limited to substantial declines in exchange rates in some economies, buttressed by the use in many cases of substantial foreign exchange reserves. Severely affected, Pakistan and Sri Lanka had to go to the International Monetary Fund for balance of payments support. Singapore and the Republic of Korea arranged credit lines with the United States Federal Reserve. The Republic of Korea also arranged bilateral credit lines with Japan and China.

Asia and the Pacific as a whole survived the financial shock of the crisis far better than the other developing regions of the world, largely because of the risk management measures and prudent macroeconomic management that the region has followed after the 1997 Asian crisis.

The blockage in global financial markets improved over the course of 2009 as the massive liquidity provided by Governments in developed countries began to show results. By mid-2009, the spread of bank-offered credit in comparison with United States Treasury Bill rates had narrowed to levels seen before the crisis (figure 4).

While the region generally weathered the financial storm, the export slowdown was more dramatic in some countries and, concomitantly, had far greater impact on their GDP growth. The double-digit export growth up to the third quarter of 2008 turned into double-digit contractions in subsequent quarters. Exporting powerhouses of

FIGURE 3. **Real GDP growth, year-on-year, in selected developing and developed countries, 2008 and 2009**

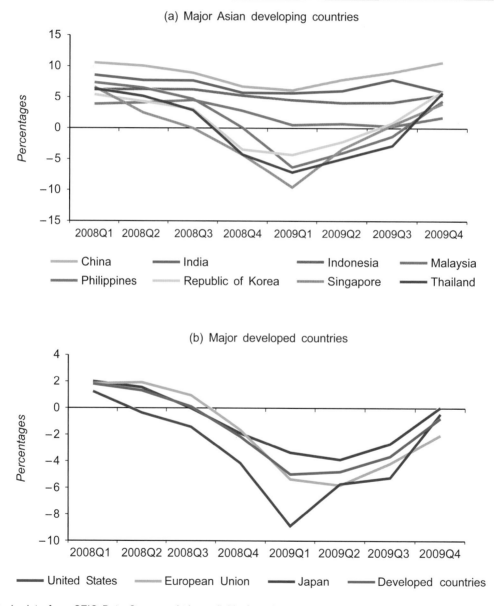

Source: Basic data from CEIC Data Company Ltd., available from http://ceicdata.com/ (accessed 5 Mar. 2010).

FIGURE 4. Spread of overnight LIBOR rates to overnight United States Federal Reserve effective fund rates, February 2007 to January 2010

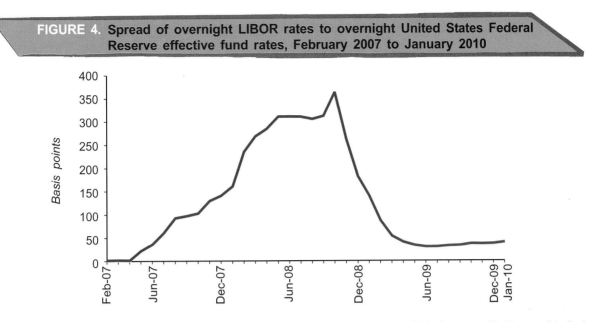

Sources: ESCAP calculations based on data from the British Banker's Association, available from www.bbalibor.com/bba/jsp/polopoly.jsp?d=1661 (accessed 5 Mar. 2010); and the United States Federal Reserve, *Federal Reserve Statistical Release*, available from www.federalreserve.gov/releases/h15/data.htm (accessed 18 Feb. 2010).

North-East and South-East Asia were hit hard (figure 5) and consequently suffered severe contractions in growth – excepting China where exports accounted for a relatively small share of GDP and where fiscal stimulus supported domestic demand.

By the second quarter of 2009, the export contraction reached a turning point and exports began to pick up again in many major economies of the region, causing the contraction in GDP growth to bottom out. Driving this stabilization and turnaround, the consumption slowdown in the world's developed countries had stabilized as governmental stimulus measures began to yield results. Personal consumption expenditure in the United States increased in the first quarter of 2009 by 0.6%; whereas it had sharply fallen in the last two quarters of 2008. By the third quarter of 2009 that rise had multiplied more than fivefold to 3.4%.[1] In tandem with the export turnaround, governmental

expansionary policies in the Asia-Pacific region took effect during the latter half of the year.

While the crisis impacted growth in GDP across the board, the experience of individual countries varied in the region. Dependence on exports to developed countries and exposure to global financial flows were key determinants. Responses to the crisis also depended very much on country circumstances. In particular, domestic demand and the availability of fiscal space drove the differences in impacts and responses to the crisis between countries, as the following paragraphs show.

Exposure to developed-country demand

The impact of the crisis was transmitted through trade shocks to the highly export-oriented economies in the Asia-Pacific region. Exports dropped especially in the first half of 2009 at rates nearly

---

[1]   United States Department of Commerce, Bureau of Economic Analysis, "Gross domestic product: third quarter 2009 (advance estimate)", press release, 29 Oct. 2009; available from www.bea.gov/newsreleases/national/gdp/gdpnewsrelease.htm.

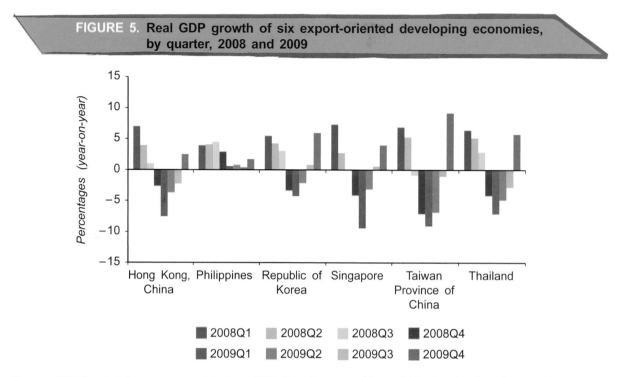

FIGURE 5. Real GDP growth of six export-oriented developing economies, by quarter, 2008 and 2009

Source: ESCAP calculations based on data from CEIC Data Company Ltd., available from http://ceicdata.com/ (accessed 5 Mar. 2010).

twice as much as and more widespread than those that followed the crisis of 1997 and the recession in 2001 after the "dot-com bubble" (figure 6). Monthly contraction rates of around 40% in the Philippines, the Russian Federation, Singapore and others were observed over that period. As income growth rates in the region waned, imports dropped even more sharply. The decline of imports in the wake of the export collapse was further evidence of the high import content of regional exports.

Exports dropped at rates nearly twice as much as those that followed the crisis of 1997

The relative movements of total imports of the United States of America and its imports from the ESCAP region reveal vulnerability to trade shocks as well as the capacity to recover from them (figure 7). Clearly the exports of devel-

oped Asian and Pacific economies to the United States fell by much more than the total imports of the United States, particularly during the first three quarters of 2008. The exports of developing Asian and Pacific economies fared better, improving their market share towards the third quarter of 2008 relative to their share in first quarter of 2007. By the first quarter of 2009, exports from those developing economies were falling in tandem with the fall in total United States imports, but an improvement was recorded for the second quarter of the year. The share in United States imports of the developed economies of the region continued to fall into the second quarter of 2009, before starting to rebound. Meanwhile those developing economies had hit bottom earlier and begun growing again by the end of the first quarter of 2009.

How selected Asian and Pacific developing economies fared in terms of competitiveness during the downturn in United States import demand can be seen more directly from the relative movement in market share (table 1). Remarkably, despite the sharp drops in exports

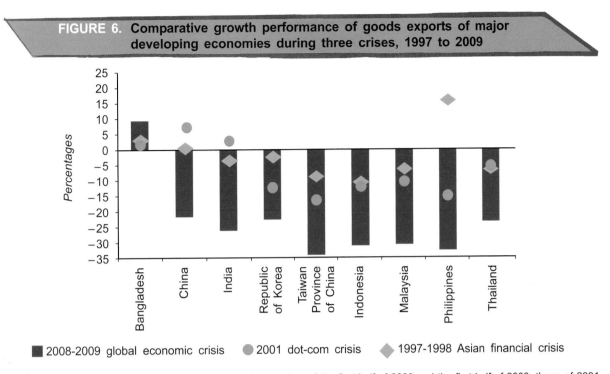

FIGURE 6. Comparative growth performance of goods exports of major developing economies during three crises, 1997 to 2009

■ 2008-2009 global economic crisis   ● 2001 dot-com crisis   ◆ 1997-1998 Asian financial crisis

Note: Growth rates of 2008 and 2009 were computed using data of the first half of 2009 and the first half of 2008; those of 2001 dot-com were computed on the basis of 2001 over 2000; and those of 1997 and 1998 were computed on the basis of 1998 over 1997.

Source: ESCAP calculations based on data from CEIC Data Company Ltd., available from http://ceicdata.com/ (accessed 16 Feb. 2010).

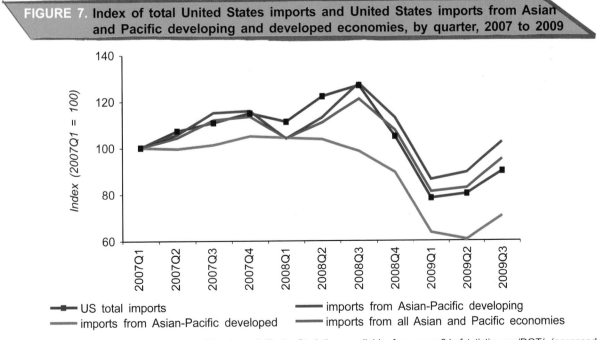

FIGURE 7. Index of total United States imports and United States imports from Asian and Pacific developing and developed economies, by quarter, 2007 to 2009

■ US total imports
imports from Asian-Pacific developing
imports from Asian-Pacific developed
imports from all Asian and Pacific economies

Source: Basic data from IMF database, *Direction of Trade Statistics,* available from www2.imfstatistics.org/DOT/ (accessed 16 Feb. 2010).

TABLE 1. Share of Asian and Pacific developing and developed economies in total United States imports, by quarter, 2007 to 2009

	2007 Q1	2007 Q2	2007 Q3	2007 Q4	2008 Q1	2008 Q2	2008 Q3	2008 Q4	2009 Q1	2009 Q2	2009 Q3
China	16.2	16.2	17.7	17.2	14.8	15.1	17.2	18.8	18.7	19.2	19.7
Indonesia	0.8	0.7	0.8	0.7	0.7	0.7	0.8	0.8	0.9	0.9	0.8
Malaysia	1.8	1.6	1.7	1.6	1.6	1.5	1.4	1.4	1.4	1.4	1.6
Philippines	0.5	0.5	0.5	0.5	0.4	0.4	0.4	0.4	0.5	0.4	0.4
Republic of Korea	2.7	2.6	2.3	2.3	2.3	2.3	2.2	2.4	2.8	2.6	2.4
Thailand	1.2	1.2	1.2	1.2	1.2	1.1	1.1	1.2	1.2	1.2	1.2
All ESCAP-region developing economies	28.4	28.0	29.5	28.7	26.5	26.3	28.6	30.6	31.3	31.7	32.4
All ESCAP-region developed economies	8.6	7.9	7.8	7.8	8.0	7.3	6.6	7.3	6.9	6.4	6.7
Total ESCAP region	37.0	35.9	37.3	36.5	34.6	33.6	35.3	37.9	38.3	38.1	39.1

Source: IMF database, *Direction of Trade Statistics,* available from www2.imfstatistics.org/DOT/ (accessed 16 Feb. 2010).

since the second quarter of 2008, almost all of those developing economies actually increased their market share in the import market of the United States during the ensuing year. China, despite the fall in total exports to the United States, saw its share in that import market increase from about 15% in the second quarter of 2008 to 19.7% in the third quarter of 2009. While total imports into the United States fell during that period, the fall in imports from the developing economies of the ESCAP region was less than that of imports from other suppliers to the United States market.

One implication is that those developing economies did not lose market competitiveness against suppliers from the rest of the world during the downturn in the United States import market, they actually gained in market share. Market competitiveness here refers to the combined effects of cost structure and exchange rate movements on export values. Asian currencies, in general, appreciated less than the United States dollar around the first quarter of 2009, thus supporting Asian market competitiveness during that period. Alternatively, the outcome could simply have been due to the product mix of exports from those developing countries to the United States which could have had relatively lower income elasticity than have

exports from the rest of the world. Further study over a longer time period could determine the causes.

Heightened risk aversion led to financial institutions increasing the cost of trade finance

---

The asset bubble burst that set off the worldwide economic crisis did not damage trade only on the demand side. The supply side, particularly through the trade credit squeeze, was also affected. Large financial institutions scaled back from dealing with emerging market risks, such as financing exports, and instead focused on bolstering their capital bases. That heightened risk aversion, coupled with the overall credit squeeze, led to financial institutions increasing the cost, as well as scaling down the volume, of trade finance. On the other hand, the case may be that a decrease in trade caused the reduction of trade finance. Hence, a drop in demand by the United States, European Union and Japan for Asian exports might naturally lead to reduced demand for trade credit, directly and along the interregional supply chain.[2] Yet another explanation[3] for the reduction of trade credit may lie in the impact of the International Convergence of Capital Measurement and Capital Standards: a Revised Framework (Basel II) on trade flows, through increased procyclicalness of trade finance. According to observers, though not specific to trade finance, the way in which Basel II classifies risk (i.e., focusing on counterparty risk – which is normally taken simply as country risk – rather than performance risk) penalizes trade finance as the risk premiums on international transactions tend to be relatively high, despite the low performance risk of trade finance.[4] Thus, during crises, when country risks (particularly with developing countries) are elevated, trade finance costs escalate, further curtailing export performance.

Given the scarcity of trade finance, the immediate response was to increase the volume of trade finance facilitation programmes of all regional development banks and the International Finance Corporation. Increased financial commitments for trade finance were similarly echoed by the Group of 20 (G-20) leaders at the London Summit of April 2009. Initiatives in the Asia-Pacific region included partnership agreements between the Asian Development Bank (ADB) and private banks (for example, Wachovia) to allow them to share risk in extending trade finance. Guarantees were extended as well as loans to trading parties. Subsequent to the pledges, the concern[5] arose that the additional commitments might not be new and that the amounts cited included ongoing commitments. In addition, it was not very clear as to what extent the regulatory and supervisory framework could be adjusted to take into account the effect of trade finance on developing country exports in an environment of shrinking trade.

The changes experienced in 2009 have resulted in decreases in current account surpluses in the region, in tandem with decreases in current account deficits in developed countries. Whether they are temporary reversals driven in many Asian economies by even sharper falls in imports, or the beginning of a long-term process of rebalancing, remains to be seen. In any case, the current account deficit of the United States has decreased quite sharply, while China has significantly pared down its trade surplus.

The crisis has sparked a debate on the role of trade in development

---

The global crisis, having impacted Asian and Pacific economies through international trade, exposed the vulnerability of the export sector of the region to developed country demand. The crisis has sparked a debate on the role of trade in development and the importance of market diversification.

Trade in a modernizing economy has always been a reliable engine of growth in much of Asia, if not in most parts of the world. The shift

---

[2]   IMF, *World Economic and Financial Surveys, Regional Economic Outlook: Asia and the Pacific: Global Crisis: the Asian Context,* May 2009 ed. (Washington, D.C.); available from www.imf.org/external/pubs/ft/reo/2009/APD/ENG/areo0509.htm.

[3]   Caliari, Aldo, *The Financial Crisis and Trade in Asia: Towards an Integrated Response in Asia.* Proceedings of the ESCAP Regional High-level Workshop on "Strengthening the Response to the Global Financial Crisis in Asia-Pacific: The Role of Monetary, Fiscal and External Debt Policies", 27 to 30 July 2009, Dhaka, Bangladesh, p. 7; citing WTO Working Group on Trade, Debt and Finance, 2008, reporting on the complaints by developing countries regarding the negative effects of biases embedded in the Basel II framework.

[4]   Chauffour, Jean-Pierre and Thomas Faroll, "Trade finance in crisis: Market adjustment or market failure?", Policy Research Working Paper 5003 (Washington, D.C.: World Bank, 2009), p. 15; available from: www-wds.worldbank.org/external/default/WDSContentServer/IW3P/IB/2009/07/20/000158349_20090720085356/Rendered/PDF/WPS5003.pdf.

[5]   Caliari, *The Financial Crisis and Trade in Asia,* p. 8.

to export-led industrialization, epitomized by the "Asian Tigers", created a demonstration effect in most of developing Asia. Over the 40 years from 1956 to 1996, the per capita incomes of the "rapidly integrating economies"[6] of Asia grew by 5%, in comparison with the world average of 1.9%.[7]

Furthermore, during the 1997 crisis, the affected Asian economies managed to export their way to recovery. Innovative production schemes like the regional tie-in to global supply chains fundamentally changed the composition of trade as well as its direction. The strategy paid off because the erstwhile growth engine of the world, the United States, maintained robust demand. Historically, growth in trade in goods has always outstripped global output growth.

Unfortunately, the reverse has also held true. As global growth has moved into negative territory, trade has plummeted more sharply. For some sectors the downturn will be harder to overcome than in the past. Since the global economy is interlinked through trade more than ever before, the impact of a fall in output on trade has become magnified. Empirical estimates[8] put the elasticity of world trade to output at 3.35, from under 2 in the 1960s. East Asia has the largest elasticity for the 12 years from 1995 to 2007, as well as the largest increase in elasticity compared to the 12-year period 1982 to 1994. With export elasticity to global growth at 4.45, the East Asian trading sector is indeed very sensitive to changes in global growth relative to other regions in the world.

What could account for the increasingly higher elasticity measures of the current decade in comparison with the earlier periods? Some ob-servers[9] say that the structure of the global production chains exacerbates the decline in merchandise trade during recessions. Trade finance might be able to provide another, partial explanation of why trade has contracted much more than global output.

The responsiveness of trade to a global downturn depends on the mix of products

---

Given the fragmentation in production systems, countries increasingly specialize in a particular process or component (that is, intermediate products) rather than a whole or final product. Countries that want to export such products need to import the parts and components. For example, China imports semiconductors from Malaysia, hard disks from the Philippines and other components from elsewhere, and assembles them into computers that are shipped to the United States. Chinese imports and exports are thus higher than if China were to produce the computers wholly from within its borders. So the responsiveness of trade of a country to a global downturn depends, in part, on its mix of products. The greater the proportion of products destined for exports that need imported inputs, the more sensitive the trading sector is to changes in global incomes. Such trade among countries linked through international production networks tends to be "double-counted" in trade statistics[10] as corroborated by the rapid increases in manufactured imports and exports in countries, such as China and Malaysia, that are heavily involved in international production networks.

---

[6] The ADB characterization of "integrating Asia" comprises the 10 countries of ASEAN and China, India, Japan, the Republic of Korea, Taiwan Province of China and Hong Kong, China.

[7] ADB, *Emerging Asian Regionalism: A Partnership for Shared Prosperity* (Manila, 2008), p. 27; available from www.aric.adb.org/emergingasianregionalism (accessed 12 Oct. 2009).

[8] Freund, Caroline, "The trade response to global downturns: Historical evidence", Policy Research Working Paper 5015 (Washington, D.C.: The World Bank, 2009), p. 6; available from http://econ.worldbank.org.

[9] Freund, "The trade response to global downturns", p. 9.

[10] UNCTAD, *Trade and Development Report 2003: Capital Accumulation, Growth and Structural Change,* (United Nations publication, Sales No. E.03.II.D.7), p. 49.

Consequently, how vulnerable to the worldwide slump in income did Asia and the Pacific become? That would depend on (a) the degree of openness of the economies in the region, (b) the market orientation of exports and (c) the product mix of trade. On the demand side, the fall in import demand of the affected economies of the United States, Europe and Japan has a direct bearing on exports from the region because of its large share of developed-country imports.

Since the crisis was transmitted through the trade channel, obviously the greater the share of the trade sector in the economy, the greater was the impact. The Asia-Pacific region is highly open and export dependent: the export sector of Asian and Pacific developing economies comprises close to 38% of GDP, which is two and a half times larger than the corresponding share of the developed economies in the region (figure

8). The subregional groupings exhibit some striking differences, however. South-East Asia, and East and North-East Asia, are the most export-dependent, while South and South-West Asia have less export dependent economies.

The phenomenal Chinese export performance during the past five years accounts for much of the increase in the ratio of exports to GDP in the East and North-East Asian subregion. By contrast, despite doubling its own ratio of exports to GDP, India with just 1% of world exports does not significantly alter the corresponding ratio in the South Asian subregion.[11]

The destination market of exports has also become an indicator of vulnerability as it came to reflect the exposure of an economy to the source of market disturbance. Measures of trade intensity are revealing here, indicating whether a region or country exports more (as a

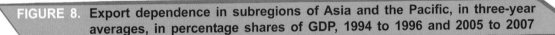

FIGURE 8. Export dependence in subregions of Asia and the Pacific, in three-year averages, in percentage shares of GDP, 1994 to 1996 and 2005 to 2007

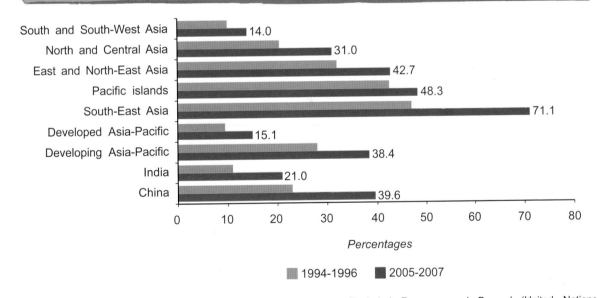

South and South-West Asia   14.0
North and Central Asia   31.0
East and North-East Asia   42.7
Pacific islands   48.3
South-East Asia   71.1
Developed Asia-Pacific   15.1
Developing Asia-Pacific   38.4
India   21.0
China   39.6

Percentages

■ 1994-1996   ■ 2005-2007

Source: ESCAP, *Asia-Pacific Trade and Investment Report 2009: Trade-led Recovery and Beyond* (United Nations publication, Sales No. E.09.II.F.19), p. 6.

---

[11]   ESCAP, *Asia-Pacific Trade and Investment Report 2009: Trade-led Recovery and Beyond* (United Nations publication, Sales No. E.09.II.F.19), p. 6; and ADB, *Asia Economic Monitor: July 2009* (Manila, 2009), available from www.aric.adb.org/asia-economic-monitor.

percentage) to a given destination than the world does on average. More specifically, the trade intensity index measures the ratio of the trade share of a particular country to a partner or region and the world trade share to the same country or region. An index value greater than 1.0 would indicate that the country's export volume to a given destination is greater than the world average. The country would thus be said to have a more intense export trade relation with that partner than does the rest of the world (table 2).

An increasing value in the index with China might therefore indicate greater trade in components and parts with China whose final destination is the United States, rather than increased Chinese dependency on itself as final consumer. Thus, one limitation of this measure is that it does not account for the trade pattern based on the intermediate goods from global production chains. For that reason, an index that deals with the product mix could be used to complement the analysis.

Economies that trade intensively with the United States and Japan are more vulnerable than others to the collapse in external demand

Given the outlook for 2010, economies that tend to trade intensively with the United States and Japan are rendered more vulnerable than others to the collapse in external demand. In favourable contrast, the Chinese and Indian economic growth rates during 2008 and much of 2009 are quite remarkable given the backdrop of the global recession. Will those two large economies be the next engines of growth in Asia and the Pacific?

China recently surpassed Germany as the largest exporter in the world. The Chinese profile looms even larger in the region as its exports and imports account for a growing proportion of the regional trade. With China emerging as the world's factory, particularly of manufactured exports, Asian and Pacific economies that have embarked on a similar export-based growth strategy could feel threatened. At the same time China's emergence, accentuated by its resilience to the global crisis, presents the opportunity of a growing market when growth in the rest of the world is anaemic, as evinced by trade deficits in 2008 with Japan, the Republic of Korea, South-East Asia and Australia.

If China imports from Asian sources for its own consumption, its domestic spending would become an important source of external demand

To what extent can China be expected to be an engine of growth in the post-crisis period for Asian and Pacific economies? Much depends on whether China imports from developing Asia for consumption purposes or simply to source inputs for its assembly operations. If China were to import from Asian sources for its own consumption, its domestic spending would become an important source of external demand. Here a few caveats should be considered in using the trade intensity indicators. First of all, the trade intensity index also picks up the trade with China in parts and components of countries but does not distinguish it from trade in goods for own consumption. Thus, exports of intermediate goods from other countries to China could well end up as part of Chinese exports to the affected economies, such as the United States. Some estimate the foreign content of China's aggregate merchandise export at between 25 to 46% in 2002 depending on the methodology used.[12] Furthermore,

---

[12] Dean, J., K.C. Fung and Z. Wang, "How vertically specialized is Chinese trade?", Bank of Finland Discussion Papers 31 (Helsinki: Bank of Finland Institute for Economies in Transition, 2008), available from www.bof.fi/NR/rdonlyres/0F367D7B-DA85-4D13-8788-9E2EF25DFBCB/0/dp3108.pdf.

TABLE 2. Trade intensity indices of Asian and Pacific economies, 2007

	Trade with US	with Japan	with China
Developing economies			
China	1.39	2.01	–
Hong Kong, China	1.25	0.51	6.44
Macao, China	2.96	0.28	2.13
Mongolia	0.25	0.16	15.60
Republic of Korea (the)	0.90	1.71	4.60
Russian Federation (the)	0.15	0.57	0.99
Bangladesh	1.89	0.29	0.17
India	1.02	0.56	1.35
Maldives	0.08	1.11	0.00
Pakistan	1.62	0.16	0.73
Sri Lanka	2.07	0.66	0.13
Cambodia	4.28	0.75	0.25
Indonesia	0.76	5.04	1.79
Malaysia	1.14	2.22	1.86
Philippines	1.58	4.22	1.03
Singapore	0.68	1.18	2.13
Thailand	0.92	2.83	2.06
Viet Nam	1.62	2.89	1.34
Developed economies			
Australia	0.37	4.09	2.56
Japan	1.50	–	3.11
New Zealand	0.85	2.29	1.16
United States	–	1.36	1.23

Notes: The index takes a value between 0 and +∞. Values greater than 1.0 indicate an "intense" trade relationship. The index utilizes export data.
Source: ESCAP, Asia-Pacific Trade and Investment Agreements Database (APTIAD) Interactive Trade Indicators; available from www.unescap.org/tid/artnet/artnet_app/iti_aptiad.aspx (accessed 6 Oct. 2009).

a study[13] estimates that the share of parts and components in total imports into China has doubled from 17.6% in 1992 to 34.3% in 2003.

Secondly, the strength of realignment in trade of Asian and Pacific developing economies with China will depend on the import intensity of the latter's domestic demand. In other words, it will depend on whether the share of final goods in the imports of China will increase relative to imports of parts and components. A study of the recent pattern of trade between China and the East and South-East Asian economies provides limited evidence that China "is becoming more of a consumer and less of an assembler".[14] The study reveals that China increased its imports from East and South-East Asia from $9.9 billion to $17.9 billion over the period from January to June 2009, when exports of the region were declining, indicating that China is providing additional external demand to its regional trading partners. Given the disparity in the magnitude of consumption spending be-

---

[13] Athukorala, P-C. and N. Yamashita, "Production fragmentation and trade integration: East Asia in a global context", *North American Journal of Economics and Finance* (Dec. 2006), vol. 17, no. 3, p. 8.
[14] ADB, *Asian Development Outlook Update: Broadening Openness for a Resilient Asia* (Manila: ADB, 2009), available from www.adb.org/Documents/Books/ADO/2009/Update/ado2009-update.pdf (accessed 5 Oct. 2009).

tween the developed countries and China, however, China could not be expected to substitute, in the short term, for the United States or European Union, in generating external demand for Asian and Pacific economies.

India has become an attractive and growing market for the region

---

In addition, by virtue of its economic performance during the crisis, India has become an attractive and growing market for the region. Unlike China, which tends to dominate in manufactured exports of finished goods, India has always been a net importer of goods with countries in the region, excepting with the Republic of Korea with which it has a positive trade balance. In 2008, for example, its trade deficit with the ASEAN countries and China approached $15 billion and $21 billion, respectively. Furthermore, Indian imports of goods from ASEAN countries grew annually by more than 25% in 2007 and 2008. As India continues to grow, its imports will provide buoyant demand in the region.

Even more significant than net trade figures in the region's trade with India might be the sharp contrast in complementarities of competitive structure. India is a world leader in services exports, especially commercial services; whereas the comparative advantage for many of the region's trading partners lies in manufactures and commodities. Hence, the ASEAN-India Trade in Goods Agreement that came into effect on 1 January 2010 and continuing negotiations in services and investments appear promising for regional integration. The agreement marks intensification of the "Look East" strategy of India and the need for ASEAN countries to engage with rapidly growing markets and to balance its relations with all major Asian economic powers.

Product mix is also important. Expected to fall first is trade in export items that require signifi-

cant imported inputs that are, in turn, characterized as having rather high intra-industry trade (IIT) indices. IIT measures the degree of overlap between imports and exports in the same commodity category, with a value of 1.0 indicating pure "intra-industry" trade and a value of 0 indicating pure "inter-industry" trade. Export commodities, such as electronics or motor vehicles that use significant quantities of imported electronic and automotive parts and components as intermediate goods, have high IIT. The higher the share of such items in a country's export profile, the more vulnerable that country to the crisis.

The surge in intra-industrial trade in electronic parts and components has underpinned much of the growth in intraregional trade in the region

---

Many economies in South-East Asia exhibit high IIT in the sectors that are cited in table 3 under categories of the Harmonized Commodity Description and Coding System (HS); the extent of outsourcing in each sector is indicated for machinery (HS Code 84), electronics (HS Code 85), motor vehicles (HS Code 87) and knitted apparel (HS Code 61). Motor vehicle production in Malaysia, the Philippines, Thailand and Indonesia is subject to extensive parts and components trade that is facilitated under the ASEAN Free Trade Agreement (AFTA). Those same South-East Asian economies exhibit very high IIT in electronics (HS Code 85), indicating a high degree of outsourcing activity. The surge in intra-industrial trade in electronic parts and components (as intermediate goods) has underpinned much of the growth in intraregional trade in the region. A softening in demand would certainly take a heavier toll on items marked by extensive trade in parts and components. Economies with high proportions of those sectors in their export profiles were thus more vulnerable to the crisis.

TABLE 3. Intra-industry trade indices of Asian and Pacific economies, by sector, 2007

Economy	Sector/Commodity Group (HS codes)			
	HS 84	HS 85	HS 87	HS 61
Developing economies				
China	0.55	0.55	0.81	0.04
Hong Kong, China	0.02	0.03	0.00	0.71
Macao, China	0.46	0.37	0.22	0.48
Mongolia	0.03	0.03	0.04	0.58
Republic of Korea (the)	0.83	0.67	0.23	0.71
Russian Federation (the)	0.26	0.22	0.16	0.00
Bangladesh	0.06	0.05	0.16	0.01
India	0.38	0.41	0.87	0.04
Pakistan	0.04	0.07	0.07	0.18
Sri Lanka	0.06	0.27	0.47	0.22
Cambodia	0.01	0.05	0.27	0.03
Indonesia	0.46	0.72	0.68	0.22
Malaysia	0.78	0.93	0.47	0.96
Philippines	0.98	0.74	0.91	0.40
Singapore	0.79	0.66	0.06	0.63
Thailand	0.80	0.92	0.55	0.12
Viet Nam	0.46	0.76	0.25	0.08
Developed economies				
Australia	0.35	0.32	0.29	0.11
Japan	0.52	0.61	0.18	0.03
New Zealand	0.49	0.50	0.07	0.19
United States	0.82	0.66	0.62	0.10

Notes: The index ranges from zero to 1.0, with zero indicating pure inter-industry trade and 1.0 indicating pure intra-industry trade. The Harmonizing Commodity Description and Coding System (HS) codes are:
61 Articles of apparel, accessories knit or crochet.
84 Nuclear reactors, boilers, machineries, etc.
85 Electrical, electronic equipment.
87 Vehicles other than railway and tramway.
Source: ESCAP, Asia-Pacific Trade and Investment Agreements Database (APTIAD) Interactive Trade Indicators; available from www.unescap.org/tid/artnet/artnet_app/iti_aptiad.aspx (accessed 7 Oct. 2009); descriptions of commodity codes come from www.trademap.org/stCorrespondingProductCodes.aspx.

Exposure to capital flows

The region experienced the first impact of the crisis through short-term capital flows, which brought instability, not unlike in 1997. Policymakers had attempted to mitigate the risk of instability by building up foreign reserves to levels that could cope with expected capital outflows. Notwithstanding policy, the manner in which the channel of capital flows operated during the global crisis was different from the case in 1997. At that time, the problem with capital flows lay more in excessive short-term foreign debt of domestic banks and other private-sector operators. However, the past decade has been notable for another aspect of capital flow build-up – that of foreign portfolio capital. Looking at net capital flows (figure 9), the collapse of 1997 and 1998 was due largely to the reversal in short-term bank loans. The global crisis of 2008 and 2009 was driven more by sharp reversals in portfolio flows, although inevitably there were also

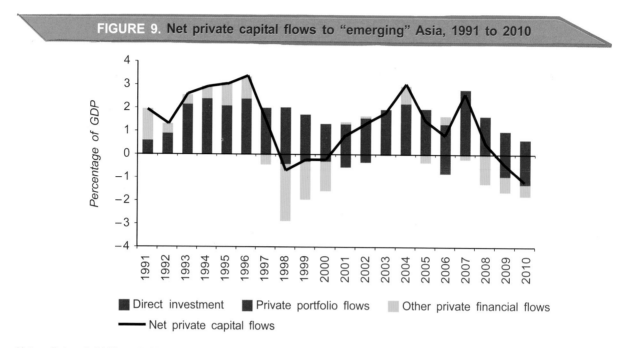

FIGURE 9. Net private capital flows to "emerging" Asia, 1991 to 2010

■ Direct investment ■ Private portfolio flows ▨ Other private financial flows
— Net private capital flows

Notes: Data of 2009 and 2010 are projections by IMF, "Emerging" Asia comprises 26 developing countries and newly industrialized economies of Asia.
Source: Based on data from IMF, *World Economic and Financial Surveys: World Economic Outlook Database,* Oct. 2009 ed., available from www.imf.org/external/pubs/ft/weo/2009/02/weodata/index.aspx (accessed 25 Feb. 2010).

retrenchments in lending by many international banks in response to the financial stresses faced by their headquarters in the United States and Europe. In contrast to the 1997 crisis, the reversal in capital flows was driven by pressures emanating from outside the region, from the problems of the financial institutions in developed countries and the increase in global risk aversion.

The region experienced the first impact of the crisis through short-term capital flows

Some major economies relatively more reliant on external borrowing for financing domestic credit creation, such as India and the Republic of Korea, were also impacted by the crisis through the channel of the global credit crunch. Notably, the corporate sector in India used significant foreign borrowings to fund expansion;[15] external commercial borrowing in India during the first quarter of FY2009 was $2.711 billion, in comparison with $4.052 billion in the first quarter of FY2008. Banks in the Republic of Korea relied on global borrowing to fund credit-dependent household spending; the country's loan-to-deposit ratio of close to 120% was the highest in the region. Reduced availability of international credit impacted growth through increased pricing of loans to fund consumption and investment, despite easing of monetary policy that all countries engaged in. The continuing dependence on foreign financing of consumption by some countries after the crisis (figure 10) has meant that the resumption of international credit flows remains an important factor in recovery.

---

[15] *The Hindu Business Line,* "Overseas borrowing gets easier for India Inc.", Chennai, India, 31 July 2009, available from www.thehindubusinessline.com/2009/07/31/stories/2009073151870100.htm.

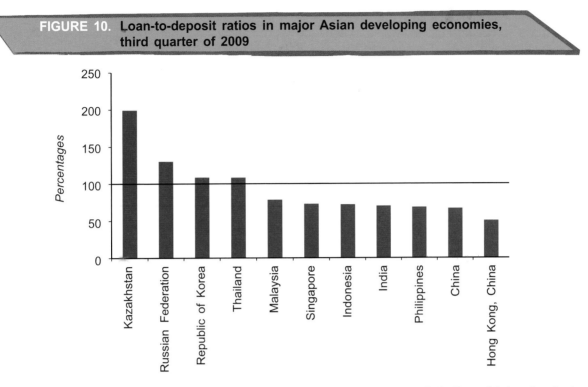

FIGURE 10. Loan-to-deposit ratios in major Asian developing economies, third quarter of 2009

Notes: Data of Kazakhstan and the Philippines refer to April 2009 and May 2009, respectively. Data of Indonesia refer to May 2009. Data of India refer to Q2 2009. Data of India refer to the credit-to-deposit ratio of scheduled commercial banks. Data of Thailand refer to the consolidated-loan-to-deposit ratio.

Sources: ESCAP staff estimation based on data from CEIC Data Company Ltd., available from http://ceicdata.com/ (accessed 29 Jan. 2010); and IMF, *Republic of Kazakhstan: 2009 Article IV Consultation – Staff Report; Supplement; and Public Information Notice on the Executive Board Discussion,* IMF Country Report No. 09/300 (Washington, D.C., 17 June 2009).

> *The critical lesson is that countries that have experienced massive portfolio capital inflows are at risk of a sudden outflow*

Any region that experiences a slowdown or reversal in foreign portfolio capital flows will inevitably suffer from a negative balance-of-payments shock in the form of exchange-rate depreciation, sharp decline in foreign exchange reserves and/or interest rate hike with deleterious effects on the domestic economy. While the Asia-Pacific region did see a sudden stop in capital flows, those economies that were running current-account surpluses were not as vulnerable as the Republic of Korea, in particular, and

India and Indonesia, which experienced some of the sharpest declines in reserves and exchange rates. Even in those economies the current-account deficits were fairly small, suggesting that the need for net capital flows to finance the deficit was fairly modest. The critical lesson is that even countries that do not require foreign capital to finance current account imbalances but have experienced massive portfolio capital inflows in previous years, and thus have a stock of gross external liabilities that could potentially be reversible, are at risk of a sudden outflow. For example, countries with large current-account surpluses, such as Singapore and Malaysia, have also experienced downward pressure on their reserves due to a reversal of some portfolio capital inflows from previous years.

Exposure to a high level of foreign portfolio capital inflows can thus create a crisis even when economic fundamentals are sound, or it can make a bad situation worse when the fundamentals are weak. Foreign portfolio capital is volatile for a host of reasons, some of which, as demonstrated by the present crisis, are driven by developments outside of the country or region in question. Moreover, once the outflow of foreign portfolio capital becomes a problem, it further undermines the confidence of international capital markets. While the current financial crisis has confirmed the importance of reserve holdings, the appropriate size of reserves remains unclear; i.e., reserve adequacy. Asia as a whole clearly holds adequate reserves in terms of its imports and short-term debt (table 4). However, as shown by the Republic of Korea and other countries, other forms of mobile capital such as portfolio flows are a concern. No proper yardstick has yet been developed to account for the potential reversibility of those other types of capital flows.[16]

TABLE 4. Foreign reserve adequacy, 1996 to 2009: outstanding year-end reserves position

Region[a] and country	Foreign reserves (in billions of US dollars)				GDP	Foreign reserves as a percentage of:							
						Short-term external debt[b]				Imports			
	1996	2007	2008	2009	2008	1996	2007	2008	2009	1996	2007	2008	2009
Developing Asia[c]	483.1	2 916.8	3 328.5	3 355	39.6	170	449	589	595	49.0	103.6	100.0	116.8
China	107.0	1 530.3	1 949.0	1 954	45.1	376	1 249	1 865	1 873	69.4	147.9	172.0	193.4
India	20.2	267.0	247.4	242	20.3	260	339	333	324	53.2	123.2	84.8	91.9
Republic of Korea	34.0	262.2	201.1	212	21.6	45	176	173	177	22.6	73.5	46.2	63.7
Other developing Asia[d]	321.9	857.3	931.0	948	48.1	145	389	502	511	48.9	66.6	63.3	74.9
Latin America	143.0	399.9	442.7	410	11.4	145	238	369	300	63.6	65.2	59.5	62.4
Brazil	58.3	179.4	192.8	186	12.0	111	292	342	329	102.7	141.8	105.5	109.5
Chile	15.0	16.8	23.1	24	13.6	201	86	113	114	78.0	35.7	37.3	46.1
Mexico	19.4	87.1	95.1	84	8.8	60	256	241	218	20.7	29.5	29.4	31.0
Central and Eastern Europe	52.6	224.2	230.4	211	15.7	504	114	107	92	38.1	34.3	29.6	38.9
Middle East	18.5	59.8	57.1	47	8.0	111	98	112	90	47.5	44.9	34.9	34.0
Russian Federation	11.3	466.8	412.5	368	25.7	42	486	509	446	16.4	208.8	141.3	144.4
Memo:													
Net oil exporters	180.5	959.5	946.3	..	19.8	200	1 050	1 862	..	67.2	108.8	89.5	..

Notes: [a] Regional aggregates are the sum of the economies listed. For 2009, data are the latest available (up to August 2009).
[b] Consolidated cross-border claims of all Bank of International Settlements reporting banks for countries outside the reporting area with a maturity of up to one year plus international debt securities outstanding with a remaining maturity of up to one year.
[c] Economies listed and other Asian developing countries.
[d] Taiwan Province of China; Hong Kong, China; Indonesia, Malaysia, the Philippines, Singapore and Thailand.
Sources: Based on data from the World Bank, *World Economic Outlook Database,* October 2009, available from www.imf.org/external/pubs/ft/weo/2009/02/weodata/weoselgr.aspx (accessed 15 Dec. 2009); Economist Intelligence Unit, Country Analysis and Forecasts, *EIU CountryData,* accessible at http://countryanalysis.eiu.com/ (accessed 15 Dec. 2009); and Bank for International Settlements, "BIS Quarterly Review: March 2010", Table 9A (available from www.bis.org/statistics/hcsv/hanx9a_1y.csv) and Table 17B (available from www.bis.org/statistics/qcsv/anx17b.csv).

---

[16] For example, see Wijnholds, J. Onno de Beaufort, and Arend Kapteyn, "Reserve adequacy in emerging market economies", IMF Working Paper WP/01/143 (Washington, D.C.: IMF, 2001), pp. 9-11.

A more precise yardstick of vulnerability could encompass the measurement of overall gross external liabilities of a country that are most clearly reversible and measurable

A more precise yardstick of vulnerability could encompass the measurement of overall gross external liabilities of a country that are most clearly reversible and measurable. The components of such an approach are short-term debt, the stock of portfolio inflows and the magnitude of imports over three months. The quantum of short-term debt and the stock of portfolio capital inflows are relevant because they can exit the country at any time, resulting in currency devaluation pressure. Similarly, the quantum of imports over three months represents the amount of reserves that flows out as financing for imports. "Gross" rather than "net" is appropriate because, if foreigners should choose to withdraw their funds, the country might not be able to coordinate accounts in order to remit its gross external assets back to the country simultaneously – particularly if the investments to and from the country are made by unconnected parties.

One hundred per cent of foreign reserves is taken as the threshold. However, the threshold is subject to a number of caveats. It may be an overestimate because the portfolio market price in distress periods may be much less than its historical value, while exchange-rate depreciations during crisis may also lessen the stock of outflow. On the other hand, the threshold may be an underestimate because some countries are also susceptible to "internal drain" – a run against domestic currency by residents. The likelihood of internal drain has increased in recent years because regulation of financial out-

flows has been liberalized in several countries across the region.

At the end of 2008, after the worst of the financial impact of the crisis, the vulnerability yardstick was not covered in full (100%) by foreign reserves in a number of countries. Of those for which data are available (figure 11), the vulnerability yardstick exceeds the stock of reserves in the Republic of Korea, Indonesia, Malaysia, Philippines and Kazakhstan. In each of those countries, the stock of foreign portfolio inflows accounted for the greatest part of the vulnerability yardstick, followed by short-term debt.

The lesson to be drawn here is that the analysis of the risks of a sudden reversal in foreign capital flows should be broadened. The traditional view of short-term debt being the main component of such flows should be tempered with the finding that portfolio capital has become increasingly important in the region, with the potential to destabilize currencies by flowing out in a similar short-term fashion.

The next question that arises is how best to deal with portfolio capital flows – a matter of much debate. An uncontrolled inflow requires a sufficient build-up of reserves to buffer sudden outflows. Building up of reserves is costly, however, because of potential exchange-rate losses as well as the loss in interest income from having to invest the funds in low-interest-earning foreign currency assets. An option would be to manage the quantum of inflow of such funds through various capital controls. The potential benefits of such controls have come increasingly under discussion owing to the lessons from this crisis about the risks of short-term capital inflows.[17] A completely open capital account is not necessarily appropriate from a cost-benefit analytical viewpoint,[18] particularly since research has suggested that the benefits of such openness are ambiguous.[19] Further-

[17]   Ostry, J. D. and others, *Capital Inflows: The Role of Controls,* Staff Position Note No. 2010/04 (Washington, D.C.: IMF, 2010), available from www.imf.org/external/pubs/cat/longres.cfm?sk=23580.0.

[18]   Rodrik, D., "The social cost of foreign exchange reserves", *International Economic Journal 20,* 2006.

[19]   For example, Kose, M.A. and others, "Financial globalization: a reappraisal", NBER Working Paper No. 12484 (Cambridge, Massachusetts: National Bureau of Economic Research, 2006); and Eichengreen, B., *Capital Flows and Crisis* (Cambridge, Massachusetts: MIT Press, 2003).

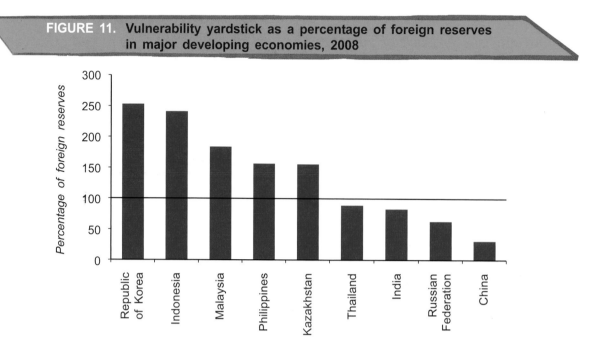

FIGURE 11. Vulnerability yardstick as a percentage of foreign reserves in major developing economies, 2008

Notes: Vulnerability yardstick is the sum of short-term debt, imports of the last quarter of the year and stock of equity and debt portfolio capital. Data on stock of foreign portfolio investments of Indonesia, Malaysia and Philippines refer to figures of 2007.

Sources: ESCAP calculations based on data from IMF, *International Financial Statistics (IFS) Online Service,* available from www.imfstatistics.org/imf/ (accessed 24 Oct. 2009) and *World Economic and Financial Surveys: World Economic Outlook Database,* Oct. 2009 ed., available from www.imf.org/external/pubs/ft/weo/2009/02/weodata/index.aspx (accessed 24 Oct. 2009); World Bank, *Quarterly External Debt Statistics* databases, available from http://web.worldbank.org/WBSITE/EXTER-NAL/DATASTATISTICS/EXTDECQEDS/0,,menuPK:1805431~pagePK:64168427~piPK:64168435~theSitePK:1805415,00.html (accessed 13 Oct. 2009); and CEIC Data Company Ltd., available from http://ceicdata.com/ (accessed 24 Oct. 2009).

more, the relevance of an international tax to moderate the volatility of portfolio flows, along the lines of the so-called Tobin tax, has been discussed in the context of problems inherent in imposing capital controls at national level.[20]

Capital markets and exchange rates: renewed inflows bring instability

The initial impact of the crisis on the region was felt through the financial markets as investors withdrew capital from equity and debt markets in a flight to safety. For highly leveraged investors, declining equity values abroad also triggered margin calls. That outflow of capital led to particularly sharp falls in markets where, taking advantage of high global liquidity, foreign investors had acquired an increasing presence. The entry of foreign capital has been encouraged by the liberalization of capital markets in the region since the 1997 crisis.[21] Financial markets in the region have seen a sharp upturn during 2009 after reaching their troughs in the early part of the year, due to renewed inflows of foreign capital. Markets have also been supported by

[20] Epstein, Gerald, "Should financial flows be regulated? Yes", United Nations DESA Working Paper No. 77, ST/ESA/2009/DWP/77, available from www.un.org/esa/desa/papers/, July 2009; and Persaud, Avinash, "We should put sand in the wheels of the market", *Financial Times,* Comment/Opinion, London, 27 Aug. 2009, available from www.ft.com/cms/s/0/08523a6a-934c-11de-b146-00144feabdc0.html.

[21] See Akyuz, Yilmaz, *The Current Global Financial Crisis and Asian Developing Countries,* ESCAP Series on Inclusive and Sustainable Development 2 (Bangkok: ESCAP, 2008), p. 3.

buoyant domestic buying spurred by borrowing in a number of countries such as China and India.

Financial markets in the region have seen a sharp upturn due to renewed inflows of foreign capital

As capital inflows have returned to the region, exchange rates have come under upward pressure after substantial depreciation since the onset of the crisis (figure 12). Notably, the Korean won appreciated around 8% over the period beginning in January 2009 to the time of this writing. Other currencies such as the Thai baht, Indian rupee and Singaporean dollar appreciated slightly. A number of currencies, particularly those most affected by the crisis such as the Korean won and Russian rouble, still remain substantially below values seen in September 2008. In any case, the fall in currency values to

their lowest point for countries in the region was generally far less than in the 1997 crisis (figure 13). One factor responsible in maintaining currency values was the use by the central banks of foreign exchange reserves in supporting currencies across the region (figure 14).

Exchange rates have come under upward pressure after substantial depreciation since the onset of the crisis

As recovery gains momentum in the region, concerns about the future strength and role of the United States dollar as a reserve currency grow, given the build-up of governmental debt and lacklustre growth. The need to engage in policies in the coming months to manage appreciation of currencies in order to encourage nascent export recovery will require Asian and

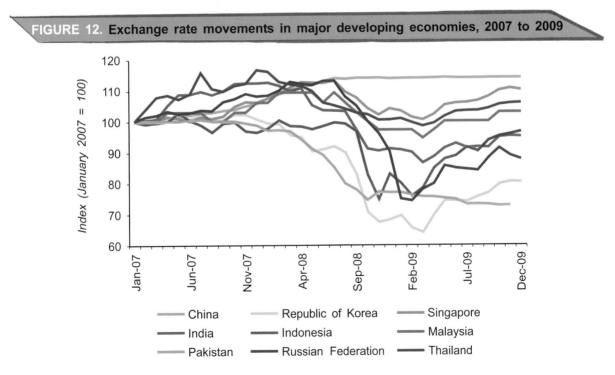

FIGURE 12. **Exchange rate movements in major developing economies, 2007 to 2009**

Legend: China, India, Pakistan, Republic of Korea, Indonesia, Russian Federation, Singapore, Malaysia, Thailand

Note: A positive trend represents appreciation and vice versa.
Source: Based on data from CEIC Data Company Ltd., available from http://ceicdata.com/ (accessed 15 Feb. 2010).

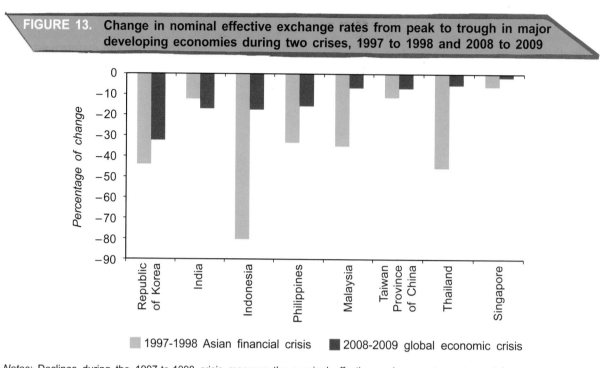

FIGURE 13. Change in nominal effective exchange rates from peak to trough in major developing economies during two crises, 1997 to 1998 and 2008 to 2009

Notes: Declines during the 1997-to-1998 crisis measure the nominal effective exchange-rate movement from peak to trough during that period. Declines for the recent crisis (2008 to 2009) measure the corresponding movement from the recent peak in 2008 to November 2009.

Source: Based on data from Bank of International Settlements databases, available from www.bis.org/statistics/eer/broad1002.xls (accessed 15 Feb. 2010).

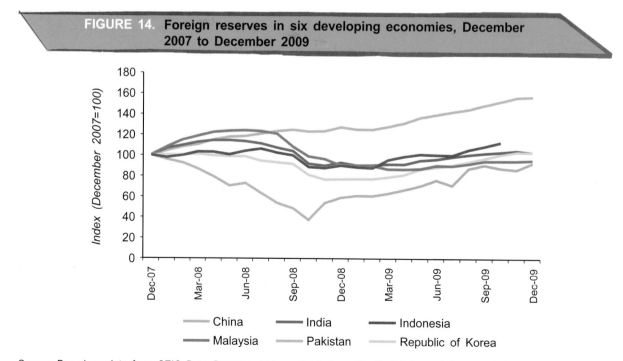

FIGURE 14. Foreign reserves in six developing economies, December 2007 to December 2009

Source: Based on data from CEIC Data Company Ltd., available from http://ceicdata.com/ (accessed 25 Feb. 2010).

Pacific Governments to make important decisions about how to reduce exposure to losses in any future investment in dollar assets. Losses would arise from reduction in values of assets due to any future dollar depreciation and from the interest rate spread between investment in dollar-denominated debt instruments compared with the interest rate paid on domestic bonds issued as part of any accompanying "sterilization". China was at the forefront of implementing alternative approaches in 2009. The central bank signed swap arrangements with numerous countries in Asia as well as farther afield in Latin America, allowing those countries to extend credit in yuan to their own importers and exporters and their trade with China to be invoiced in yuan rather than dollars.

Emerging reorientation of foreign direct investment

In common with other capital flows, foreign direct investment (FDI) in the region was significantly impacted during the crisis (figure 15). China, for example, attracted 20% less FDI from January to July 2009 compared with the corresponding period in 2008.[22] Similarly, FDI in India from April to June 2009 was down 30% compared with the corresponding period in 2008.[23] Developed-country foreign enterprises did not pursue investments abroad for several reasons – downward adjustment in expectations of profitability of the investment, the need to save funds for difficulties faced in their home markets in developed countries, and difficulty in obtaining financing due to the credit crunch. There will therefore be some reorientation in the

sources of FDI, as more investment comes from enterprises of countries within the region that are relatively profitable.

In the medium term, the crisis is likely to increase the relative importance of FDI from the region

---

Reorientation in FDI is one aspect of a general increase in the importance of outbound FDI from the region. FDI outflows from South, East, and South-East Asia in 2008 increased by 7% to $186 billion.[24] Here, again, the history of China's outbound investment flows is spectacular, albeit short.[25] Until 2004 it had remained insignificant, but by 2007 had increased to $25 billion, only to double to more than $50 billion in 2008. There was some fall in outbound FDI in late 2008 and early 2009 due to the crisis, as the credit crunch made financing of such acquisitions more difficult. Outbound FDI from India in 2008, for example, was down by 7% to under $17 billion, the first absolute fall in outbound FDI from the country since 1999. Similarly the first half of 2009 saw outbound investments from the country fall by 65% to under $3 billion compared with the corresponding period in 2008.[26] In the medium term, the crisis is likely to increase the relative importance of FDI from the region as companies exploit the relative weakness of enterprises in the developed world to acquire some of their assets, either in the developed world or of subsidiaries in developing countries. Some of the largest invest-

---

22 Terence Poon, "Foreign direct investment in China continues to slide", *Wall Street Journal, Asia* ed., Economy sec. (online), 18 Aug. 2009; available from http://online.wsj.com/article/SB125047781996935959.html?KEYWORDS=%22foreign+direct+investment+in+china+continues+to+slide%22.

23 *Economic Times,* "FDI increased 8% in June to $2.58 bn", News sec., Delhi, 19 Aug. 2009, available from http://economictimes.indiatimes.com/News/Economy/Finance/FDI-increased-8-in-June-to-258-bn/articleshow/4909780.cms.

24 UNCTAD, *World Investment Report 2009: Transnational Corporations, Agricultural Production and Development* (United Nations publication, Sales No. E.09.II.D.15), p. xxiii.

25 Rosen, Daniel H., and Thilo Hanemann, "China's changing outbound foreign direct investment profile: drivers and policy implications", Policy Brief No. PB09-14 (Washington, D.C.: Peterson Institute for International Economics, 2009).

26 *Emirates Business 24-7,* "Domestic growth may help India's outward FDI", Dubai, available from www.business24-7.ae/Articles/2009/8/Pages/18082009/08192009_feb4d07748b44a9da4abc69e871fac2c.aspx.

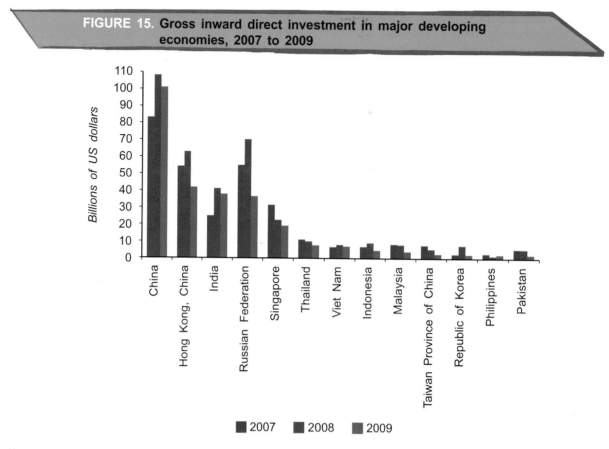

FIGURE 15. Gross inward direct investment in major developing economies, 2007 to 2009

■ 2007 ■ 2008 ■ 2009

Note: Inward direct investment figures for 2009 are estimates.

Sources: UNCTAD, *World Investment Report 2009: Transnational Corporations, Agricultural Production and Development* (United Nations publication, Sales No. E.09.II.D.15), p. 249; Economist Intelligence Unit, Country Analysis and Forecasts, *EIU CountryData,* accessible at http://countryanalysis.eiu.com/ (accessed 22 Feb. 2010).

ments made during this window of opportunity have been in the financial sphere, with banks and sovereign wealth funds from the region acquiring developed-country assets. Examples include the purchase of ING's Asian operations by Overseas-Chinese Banking Corporation Limited of Singapore in October 2009 and China Investment Corporation's purchase of additional shares in Morgan Stanley in June 2009. Furthermore, as the limits of the region's old growth model based on exports of manufactures become apparent, companies will try to capture a greater share of the most lucrative value-added activities in the international production

chain by increasingly investing abroad. For example, in China, outbound FDI is improving trading infrastructure through the establishment of foreign offices that will improve logistical services for China's trading firms. At the same time, other aspects driving the increase in outbound FDI from the region, such as the ambition to secure natural resource assets to drive high economic growth and to capture production in the lower-wage countries, will continue both within the region and beyond. For example, flows to Africa grew to a record $88 billion in 2008, driven by natural resource investment and with an increasing role of Asian investors.[27]

---

[27] AFP [Agence France-Presse], "Global crisis hits African investment: UN", *News on African Politics*, AFP global ed., 18 Sept. 2009, available from www.africanpoliticsinfo.com/article/674708/?k=j83s12y12h94s27k02.

Evolving impacts on jobs and income

As a region with heavy trade dependency, the collapse in aggregate demand from developed countries has led to factory closures and massive job losses in many of the key export manufacturing industries in the region, including textiles, garments, electronics and autos. By 2009 the number of unemployed in the Asia-Pacific region had increased by 10 million in comparison with 2007, bringing the unemployment rate up to 5.0%.[28] While the average unemployment rate of the region is below that of the countries of the Organisation for Economic Cooperation and Development (OECD), which recorded an average rate of 8.2% in the second quarter of 2009,[29] unemployment in developing economies of Asia has particularly worrisome features.

As the region with the lowest level of public expenditure on social protection millions could slip back into poverty within months or even days

Increases in unemployment in developing countries exert far greater socio-political repercussions than in developed countries because of insufficient social protection programmes. As the region with the lowest level of public expenditure on social protection (figure 16), the millions who have spent decades working their way out of poverty could slip back into poverty within

months or even days, if their personal savings evaporate. Even before the crisis, the proportion of working poor in terms of employed workers earning less than $2 per day as a share of total employment was as high as 80.1% in South Asia in 2007.[30] Although the Asia-Pacific region has made great strides in reducing absolute poverty during the past two decades, most workers earn an income just above the poverty line and are in danger of falling back into poverty. On the basis of estimated GDP growth rates in the region, the current crisis could trap an additional 21 million people below the poverty line of $1.25 per day and 25 million based on the $2-per-day poverty line between 2009 and 2010.[31] When societies are under stress, abuse and violence against women, children and youth are exacerbated.[32] Often girls, more than boys, bear the brunt of social fallout that can last far beyond the crisis itself.

Recently available data from the region confirm that more workers shifted into vulnerable employment during the crisis

Unemployment is untenable for many workers who have lost their jobs or whose income is reduced in the absence of social protection systems. Shifting to vulnerable and informal employment is often the only means of survival for low-skilled workers at the bottom of the income

[28]   ILO, Economic and Labour Market Analysis Department, *Trends Econometric Models* (information available from www.ilo.org/empelm/what/projects/lang--en/WCMS_114246/index.htm), October 2009.

[29]   OECD, "Harmonised unemployment rates: news release, January 2010" (Paris: OECD, 2010), p. 2.

[30]   ILO, Economic and Labour Market Analysis Department, *Key Indicators of the Labour Market* (KILM), 6th ed., available from http://kilm.ilo.org/KILMnetBeta/default2.asp (accessed 4 Feb. 2010).

[31]   ESCAP, ADB and UNDP, *Achieving the Millennium Development Goals in an Era of Global Uncertainty, Asia-Pacific Regional Report 2009/10* (United Nations publication, Sales No. E.10.II.F.10), p. 31; available from www.mdgasiapacific.org/regional-report-2009-10.

[32]   See Heyzer, N. and M. Khor, "Globalization and the way forward", Development Outreach "Speaker's Corner" (Washington, D.C.: World Bank, 2009); and Knowles, J.C., E.M. Pernia and M. Racelis, "Social consequences of the financial crisis in Asia: the deeper crisis", Economic and Development Resource Center Briefing Notes no.16 (Manila: Asian Development Bank, 1999).

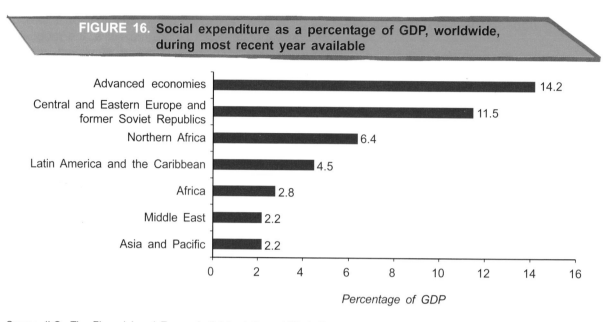

FIGURE 16. Social expenditure as a percentage of GDP, worldwide, during most recent year available

Source: ILO, *The Financial and Economic Crisis: A Decent Work Response* (Geneva, 2009).

ladder who need to support families. People try to cope by shifting from urban to rural employment and to informal and short-term itinerant jobs, many of them falling prey to exploitative and abusive employment. Unemployment figures in Asia and the Pacific are a crude measure that grossly underestimate the fallout from the crisis. Lack of timely and reliable information compounds the challenge of assessing the labour market impacts of the crisis. Many countries in the region still do not have labour market surveys; some like India might conduct such surveys infrequently, but even then the task can be complicated by geographic vastness or large populations. Information that likely reflects the real nature of the desperation that has followed the crisis emerges from reports, such as the example from China that over 20 million rural migrants have returned home after failing to find jobs in the city.[33] Also, recently available data from the region confirm that more workers shifted into vulnerable employment during the crisis. For example, first quarter 2009 figures for Thailand show that the number of wage employees grew by 0.6% (solely as a result of expansion in Government employment), whereas the number of own-account and contributing family members increased by 3.2% and 3.3% respectively.[34] Similarly in Indonesia, the number of casual workers not in agriculture increased by approximately 7.3% between February 2008 and February 2009.[35] For the region as a whole, vulnerable employment could have increased by as much as 47.5 million between 2007 and 2009, adding to the estimated 1.07 billion workers (60.7% of all workers in the region) who are classified as having been in vulnerable employment in 2008.[36]

---

[33] Xinhua News, "20 million jobless migrant workers return home", 2 February 2009, available from http://news.xinhuanet.com/english/2009-02/02/content_10750749.htm.

[34] ILO, "Protecting people, promoting jobs: A survey of country employment and social protection policy responses to the global economic crisis", presented to the G-20 Leaders' Summit, Pittsburgh, 24-25 September 2009; p. 12.

[35] Chatani, Kazutoshi and Kee Beom Kim, *Labour and Social Trends in Indonesia 2009: Recovery and Beyond through Decent Work* (Jakarta: ILO, 2009), p. 9; available from www.ilo.org/jakarta/whatwedo/publications/lang--en/docName--WCMS_119134/index.htm.

[36] ILO, *Trends Econometric Models,* October 2009.

As export-oriented manufacturing of garments and electronics was among the sectors hardest hit by the global crisis, women workers in the region, who represent a disproportionately large share of the workers in manufacturing, are especially vulnerable to unemployment. In the Philippines female workers account for more than half the total workforce in electronics manufacturing, while in Bangladesh they form 85% of the workforce in garment manufacturing.[37] In Thailand, female workers in manufacturing decreased by close to 130,000 (year-on-year) in the fourth quarter of 2008, accounting for 63.2% of the total decrease in employment in that industry.[38] Even in the Republic of Korea, where the increase in unemployed men was higher than that for women from June 2008 to June 2009, the unemployment rate for women was catching up with that for men in the latter months of 2009. For all of Asia and the Pacific, the number of unemployed women is estimated to have increased during 2009 by at least 5.7%, in comparison with 4.9% for men.[39]

Joblessness among youth is also a major challenge as labour markets become increasingly hostile. Besides reducing overall family income levels, prolonged unemployment of young people can exacerbate social tensions, including rises in suicide and crime rates. In countries with young populations, youth unemployment has risen from already high levels. In the Philippines, for example, youth unemployment increased by 5.9% in January 2009 year-on-year. In Japan, notwithstanding its narrow youth base, the year-on-year increase in youth unemployment was 23.4% in April 2009.[40] An estimated 51 million new jobs need to be created to absorb Asian labour force growth over 2009 and 2010; Asian youth may hence be heading into a period of prolonged unemployment that holds negative consequences not only for the unemployed themselves, but for the economies whose growth and development depend on utilizing human resources optimally.

Historically, severe economic recessions have often led to irreversible changes in the labour market and permanent job losses

---

Historically, severe economic recessions have often led to irreversible changes in the labour market and permanent job losses. Figure 17 shows the labour market trends of selected Asian economies that were most affected by the Asian financial crisis in 1997; namely Hong Kong, China; and Thailand, Indonesia and the Republic of Korea. Since that crisis, unemployment rates in Hong Kong, China; and Republic of Korea and Indonesia have never fully recovered to their pre-crisis levels. Between 1998 and 2007 a number of negative shocks contributed to fluctuation in unemployment rates in those economies, including the outbreak of severe acute respiratory syndrome (SARS; especially in Hong Kong, China) and the bursting of the dotcom bubble; however, the evidence strongly suggests that the Asian financial crisis triggered and/or accelerated structural changes in those economies that have led to a permanent increase in the natural rate of unemployment. In the current crisis, slow recovery in the United States and Europe may compound cyclical unemployment with structural unemployment that arises from excess capacity in the export manufacturing sectors. In the long run, structural adjustments in the labour market generate efficiency and gains in productivity; however, short-run policy instruments will be needed during the transition period to support training requirements and provide a social safety net for disadvantaged and vulnerable populations.

---

37   Newfarmer, Richard, "The financial crisis, trade and effects on women", Presentation at workshop on "Women leading change: Traction for change", Geneva, 4 March 2009.
38   ILO, "Protecting people, promoting jobs", p. 8.
39   Ibid.
40   Ibid., p. 9.

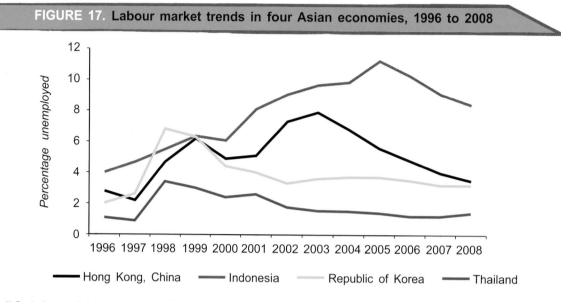

FIGURE 17. Labour market trends in four Asian economies, 1996 to 2008

Source: ILO, *Laborsta* database, available from www.laborta.ilo.org (accessed 18 Jan. 2010).

The ILO estimates that the G-20 countries used discretionary fiscal expansion policies in 2009, together with automatic stabilizers, to create or save between 7 and 11 million jobs; that represents between 29 and 43% of total unemployment in G-20 countries in the first half of 2009.[41] A similar study by the OECD on the impact of fiscal stimulus policies on employment presents similar findings. In 2010, for the 19 OECD countries in the study, the employment impact ranged between 0.8 and 1.4%, representing between 3.2 and 5.5 million jobs.[42] In Latin America, infrastructure spending, which is a large component of most fiscal stimulus packages, is said to have the potential to create up to 200,000 direct jobs for every $1 billion spent, whereas 500,000 new jobs can be created by spending the same amount on labour-intensive rural projects.[43] In the Asia-Pacific region, the ILO estimates that one million jobs can be created in Indonesia with the $1.2 billion allocated for infrastructure

spending, by using labour-intensive methods in half of the projects.[44]

Recovery in the labour market can trail behind economic recovery by as long as 4 or 5 years. Making up for lost ground in the struggle against poverty could take even longer

From the onset of the global economic crisis, many Governments in Asia and the Pacific have responded to the worsening employment situation with a wide range of measures. Recent data from the region show signs of stabilization in the labour market with unemployment rates having reached a peak in 2009 (figure 18); previous financial and economic crises, nonetheless, indicate that recovery in the labour

---

[41] ILO, "Protecting people, promoting jobs", p. 12.
[42] OECD, *OECD Employment Outlook 2009: Tackling the Jobs Crisis* (Paris: 2009), p. 31.
[43] ILO, "Protecting people, promoting jobs", p. 25.
[44] Ibid., p. 26.

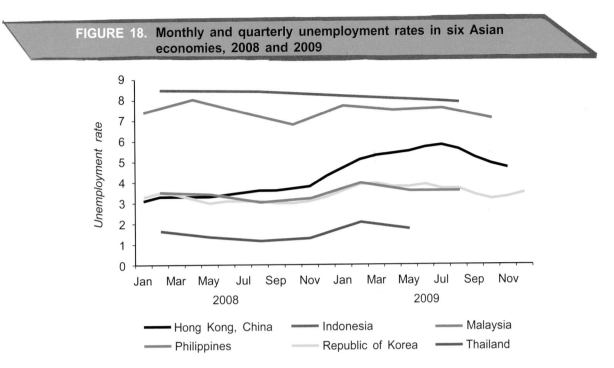

FIGURE 18. Monthly and quarterly unemployment rates in six Asian economies, 2008 and 2009

Source: ILO, *Laborsta* database, available from www.laborta.ilo.org (accessed 18 Jan. 2010).

market can trail behind economic recovery by as long as 4 or 5 years. Making up for lost ground in the struggle against poverty could take even longer, since increases in informality are difficult to reverse. Real wages as well as labour productivity take time to recover. The appropriate mix of macroeconomic policies is therefore an essential prerequisite, with labour market reforms and allocation of resources for building effective social protection systems.

Migration and remittances: bucking the pressures

During the past two decades, remittances have become an increasingly important source of external development finance, supporting the balance of payments and contributing to the gross national product. For poor households they provide a vital lifeline – they help in developing human capital by contributing to education and

healthcare needs and they foster entrepreneurial development through investments in businesses, especially during economic crises and natural disasters. In the major remittance-recipient economies of the Philippines, Bangladesh and Nepal, remittances grew strongly in 2008 and continued to grow throughout 2009 despite the economic crisis, although at a much slower rate in comparison with 2008 rates (figure 19). Pakistan curiously experienced an accelerated growth rate of remittances in 2009, which was first thought to have come from migrant workers returning home with their savings after losing their jobs in host countries. However, no evidence of large-scale return of workers supported that assumption, so the jump in remittances is more likely to have been a result of Government intervention such as the Pakistan Remittance Initiative, which encouraged transmittal of remittances through formally recorded channels. Also, the depreciation of the Pakistan rupee attracted remittance inflows for investment purposes.[45]

---

[45]   Khan, Ashfaque, "Role of remittances", *The News International* (Pakistan), 8 Sept. 2009, available from www.thenews.com.pk/editorial_detail.asp?id=197238.

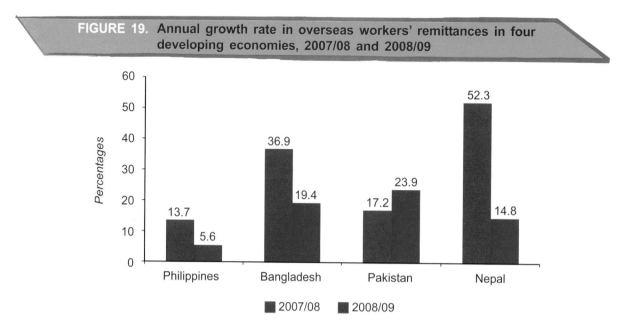

FIGURE 19. Annual growth rate in overseas workers' remittances in four developing economies, 2007/08 and 2008/09

Source: World Bank database; compiled by Migration and Remittances Team, Development Prospects Group, World Bank, available from http://econ.worldbank.org/WBSITE/EXTERNAL/EXTDEC/EXTDECPROSPECTS/0,,contentMDK:21122856~pagePK:64165401~piPK:64165026~theSitePK:476883,00.html (accessed 5 Mar. 2010).

In the major remittance-recipient economies, remittances grew strongly in 2008 and continued to grow throughout 2009 despite the economic crisis

---

As labour-market conditions are expected to remain depressed in most destination countries, pressure may grow in those countries to protect domestic jobs from migrants

---

Owing to the global reach of the crisis and the severe economic recession affecting the major remittance-sending countries, total remittances to the Asia-Pacific region are expected to fall by 1.5% in East Asia and the Pacific and 1.8% in South Asia in 2009.[46] Nonetheless, remittances are proving to be by far the most resilient source of foreign-exchange earnings, in comparison with other capital flows to developing countries which have fallen dramatically since the beginning of the crisis.

The resilience of remittance flows to Asian and Pacific countries has been attributed to the comparatively stable migrant populations in a wide spread of destination countries, including neighbouring Asian or Pacific economies and countries of the Cooperation Council for the Arab States of the Gulf (GCC) that fared better during the economic crisis than did the United States and developed Europe. Given the growth in unemployment in most of those countries, however, the critical question is what will hap-

---

[46]   Ratha, D., S. Mohapatra and Ani Silwal, "Migration and remittance trends 2009: a better-than-expected outcome so far, but significant risks ahead", *Migration and Development Brief 11* (Washington D.C.: World Bank, 2009), p. 14.

pen to those workers. So far, no evidence suggests that the recession is leading to a mass return of workers.[47] The latest available data from the Philippines and Nepal show a reduction in departures of new workers from their home country, and, for Bangladesh, a vast reduction in the growth rate of migrant worker outflows (5% increase in 2008 compared to 118% increase in 2007).[48] As labour-market conditions are expected to remain depressed in most destination countries, pressure may grow in those countries to protect domestic jobs from migrants. Already an increasing number of countries have introduced policies to restrict migrant workers' access to labour markets. For example, in January 2009, Malaysian authorities instituted a freeze on the issue of work permits to foreign workers in manufacturing and services; in February 2009, the Government of the Republic of Korea stopped issuing new visas to temporary migrant workers.[49] The Russian Federation and the United Kingdom have enacted similar legislation.[50]

Recognizing how devastating could be the consequences of large numbers of returnees, Governments in some of the major migrant-sending countries in the region have taken measures to counteract negative impacts on migrant workers. The Philippines has responded with an aggressive labour-export strategy to identify areas with a high demand for labour and negotiate new bilateral labour migration agreements with those countries. The Government opened the Filipino Expatriate Livelihood Support Fund[51] to help returning migrants find new jobs. As patterns of migration from and within Asia and the Pacific will continue to be affected by the growth slowdown,

such support programmes need to be sustained well into the economic recovery process.

Domestic demand and fiscal space shaping responses

Many Asian and Pacific economies have had either substantial domestic demand or healthy fiscal resources to mitigate the impact of the global crisis. Where domestic demand accounts for a large share of GDP growth,[52] such as in India, the Philippines, Viet Nam and Indonesia, the economy has displayed relatively robust and positive growth performance (figure 20). China, a major exporter, has been cushioned by the second largest governmental spending programme of the world in absolute terms and the largest as a percentage of GDP, permitted by the State's sound fiscal position and accumulated reserves. The exceptionally large fiscal stimulus in China has been crucial in global efforts to combat global recession. Other Governments in the region have also managed to contain the depth of their slowdowns through public spending programmes aimed at employment creation and support to domestic demand. A quantitative analysis reported in box 1 shows that fiscal stimulus programmes indeed helped in offsetting to some extent the loss of exports. In the absence of these packages the GDP growth in 2009 would have dropped by 7.8 percentage points but actually dropped by only 4.2 percentage points.

The unprecedented scale of Government spending coupled with declining tax revenues, typical of recessions, led to decline among all major developing economies[53] in the region in their

---

[47] Awad, Ibrahim, *The Global Economic Crisis and Migrant Workers: Impact and Response* (Geneva: ILO, 2009), p. ix.

[48] Fix, M. and others, *Migration and the Global Recession* (Washington, D.C.: Migration Policy Institute, 2009), p. 41.

[49] Abella, Manolo and Geoffrey Ducanes, "The effect of the global economic crisis on Asian migrant workers and Governments' responses", Technical Note (Bangkok: ILO Regional Office for Asia and the Pacific, 2009), pp. 9-10.

[50] Awad, *The Global Economic Crisis and Migrant Workers,* pp. 47-48.

[51] Philippine Information Agency, "Gov't earmarks P1-B for Fil-Expat Livelihood Support Fund, PGMA tells OFWs in Riyadh", press release, 5 Feb. 2009, available from www.pia.gov.ph/?m=12&sec=reader&rp=1&fi=p090205.htm&no=8&date=.

[52] See chapter 3 for a discussion on the lacunae in using net exports as a measure of contribution to GDP.

[53] Regarding the data on fiscal balances, the major developing economies refer, because of limited data availability, to 11 major developing economies in the ESCAP region.

FIGURE 20. Contributions of domestic demand, exports and imports to real GDP growth in major Asian developing economies, 2008 and 2009

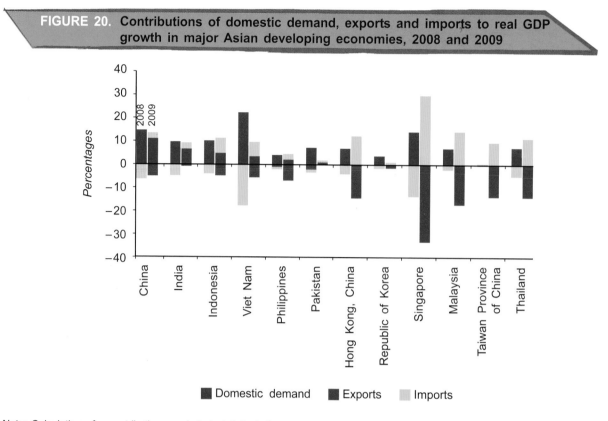

■ Domestic demand ■ Exports ▨ Imports

Note: Calculations for contributions excluded statistical discrepancy.
Source: ESCAP calculations based on Economist Intelligence Unit, Country Analysis and Forecasts, *EIU CountryData,* accessible from http://countryanalysis.eiu.com/ (accessed 5 Feb. 2010).

fiscal balances as a percentage of GDP in the last quarter of 2008. Rising budget deficits required increasing funding of Government spending by the issuance of Government bonds. The value of local currency bonds outstanding across emerging markets in East Asia rose by 12.8% to $3,940 billion in the first half of 2009 in comparison with the corresponding period of the year before.[54] Apart from Government funding of stimulus spending, local currency bonds were issued by corporate borrowers wishing to raise funds for relatively robust domestic operations in some economies in the region and to reduce exposure to possible volatility from dollar and euro funding.

> *Governments in the region have managed to contain the depth of their slowdowns through public spending programmes aimed at employment creation and support to domestic demand*

Common elements in fiscal packages across the region have been infrastructure spending, cash transfers and tax cuts. While large infrastructural projects featured prominently in the package for

---

[54] Cookson, Robert, "East Asia debt market 'underdeveloped'", *Financial Times,* 15 Sept. 2009, available from www.ft.com/cms/s/0/95b0bbce-a225-11de-9caa-00144feabdc0.html.

BOX 1. Assessing the impact of expected downturns in export growth

As a first approximation, the impact of the 2009 downturn in export growth on GDP is estimated for a selection of economies in the Asian and Pacific region. The exercise utilizes estimates of short-term multiplier effects from the Global Macro Model of Oxford Economics Ltd.[a] Those effects take into account (a) import leakages and knock-on effects of changes in aggregate demand components in various sectors of the economy and (b) feedback effects from other economies included in the model. As shown in the appendix for a group of 11 Asian economies, GDP declines on average $0.88 for each $1.00 lost in exports. Similarly, every $1 increase in public spending, private consumption and private investment is associated with GDP increases of, respectively, $0.99, $0.98 and $0.83. The multiplier effects of exports and private investment are lower because of the higher import content of such expenditures.

The estimated GDP impacts of the 2009 drop in exports in the selected Asian economies are calculated in table 5. The figures in column 4 of the table represent how much GDP would have dropped in 2009 as a consequence of the shortfall in exports from their past trends. This exercise is one of comparative static in which the shortfall in exports is the only factor affecting output that is considered.

The estimated impact of the export shortfall on GDP growth, as shown in column 4, is estimated for each country as

$$\frac{\Delta GDP}{GDP} = m_X \left[\left(\frac{\Delta X}{X} \right)_{2009} - \left(\frac{\Delta X}{X} \right)_{2001-07} \right] \frac{X}{GDP},$$

where m_X is the export multiplier shown in the appendix table 6 and the term in brackets is the shortfall in the rate of growth of exports between 2009 and the average for 2001 to 2007, shown in column 3. Column 5 shows the impact on GDP in billions of United States dollars of 2008.[b]

Table 5 shows that if the shortfall of exports had been the only adverse effect on GDP, and if there had been no compensatory policy measures, GDP growth should have dropped by 7.8% in 2009. However, the actual shortfall in GDP growth that year was only 4.2%, compared to the higher levels of the trend from 2001 to 2007. The disparity is partly explained by the implementation of large fiscal stimulus packages in several of the 11 Asian countries. The sizes of such packages (column 6) were roughly sufficient or exceeded the GDP shortfall in China, India, Japan, the Republic of Korea and Thailand. In just the first two of those countries, however, the packages managed to keep GDP growth at relatively high levels in 2009 (8.7% in China and 7.2% in India). A possible explanation is that other components of aggregate demand, such as autonomous consumption and investment, were adversely affected by the crisis in Japan, the Republic of Korea and Thailand.

---

[a] The Global Macro Model is a traditional Mundell-Fleming type of global macroeconomic model with the standard demand and supply equations. The major linkages of this type of model are external trade, financial markets, monetary aggregates (such as interest rates) and commodity prices (such as oil prices). In the long run, each of the economies behaves like the textbook description of a single-sector economy under Cobb-Douglas technology in equilibrium.

[b] Column 5 is obtained by multiplying column 4 by the nominal GDP of 2008.

(Continued on next page)

BOX 1. *(continued)*

TABLE 5. Impact of the 2009 shortfall in exports on GDP of major Asian economies

	Average annual growth rate of real exports of goods and services (per cent)		Shortfall in exports due to crisis (1) − (2) (per cent)	Estimated impact on the 2009 GDP: Comparative statics exercise		Memo item: size of fiscal stimulus packages ($ billion)
	2001-07 1	2009 2	3	(per cent) 4	($ billion) 5	6
China	17.8	−8.8	−26.6	−9.9	430	585
Hong Kong, China	10.7	−10.5	−21.3	−28.8	62	11
India	16.0	−2.8	−18.8	−3.2	40	38
Indonesia	9.3	−10.4	−19.7	−7.7	39	12
Japan	9.1	−24.6	−33.7	−5.8	287	336
Malaysia	8.0	−11.3	−23.6	−11.7	26	19
Philippines	8.1	−12.7	−20.7	−6.1	10	7
Republic of Korea	12.3	−1.2	−9.3	−3.5	33	53
Singapore	12.3	−11.5	−23.8	−27.2	49	14
Taiwan Province of China	10.5	−12.2	−22.7	−9.2	37	15
Thailand	7.6	−13.8	−21.4	−10.4	29	44
Weighted average/ Sum	12.8	−13.9	−26.8	−7.8	1 042	1 134

Memo item: Increase in demand side components to make up for the impact on GDP

Public spending	1 074
Private consumption	1 123
Private investment	1 256

Notes: Estimates for 2009 figures. GDP in United States dollars of 2008 used as weights in weighted averages. Figures for public spending, private consumption and private investment are estimates of increases needed to compensate for the estimated GDP shortfall for the 11 countries; calculations use estimated the multipliers for each of those domestic demand components shown in the appendix.

Sources: ESCAP calculations based on data from the United Nations Statistics Division, *National Accounts Main Aggregates Database* (accessed 24 Feb. 2010); and Economist Intelligence Unit, Country Analysis and Forecasts, *EIU CountryData,* accessible at http://countryanalysis.eiu.com/ (accessed 24 Feb. 2010).

The 2009 shortfall in exports was extreme and is unlikely to be repeated. Notwithstanding, a return to business-as-usual export growth rates is also very unlikely. From 2001 to 2007, real exports of the 11 selected countries in table 5 grew at an annual average rate of 12.8%. In constant 2008 prices they more than doubled in value from $2.3 trillion in 2001 to $4.8 trillion in 2007. They fell, however, to $4.5 trillion in 2009, as shown in Figure 21, and are expected to grow at slower rates in coming years.

Figure 21 displays two recent forecasts: one by the Economist Intelligence Unit (EIU, in red) and another by Oxford Economics Ltd. (OE, in blue) that take into consideration average annual rates of export growth of, respectively, 7.0% and 9.3% from 2011 to 2014. To highlight the impact of the expected slowdown in export growth, a projection of exports from 2011 onward growing at the historical average of the 2001-to-2007 growth rates is also shown in the figure (in grey).

(Continued on next page)

BOX 1. *(continued)*

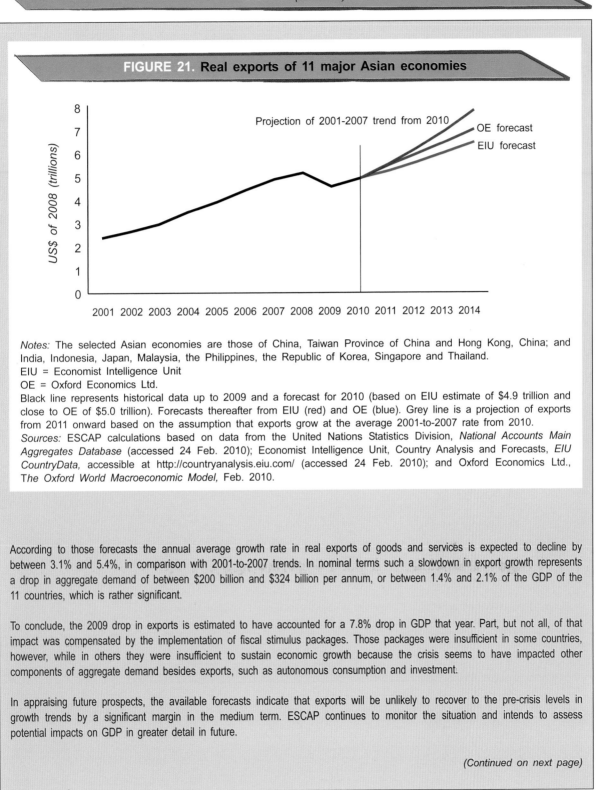

FIGURE 21. Real exports of 11 major Asian economies

Notes: The selected Asian economies are those of China, Taiwan Province of China and Hong Kong, China; and India, Indonesia, Japan, Malaysia, the Philippines, the Republic of Korea, Singapore and Thailand.
EIU = Economist Intelligence Unit
OE = Oxford Economics Ltd.
Black line represents historical data up to 2009 and a forecast for 2010 (based on EIU estimate of $4.9 trillion and close to OE of $5.0 trillion). Forecasts thereafter from EIU (red) and OE (blue). Grey line is a projection of exports from 2011 onward based on the assumption that exports grow at the average 2001-to-2007 rate from 2010.
Sources: ESCAP calculations based on data from the United Nations Statistics Division, *National Accounts Main Aggregates Database* (accessed 24 Feb. 2010); Economist Intelligence Unit, Country Analysis and Forecasts, *EIU CountryData,* accessible at http://countryanalysis.eiu.com/ (accessed 24 Feb. 2010); and Oxford Economics Ltd., T*he Oxford World Macroeconomic Model,* Feb. 2010.

According to those forecasts the annual average growth rate in real exports of goods and services is expected to decline by between 3.1% and 5.4%, in comparison with 2001-to-2007 trends. In nominal terms such a slowdown in export growth represents a drop in aggregate demand of between $200 billion and $324 billion per annum, or between 1.4% and 2.1% of the GDP of the 11 countries, which is rather significant.

To conclude, the 2009 drop in exports is estimated to have accounted for a 7.8% drop in GDP that year. Part, but not all, of that impact was compensated by the implementation of fiscal stimulus packages. Those packages were insufficient in some countries, however, while in others they were insufficient to sustain economic growth because the crisis seems to have impacted other components of aggregate demand besides exports, such as autonomous consumption and investment.

In appraising future prospects, the available forecasts indicate that exports will be unlikely to recover to the pre-crisis levels in growth trends by a significant margin in the medium term. ESCAP continues to monitor the situation and intends to assess potential impacts on GDP in greater detail in future.

(Continued on next page)

BOX 1. *(continued)*

Appendix: Estimated short-term multiplier effects

Table 6 displays the estimated short-term multiplier effects of different aggregate demand components in 11 different Asian economies. Those effects are calculated from the Global Macro Model of Oxford Economics Ltd. as the average increase in real GDP during a single year in response to an increase of $1 in each demand component during the four quarters of that year. For instance, the 0.66 multiplier for exports in the case of China means that a $1 increase in exports in a given year contributes an additional $0.66 to the country's GDP during that year.

TABLE 6. Estimated multiplier effects of aggregate demand components

	Exports	Public spending[a]	Private consumption	Private investment
China	0.66	1.10	1.05	0.89
Hong Kong, China	0.65	0.89	0.86	0.88
India	0.79	1.00	0.63	0.58
Indonesia	0.79	0.76	0.66	0.71
Japan	1.08	0.98	1.14	0.85
Malaysia	0.42	1.13	1.03	0.91
Philippines	0.63	1.03	0.75	1.01
Republic of Korea	0.82	0.87	0.74	0.80
Singapore	0.44	0.65	0.58	0.63
Taiwan Province of China	0.58	0.68	0.56	0.70
Thailand	0.67	1.02	0.88	0.95
Weighted average[b]	0.83	0.99	0.98	0.83

Notes: [a] Governmental consumption expenditure and public gross fixed-capital formation.
[b] GDP in current United States dollars of 2008 used as weights.
Source: ESCAP calculations based on Oxford Economics Ltd., *The Oxford World Macroeconomic Model,* Feb. 2010.

China, as well as in subsequent packages introduced, by among others, Thailand, Malaysia and Viet Nam, the focus so far has been on spending measures that can be delivered quickly. China implemented significant spending on social sectors and introduced measures that helped sustain domestic private consumption at a level comparable to that in 2008, including tax breaks and other forms of incentives for automobile and electronics purchases, increases in pensions and introduction of a rural pension programme. Income and business taxes were also cut by, among others, Viet Nam, Indonesia, Malaysia, Thailand, India, Japan, the Republic of Korea and Singapore. Cash transfer programmes have been undertaken by the Philippines, Thailand, Japan, Singapore, and Taiwan Province of China. Subsidies for transport, technical innovation and the poor have increased, as well as spending on education and healthcare. Measures to increase consumption have had the greatest growth multiplier effect in consumption-led economies, as they are proportional to the size of consumption as a portion of GDP in an economy. Thus, consumption-boosting measures in such export-dependent economies as those of China and South-East Asia would not have as great an effect. Small, open trading economies also experience significant leakage of any stimulus spending through increased imports, implying that stimulus can play only a limited role in reviving growth until global demand recovers.

Other than the impact of reduced private consumption in developed countries on exports of the Asia-Pacific region, the choice of component of fiscal spending in developed countries also has an impact on import demand as well as in comparison with direct measures to increase private consumption spending. Government spending on public investment would have a lower impact on imports due to the import composition of such spending, whereas spending on Government salaries would feed through to consumption, as would direct cash transfers to consumers.

To the extent that comparatively robust consumption in the region is directed to developed country exports, developed economies can spur some of their own revival through the export channel. Such is the case particularly for commodities producers like Australia. However, import demand from the region, most importantly from China and especially import demand for goods used for infrastructure development in the country supported by fiscal stimulus, is also sustaining exports of manufactured goods from developed countries. For example, China overtook the United States as the leading export market for Japan during the first half of 2009,[55] indicating a notable realignment in the relative importance to Japan of the Chinese and American markets. While Chinese demand for imports from Japan fell during the period, import demand from the United States for Japanese products fell even more. Recovery in Europe has also been aided by demand from the region. Exports of the 16 Euro Zone economies to East Asia rose by 16.3% in the second quarter of 2009, in comparison with a 14.4% drop during the first quarter.[56]

Monetary policies played a far smaller role than fiscal policies in supporting domestic demand

Apart from wide-ranging fiscal measures, central banks have adopted very loose monetary policies. Apart from interest rates set at near-zero levels in many cases (figure 22), Government guarantees have been extended on bank deposits and direct interventions to increase money supply have emerged in countries experiencing deflationary pressures. While monetary policies have been accommodative across most of the region, they played a far smaller role than fiscal policies in supporting domestic demand, for the following reasons. First, interest rates in many countries were already low before the crisis, thus reducing policy leverage to stimulate the economy, while in some other countries relatively high inflationary pressures remained, de-

55   IMF, *Direction of Trade Statistics*, available from www2.imfstatistics.org/DOT/ (accessed 7 Jan. 2010).
56   Ibid., East Asia refers to China; Hong Kong, China; Macao, China; Japan; Republic of Korea; and Mongolia.

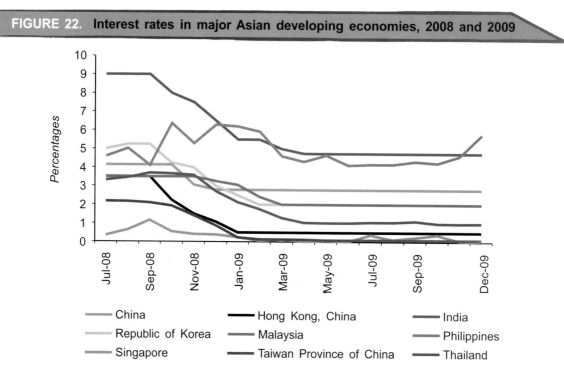

FIGURE 22. Interest rates in major Asian developing economies, 2008 and 2009

Notes: China: Central Bank base rate less than 20 days. Hong Kong, China: Discount Window base rate. India: Repo rates (Reserve Bank of India). Republic of Korea: Base rate (Bank of Korea). Malaysia: Interbank overnight, weighted average. Philippines: One-week interbank rate. Singapore: Overnight interbank rate, period average. Taiwan Province of China: Interbank rate. Thailand: Interbank overnight rate.
Source: ESCAP calculations based on data from CEIC Data Company Ltd., available from http://ceicdata.com/ (accessed 25 Feb. 2010).

spite the economic slowdown. Second, despite greater availability of liquidity, banks remained unwilling to lend, for example to exporters, in an uncertain external environment.

> *The key question is whether the rebound can be converted to sustained recovery*

While growth has started to recover in the region, the concern is that much of the recovery remains dependent on support policies of Governments and growth has yet to become self-sustaining. Furthermore, the base effect of year-on-year comparisons with sharp GDP contractions late in 2008 and early in 2009 will result in data that show strong rebounds. The key question is whether the rebound can be converted to sustained recovery. Growth in recent years for many export-led economies was supported by the debt-fuelled excessive consumption of developed countries, particularly the United States. Such consumption is unlikely to return to its previous levels, as consumers work off their debt overhang in coming years and subsequently are not able to acquire debt burdens of the scale seen in the past. Total outstanding consumer credit in the United States reversed its expansion in the fourth quarter of 2008 and thereafter decreased throughout 2009.[57] The fis-

---

[57] Data as of third quarter of 2009 from United States Federal Reserve, *Federal Reserve Statistical Release,* available from www.federalreserve.gov/releases/g19/20091207/ (accessed 7 Dec. 2009).

cal and monetary policies which sustained much of the early part of the recovery seen in developed countries are by their nature time-limited measures. A long-term consumption slowdown in developed countries can therefore be expected. Furthermore, given the enormity of the global macroeconomic imbalances and their convergence with environmental stresses and growing social disparities and geopolitical tensions, a return to business-as-usual scenarios may eventually bring about the systemic collapse that was so narrowly averted in 2008. Fundamental changes to unwind global macroeconomic, social and environmental imbalances of the past are inevitable and desirable.

GROWTH OUTLOOK FOR 2010

Recovery underway

Strong support from expansionary policies helped Asian and Pacific economies to reverse their declines by the second half of 2009. A notable recovery is expected in 2010. For the developing economies of the region, GDP is expected to grow by 7.0% in 2010, following an estimated growth of 4.0% of the previous year (figure 23 and table 7).

Strong support from expansionary policies helped Asian and Pacific economies to reverse their declines by the second half of 2009

Backdrop for 2010 forecast

The foregoing forecasts are based on the assumption that the world economy can stay firmly on its current track of stabilization. The assumption is that the United States can resume growth, at around 2.5% in 2010, after the severe setback of -2.4% estimated for 2009. The European Union faced a steeper decline in 2009, at an estimated rate of -4.0%. In 2010, the European Union is assumed to be able to recover growth of around 0.8%. The economic

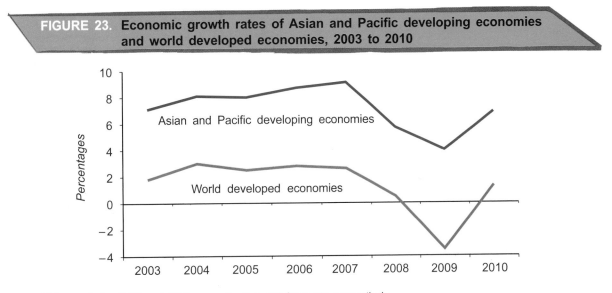

FIGURE 23. Economic growth rates of Asian and Pacific developing economies and world developed economies, 2003 to 2010

Note: GDP growth for 2009 and 2010 are estimates and forecasts, respectively.
Sources: ESCAP calculations based on data from national sources; IMF, *International Financial Statistics (IFS) Online Service,* available from www.imfstatistics.org/imf/ (accessed 15 Sep. 2009); ADB, *Key Indicators for Asia and the Pacific 2009,* available from www.adb.org/Documents/Books/Key_Indicators/2009/default.asp (accessed 1 Oct. 2009); website of the Interstate Statistical Committee of the Commonwealth of Independent States, www.cisstat.com (accessed 22 Mar. 2010); and ESCAP estimates. Figures for world developed economies come from United Nations, *World Economic Situation and Prospects 2010* (United Nations publication, Sales No. E.10.II.C.2.).

TABLE 7. Rates of economic growth and inflation of Asian and Pacific economies, in percentages, 2008 to 2010

	Real GDP growth[a]			Inflation[b]		
	2008	2009[c]	2010[d]	2008	2009[c]	2010[d]
East and North-East Asia[e]	**2.1**	**−1.1**	**4.0**	**3.5**	**−0.3**	**1.0**
China	9.0	8.7	9.5	5.9	−0.7	2.5
Democratic People's Republic of Korea (the)	3.7	..	..	..	..	..
Hong Kong, China	2.4	−1.9	4.5	4.3	0.5	1.9
Japan	−1.2	−5.2	1.3	1.4	−1.4	−0.5
Macao, China	12.9	1.3	..	8.6	1.2	..
Mongolia	8.9	0.5	6.5	28.0	7.0	7.9
Republic of Korea (the)	2.2	0.2	5.2	4.7	2.8	2.5
Russian Federation (the)	5.6	−7.9	3.5	14.1	11.7	8.1
Taiwan Province of China	0.7	−1.9	4.5	3.5	−0.9	1.3
North and Central Asia	**5.8**	**−5.8**	**3.7**	**14.4**	**10.7**	**7.9**
Armenia	6.8	−14.4	1.5	9.0	3.4	4.0
Azerbaijan	10.8	9.3	7.0	20.8	1.5	6.0
Georgia	2.1	−4.0	2.0	10.0	1.7	5.5
Kazakhstan	3.3	1.0	2.0	17.0	7.3	7.0
Kyrgyzstan	7.6	2.3	3.0	24.5	6.8	8.6
Russian Federation (the)	5.6	−7.9	3.5	14.1	11.7	8.1
Tajikistan	7.9	3.4	3.5	20.4	6.4	8.0
Turkmenistan	9.8	6.1	7.0	13.0	10.0	12.0
Uzbekistan	9.0	8.1	8.0	12.7	8.0	8.5
Oceania[e]	**2.0**	**1.0**	**2.3**	**4.4**	**1.9**	**2.5**
Australia	2.3	1.2	2.4	4.4	1.8	2.5
Cook Islands (the)	−1.2	−0.1	0.8	7.8	6.5	6.3
Fiji	−0.1	−2.5	1.9	7.7	3.7	3.4
Kiribati	3.4	1.5	0.8	18.6	6.6	5.9
Marshall Islands (the)	−2.0	0.5	0.5	17.5	9.6	5.9
Micronesia (Federated States of)	−1.0	0.5	0.5	6.8	2.9	7.4
Nauru	1.0	1.0	2.0	4.5	1.8	2.3
New Zealand	−0.5	−0.5	1.8	4.0	2.1	2.0
Palau	−1.0	−3.0	−1.0	12.0	5.2	6.7
Papua New Guinea	6.7	4.5	8.5	10.6	6.9	7.1
Samoa	−4.9	−0.8	0.5	11.5	6.1	6.9
Solomon Islands	6.9	0.4	2.4	17.2	8.0	7.0
Tonga	1.2	0.4	0.4	10.4	1.6	1.9
Tuvalu	1.5	1.0	1.6	5.3	3.8	3.5
Vanuatu	6.6	3.0	4.6	4.8	4.5	5.0
South and South-West Asia[f]	**4.7**	**2.9**	**6.1**	**11.5**	**11.2**	**8.4**
Afghanistan	3.4	15.1	7.6	26.8	−10.0	8.4
Bangladesh	6.2	5.9	6.0	9.9	6.7	6.0
Bhutan	5.0	5.7	6.6	6.3	7.2	8.4
India	6.7	7.2	8.3	9.1	11.9	7.5
Iran (Islamic Republic of)	3.3	2.0	5.0	25.5	16.0	15.0
Maldives	5.8	−2.6	2.1	12.3	8.5	6.0
Nepal	5.3	4.7	3.5	7.7	13.2	7.5
Pakistan	4.1	2.0	3.2	12.0	20.8	12.0
Sri Lanka	6.0	3.5	6.0	22.6	3.4	8.6
Turkey	0.9	−6.0	3.0	10.4	6.3	7.2

(Continued on next page)

TABLE 7. *(continued)*

	Real GDP growth[a]			Inflation[b]		
	2008	**2009**[c]	**2010**[d]	**2008**	**2009**[c]	**2010**[d]
South-East Asia	**4.0**	**0.6**	**5.1**	**8.6**	**2.1**	**4.1**
Brunei Darussalam	−1.9	−0.5	0.6	2.7	1.2	1.2
Cambodia	6.7	0.0	4.0	25.0	−0.8	5.0
Indonesia	6.1	4.5	5.5	10.1	4.6	5.3
Lao People's Democratic Republic (the)	7.9	5.4	6.0	7.6	0.2	5.0
Malaysia	4.6	−1.7	5.0	5.4	0.6	2.0
Myanmar	2.0	2.0	3.1	26.8	6.5	10.4
Philippines (the)	3.8	0.9	3.5	9.3	3.3	4.7
Singapore	1.1	−2.0	7.0	6.6	0.6	2.3
Thailand	2.5	−2.3	4.0	5.5	−0.8	3.5
Timor-Leste	12.8	7.4	7.5	7.6	1.3	4.0
Viet Nam	6.2	5.3	5.8	23.1	7.0	10.3
Developing economies[g]	**5.7**	**4.0**	**7.0**	**7.3**	**3.1**	**4.1**
- " - " - excluding China and India	2.7	−0.6	4.7	8.0	3.8	4.5
Developed economies[h]	**−0.9**	**−4.6**	**1.4**	**1.7**	**−1.1**	**−0.2**
Pacific island developing economies[i]	**3.8**	**1.9**	**5.3**	**10.1**	**6.3**	**6.4**

Notes: [a] Calculations are based on GDP figures at market prices in United States dollars in 2007 (at 2000 prices) used as weights to calculate the regional and subregional growth rates.

[b] Changes in the consumer price index.

[c] Estimates.

[d] Forecasts (as of 15 April 2010).

[e] Estimates for 2009 and forecasts for 2010 are available for selected economies.

[f] The estimates and forecasts for countries relate to fiscal years defined as follows: 2008 refers to the fiscal year spanning 1 April 2008 to 31 March 2009 in India; 21 March 2008 to 20 March 2009 in the Islamic Republic of Iran; 1 July 2007 to 30 June 2008 in Bangladesh and Pakistan and 16 July 2007 to 15 July 2008 in Nepal.

[g] Developing Asian and Pacific economies comprise 37 independent economies in the region, excluding North and Central Asia (the Commonwealth of Independent States).

[h] Developed Asian and Pacific economies comprise Australia, Japan and New Zealand.

[i] Pacific island developing economies refers to 13 economies listed under Oceania, excluding Australia and New Zealand.

Sources: ESCAP calculations based on data from national sources; IMF, *International Financial Statistics (IFS) Online Service,* available from www.imfstatistics.org/imf/ (accessed 29 Sep. 2009); ADB, *Key Indicators for Asia and the Pacific 2009,* available from www.adb.org/Documents/Books/Key_Indicators/2009/default.asp (accessed 1 Oct. 2009); CEIC Data Company Ltd., available from http://ceicdata.com/; website of the Interstate Statistical Committee of the Commonwealth of Independent States, www.cisstat.com (accessed 22 Mar. 2010); and ESCAP estimates.

contraction in Japan was equally pronounced in 2009, with GDP falling by an estimated 5.2%. The Japanese economy is expected to resume growth in 2010 of 1.3%.

Monetary policy has remained loose since the outbreak of the global financial crisis. The loose stance is expected to prevail until mid-2010, with authorities not likely to make bold moves on interest rates before signs of solid recovery

are clear. The United States Federal Reserve Board is expected to keep its target rate at a very low level, from 0 to 0.25%, during the first half of 2010 and gradually increase it during the second half. Similarly, the European Central Bank is expected to hold the main refinancing rate at 1%. The European Central Bank is not expected to raise interest rates ahead of the United States. The Bank of Japan has been keeping its uncollateralized overnight call rate at

0.1% since December 2008. Given the deep setback in economic performance, the Bank of Japan is unlikely to revert to monetary tightening until the end of 2010.

Regarding key exchange rates, the United States dollar weakened notably during 2009, falling to an average of 90 yen and 0.67 euro in the fourth quarter of 2009, from 96 yen and 0.76 euro in the same quarter of 2008. The dollar is expected to appreciate, albeit very mildly and gradually, in 2010, owing to the economic recovery. The dollar should edge up to around 100 yen by the end of 2010 and hover around 0.7 euro during the year.

Oil prices have corrected noticeably during 2009, notwithstanding fluctuations. During 2009 the oil price averaged around $62 per barrel or 37% below its average level of 2008. The oil price is expected to pick up to around $75

to $80 per barrel on average during 2010, reflecting increased economic activity and hence increased demand for oil but still a weak dollar.

Different paces of expansion

Against such a background, the forecast is that growth in the developing economies of Asia and the Pacific will pick up to 7.0% in 2010, signifying a notable recovery from growth of 4.0% in 2009 (figure 24). Yet, the pace of recovery will vary across the subregions as will be discussed in chapter 2. South and South-West Asia will lead the recovery and is forecast to grow by 6.1% in 2010, after a growth of 2.9% in 2009, while North and Central Asia will experience the largest rebound. The sharp downturn of the Russian Federation saw growth in the subregion decelerate in 2009, to -5.8%, but positive growth is expected to return in 2010, at 3.7%.

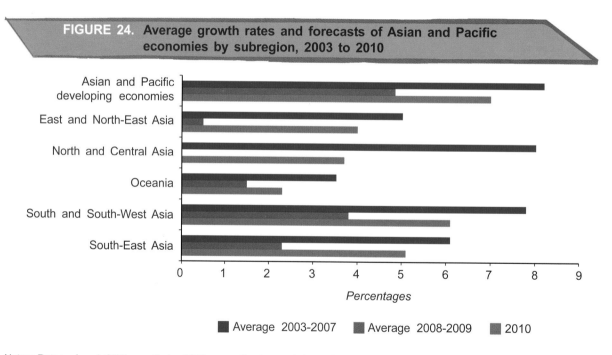

FIGURE 24. Average growth rates and forecasts of Asian and Pacific economies by subregion, 2003 to 2010

Percentages

■ Average 2003-2007   ■ Average 2008-2009   ■ 2010

Notes: Rates of real GDP growth for 2009 are estimates and those for 2010 are forecasts (as of 15 April 2010). Asian and Pacific developing economies comprise 37 economies (excluding North and Central Asia). The calculations are based on the weighted average of GDP figures in United States dollars in 2007 (at 2000 prices).

Sources: ESCAP calculations based on national sources; IMF, *International Financial Statistics (IFS) Online Service,* available from www.imfstatistics.org/imf/ (accessed 29 Feb. 2009); ADB, *Key Indicators for Asia and the Pacific 2009,* available from www.adb.org/Documents/Books/Key_Indicators/2009/default.asp (accessed 1 Oct. 2009); CEIC Data Company Ltd., available from http://ceicdata.com/; and website of the Interstate Statistical Committee of the Commonwealth of Independent States, www.cisstat.com (accessed 22 Mar. 2010); and ESCAP estimates.

Downside risks persist

While recovery in the developed world will likely be well managed by policymakers, deep uncertainties persist about the pace of recovery in the United States. Economic activities continue to pick up, but some indicators, notably rising unemployment, have increased the complexity of managing macroeconomic policies. Continued fiscal expansion will not be sustainable and has been exerting pressure on fiscal balances. However, as the Government turns off the fiscal throttle, private-sector growth drivers may not be strong enough and the economy could fall back quickly into a double-dip recession, thereby sparking a new cycle of fiscal expansion.

Pressure is growing for protectionist measures in developed countries but also potentially in developing countries, which is of great concern for recovery in Asia and the Pacific

---

A growing concern is the impact of sharply increased Government borrowing in major developed economies. Early in 2010 the perceived difficulties of Greece in repaying its Government debt came to the fore; in coming years other economies in the European Union may be facing similar problems. The impact on Asian and Pacific countries would emerge through reduced import demand from developed economies, because of curtailment of their GDP growth. Belt-tightening policies would be imposed as part of measures to pare Government debt; that would bring on a slowdown and borrowing costs would likely increase through fears of default. Furthermore, growth would be impacted if financial institutions in Europe, which hold a substantial amount of Government debt, cut lending to the corporate sector in Europe in order to retain additional reserves in case of bond defaults. If growth fails to recover in affected countries, debt payments would swallow an increasing share of Government budgets, resulting in a vicious downward growth cycle as Governments were left with fewer resources to stimulate their economies.

On the other hand, if expansionary policies in Asia and the Pacific turn out to be pro-cyclical, inflation will neutralize the incipient growth process, moving economies into recession as Governments normalize exceptionally loose monetary policy and raise interest rates. Similarly with the exit strategy needed for fiscal policy, the timing and magnitude of monetary policy reversal would also affect the prevailing forecast.

Countries across the Asia-Pacific region have begun to reverse their monetary stance in recent months. The dilemma for the region is that if they adopt a much tighter monetary policy than their major trading partners, in particular the United States, it will attract capital inflows and further fuel the appreciation of Asian currencies against the United States dollar. As a result, exports may experience renewed difficulties that would, given the importance of external demand in the region, negatively affect the overall forecast of economic growth.

Pressure is growing for protectionist measures in developed countries but also potentially in developing countries, which is of great concern for recovery in Asia and the Pacific. The first protectionist initiative during the crisis was the "Buy American" clause in the stimulus package of the United States. One novel aspect of protectionism in the crisis has been the role of subsidies to financial institutions and manufacturing companies, particularly the automotive sector, in the United States and Europe. Subsidy programmes and other forms of preferential treatment given as part of bailout packages could significantly alter competitive conditions of trade for some time to come by skewing the playing field against Asian and Pacific enterprises that do not benefit from such subsidies.[58]

---

[58]   Khor, Martin, *Trade: Protectionism on the rise hits developing countries hardest,* Third World Network Info Service on WTO and Trade Issues, Penang, Malaysia, 11 February 2009; available from www.twnside.org.sg/title2/wto.info/2009/twninfo20090208.htm.

As the impact on developed countries has increased, a number of prominent trade disputes have arisen, for example, one has been the imposition of duties on tyres from China by the United States in September 2009, which will be adjudicated at the World Trade Organization.

Another threat, albeit one that has receded more recently, is the H1N1 influenza and the possibility that it could become more virulent some time in the fufure. Following the outbreak of H1N1 influenza, the World Health Organization raised its pandemic flu alert to level 6, its highest level, in mid-2009. There is still no sign that the alert will be lifted in the near future, signifying the continued presence of the risk of spread of pandemic flu. Should the pandemic intensify, it would inevitably destabilize economic recovery by dampening consumer and investment behaviour. Impacts on tourism and related industries and services would also be detrimental.

BALANCING GROWTH WITH STABILITY

Beyond the immediate risks to the speed and sustainability of recovery, fundamental concerns exist about the nature of the recovery process and whether it will resurrect old challenges as well as create new obstacles for years to come. A complex set of policy challenges lie ahead. They are discussed below and in chapter 3 in the context of inclusive and sustainable development.

Inflation threatens from demand and supply sides

The main short-term threat to growth in Asia and the Pacific is the return of inflationary pressures as recovery gathers steam. Countries will have to balance the risks of setting off an inflationary spiral with long-term negative consequences and of halting the short-term growth

recovery trend prematurely. Critical decisions for each economy will be when and how to turn off fiscal stimulus and accommodative monetary policy.

Critical decisions for each economy will be when and how to turn off fiscal stimulus and accommodative monetary policy

Inflationary pressure has fallen significantly since the last quarter of 2008 in tandem with the downturn in domestic economic activity (figure 25). The level and degree of fall in inflation diverged considerably across economies, depending on the degree to which they had been exposed to the global slowdown. Export-oriented economies such as those of South-East Asia experienced the lowest levels of inflation, whereas more domestic-demand-led economies such as India and Indonesia continued to display comparatively higher levels. Other than country-dependent, demand-side factors, reduction in price growth across all countries was attributable to lower imported inflation from declining global oil and food prices in the early part of 2009. The crude oil price averaged around $52 per barrel in the first half of 2009, in comparison with an average of $97 in 2008. The continuing existence of fuel subsidies in such economies as India, Indonesia, Malaysia and China has, however, diminished the magnitude of oil price falls for consumers. International food prices also fell, by around 30% during the first half of 2009 in comparison with levels of the preceding year.[59] Nevertheless, as food prices remain dependent on domestic factors in many cases, countries such as India experienced food price rises even when food was falling in price elsewhere.

---

[59] Food and Agriculture Organization of the United Nations, *World Food Situation,* available from www.fao.org/worldfoodsituation/FoodPricesIndex/en/ (accessed 20 Dec. 2009).

FIGURE 25. Consumer price inflation, year-on-year, in major Asian developing economies, 2008 and 2009

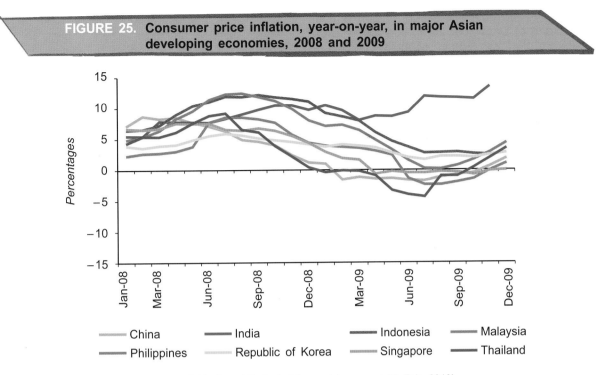

Source: CEIC Data Company Ltd., available from http://ceicdata.com/ (accessed 20 Feb. 2010).

Economies such as those of Singapore, Thailand and Taiwan Province of China experienced deep GDP contractions with various degrees of deflationary pressure early in 2009. That phenomenon proved to be short-lived as economic recovery led to rising domestic demand and assuaged earlier fears of a deflationary spiral. Inflation rates had fallen from the start of the crisis but by July of 2009 had stabilized in many countries and began moving upward in subsequent months. India was the first major economy to witness rising prices, since March 2009. In view of the growing inflationary pressures, the Reserve Bank of India increased the statutory liquidity ratio of commercial banks in October 2009, increased the reserve requirement of banks in January 2010, and increased the repo and reverse repurchase rates in March 2010. In January 2010, China also moved to tighten monetary policy in response to increasing inflation through an increase in reserve re-

quirements and increased interest rate for three-month and one-year Government bills. In March 2010, Malaysia increased its overnight policy interest-rate while Australia raised its cash interest rate.

A key factor behind rising prices is the return of supply-side pressure from commodity price volatility

Other than the increasing demand-side inflationary pressures, a key factor behind rising prices is the return of supply-side pressure from commodity price volatility. The *Economic and Social Survey of Asia and the Pacific 2009*[60] highlighted that issue for policymakers to beware of in the post-crisis phase. Oil prices increased

[60] ESCAP, *Economic and Social Survey of Asia and the Pacific 2009* (United Nations publication, Sales No. E.09.II.F.11).

dramatically during 2009. Since its lowest point at the end of December 2008, benchmark Brent crude oil had more than doubled in price to over $70 by the end of August 2009. Consequently the food-fuel link could influence key food prices upwards. The reasons for the rise in oil prices are open to debate, especially when recessionary forces prevail. The increase has in part been attributed to speculation in the oil market.[61] The large amount of liquidity available to financial investors, coupled with the belief that oil prices should be moving upwards on fundamental demand-supply factors, have also played their part. The absence of a clear endpoint in the current situation might feed speculative forces further.

A return to high food prices would follow quickly, a possibility that merits close monitoring. Other possible influences to a return of high food prices would include the weather – India, among other countries, has witnessed a disappointing monsoon season. Sugar prices have climbed to record highs in India owing to the shortfall in the sugar crop and to production decrease in Brazil, the world's other leading producer. The impact on rice production could be even more significant – Asian and Pacific demand for rice as a consequence of harvest shortfalls would be a key concern for prices. While governmental rice stocks exist in some countries, they are finite; the impact on intraregional rice trade will depend on the impact of decreased rains on the crop.

Prices may also be affected by increased food demand in line with economic recovery. As the recovery may arrive at different times across the region, early recovery in large economies that are not food-self-sufficient could stimulate increases in food prices that, in combination with declining growth, would be especially damaging for the poorest and most vulnerable

sections of the population. Higher food prices would have a far more direct impact on the poorest people of the region, impacting poverty, exacerbating inequality and levels of malnutrition, illness, infant and maternal mortality that would extend the poverty trap for long periods. The question will be how the region would respond to any situation of sudden and excessive food price rise. In the previous episode immediately before the economic crisis, food producing countries suspended trade in some cases to safeguard domestic supply. Such reactive responses do not solve fundamental demand and supply imbalances. They aggravate hoarding, rent-seeking and self-perpetuating price rises.

Increases in food prices would be especially damaging for the poorest and most vulnerable in the region

One option to deal with such a risk is a regional rice bank. A permanent East Asian emergency rice reserve is being discussed by ASEAN+3 as a follow-up to its ongoing East Asia Emergency Rice Reserve Pilot Project.[62] The pilot project, which has existed since 2004, is a system of mutual assistance for sharing of rice stocks among the 13 countries of ASEAN+3 that aims as well to contribute to rice price stability in the region. Another positive initiative is the agreement, since 2007, to establish the South Asian Association for Regional Cooperation (SAARC) Food Bank. It would maintain food reserves and support national as well as regional food security through collective action among member countries. The SAARC Food Bank would also foster intercountry partnerships and regional integration.

---

[61] For example, see Paul Krugman, "Oil speculation", *New York Times,* Opinion sec., 8 July 2009; and UNCTAD, *Trade and Development Report 2009: Responding to the Global Crisis, Climate Change Mitigation and Development* (United Nations publication, Sales No. E.09.II.D.16).

[62] Chairman's statement at the 10th ASEAN Plus Three Foreign Ministers Meeting, 22 July 2009, held at Phuket, Thailand; available from www.aseansec.org/PR-42AMM-Chairman-Statement-ASEAN+3.pdf.

Nonetheless, as ESCAP has observed in a previous edition of the *Survey*,[63] the region has yet to take adequate measures to encourage long-term increase in food production. Rising populations and increased consumer wealth in developing countries will continue to advance thus raising the policy imperative of reversing the long-term neglect of agriculture that was clear immediately prior to the crisis in 2008.

Asset bubbles build up

Abundant foreign capital buoyed by liquidity support provided to financial institutions in developed countries has been attracted to the Asia-Pacific region in recent months because of its comparatively strong growth prospects. Looking forward, as the inflows grow in scale, the risk also grows that unexpected change in interest rates, or a sudden appreciation of the dollar, could simultaneously cause capital to exit from target countries and financial asset classes in the region, precipitously bringing down asset prices and exchange rates. How to manage the benefits from foreign portfolio investments and minimize the risks that they bring to macroeconomic stability remains a huge challenge for the region. The risk remains of asset price bubbles forming in particular sectors with consequent risks for domestic financial sectors and overall macroeconomic stability.

Liquidity has been injected into the United States financial sector with the Federal Reserve purchases of mortgage-backed securities and other agency debt. The scale of such liquidity support is seen from the Government targets for such purchases, of $1.25 trillion and $175 billion respectively by the first quarter of 2010.[64] Foreign capital has been abundant as well due to the rise of the dollar "carry trade", with borrowings at low dollar interest rates for investment in economies where appreciation expectations are strong and interest rates comparatively higher. The situation resembles that in Japan from mid-2005 onwards, where near-zero interest rates in support of domestic recovery led to the use of the yen as the carry trade currency of choice. Countries in this region have been particularly susceptible to the carry trade as expectations of recovery earlier than in other parts of the world have caused interest rate and exchange rate rises, thereby offering more attractive differentials for carry trades than exist in other regions.

Asset price bubbles are bringing risks for domestic financial sectors and overall macroeconomic stability

---

Domestic capital has also been attracted to regional asset markets by liquidity addition at the national level in a number of developing countries in the region as part of monetary stimulus policies during the crisis. Credit provision (figure 26) and asset prices in a number of economies have increased substantially following declines early in the crisis, notably in China, India and the Russian Federation (figure 27). For example, during February 2010 the value of property sales in 70 major cities in China surged 10.7% year-on-year.[65] In comparison with the figures at the year's end in 2008, the Chinese Shanghai Composite Index and Indian BSE30 had jumped by 67.6% and 70.3%, respectively, by the end of February 2010.

---

[63] ESCAP, *Economic and Social Survey of Asia and the Pacific 2008* (United Nations publication, Sales No. E.08.II.F.7), chap. 3, "Unequal benefits of growth – agriculture left behind"; and ESCAP, *Sustainable Agriculture and Food Security in Asia and the Pacific,* Theme Study 2009 (Bangkok: 2009).

[64] United States Federal Reserve, "Minutes of the Federal Open Market Committee", 3-4 November 2009 (Washington, D.C.: Board of Governors of the Federal Reserve System), available from www.federalreserve.gov/monetarypolicy/files/fomcminutes20091104.pdf.

[65] *China Daily*, "Real estate prices rise at record pace", Beijing, 11 Mar. 2010, available from www.chinadaily.com.cn/china/2010-03/11/content_9570137.htm.

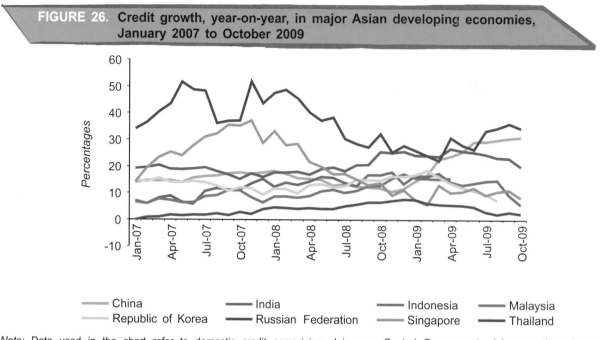

FIGURE 26. Credit growth, year-on-year, in major Asian developing economies, January 2007 to October 2009

China ── India ── Indonesia ── Malaysia
Republic of Korea ── Russian Federation ── Singapore ── Thailand

Note: Data used in the chart refer to domestic credit comprising claims on Central Government, claims on the private sector and claims on other financial institutions.
Source: ESCAP calculations based on data from IMF, *International Financial Statistics (IFS) Online Service,* available from www.imfstatistics.org/imf/ (accessed 20 Jan. 2010).

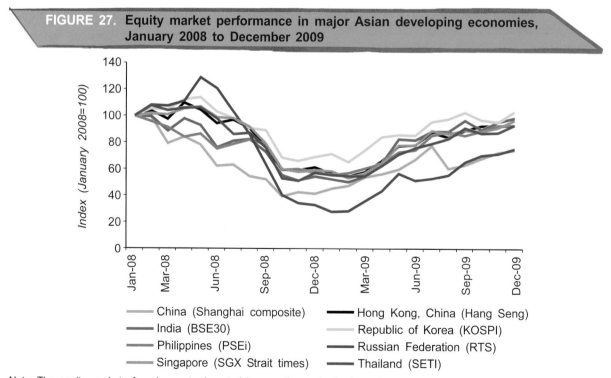

FIGURE 27. Equity market performance in major Asian developing economies, January 2008 to December 2009

China (Shanghai composite) ── Hong Kong, China (Hang Seng)
India (BSE30) ── Republic of Korea (KOSPI)
Philippines (PSEi) ── Russian Federation (RTS)
Singapore (SGX Strait times) ── Thailand (SETI)

Note: The equity market of each country is noted in parentheses in the legend.
Source: ESCAP calculations based on data from CEIC Data Company Ltd., available from http://ceicdata.com/ (accessed 20 Feb. 2010).

Other than credit being directed to domestic asset purchases, there are risks from excessive lending to export enterprises, a sector that was previously regarded as dependable but may be less so in coming years. With the outlook for exports possibly less favourable than in the past, the failure of such enterprises in any large number could jeopardize domestic banking sectors, similar to a sharp downturn in domestic asset prices. Such a development would markedly increase non-performing loans of domestic banks and in turn put their operations in jeopardy.

Riding on the expectations of an early and strong recovery, equity markets began to climb during the early part of 2009. In some cases,

stock markets have since come close to peak levels seen immediately before the crisis. Furthermore, falls in the region's major markets before the beginning of their recovery were far less, except for China, than those witnessed in the 1997 crisis (figure 28). Consequently, in global terms, Asian equity markets have seen one of the greatest post-crisis recoveries of all developing country regions (figure 29), reflecting investor expectations of comparatively healthy growth prospects in relation with other regions.

Asset markets are considered to be a leading indicator of future economic performance; hence, the recovery in prices appears to reflect investors' anticipations that growth will return to

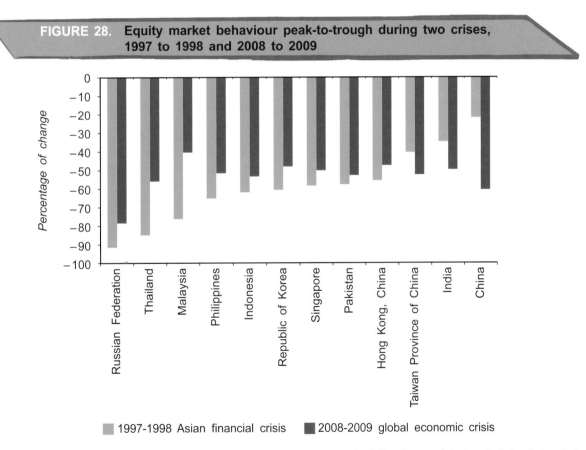

FIGURE 28. **Equity market behaviour peak-to-trough during two crises, 1997 to 1998 and 2008 to 2009**

1997-1998 Asian financial crisis   2008-2009 global economic crisis

Notes: Declines during the 1997-to-1998 crisis measure major stock market index falling from peak to trough during that period. Declines for the recent crisis (2008 to 2009) measure the corresponding movement from peak in 2008 to November 2009.
Source: Based on data from CEIC Data Company Ltd., available from http://ceicdata.com/ (accessed 15 Feb. 2010).

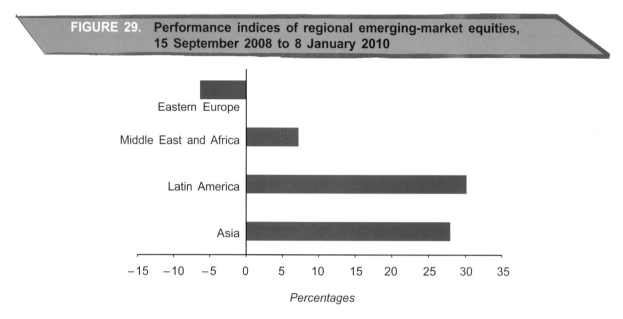

FIGURE 29. Performance indices of regional emerging-market equities, 15 September 2008 to 8 January 2010

Percentages

Source: Based on data from MSCI Barra, available from http://www.mscibarra.com/products/indices/international_equity_indices/gimi/stdindex/performance.html (accessed 11 Jan. 2010).

the Asia-Pacific region. The optimism of investors[66] about future recovery may be excessive, being driven by the need to invest buoyant funds available from the unprecedented governmental injection of liquidity into the financial sector in developed countries as well as by excessive domestic liquidity creation. Consequently, volatility may continue in financial markets carrying risks for domestic financial sectors and overall macroeconomic stability. Hence, the governments may consider managing capital flows through various types of capital controls.

Avoiding premature exit

The recovery phase for economies in the region presents the critical challenge for policymakers of deciding when and how to exit from the stimulus programmes that have supported growth since the crisis. While continuing with stimulus policies in a climate of incipient growth recovery would likely lead to some inflationary

and fiscal pressures, the overwhelming priority for policymakers should be to continue stimulating economies until the self-perpetuating motors of growth are firmly entrenched.

Risks have accompanied the incipient growth recovery, the most acute being inflationary pressures. The other consequence of the substantial government support has been increases in budget deficits across the region. Resolving the consequences of deficits will be a medium-term challenge; for most of the region such deficits were, in any case, an aberration from otherwise prudent fiscal policies. The relatively stable macroeconomic fundamentals of most countries mean that their increased levels of borrowing are sustainable and can be paid off over time. So, while fiscal pressure is undoubtedly a challenge, the key short-term concern for the region remains inflationary pressures.

The recovery cannot be said to have been re-ignited in full measure as yet. Growth still de-

---

[66] Pilling, David, "Mixed signals from Asia's animal spirits", *Financial Times,* 14 May 2009, available from www.ft.com/cm/s/0/2ba14cd2-3fef-11de-9ced-00144feabdc0.html.

pends largely on government spending and investment from stimulus policies. With continued weakness in developed-country markets, the previous growth engine of exports remains subdued for many economies. In such a climate, a premature withdrawal of fiscal stimulus could have severe consequences for the growth of economies in the region, and therefore for the livelihoods of their poorest and most vulnerable citizens.

The overwhelming priority for policymakers should be to continue stimulating economies until the self-perpetuating motors of growth are firmly entrenched

In the balance of risks, Asian and Pacific economies should aim to sustain growth rather than manage inflation. Policymakers should guard against premature exit from stimulus policies until growth becomes more self-sustaining. When exit policies are enacted, the mix between fiscal and monetary policies will be important for the twin tasks of sustaining growth while managing inflation. In that pursuit, monetary tightening could play the most effective role in controlling price pressures because it could act directly on credit build-up.

While decisions on timing the exit from stimulus policies depend on national circumstances, a key role remains for regional coordination: to prevent negative macroeconomic repercussions due to regional diversity in policies. For example, monetary tightening through an increase in interest rates in the absence of such a rise in other economies will attract portfolio flows and

serve to increase inflationary pressures. Foreign portfolio inflows would also lead to exchange-rate pressure that would endanger the recovery of exports.

Sustaining Asia's dynamism

The fundamental long-term challenge for maintaining growth in the Asia-Pacific region is to complement the engine of exports to developed countries, especially the United States. Under current projections, the import demand of the United States is unlikely to resume its pre-crisis growth trajectory, as its debt-driven consumption is constrained (see box 1). The effects in the region will vary according to the degree of export-dependence of each country and its exposure to the United States market.

Countries that can boost their domestic demand to significant levels may use that channel to replace the loss in the export contribution to growth. For smaller export-dependent economies in the region, a clear route for mitigating the decline in the role of exports to developed countries is to increase their share of intraregional trade to benefit from the domestic demand of their larger neighbours. Stimulus measures have temporarily increased governmental investment and consumption in a number of countries. Fiscal stimulus in some has also increased private consumption through the provision of funds directly to consumers. However, for domestic and regional demand to increase its contribution beyond such temporary fillips, policy measures are needed that can induce long-term structural rebalancing of economies. Such a strategy would address a number of critical global and regional imbalances and begin to chart the way forward, as discussed in Chapter 4.

"The prospects of convergence, which seemed bright before the crisis, have receded. We must take steps to counter these developments and restore the momentum of growth in the developing world"

Manmohan Singh
Prime Minister of India

CRISIS AND REBOUND: THE DIFFERENTIATED IMPACTS, POLICY RESPONSES AND OUTLOOK AT THE SUBREGIONAL LEVEL

2

As the first global economic contraction in modern times hit Asia and the Pacific late in 2008, economic growth among developing economies of the region decelerated sharply from a pre-crisis level of 9.1% in 2007 to 4.0% in 2009. That the growth rate remained positive was due to continuing rapid growth in China (8.7%) and India (7.2%). However, if those two powerhouses are excluded, growth of developing economies in the rest of the region contracted to 0.6%, much the same as in the rest of the world. The synchronized impact of the global crisis is shown in figure 30.

Comparison of crisis-period growth (2008 and 2009) with pre-crisis growth trends (that is, the five-year average annual growth from 2003 to 2007) reveals that almost all economies experienced various degrees of deceleration in growth from their pre-crisis performance (figure 31). Japan, Fiji, Palau and Samoa were the most severely hit, followed by Armenia, Cook Islands, Georgia, the Marshall Islands, New Zealand, the Russian Federation, Taiwan Province of China, Singapore and Turkey.

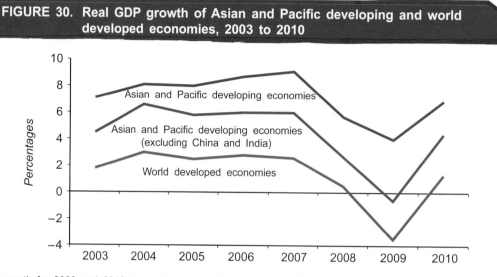

FIGURE 30. Real GDP growth of Asian and Pacific developing and world developed economies, 2003 to 2010

Note: GDP growth for 2009 and 2010 are estimates and forecasts, respectively.

Sources: ESCAP calculations based on national sources; IMF, *International Financial Statistics (IFS) Online Service,* available from www.imfstatistics.org/imf/ (accessed 29 Sept. 2009); ADB, *Key Indicators for Asia and the Pacific 2009,* available from www.adb.org/Documents/Books/Key_Indicators/2009/default.asp (accessed 22 Mar. 2010); Interstate Statistical Committee of the Commonwealth of Independent States, available from www.cisstat.com (accessed 22 Mar. 2010); and ESCAP estimates and forecasts. Figures for developed economies from United Nations, *World Economic Situation and Prospects 2010* (United Nations publication, Sales No. E.10.II.C.2.).

The grim performance notwithstanding, clear signs of a rebound emerged across the region towards the end of 2009. Central to such better-than-expected performance was the domestic demand response to aggressive pump-priming. Business should not simply resume as usual – Governments have helped prevent a meltdown, but they will find it much trickier to steer their economies back to their pre-crisis growth rate. They first need to address imbalances and shift to a more sustainable and inclusive development paradigm.

Central to such better-than-expected performance was the domestic demand response to aggressive pump-priming

---

As a basis for understanding the range of required policy responses, this chapter examines the patterns of crisis impact and recovery across five subregions of Asia and the Pacific. The extent of the impact in each economy

hinged on a number of factors, including its initial conditions, the breadth and depth of its integration with the global economy, and the speed and intensity of the Government's countercyclical measures.

EAST AND NORTH-EAST ASIA

The East and North-East Asian subregion spans diverse economic systems as well as the development spectrum: from the centrally planned Democratic People's Republic of Korea to three economies in transition away from centrally planned systems, to market economies at advanced stages of development; and, at its eastern extreme, Asia's only developed country, Japan.

The diversity enhances economic complementarity and generates a potential for expanding and deepening a wide range of economic relations: from the Japanese capital- and technology-intensive economy, to Chinese labour-intensiveness to Mongolian and Russian Federation resource-abundant economies. China is the subregional growth engine as well as one of the

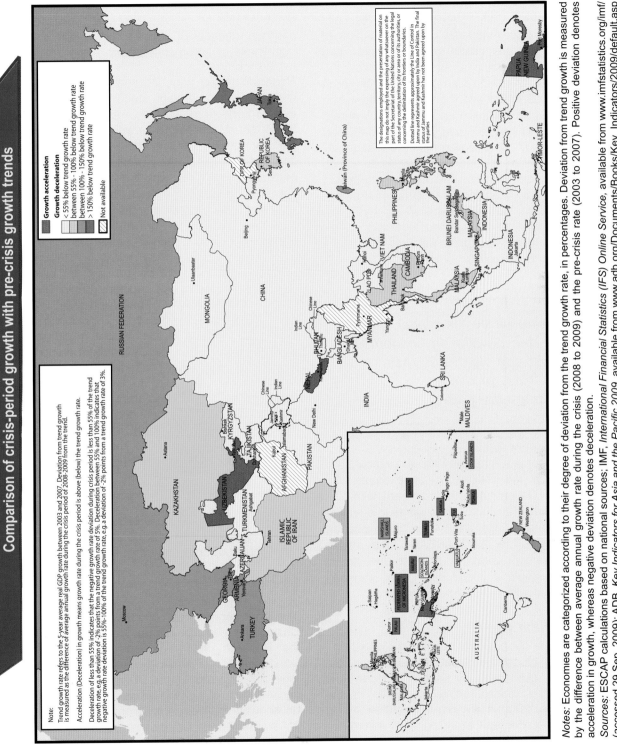

FIGURE 31. Map of growth deceleration among Asian and Pacific economies: Comparison of crisis-period growth with pre-crisis growth trends

Note:

Trend growth rate refers to the 5-year average real GDP growth between 2003 and 2007. Deviation from trend growth is measured as the difference of average annual growth rate during the crisis period of 2008-2009 from the trend.

Acceleration (Deceleration) in growth means growth rate during the crisis period is above (below) the trend growth rate.

Deceleration of less than 55% indicates that the negative growth rate deviation during crisis period is less than 55% of the trend growth rate, e.g. a deviation of -2% points from a trend growth rate of 5%. Deceleration between 55% and 100% indicates that negative growth rate deviation is 55%-100% of the trend growth rate, e.g. a deviation of -2% points from a trend growth rate of 3%.

Growth acceleration

Growth deceleration

- < 55% below trend growth rate
- between 55% - 100% below trend growth rate
- between 100% - 150% below trend growth rate
- > 150% below trend growth rate
- Not available

The designations employed and the presentation of material on this map do not imply the expressing of any whatsoever on the part of the Secretariat of the United Nations concerning the legal status of any country, territory, city or area or of its authorities, or concerning the delimitation of its frontiers or boundaries.

Dotted line represents approximately the Line of Control in Jammu and Kashmir agreed upon by India and Pakistan. The final status of Jammu and Kashmir has not been agreed upon by the parties.

Notes: Economies are categorized according to their degree of deviation from the trend growth rate, in percentages. Deviation from trend growth is measured by the difference between average annual growth rate during the crisis (2008 to 2009) and the pre-crisis rate (2003 to 2007). Positive deviation denotes acceleration in growth, whereas negative deviation denotes deceleration.

Sources: ESCAP calculations based on national sources; IMF, *International Financial Statistics (IFS) Online Service*, available from www.imfstatistics.org/imf/ (accessed 29 Sep. 2009); ADB, *Key Indicators for Asia and the Pacific 2009*, available from www.adb.org/Documents/Books/Key_Indicators/2009/default.asp (accessed 1 Oct. 2009); CEIC Data Company Ltd., available from http://ceicdata.com; website of the Interstate Statistical Committee of the Commonwealth of Independent States, available from www.cisstat.com (accessed 22 Mar. 2010); and ESCAP estimates.

world's fastest-growing economies – consistently so. While vertically and horizontally integrated production networks have deepened economic relations among China, Japan and the Republic of Korea, linkages with the other economies of the subregion are much less developed and harbour a huge potential for future growth. Importantly, perhaps as a sign of more to come, in October 2009 China and the Russian Federation signed a $4 billion trade and investment agreement that included oil, gas, raw materials and engineering. The two Governments envisage expanding Russian oil and gas exports to China and cooperation between them in extracting and processing raw materials. The Russian Federation is one of the main suppliers of hydrocarbons to China, while its technology and investment agreement with China will help modernize its own Far East region.

After being hit by the global financial crisis, the developing economies in East and North-East Asia, led by China, recovered swiftly in the latter part of 2009

Other economies are likewise extending their links outside the subregion; for example, the Mongolian Government has agreed with the Ivanhoe Mines/Rio Tinto consortium a development scheme for the giant Oyu Tolgoi copper-gold deposit. The 2009 ASEAN-China Investment Agreement aims to promote investment flows and create a liberal, facilitative, transparent and competitive investment regime.

Impact of the crisis

After being hit by the global financial crisis, the developing economies in East and North-East Asia, led by China, recovered swiftly in the latter part of 2009. Their inherent resilience and their unprecedented expansionary macroeconomic policies are key. Although the export sector has continued to struggle, the downturn has largely been cushioned by domestic demand.

Monetary authorities have also enjoyed greater flexibility, since lower food and energy prices have helped reduce inflation. Japan, however, remained under greater pressure because its previous decade of recession has left it with high levels of accumulated debt.

Rebound under way. Between 2008 and 2009, growth in the subregion decelerated into negative territory, from 2.1% to -1.1% (table 8 and figure 32). Much of the slowdown took place in the first half of 2009, at the peak of the global financial crisis. A further dampener, in the second quarter of 2009, was the outbreak of H1N1 influenza, whose severity at that time was unknown. Figure 32 reveals the scale of the deceleration, with GDP growth declining rapidly during the first and second quarters of 2009.

In China, the deceleration brought the slowest growth since records of quarterly growth began in the 1990s. However, urban fixed-asset investment, which had increased by 26% during both 2007 and 2008, rose even more quickly – by 31% in 2009 – after the Government responded with its fiscal stimulus package. Household consumption also continued to grow, though retail sales growth decelerated from 22% in 2008 to 16% in 2009. The pronounced rebound of 80% in the stock market brought recovery of all the ground it had lost due to the crisis, spurring growth to reach 8.7% in 2009.

In China, the deceleration brought the slowest growth since records of quarterly growth began in the 1990s

---

The four economies of Taiwan Province of China; Hong Kong, China; Macao, China; and the Republic of Korea also experienced their worst contraction since the Asian financial turmoil of 1998 (table 8). Nevertheless, by the second half of 2009, a rebound was clearly under way in their subregion. By the end of 2009, the Korea Composite Stock Price Index was 50% higher than a year earlier and 56% above its trough of November 2008, while much smaller declines were recorded than during the

TABLE 8. Rate of economic growth and inflation in East and North-East Asian economies, 2008 to 2010

(Percentages)

	Real GDP growth			Inflation[a]		
	2008	2009[b]	2010[c]	2008	2009[b]	2010[c]
East and North-East Asia[d]	**2.1**	**−1.1**	**4.0**	**3.5**	**−0.3**	**1.0**
China	9.0	8.7	9.5	5.9	−0.7	2.5
Democratic People's Republic of Korea	3.7	..	..	..	..	..
Hong Kong, China	2.4	−1.9	4.5	4.3	0.5	1.9
Japan	−1.2	−5.2	1.3	1.4	−1.4	−0.5
Macao, China	12.9	1.3	..	8.6	1.2	..
Mongolia	8.9	0.5	6.5	28.0	7.0	7.9
Republic of Korea (the)	2.2	0.2	5.2	4.7	2.8	2.5
Russian Federation (the)	5.6	−7.9	3.5	14.1	11.7	8.1
Taiwan Province of China	0.7	−1.9	4.5	3.5	−0.9	1.3

Notes: [a] Changes in the consumer price index. [b] Estimates. [c] Forecasts (as of 15 April 2010). [d] Subregional calculations based on GDP figures at market prices in United States dollars in 2007 (at 2000 prices), used as weights to calculate the subregional growth rates.

Sources: ESCAP calculations based on national sources; IMF, *International Financial Statistics (IFS) Online Service,* available from www.imfstatistics.org/imf/ (accessed 29 Sep. 2009); ADB, *Key Indicators for Asia and the Pacific 2009,* available from www.adb.org/Documents/Books/Key_Indicators/2009/default.asp (accessed 1 Oct. 2009); Interstate Statistical Committee of the Commonwealth of Independent States, available from www.cisstat.com (accessed 22 Mar. 2010); and CEIC Data Company Ltd., available from http://ceicdata.com/; and ESCAP estimates.

FIGURE 32. Real GDP growth, year-on-year, of major East and North-East Asian economies, 2008 and 2009

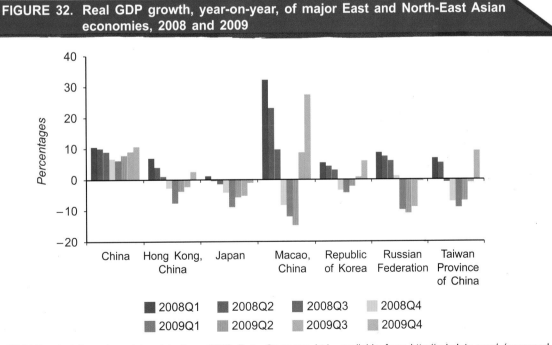

Source: ESCAP calculations based on data from CEIC Data Company Ltd., available from http://ceicdata.com/ (accessed 5 Mar. 2010).

previous year in both consumption and investment. Similarly, in Hong Kong, China, the fall in GDP was 7.5% during the first quarter but had narrowed down to 3.7% in the second quarter; by the third quarter it was down to 2.2%. In Macao, China, revenue from the gaming and entertainment sector fell by 10% within the first seven months of 2009, with a 15% year-on-year drop in GDP in the second quarter of 2009. By the third quarter however, a number of multibillion-dollar investment projects that had been put on hold, started to pick up slowly.

Although the economy of Mongolia is relatively less integrated with the rest of the subregion, it also experienced a sharp drop in economic growth, from a robust 8.9% to 0.5% between 2008 and 2009. Lower commodity prices for some of its principal exports contributed to the sharp deceleration.

Japan experienced average pre-crisis growth of 2.1% during the period 2003 to 2007; but growth started to fall as early as the second quarter of 2008, when it was 0.4% lower than in the previous year, and continued to slide in the first quarter of 2009, by 8.9% year-on-year. Over the whole of 2009, the economy shrank by 5.2%, with deterioration in almost all economic indicators – not only in exports, but also in private consumption, which makes up almost 60% of GDP. Already weak prior to the crisis, consumption fell steadily along with wage income and employment. Private investment contracted at an unprecedented pace.

Deflationary pressures key concern. Lack of inflationary pressure in the subregion going into the crisis permitted accommodative monetary policies as part of stimulus measures. Deflationary pressures were much more evident in this subregion than in others, following marked corrections in oil and food prices (table 8) and excess capacity. In February 2009, consumer prices in China fell to -1.6% from a year earlier, while over the whole year prices declined to -0.7%. Housing costs showed the greatest downward adjustment among major expenditure items, owing to the consolidation in the property market. In Hong Kong, China, deflation emerged in mid-2009, after months of downward price adjustments. More dramatically, in

Japan, while consumer price inflation hovered around 0%, producer price inflation swung from 4.5% in 2008 to an estimated -5.2% in 2009, bringing back deflationary pressures that had plagued the Japanese economy for more than a decade. Mongolia exhibited a relatively high inflation rate, estimated at 7.0%, a significant deceleration in comparison with 28.0% of 2008.

The Russian Federation and Mongolia were affected not only by the volume decreases but also by the sharp fall in international commodity prices

---

The crisis largely impacted East and North-East Asia through trade channels, with plunges in import demand from developed countries amounting to over 25% for Japan and the United States, and the European Union. Furthermore, the Russian Federation and Mongolia were affected not only by the volume decreases but also by the sharp fall in international commodity prices (figures 33 and 34). The decline in exports was already evident by the end of 2008 and exports fell steeply in the first half of 2009. Year-on-year decreases in merchandise trade were around 20% in China, the Republic of Korea and Hong Kong, China; in Japan and Taiwan Province of China they reached over 30%; in Mongolia, 40%, and in Macao, China a notable 55%. The export of services also declined, evident in a slowing in the growth in tourist arrivals. The sharpest decline was in transport-related and other services that also reflected the drop in merchandise trade, since in the more advanced economies an important share of merchandise trade is captured by services.

The major products of East and North-East Asia were clearly sensitive to the slowdown in demand from developed countries, to a much greater extent than in economies in other subregions that weathered the export contractions better because of their exports of low-cost/low-technology manufactured goods, or because of windfall gains in commodity price rises. Cases in point are Bangladeshi garment exports and Uzbekistani gold

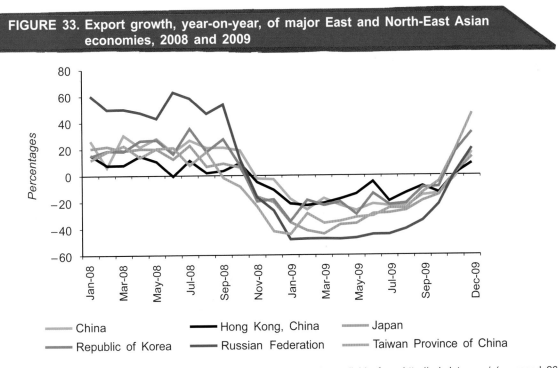

FIGURE 33. Export growth, year-on-year, of major East and North-East Asian economies, 2008 and 2009

Source: ESCAP calculations based on data from CEIC Data Company Ltd., available from http://ceicdata.com/ (accessed 26 Feb. 2010).

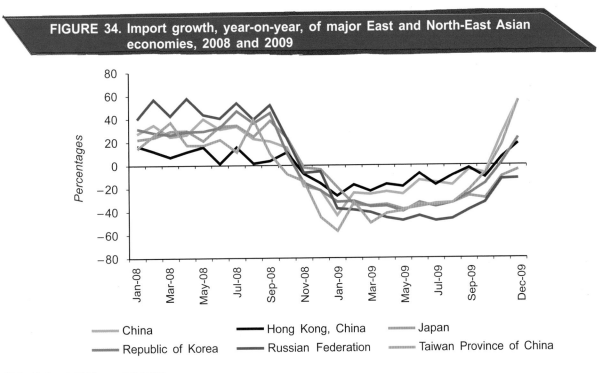

FIGURE 34. Import growth, year-on-year, of major East and North-East Asian economies, 2008 and 2009

Note: Data of 2009 are estimates.
Source: ESCAP calculations based on data from CEIC Data Company Ltd., available from http://ceicdata.com/ (accessed 26 Feb. 2010).

exports. East and North-East Asian specialization in medium- and high-technology manufactured goods as well as fuel and metal commodity products led to the initial severity of the negative export impact of the global crisis.

On the import side, in tandem with export declines, demand for raw materials and intermediates for export-oriented production saw sharp declines. Commodity prices fell at the same time, so current accounts were only moderately affected (figure 35). All economies remained in positive territory with the exception of Mongolia, because of the unfavourable world prices for its principal exports and import dependence. Some economies, notably the Republic of Korea, even improved while others experienced modest deterioration.

Renewed inflows challenge policy. The global crisis affected inward flows of foreign direct investment (FDI) in East and North-East Asia. China has exhibited the most dynamism, having

seen robust FDI growth of 15% in 2007 and 30% in 2008. But in 2009, FDI declined by 13%. Thanks to the current account surplus, however, reserves built up even more rapidly; by the end of 2009, Chinese foreign assets surpassed $2.4 trillion, the highest in the world.

The Republic of Korea also received net capital inflows, attributable mainly to massive inflows of portfolio investment that more than offset the net outflows related to direct investment, derivatives and other investments. In 2008, the country had net portfolio outflows of $2.4 billion. In 2009 net portfolio inflows reached $51 billion, helping foreign reserve assets rise by over $65 billion, in conjunction with the current account surplus.

Other economies of the subregion are also faced with the challenge of how to maximize the benefits of capital inflows while reducing their destabilizing effects. In 2009, for example, Hong Kong, China recorded net capital inflows associated with financial derivatives and other investments that exceeded the net outflows in

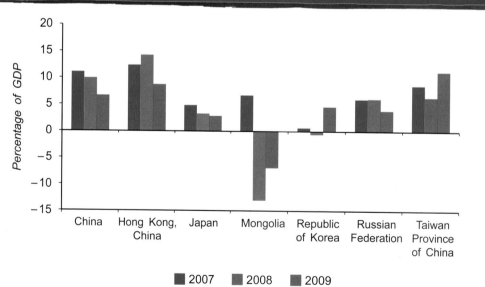

FIGURE 35. Current account balance as a percentage of GDP in major East and North-East Asian economies, 2007 to 2009

■ 2007 ■ 2008 ■ 2009

Note: Data for 2009 are estimates.
Sources: ESCAP calculations based on data from IMF, *International Financial Statistics (IFS) Online Service,* available from www.imfstatistics.org/imf/ (accessed 3 Nov. 2009); and *World Economic and Financial Surveys: World Economic Outlook Database,* Oct. 2009 ed., available from www.imf.org/external/pubs/ft/weo/2009/02/weodata/index.aspx (accessed 3 Nov. 2009); and ESCAP estimates.

direct and portfolio investment. Combined with its current account surplus, by 2009 foreign reserve assets had exceeded $250 billion.

Mongolia also witnessed capital inflows that enabled it to offset a current account deficit in the second quarter of 2009. By mid-2009, foreign reserves stood at about $650 million

---

In the case of Taiwan Province of China, net capital inflows in the first half of 2009 came mainly from the net inflows of other investment and financial derivatives. They offset the net outflows of direct and portfolio investment that had resulted from increased investment overseas. Coupled with current account surplus, foreign reserve assets continued to accumulate to over $300 billion by mid-2009.

Mongolia also witnessed capital inflows that enabled it to offset a current account deficit in the second quarter of 2009. By mid-2009, foreign reserves stood at about $650 million.

Appreciating currencies. In China, in the first half of 2008, the Central Bank ceased floating the yuan within a band, that had led to notable appreciation. During 2009, however, despite the increase in capital inflows, the yuan remained largely stable at around 6.8 per United States dollar. Stability in the exchange rate, as the US dollar weakened, helped maintain export competitiveness in third markets. However, with continuing surpluses in capital and current accounts, China continues to face pressures for appreciation.

The Korean won, by contrast, regained value during 2009, rising by 18% – a consequence of surplus in the current account, inflows of portfolio capital and improved access to foreign credit markets. The Japanese yen appreciated by over 20% from its low in mid-2008. Both Japan and the Republic of Korea, however, became less competitive in the Chinese market and elsewhere because of the stability of the yuan. China takes a major share of exports of both of those countries, so exchange rate movements

dampened intraregional trade in 2009. The New Taiwan dollar experienced mild appreciation of 3% over 2009 against the United States dollar. Under the Linked Exchange Rate system, the Hong Kong dollar remained stable. The largest appreciation – almost 20% during 2009 – was that of the Russian rouble, reflecting the Government's monetary policy which helped avoid uncontrolled currency depreciation.

On the other hand, towards the end of 2008, the Mongolian tugrik lost over 25% of its value against the United States dollar. The Bank of Mongolia responded with a rise in interest rates. By end-2009 the tugrik was 8% higher than its March trough.

Policy responses

Low inflation levels enabled Governments to support aggressive fiscal spending with accommodative monetary policies. At the end of 2008, Japan, for example, lowered the policy interest rate by 0.5% to a token 0.1%. From October 2008, the Bank of Korea cut its policy rate six times in a row, reducing it by 325 basis points to a record low of 2%. Similarly, Hong Kong, China and Taiwan Province of China kept interest rates at rock-bottom levels – at 0.5% and 0.1%, respectively (figure 36).

Low inflation levels enabled Governments to support aggressive fiscal spending with accommodative monetary policies

---

At such rates, little room remains for further cuts to support private lending. China is a special case – the Government could direct increases in bank lending. In general each country's capacity to undertake effective stimulus was due to the considerable fiscal space available before the crisis for Government spending. The subregion displayed some of the largest fiscal spending programmes in the world as a percentage of GDP, particularly those of China, the Republic of Korea and Japan.

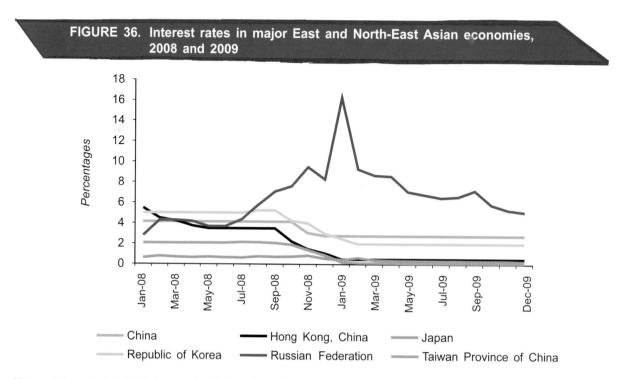

FIGURE 36. Interest rates in major East and North-East Asian economies, 2008 and 2009

Notes: China: Central Bank base rate of less than 20 days; Hong Kong, China: Discount Window base rate; Japan: Interbank rate of one month; Republic of Korea: Base rate (Bank of Korea); Russian Federation: Overnight interbank rate; Taiwan Province of China: Interbank overnight rate.
Source: CEIC Data Company Ltd., available from http://ceicdata.com/ (accessed 25 Feb. 2010).

> *The Republic of Korea and China have been notable for including significant initiatives to achieve the twin goals of promoting the emerging field of "green" technology as well as shifting domestic consumption and production patterns to a more environmentally sustainable path*

Stimulus policies across the subregion have displayed some positive signs of moving economies to a new growth trajectory based on new industrial sectors and more inclusive and sustainable demand. The Republic of Korea and China have been notable for including significant initiatives to achieve the twin goals of promoting the emerging field of "green" technology as well as shifting domestic consumption and production patterns to a more environmentally sustainable path. The Republic of Korea had the world's largest component of a stimulus programme dedicated to environment-related projects, accounting for 79% of its total stimulus spending, China was second globally with 34%.[67] Also in 2009 the Republic of Korea initiated a five-year plan to move its economy decisively towards a low-carbon, "green-growth" vision of development. Earlier China had incorporated significant environment-related spending into its 11th Five-Year Plan (2006 to 2010).

---

[67] UNEP, *Global Green New Deal: An Update for the G20 Pittsburgh Summit,* September 2009; available from www.unep.org/pdf/G20_policy_brief_Final.pdf.

Unwinding expansionary policies. While aggressive fiscal stimulus was possible because of the accumulated budget surpluses, the scale of spending has inevitably put pressure on budgets going forward (figure 37). During the recovery phase, Governments have begun to consider the timing and prioritization of their exit strategies to ensure fiscal probity without endangering renewed growth momentum. Other than the impact on Governmental budgets, delay in removing stimulus creates the risk of asset price bubbles across many economies in the subregion. Property markets in China, the Republic of Korea and Hong Kong, China have seen rapid price rises over 2009.

Tightening monetary policies across the subregion to reduce the build-up in asset prices would need coordination, since any mismatch between economies is likely to lead to significant fluctuations in exchange rates. If Governments raise interest rates ahead of their trading partners, particularly the United States, they would see their currencies continue to strengthen, possibly retarding exports and choking off recovery. On the other hand, coordination in tightening monetary policy is complicated by varied growth performance across the subregion. Resilient economies would face greater demand-side pressure for monetary tightening, whereas economies that have just begun to see growth recovery might need to maintain supportive monetary policies.

Tightening monetary policies across the subregion to reduce the build-up in asset prices would need coordination, since any mismatch between economies is likely to lead to significant fluctuations in exchange rates

Policy coordination accelerates. East and North-East Asian countries were notable among other parts of the ESCAP region for taking the lead in policy cooperation to combat impacts of

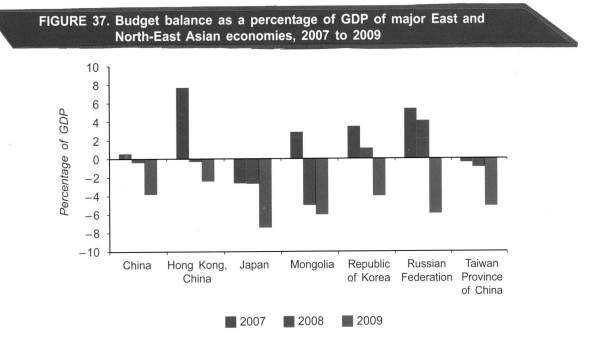

FIGURE 37. Budget balance as a percentage of GDP of major East and North-East Asian economies, 2007 to 2009

■ 2007   ■ 2008   ■ 2009

Note: Budget balance for Mongolia and Russian Federation includes grants.
Sources: ADB, *Key Indicators for Asia and the Pacific 2009,* available from www.adb.org/Documents/Books/Key_Indicators/2009/default.asp (accessed 3 Nov. 2009); and ESCAP estimates.

the crisis. Cooperation moved to new heights among the major economies of Japan, China, the Republic of Korea and the Russian Federation. The three first-named played a leading role in 2009 in the financial response of Asia and the Pacific to the crisis through the multilateralization of the ASEAN+3 Chiang Mai Initiative, as well as the expansion of bilateral currency swap arrangements between the Republic of Korea and the other two East Asian economies in late 2008.[68] The Russian Federation and China have deepened their cooperation through the Shanghai Cooperation Organisation framework as well as on a bilateral basis. In October 2009, the two economies moved towards deeper integration in trade and investment related to the supply of energy from the Russian Federation to China, an area of enormous future potential in subregional cooperation. The two economies have also been at the forefront of proposals to expand the system of world reserve currencies and increase the use of IMF special drawing rights (SDRs).[69]

Outlook and policy challenges

By mid-2009 all economies were showing signs of a rebound. Growth is forecast to rise from the setback of -1.1% in 2009 to 4.0% in 2010 (table 8). Yet risks remain – the recent rebound could quickly turn into a second dip if global financial weakness returns, or if Governments exit prematurely from expansionary macroeconomic policies, and the private sector does not fill the investment gap. The key question is how to turn the recent rebound into a sustained recovery.

From rebound to sustainable recovery. Developments in the East and North-East subregion remain strongly influenced by China. If China is taken out of the equation, the growth rate for the rest of the subregion is below that of other Asia-Pacific subregions. Stimulus spending by China has increased domestic investment and consumption and therefore increased the demand for imports from the subregion. For example, China in 2009 became the most important Japanese trading partner, overtaking the United States. Similarly, the increase in exports of the Republic of Korea to China in 2009 served to replace much of the loss in exports to developed countries.[70] Such developments point to a possible trend in the medium term among neighbouring economies – that of supplying goods destined for final demand in China rather than for processing and export by China to supply final demand in developed countries.

China is expected to continue to lead growth, expanding by 9.5% in 2010, with investment in infrastructure helping to remove supply-side constraints and spur even faster growth beyond 2010. A brighter economic outlook should also encourage further investment by the private sector. China is likely to emerge in 2010 as the world's second-largest economy.

Much depends on what happens in Japan. Even though Japan should benefit from a revival in external demand and achieve positive growth of 1.3% in 2010, domestic demand remains weak and business investment has yet to sustain recovery. Consequently, Japan and other developed countries appear to be converging in an equilibrium of slower growth. That would hinder the return of East and North-East Asian economies to high growth unless they can consume more, save less and integrate more quickly among themselves and with other rapidly growing Asian and Pacific economies, notably that of India. Much remains to be done in liberalizing trade and investment and removing regulatory bottlenecks while improving employment conditions in order to help boost private consumption.

---

[68] Sim, William and Nipa Piboontanasawat, "South Korea, China, Japan agree on currency swaps for stability", *Bloomberg*, 12 December 2009; available from www.bloomberg.com/apps/news?pid=20601089&sid=aMtclSyeEF8E.

[69] Xinhua, "Russia, China hold similar positions on financial reform", *China Daily*, 31 March 2009; available from www.chinadaily.com.cn/china/g20/2009-03/31/content_7633245.htm.

[70] Chang-mock, Shin, "Korea focus: retrospect on Korean economy in 2009", CEO Information No. 736 (Seoul: Samsung Economic Research Institute, 23 December 2009); available from www.koreafocus.or.kr/design2/layout/content_print.asp?group_id=102863.

BOX 2. Potential for economic cooperation: the Democratic People's Republic of Korea

After two years of recession, the Democratic People's Republic of Korea[a] showed positive economic growth in 2008; yet growth remains constrained. The global financial crisis appears to have had limited, if any, impact on the economy, given the limited integration of the economy with the external world. The country has suffered its own financial difficulties: the complications arising from a revaluation of its currency in November 2009. Inflation has followed, causing severe difficulties for poorer sections of the population in purchasing necessary goods.

Trade flows remain small. It is estimated that imports continue to outpace exports resulting in a trade deficit of around $1.5 billion in 2008. Investment is hampered by foreign exchange constraints that limit the import of capital goods needed for technological upgrading. Other constraints such as outdated trade laws and the lack of comprehensive and coherent foreign investments policy remain to be addressed.

Insufficient availability of energy has been a major constraint for sustainable economic growth and social welfare. Considerable unexploited resources remain; only 30% of hydropower resources have been developed, representing nearly half of the electricity used by industry. No oil or natural gas is produced, requiring that they or their refined products be imported.

Difficulties in the agricultural sector and their impact on food security for the population have been of great concern. Food production fell sharply over the past decade. In addition to geographical and climatic constraints, production during both the agricultural seasons has been severely limited by input shortages of mechanized equipment; quality seeds, fertilizer, pesticides, fuel and plastic sheeting, as well as labour. In recent years food imports have been reduced in a disturbing trend to offset the cereal shortfall, presenting further challenges for vulnerable groups within the country. Safety-net programmes that improve access to basic food and other essentials are critical for households unable to meet their essential needs through their own production, purchase or traditional coping mechanisms.

On a more positive note, the major trading partners of Democratic People's Republic of Korea are its neighbouring economies, namely those of the Republic of Korea, China and the Russian Federation. Being located between the well-established transport systems of those trading partners, the potential for transit of goods by rail and road is big, as is broader economic cooperation between Democratic People's Republic of Korea and North-East Asia. It was also reported recently that the country has upgraded the status of a free trade zone near its border with China and Russian Federation, that potentially will boost foreign investment.

---

[a]   Despite the paucity of reliable information for some economies, the current survey endeavours to cover all members of ESCAP, including the Democratic People's Republic of Korea. However, in the absence of comprehensive economic and social data, it is very difficult to present a complete and accurate macroeconomic picture. The information here was obtained from secondary sources.

Benefiting from strong growth in China, the Republic of Korea is expected to resume positive growth in 2010, at a rate of around 5.2%. Taiwan Province of China should also be able to take advantage of economic growth in the region and grow by around 4.5% in 2010, though this will depend on the performance of the all-important export sector. Hong Kong, China, given its closer integration with the Chinese economy, should benefit from a strong performance in China and be able to grow by 4.5% in 2010. Mongolia should benefit from the Oyu Tolgoi investment. Its economy should expand by 6.5% in 2010.

NORTH AND CENTRAL ASIA

North and Central Asia is the subregion worst affected by the global economic crisis. In 2008 its economy had grown by 5.8%; in 2009, following the crisis, its economy shrank by 5.8% (table 9). Millions of people who had recently moved out of poverty saw themselves slide quickly back while unemployment rose, real wages declined and prices of basic necessities shot up. Countries that depended on foreign-exchange remittances also came under pressure as a result of the shrinking economy in the two main migrant

TABLE 9. Rate of economic growth and inflation in North and Central Asian economies, 2008 to 2010

(Percentages)

	Real GDP growth			Inflation[a]		
	2008	2009[b]	2010[c]	2008	2009[b]	2010[c]
North and Central Asia[d]	**5.8**	**−5.8**	**3.7**	**14.4**	**10.7**	**7.9**
Armenia	6.8	−14.4	1.5	9.0	3.4	4.0
Azerbaijan	10.8	9.3	7.0	20.8	1.5	6.0
Georgia	2.1	−4.0	2.0	10.0	1.7	5.5
Kazakhstan	3.3	1.0	2.0	17.0	7.3	7.0
Kyrgyzstan	7.6	2.3	3.0	24.5	6.8	8.6
Russian Federation	5.6	−7.9	3.5	14.1	11.7	8.1
Tajikistan	7.9	3.4	3.5	20.4	6.4	8.0
Turkmenistan	9.8	6.1	7.0	13.0	10.0	12.0
Uzbekistan	9.0	8.1	8.0	12.7	8.0	8.5

Notes: [a] Refer to percentage changes in the consumer price index. [b] Estimates. [c] Forecasts (as of 15 April 2010). [d] Calculations are based on GDP figures at market prices in United States dollars in 2007 (at 2000 prices) used as weights to calculate the subregional growth rates.

Sources: ESCAP calculations, based on data from the Interstate Statistical Committee of the Commonwealth of Independent States, www.cisstat.com (accessed 22 Mar. 2010); and IMF, *World Economic and Financial Surveys: World Economic Outlook Database,* Oct. 2009 ed., available from www.imf.org/external/pubs/ft/weo/2009/02/weodata/index.aspx (accessed 3 Nov. 2009); and ESCAP estimates.

destination countries of the Russian Federation and Kazakhstan. Decline in remittances in most Central Asian countries, became a channel of instability and declined economic growth, unlike for the rest of Asia and the Pacific where workers' remittances showed more resilience and support for domestic demand.

The five net fuel exporters suffered a steep decline in export revenue as a result of lower oil prices. All have since seen inflation fall, often because of lower prices for food and oil; nevertheless inflation rates remain stubbornly high in a number of countries and can be expected to continue to face upward pressures as demand picks up.

Overall, the crisis brought vulnerabilities to the fore that should be carefully tracked and for which remedial policy responses are essential. For workers and families, the recovery process will be long and slow.

In 2009 Governments faced two main tasks. The most immediate was to contain the worst of the socioeconomic fallout. As was the case in other subregions, North and Central Asian countries adopted expansionary fiscal and monetary policies, combined with measures to stabilize their banking sectors. Governments had little choice but to meet their pledges to increase social spending and finance ongoing infrastructure projects, leading to widened fiscal deficits.

The second task was to maintain their resolve in market reforms – just when some of the basic market-economy fundamentals were being questioned all over the world. Despite the temptation to turn their backs on previous policies, Governments on the whole did not waver and continued their market reforms. In fact, reforms in the financial and banking sectors, combined with cautious macroeconomic management policies over the past decade, improved their overall resilience to financial crisis. Many economies from the subregion showed they were better prepared for a financial crisis than during the last one of 1997.

Impact of the crisis

Economic growth has been mixed. The crisis impacted the Russian Federation severely, where lack of access to international financing during the early part of the crisis was further exacerbated by the sharp declines in commodity prices. Furthermore, its deep economic and socio-political ties with the rest of the subregion left no country unaffected. Armenia, suffering a 14.4% decline in growth, was the worst affected economy, not only in the subregion but the entire Asia-Pacific region. The orientation of the Russian Federation to Europe and other developed markets had increased over time and left it vulnerable, as trade, investment and financial flows from developed countries plummeted. A sharp fall in remittances from Armenians working abroad caused much hardship, given that in 2008 remittances accounted for a 8.9% share of its GDP. Consequently, the remittance-fuelled construction boom halted sharply, with the sector contracting by more than 50% during the first three quarters of 2009.

Reforms in the financial and banking sectors, combined with cautious macroeconomic management policies over the past decade, improved their overall resilience to financial crisis

---

Kazakhstan is one of five net exporters of fuel in the subregion with an economy highly dependent on oil revenues. It was impacted heavily by the crisis as well as reduced oil and other commodity prices. GDP was expected to grow by 1% in 2009. From mid-2009, however, Kazakhstan experienced a deceleration in the pace of decline in industrial production, being the first sign that the Government's stimulus package for industrial and infrastructure projects including small- and medium-scale enterprises was yielding a positive effect.

Georgia also featured among those countries of the subregion that experienced negative economic growth, due to its relatively high exposure to the crisis-hit developed countries and the collapse in demand for its foodstuffs and manufactured exports. Domestic instability further exacerbated lacklustre economic performance.

On a more positive note, Azerbaijan, Turkmenistan and Uzbekistan emerged as the fastest-growing economies in the subregion. They are relatively less open and thus rather more reliant on domestic demand for economic growth. They also have had the fiscal space to implement countercyclical measures. Uzbekistan is one of the fastest-growing economy of all, buoyed by increases in the price of gold and a good grain harvest. Industrial output has led the recent developments, growing by 9% in 2009, with gross fixed investment particularly in the construction sector growing by about 30%. Household consumption has remained strong, with a growth in retail trade of 16.6%. In fact, growth in private consumption could have been higher except for the decline in remittance inflows from workers in the Russian Federation and Kazakhstan. In Azerbaijan, expansion in the industrial sector has made a major contribution to economic growth.

Increased grain harvests over the year provided relief, particularly for those countries that experienced high unemployment, helping to ensure supplies for their own people and exporting to countries outside the subregion such as Afghanistan. For both the Russian Federation and Kazakhstan, exports of wheat and fuel continued to play a key role in subregional trade.

Inflation decelerated. After having experienced the highest inflation rates seen in recent years in 2008, inflation decelerated in 2009 across all countries owing to weakened domestic demand and reduced commodity prices, particularly for energy and food. Notwithstanding that trend, inflation is expected to remain stubbornly high, at or close to double digit-levels, particularly in the Russian Federation and Turkmenistan (table 9). In Kyrgyzstan, consumer price inflation decelerated from 24.5% in 2008 to 6.8.% in 2009. However, continuing power shortages and a doubling in the cost of gas imports are expected to create significant upward pressure on inflation in 2010. The Government of Turkmenistan has tried to control inflation by reducing the amount of cash in circulation through a currency reform process, given its underdeveloped capital and money markets and the lack of alternative monetary policy tools at its disposal.

In contrast, inflation in Armenia, Azerbaijan and Georgia remained at modest levels (table 9). For Armenia and Georgia, it was symptomatic of the steep decline in economic activity. In contrast, Azerbaijan experienced high growth. Inflation there in 2008 peaked at 20.8%, its highest of the past decade. The 2009 rate of 1.5% was the result of weak growth in domestic demand and reduced international oil prices. Recent rises in fuel and basic utility prices and increased cost of imported goods could soon drive the inflation rate up again.

Economic crisis resulted in a sharp decline in current account and foreign trade surpluses across the region (figure 38). The impacts varied among the more closed economies that were less affected. Stagnant real wage growth and limited access to credit brought a sharp drop in imports. However, continued import dependence on essential food products, as well as machinery and equipment to complete hydrocarbon projects and improve infrastructure, resulted in declines in imports that were less than those in exports. Trade deficits therefore widened across the entire subregion (table 10). Surpluses on the current transfers and income accounts also fell, as lower inflows of remittances and other private transfers further exacerbated balance of payment pressures.

The current-account surplus of Turkmenistan remained positive in 2009 (figure 38) despite disruptions in natural gas exports to the Russian Federation. Nevertheless, that surplus was

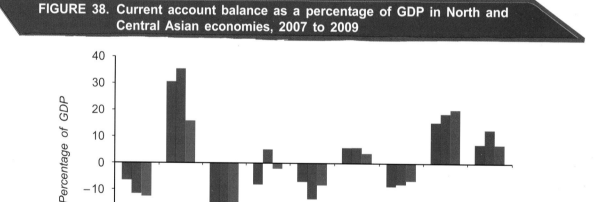

FIGURE 38. Current account balance as a percentage of GDP in North and Central Asian economies, 2007 to 2009

Note: Data for 2009 are estimates.
Sources: IMF, *International Financial Statistics (IFS) Online Service,* available from www.imfstatistics.org/imf/, (accessed 3 Nov. 2009); and *World Economic and Financial Surveys: World Economic Outlook Database,* Oct. 2009 ed., available from www.imf.org/external/pubs/ft/weo/2009/02/weodata/index.aspx (accessed 3 Nov. 2009); and ESCAP estimates.

TABLE 10. Trade performance of North and Central Asian economies, in percentages, 2007 to 2009

| | Growth rates | | | | | |
| | Exports | | | Imports | | |
	2007	2008	2009	2007	2008	2009
Armenia	17.0	−8.3	−34.0	49.1	35.4	−25.3
Azerbaijan	63.4	43.8	−69.2	14.7	25.3	−14.6
Georgia[a]	31.6	21.4	−35.3	41.8	20.9	−37.7
Kazakhstan	24.8	49.1	−39.3	38.3	15.7	−25.0
Kyrgyzstan	45.8	24.3	−22.4	55.6	46.1	−25.3
Russian Federation	16.8	32.9	−35.5	45.0	33.7	−37.3
Tajikistan	4.9	−4.2	−28.3	42.5	33.2	−21.5
Turkmenistan[b,c]	12.9	52.7	−46.6	41.5	54.8	−28.8
Uzbekistan[b,c]	42.9	29.2	−3.8	49.2	23.4	19.5

Notes: [a] 2009 data refer to first 2 quarters.
    [b] Import value in f.o.b.
    [c] Figures for 2008 and 2009 are EIU estimates for whole year.
Sources: Interstate Statistical Committee of the Commonwealth of Independent States, www.cisstat.com (accessed 29 Mar. 2010); and Economist Intelligence Unit, Country Analysis and Forecasts, Country Analysis Services, *Country Reports,* accessible at http://countryanalysis.eiu.com/, various issues, 2010.

expected to account for 20.4% of GDP as gas exports resumed and tensions eased by year-end. Exports to China and the Islamic Republic of Iran increased. Similarly, in Uzbekistan, rising global prices on its principal exports of gold, gas, and cotton were expected to sustain the export revenues in 2009. Hydrocarbons also became a more important source of income than in the past. Uzbekistan benefited from a renegotiated agreement with the Russian Federation regarding natural gas exports, with the result that it was the only country that experienced slower declines in exports in 2009.

FDI inflows remained a key priority and continued to play a key role in developing and modernizing the economies of North and Central Asia in 2009. However, a more difficult international economic environment limited new FDI into the subregion. Tight credit conditions and the economic downturn adversely impacted FDI flows into the Russian Federation. FDI in non-financial sectors fell by more than 50% to $17.3 billion in the first half of 2009, compared with $39.6 billion received in the first six months of 2008. Similarly in Georgia, FDI declined from $1.5 billion in the first four months of 2008 to $972 million in the corresponding period of 2009.

Remittances made a major socio-economic contribution in low-income countries accounting for one third and one quarter of GDP in Tajikistan and Kyrgyzstan, respectively in 2008 (table 11).

Up to one third of Tajikistan migrants are estimated to have returned home in 2009 and remittance inflows could have fallen by 60%. A 30% fall in remittance inflows was expected in Kyrgyzstan in 2009.

Policy responses

Governments reacted quickly to the crisis by implementing expansionary monetary and fiscal policies, in line with expansionary policies implemented at the global level. As the crisis evolved and Governments assumed more active man-

TABLE 11. Receipts of workers' remittances[a] in major North and Central Asian economies, 2006 to 2008

	Amount (million $)			Percentage of GDP		
	2006	2007	2008	2006	2007	2008
Armenia	658.1	845.9	1 062.1	10.3	9.2	8.9
Azerbaijan	812.5	1 287.3	1 554.3	3.9	4.1	3.4
Georgia	485.3	695.7	732.1	6.3	6.8	5.7
Kazakhstan	187.5	223	191.5	0.2	0.2	0.1
Kyrgyzstan	481.2	714.8	1 232.4	17.0	19.1	24.4
Tajikistan	1 018.8	1 690.8	1 750.0	36.2	45.5	34.1
Turkmenistan	..	..	..	..	..	..
Uzbekistan	..	..	..	..	..	..

Note: [a] Including compensation of employees.

Source: ADB, *Key Indicators for Asia and the Pacific 2009,* available from www.adb.org/Documents/Books/Key_Indicators/2009/default.asp.

agement of the economy, policy debate intensified on what that might mean for the role of the State in a market economy. How should Governments direct and regulate the economy in order to temper the excesses and instabilities to which unbridled capitalism was prone? – while also enhancing openness and transparency in governance and consultative processes among all stakeholders. The challenges were a reminder of the complex issues that will remain after the crisis subsides.

Remittances made a major socio-economic contribution in low-income countries

---

In 2009, as in other subregions, substantial increases in State spending were directed at countering the adverse impact of the crisis on the economic security and social wellbeing of the peoples of the subregion. Public investments in large infrastructure projects accelerated. However, the substantial declines in remittance inflows created serious difficulties for poor households that for years had come to depend on remittances as a way of coping with poverty.

Most countries had to augment their funding of social assistance, social insurance and nutrition programmes while implementing additional measures to protect the delivery of essential social services.

The crisis exacerbated longstanding imbalances in public pension systems. Sharp declines in economic growth and high unemployment reduced revenue contributions at the same time that expenditures were increasing and values on the asset side of balance sheets were dropping rapidly. A concomitant challenge arose from the decline in commodity prices. In countries that are resource dependent, the flow of public revenues is closely associated with commodity prices. Even though oil-producing and exporting countries entered the crisis with significant fiscal space, fiscal deficits rose sharply in those countries. The Russian Federation, having accumulated relatively large reserves in stabilization funds during the period of high commodity prices that preceded the global crisis, implemented one of the largest countercyclical packages in the world (at 7.2% of 2008 GDP) and consequently saw fiscal deficits rise sharply for the first time since 2000.

Other countries entered the crisis with constrained fiscal space. In Armenia, the budget deficit rose from 1.2% of GDP in 2008 to 6.6%

in 2009. The Government had to raise the legal maximum permitted budget deficit so that it could accommodate the spending increases for social and other support programmes (figure 39). The deficit in Georgia rose to 8.9% in 2009, compared with an already high deficit of 6.3% of GDP recorded in 2008. Despite higher revenues received from corporate profit tax linked to rising oil prices, Azerbaijan is expected to record one of the highest fiscal deficit of the subregion in 2009, because of continued expenditure increases on social spending and large infrastructure projects. Any shortfall in donor financial support, arising from the impact of the crisis and the deepening debt problems in some countries of the European Union, is of major concern to all of them.

Accommodative monetary policy. Governments in the subregion aimed at two key targets in monetary policy: curbing inflation and

providing exchange-rate stability. Central banks had to reduce interest rates to alleviate the burdens of domestic businesses that ranged from wide interest-rate spreads from high crisis-related business risks, to low capitalization of businesses, to overall weak institutional capacity. At the same time, declining commodity prices, combined with weak demand, dampened inflationary pressures and allowed for monetary policy to focus on maintaining financial stability and supporting domestic economic activity.

As capital flows reversed, strong downward pressures on exchange rates emerged in most countries of the subregion (figure 40). In the Russian Federation, monetary policy in 2009 was aimed at avoiding a large, uncontrolled devaluation of the rouble and maintaining a nominally stable rate of exchange for the rouble against a dual-currency basket of a 55:45, dollar-to-euro proportion. As the rouble stabilized,

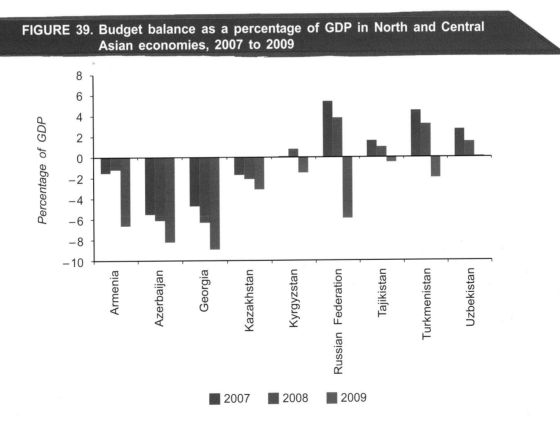

FIGURE 39. Budget balance as a percentage of GDP in North and Central Asian economies, 2007 to 2009

■ 2007   ■ 2008   ■ 2009

Note: Data for 2009 are estimates.
Sources: ADB, *Key Indicators for Asia and the Pacific 2009,* available from www.adb.org/Documents/Books/Key_Indicators/2009/default.asp (accessed 3 Nov. 2009); and ESCAP estimates.

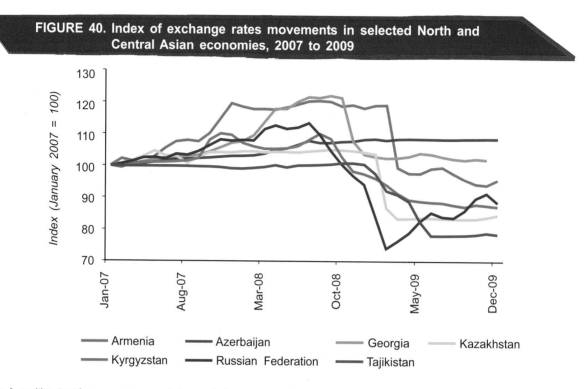

FIGURE 40. Index of exchange rates movements in selected North and Central Asian economies, 2007 to 2009

——— Armenia ——— Azerbaijan ⋯⋯⋯ Georgia ——— Kazakhstan
——— Kyrgyzstan ——— Russian Federation ——— Tajikistan

Note: A positive trend represents appreciation and vice versa.
Source: ESCAP calculations based on data from IMF, *International Financial Statistics (IFS) Online Service,* available from www.imfstatistics.org/imf/ (accessed 26 Feb. 2010).

and more recently appreciated, the Russian central bank cut its refinancing rate by 425 basis points to 8.75% and reduced cash reserve requirements to improve liquidity in the domestic economy.

Similarly in Kazakhstan, falling inflation and weak domestic demand provided space to loosen monetary policy in 2009. The Government intervened quickly to stabilize liquidity shortages in the banking sector. Another concern was the possibility that tight credit markets could dampen growth in the non-oil economy, thereby jeopardizing diversification targets in the "Kazakhstan 2030" development strategy. Consequently, the National Bank of Kazakhstan cut the refinancing rate to 7% and reduced cash reserve requirements for commercial banks. Its decision to allow the trading band of the tenge to widen to a range of 127.5 to 165.0 beginning from 5 February 2010 is likely to lead to an appreciation of the domestic currency that will help offset local demand for foreign currency.

The Government intervened quickly to stabilize the slowdown in credit growth.

Reform agenda and integration. Much of the rapid economic development in the subregion prior to the global crisis has resulted from increased integration with other developing as well as developed countries – mainly through trade and investment, particularly in natural resources, as well as remittances. Foreign exchange earnings rose substantially, enabling the countries of the subregion to boost imports and achieve high GDP growth. During the crisis, despite rising protectionist pressures and the temptation to reverse externally oriented growth policies, countries generally maintained their commitment to keeping trade, investment, finance and labour markets open. Reforms to improve the business climate and to encourage FDI continued. Kyrgyzstan moved up the global ranking from 80 to 41 in ease of doing business, by having implemented reforms in 7 out of the 10 areas measured in the report "Doing Business 2010".[71] Furthermore, countries in the process of accession to WTO continued their efforts, despite the complexities. The Russian Federation, notwithstanding an accession process almost 20 years long, remains committed to join, at the same time pursuing other trade agreements – for example, the Customs Union with Kazakhstan and Belarus (box 3). Attention has already focused on economies in Asia and the Pacific because of growing complementarities. In December 2009, the Russian Federation opened its Siberian oil export route which is expected to carry annually 80 million tons of oil eastwards. The Russian Federation has also emerged as an important supplier of liquefied natural gas to Asia.

Outlook and policy challenges

The growth prospects of the economies in North and Central Asia in 2010 depend on trends in global commodity prices and the performance of the Russian Federation and Kazakhstan, which are the largest trading partners, important investors and major sources of remittances for other economies in the subregion. A return to positive growth is expected in all countries and, for the subregion as a whole, the growth rate for 2010 is forecast at 3.7%.

Strong domestic demand and increased oil and gas production should enable the economy of the Russian Federation to continue its expan-

---

BOX 3. Creating a "Eurasian Union": the Russian Federation, Kazakhstan, and Belarus

Subregional economic cooperation and trade in North and Central Asia broadened in 2009 when the Russian Federation and Kazakhstan together with Belarus, another member of the Eurasian Economic Community (EurAsEC; but not an ESCAP member country), agreed to create a Customs Union to facilitate trade among the three of them, improve the competitiveness of their products in world and Asian markets, and open new joint investment opportunities.[a] The Customs Union started functioning on 1 January 2010 with common external tariffs, common principles in macroeconomic management and competition policies, and common approaches in subsidizing industrial and agricultural products. The Union is ready to admit other EurAsEC countries. Kyrgyzstan and Tajikistan are expected to join. The Union aims to become part of the agreed Single Economic Space (SES)[b] by 2012, that in turn aims to merge within a "Eurasian Union" of the three economies thereafter.

The Customs Union aims to exploit mutual complementarities that could help create economies of scale and increase the region's attractiveness as an investment area. Consequently the Union's GDP is expected to rise 15% by 2015. The Russian Federation plays a leading role in bilateral trade with other members of the Union. It accounts for about one tenth of Kazakh exports and more than one third of Belarusian exports. It provides more than 35% of Kazakh imports and more than 60% of Belarusian imports. Kazakhstan and the Russian Federation have substantial hydrocarbon deposits that form their principal export prospects.

The three Customs Union members possess rich deposits of ferrous, non-ferrous and precious metals, and hydropower resources. They share comparative advantages in the production of grains, meat and dairy products and could be self-sufficient in food. Their wheat exports account for 17% of global wheat exports. Their combined human-resource base includes high levels of education and scientific and technical potential. The Customs Union has a combined market of 170 million people.

Notes: [a] Eurasian Economic Community, "About EurAsEC", available from www.evrazes.com/en/about/ (accessed 1 Apr. 2010).
       [b] Resolution No. 374 of the EurAsEC Interstate Council, Concept of Establishment of the Common Transport Space of the Eurasian Economic Community, 25 February 2008, available from www.evrazes.com/docs/view/156 (accessed 1 Apr. 2010).

---

[71] World Bank, *Doing Business 2010: Reforming through Difficult Times* (Washington, D.C.: World Bank, 2009); available from www.doingbusiness.org/documents/fullreport/2010/DB10-full-report.pdf.

sion at 3.5% in 2010. However, inflationary pressures could persist, however, because of marked deterioration in fiscal deficits, rising capital inflows and stronger domestic demand. In Kazakhstan, positive economic growth of 2% is forecast in 2010 owing to continued strong investment in oil-sector projects and rising prices for hydrocarbons and metals. The fastest growing economies are expected to be those of Turkmenistan and Azerbaijan at 7%, and Uzbekistan at 8%. Kyrgyzstan and Tajikistan are expected to develop their energy resources and infrastructure and to increase energy self-sufficiency with technical and financial assistance from the Russian Federation. They will need additional international assistance to sustain economic development and solve problems of poverty, infrastructure repair and capacity-building. GDP growth of both economies is expected to accelerate to about 3.0% or more in 2010.

The growth prospects of the economies in North and Central Asia in 2010 depend on trends in global commodity prices and the performance of the Russian Federation and Kazakhstan

---

Looking beyond 2010, the subregion is expected to expand trade and investment cooperation with the rest of Asia and the Pacific. Complementarities between countries rich in natural resources and energy, and those experiencing a rapid demand for such resources, will drive the process. Cooperative agreements are expected to increase and could include science and technology aspects, with a particular focus on drawing from experience and expertise available in East Asia regarding adapting to and mitigating climate-change challenges. Improving environmental management in water, agriculture and energy resources, and building up a low-carbon infrastructure that is less resource-intensive are promising new growth areas of the future that should deepen relations with the rest of Asia and the Pacific.

OCEANIA

Many of the characteristics of Pacific island economies have always impeded their development: their geography, narrow resource bases, frequent natural disasters and fragile ecosystems that are vulnerable to rising sea levels. Those characteristics cannot be changed. Yet, signs are emerging that some of the givens are being reshaped to enable the subregion to sustain and diversify its pattern of growth.

The crisis was transmitted to Oceania through declining demand for exports, falls in tourism and remittance earnings, etc

---

Pacific countries have benefited increasingly from development of tourism and related transport services as well as remittances that provide resource for business investment and support to poor households. Some have benefited from windfall gains in high, albeit sharply fluctuating, commodity prices. But as they grow more dependent on those income sources, they become more vulnerable to global economic shocks.

In this crisis, the major economic and trade partners were the hardest hit. From within the subregion Australia and New Zealand which are key economic partners of Pacific economies, also experienced marked slowdowns. Not surprisingly, the crisis was transmitted to Oceania through declining demand for exports, falls in tourism and remittance earnings, and the changes in oil prices, since they have high transportation costs. For some Pacific island countries, incomes from off-shore trust funds were reduced as well. The challenge ahead is to find ways to continue diversifying their economies while managing any resulting instabilities.

Impact of the crisis

GDP growth in the subregion was 2.0% in 2008, but slowed to 1.0% in 2009 (table 12).

the kina against major trading partners' currencies (for example, the Australian dollar). Similarly, inflationary pressures remain in the Solomon Islands and Samoa, where the respective Governments have incurred large expenditure and currencies have depreciated.

In Nauru, the Australian inflation rate has been used as a proxy since the country uses the Australian dollar as its currency and Australia supplies about 60% of its imports. Recently the Nauru Bureau of Statistics started to compile its own consumer price index, which indicates much higher inflation than that in Australia. Particularly high levels were recorded for clothing (62.5%) and food (12.5%) from January to August 2009.

External sector affected by volatilities in commodity prices, tourism and remittances

While a handful of countries enjoy sizeable earnings from commodity exports, many island countries in Oceania are characterized by balance-of-payment deficits with disproportionately large imports compared to merchandise exports. Tourism earnings, remittances and income from trust funds are not enough to offset the structural trade imbalance fully. For instance, Samoan exports account for only a small share (4% to 5%) of imports; the huge deficit in merchandise trade is partly offset by tourism, and largely offset by remittances. Still, the current account remains in deficit (figure 41).

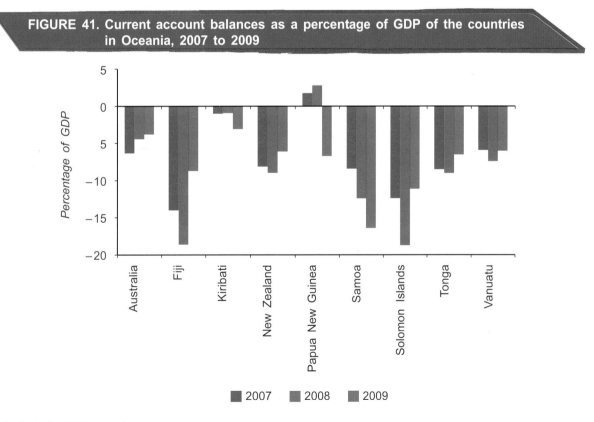

FIGURE 41. Current account balances as a percentage of GDP of the countries in Oceania, 2007 to 2009

■ 2007   ■ 2008   ■ 2009

Note: Data for 2009 are estimates.
Sources: ESCAP calculations based on data from IMF, *World Economic and Financial Surveys: World Economic Outlook Database,* Oct. 2009 ed., available from www.imf.org/external/pubs/ft/weo/2009/02/weodata/index.aspx (accessed 9 Nov. 2009 for Australia, Fiji, Kiribati, New Zealand, Papua New Guinea, Solomon Islands and Vanuatu); and ADB, *Key Indicators for Asia and the Pacific 2009* (Manila, 2009), available from www.adb.org/Documents/Books/Key_Indicators/2009/default.asp (accessed 9 Nov. 2009 for Tonga).

Fuel and food account for a large share of the imports for many countries in Oceania. The recent volatility in commodity prices has significantly affected their imports and thus their trade balances. For example, Fijian merchandise imports increased by almost 25% due to higher costs for petroleum products in 2008, followed by a fall by 30% over the first 9 months of 2009, owing to lower prices of international commodities and fuels. Similar situations prevailed in many of the other island countries. Growth of Vanuatu imports in 2008 also reflected the increase of commodity prices as well as increase in imports of capital equipment in connection with major infrastructure projects.

On the other hand, some commodity exporters (Australia, New Zealand, Papua New Guinea, Solomon Islands and Vanuatu) benefited from high commodity prices during 2008. Declines in primary commodity prices towards the end of 2008 (table 13) slashed export revenues, albeit with variations. For instance, high prices for gold, Arabica coffee and cocoa benefited Papua New Guinea, offsetting declines in revenue from other primary exports such as petroleum and copper. Palm oil and copra exporters such as Solomon Islands and Vanuatu also benefited because of increases in prices for bio-fuels.

The recent growth in visitor numbers and revenue earnings from tourism has supported economic growth in the Cook Islands, the Federated States of Micronesia, Fiji, Palau, Samoa, Solomon Islands, Tonga and Vanuatu, turning tourism into one of their most important income-generating sectors (table 14). The extent of the tourism sectoral contribution hinged on a combination of factors including: (a) the economic health and pattern of consumer spending of mostly developed economies which account for the lion's share of tourist arrivals in the Pacific; (b) price competitiveness including exchange rates against the visitors' home currencies; (c) transportation links; (d) recent natural disasters; and (e) political stability of the host country.

The global crisis and the consequent reduction in consumer spending led to falling tourist arrivals in the Pacific. For instance, reduction of tourism income in the Federated States of Micronesia and Palau is largely due to the downturn in United States and Japanese consumer spending. Yet visitors from Australia and New Zealand, who account for one third of arrivals in major Pacific destinations,[76] started to pick up in the latter half of 2009, supporting countries such as Fiji, Samoa and Vanuatu.

TABLE 13. Recent international primary commodity prices, 2007 to 2009

	2007	2008	2009
Crude oil ($ per barrel, average spot price)	71.12	96.99	61.76
Copper ($ per metric tonne)	7 118	6 956	5 150
Gold ($ per troy ounce)	697	872	973
Sawnwood Malaysian ($ per cubic metre)	806.3	889.1	805.5
Sugar; EC import price (US cents per kg)	68.09	69.69	52.44
Cocoa (US cents/kg)	195.2	257.7	288.9
Coffee, Arabica (US cents/kg)	272.4	308.2	317.1
Palm oil ($ per metric tonne)	780	949	683

Source: Based on data from World Bank Commodity Price Data (Pink Sheet), March 2010, available from http://go.worldbank.org/MD63QUPAF1 (accessed 9 Mar. 2010).

---

[76] ADB, *Pacific Economic Monitor,* No. 4, February 2010; available from www.adb.org/Documents/Reports/Pac Monitor/pem-issue04.asp.

TABLE 14. Total visitor arrivals in selected Pacific island economies, in thousands of people, 2004 to 2009

	2004	2005	2006	2007	2008	2009
Fiji	504.1	545.2	548.6	539.9	585.0	140.1[a]
Papua New Guinea	58.0	68.0	77.7	104.1	120.1	
Samoa	98.2	101.8	115.9	122.3	121.5	71.1[b]
Solomon Islands	5.6	9.4	11.5	15.2	22.0	4.4[c]
Tonga	51.9	53.3	52.8	67.1	61.5	30.6[d,e]
Vanuatu	98.5	125.6	154.1	167.1	196.7	65.6[c]

Notes: Includes day visitors.
[a] January-April   [b] January-July
[c] January-March   [d] Estimate
[e] January-June

Sources: Based on data from Samoa Ministry of Finance, *Quarterly Economic Review,* Issue No 45: Apr-Jun 2009, October 2009, available from www.mof.gov.ws/uploads/quarterly_economic_review_iss_45.pdf; Fiji Island Bureau of Statistics, accessible from www.statsfiji.gov.fj/, and visitors arrivals, accessible from www.statsfiji.gov.fj/Tourism/Visitor_Arrivals.htm; Papua New Guinea National Statistics Office, available from www.nso.gov.pg/, and visitors arrival (up to 2005) www.nso.gov.pg/Tourism/tourism.htm; Solomon Island Statistic office, accessible from www.spc.int/prism/Country/SB/Stats/; migration and tourism, available from www.spc.int/prism/Country/SB/Stats/Migration%20and%20Tourism/Tour-Index.htm; Tonga Department of Statistics, available from www.spc.int/prism/Country/TO/stats/; and Vanuatu National Statistics Office, tourism statistics, available from   www.spc.int/prism/country/vu/stats/TOURISM/tourism-index.htm.

Australia is also the main source of visitors for Papua New Guinea, Kiribati and Solomon islands although the extent of the contribution of tourism to the economy is still limited.

Exchange rate movements have also had a differentiated impact on the tourism in the Pacific subregion. For instance, the 25% decline in tourist arrivals in Fiji at the start of 2009 was mainly due to a sharp appreciation of the Fijian dollar against the Australian dollar (14%) between June 2008 and the first quarter of 2009. A 20% devaluation of the Fijian dollar in April 2009 led to a rebound in tourist arrivals. The higher tourist arrivals in Samoa during the first seven months of 2009 likely reflect the depreciation of the Samoan Tala relative to the Australian and New Zealand dollars in the first half of 2009.

Restructuring of the Pacific airline industry and increased connections to major tourist source countries, accompanied by competitive airfares, have encouraged tourism in Samoa and Vanuatu in recent years. Papua New Guinea also followed suit by partly opening up its international airline services. The closure of a charter-flight operator from Taiwan Province of China to Palau led, however, to a significant reduction in visitors from the second largest source of visitors to Palau.

Similar to tourism, in recent years remittances have become a major source of income in Pacific island countries (table 15) with Australia, New Zealand and the United States absorbing the largest share of workers. For Tuvalu and Kiribati, remittances depend heavily on seafarers' employment in merchant shipping; the sharp downturn in global trade flows in the first quarter of 2009 have adversely affected them. Although the Australian economy was less badly affected, higher unemployment may have depressed prospects for new migrant workers.

Samoa and Tonga, with GDP ratios of remittance inflows of 25.8 and 37.7% in 2008, respectively, are particularly exposed. The National Reserve Bank of Tonga estimates that remittances fell by 14% and tourist receipts by 5.9% in the year to June 2009. Tuvalu, Kiribati and Fiji are relatively less reliant on remittances. Samoan remittances continued to grow in the first half of 2009 and expected to continue further, with a considerable increase in funds sent home to families in the aftermath of the tsunami.

TABLE 15. Remittances inflows as a percentage of GDP in selected Pacific island economies, 2000 to 2008

	2000	2001	2002	2003	2004	2005	2006	2007	2008
Fiji	1.4	1.4	1.3	5.3	6.3	6.2	5.2	4.9	5.0
Kiribati	15.0	15.5	14.5	12.0	7.0	6.6	6.5	5.1	6.9
Papua New Guinea	0.2	0.2	0.4	0.4	0.4	0.3	0.2	0.2	0.2
Samoa	19.4	18.8	17.0	14.0	22.8	25.2	24.0	22.0	25.8
Solomon Islands	0.5	0.5	0.6	1.2	2.3	1.7	4.5	3.8	3.2
Tonga	30.1	39.0	44.3	32.6	34.0	30.6	30.5	39.4	37.7
Vanuatu	14.3	22.6	3.5	3.2	1.5	1.4	1.2	1.1	1.2

Sources: Based on data from World Bank Migration and Remittances Data accessible from http://econ.worldbank.org/ WBSITE/EXTERNAL/EXTDEC/EXTDECPROSPECTS/0,,contentMDK:21122856~menuPK:5963309~pagePK:64165401~piPK: 64165026~theSitePK:476883,00.html (accessed 9 Mar. 2010); and *World Development Indicators* online, available from http://ddp-ext.worldbank.org/ext/DDPQQ/member.do?method=getMembers&userid=1&queryId=6 (accessed 9 Mar. 2010).

In 2007 New Zealand launched its Recognized Seasonal Employer scheme for temporary employment of up to 5,000 migrant workers in seasonal activities, particularly fruit picking. All Pacific countries (except Fiji) were to be eligible, with initial focus on five countries: Kiribati, Samoa, Tonga, Tuvalu and Vanuatu. While the scale was limited, the scheme benefited Pacific islands in terms of household and village-level savings and the acquisition of skills and a work ethic. Australia also announced the similar Pacific Seasonal Worker Pilot in 2008, involving temporary migrants from Kiribati, Papua New Guinea, Samoa, Tonga and Vanuatu, with an annual visa quota of 2,500. Again numbers were small, particularly for a larger country such as Papua New Guinea, but the positive impacts from the returning workers could be important with respect to business start-ups, work ethic and expectations about public services. The pilot programme was to be evaluated at the end of 2009 to determine whether the scheme would be renewed and/or expanded beyond the five countries.

Trust funds lose value

Small atoll countries (Kiribati, the Marshall Islands, the Federated States of Micronesia, Palau and Tuvalu) with trust funds that serve as a main source of Government revenue were affected by the crisis. For instance, the value of the Marshall Islands Compact Trust Fund and the Kiribati Revenue Equalization Reserve Fund declined by an estimated 20% during 2008. The losses combined with increased need for fiscal expenditure added to a weakening of the fiscal states in those countries.

Imports in Australia and New Zealand decline sharply

Australia and New Zealand are the major destinations of export products for many Pacific island countries. Around 45% of Papua New Guinean and Samoan exports were destined for Australia in 2007 even though their shares in its imports were negligible. A sharp fall of imports in 2009 in Australia and New Zealand had a significant, albeit varied, impact on many of the Pacific island countries. Australian imports from Samoa halved between 2008 and 2009, while those from Kiribati contracted by 10%.

Policy responses

Policy options and responses to the crisis varied significantly across Oceania. In struggling with rising food and fuel import costs, many Pacific island Governments had implemented measures aimed at providing relief to low-income households, such as reducing customs duties and value-added tax (VAT) on selected consumer goods, and reducing taxes on fuel for transport that in turn reduced public revenues and increased budget deficits. Most of the Governments therefore entered the crisis in weakened positions.

In contrast, the developed economies of Australia and New Zealand had room for large fiscal stimulus packages. Having enjoyed fiscal surpluses in the recent past, their fiscal positions were much better than those of many OECD countries. That in turn brought benefits to Pacific island economies as deep recession was pre-empted in their key trading and economic partners. Australia launched a large fiscal stimulus package that included a $21 billion cash handout to households and public investments in school buildings and public housing. Similarly, in New Zealand a large fiscal stimulus package brought a decade-long record of fiscal surplus to an end in 2009: tax revenues fell because of falling corporate profits as well as personal income tax cuts, while expenditures jumped because of fiscal stimulus and increases in payment of unemployment benefits.

Australia and New Zealand had room for large fiscal stimulus packages

---

Australia and New Zealand also responded to the economic downturn by easing monetary policy. The Reserve Bank of New Zealand drastically cut the official cash rate from the peak of 8.25% in June 2008 to 2.5% by April 2009. Similarly, the Reserve Bank of Australia (RBA) cut the cash rate from 7.25% in March 2008 to 3% by April 2009. However, as economic contraction started to recede, the RBA turned to monetary tightening in October to pre-empt excessive inflation, in the first example of monetary tightening among developed economies.

Unique developments and constraints

Following policy responses in the rest of the world, Pacific island Governments had four options for tackling the effects of the global crisis and its myriad ramifications, although not all of them were available for some countries: (a) fiscal stimulus to boost domestic demand; (b) monetary expansion to boost aggregate domestic demand as a substitute for the reduction in external demand; (c) targeted assistance to the most vulnerable population groups; and (d) competitive devaluations in countries that had their own currencies (Fiji, Papua New Guinea, Samoa, Solomon Islands, Tonga and Vanuatu). Pacific island economies were in unique situations, especially as regards the policy space to adopt any of the above options, either alone or in combination as crisis-mitigating packages. Complexities arose that consequently are unique as well.

Some countries employed fiscal stimulus to boost aggregate demand. For example, Samoa prepared for sharp increases in fiscal deficits in FY2008/09 and FY2009/10 with increases in capital expenditure, a stimulus package focused on infrastructure, relying on Asian Development Bank concessional lending and donor grants. However, as the need for financial resources for post-tsunami rehabilitation increased, priorities changed rapidly.

The ability to finance a fiscal stimulus depends on a country's capacity to borrow, which in turn depends on the size of the existing public debt and its creditworthiness. Pacific island Governments, apart from Papua New Guinea and Vanuatu, are not in a very good position to borrow; hence their need to rely heavily on concessional lending from international development agencies and donor grants. Vanuatu had paid down its public debt through the period of strong economic growth and managed to be in budget balance in 2009. Fiji, by contrast, increased its budget deficit from a target level of 2% to 3%. Fiji had been trying to create room for more infrastructural spending by reducing the size of its public service. However, the reduction of revenue in the first half of 2009 had led to a cutback in expenditure. The Government's ability to finance a stimulus package was limited because of the constraints on its ability to borrow and to access donor grant monies. Tonga was also in a poor position to fund a stimulus package, although to some extent its rehabilitation of the commercial area of Niku'alofa, which is funded by concessional loans from China and donor funding, has functioned as an infrastructural stimulus package.

As for the second policy option, several developing States in Oceania effectively do not have an independent monetary or exchange-rate policy, since they use the United States dollar (Palau, the Marshall Islands and the Federated States of Micronesia) or Australian dollar (Kiribati, Nauru and Tuvalu) as legal tender. In countries with their own currencies, some form of monetary policy action was taken to boost aggregate demand (except Papua New Guinea). Money markets are underdeveloped, however, so demand for credit is not very responsive to changes in interest rates. Consequently, central banks in the Pacific do not emphasize interest rates as a monetary policy instrument. Expansion of the money supply is used instead as the major instrument in, for example, Fiji, Samoa, the Solomon Islands and Vanuatu. Commercial banks are also encouraged to lend, as was the case with Fiji and Solomon Islands. Effectiveness of the latter instrument is limited, inasmuch as few profitable investment opportunities are on offer. Tonga in particular has not been able to engage in credit expansion, as it has been trying to bring under control a credit "bubble" that developed over recent years through rapid expansion of the money supply.

Pacific island Governments had limited options for tackling the effects of the global crisis

---

As far as targeted assistance for the vulnerable is concerned, Fiji provided relief through removal of customs duties and VAT on key consumer goods while the income tax threshold was increased. Subsidies were provided to bus operators while bus fares for school children were paid by the Government. Tonga removed import duties on some food items and on fuel for domestic shipping and air transport. Papua New Guinea also reduced the tax on petroleum to provide relief from higher fuel prices.

Movements in exchange rates have played an important, though not well-recognized role in the performance of the developing States in

Oceania – particularly the exchange rate of the Australian and New Zealand currencies against the United States dollar. Their depreciation in the latter half of 2008 led to a loss in price competitiveness for some Pacific countries, even though it alleviated pressure on import bills.

Devaluation of Fiji in April 2009 increased competitiveness and helped to offset the decline in the EU price paid for its sugar exports, while it increased the value of remittances in domestic currency and foreign reserves as well. Devaluation, however, increases the cost of imports in local currency terms and it stimulates inflation, as well as the local currency size of the external debt, and debt servicing costs. Consequently any increase in budget expenditure is eventually squeezed out.

Outlook and policy challenges

In 2010 economic growth of 2.4% and 1.8% is anticipated in Australia and New Zealand, respectively, that will in turn improve the growth prospects of many Pacific island economies through greater tourism receipts and remittance earnings. Strong growth is also expected in Papua New Guinea from rising commodity prices and growth in domestic demand. Altogether the economies of the Oceania region are expected to grow by 2.3% in 2010, up from 1.0% in 2009.

Risks nonetheless hover in the near term: rising commodity prices put upward pressure on inflation, while rising import bills run down foreign exchange reserves. Any slippage in the global economy would hit the region hard. Hence, considering the risks in tandem with the vulnerabilities unique to this subregion, not the least of which are the increasingly frequent, severe natural disasters, forecasting remains a highly inexact enterprise.

Looking beyond 2010, developments in information and communication technology are generating new sources of economic growth that will help bridge the geographical isolation that has for so long kept Oceania apart from the rest of Asia and the Pacific (Box 4).

BOX 4. Connectivity in the Pacific

Pacific island economies have had basic international telecommunication connectivity since the 1970s. However, the Pacific has recorded the slowest growth in mobile telephone expansion in the Asian and Pacific region, with 4 users per 100 persons, compared to 39 per 100 for the Asian-Pacific region. Information and communication technology (ICT) penetration is concentrated mainly around major population centres, limited by the high costs of international and domestic bandwidth.

For small economies, cable was considered unaffordable. Only a few countries, namely Fiji, Guam, New Caledonia, Papua New Guinea, and recently American Samoa and Samoa, have access to the global backbone through submarine fibre cables.

However, as investments are being undertaken to redeploy underused cable networks, more Pacific island developing economies will get connections. Papua New Guinea, for example, has been using retired cables to redeploy part of the Pacific Rim West cable to Port Moresby. Similar initiatives include the Pacific Rim East cable which runs from New Zealand to Hawaii and is used to connect American Samoa and Samoa to the global telecommunications infrastructure networks. Another project is the South Pacific Island Network, an eastbound submarine cable running from New Caledonia to French Polynesia and New Zealand, with landing points in Vanuatu, Wallis, Samoa and American Samoa. With the completion of all the intra-regional ICT infrastructure initiatives, Pacific countries will in future be able to capitalize on more available bandwidth.

For small islands where the cost of cable connectivity remains unjustifiable economically, satellite and wireless with their scalability and flexible rollout are providing additional choice. The University of the South Pacific, for example, has a satellite-based distance learning network which connects its main campus in Suva, Fiji to extension centres in 12 Pacific island countries. In many business and community centres, satellite services with low-cost, very-small-aperture terminals are being complemented by wireless mobile and internet services. T. Digicel South Pacific claims to be the fastest-growing mobile operator in the Pacific, expanding services in Samoa, Papua New Guinea, Tonga, Fiji and Vanuatu. Other islands connectivity is under way.

The Pacific can continue to expand connectivity in future by blending cable, satellite and wireless technologies. For this purpose it will be important to foster cooperation among Pacific island developing economies to bring about synergies between cable and satellite linkages. By harmonizing the mix of national policies, the subregional market can grow and enable telecommunication service providers to reach larger numbers of users through their investments. For that purpose the Pacific Plan includes a digital strategy for exploiting ICT for sustainable socio-economic development.

SOUTH AND SOUTH-WEST ASIA

The global crisis affected South and South-West Asia less than other subregions. GDP growth remained generally positive although exports declined substantially and capital inflows were reduced (table 16). The national economies depend much more on domestic than on external demand. They rely for employment mostly on agriculture which has held up well overall and thus dampened the worst of the crisis fallout.

Of greater concern is the sharp increase in food and fuel prices in 2008 which created numerous hardships for the peoples of the subregion. As inflation impacts the poor disproportionately, it is a serious problem for countries with a high incidence of poverty. Even though inflation rates decelerated in 2009, food prices remained high and upward pressures are re-emerging.

Controlling inflation is and will remain the key macroeconomic challenge for the subregion. Another key challenge is the adverse impact of security problems ranging from internal conflicts to terrorist attacks linked with geopolitical tensions, all of which impinge on macroeconomic performance and poverty reduction.

Impact of the crisis

Both the global crisis and deteriorating security situation in some countries saw economic growth come under pressure in 2009, decelerating to 2.9% as compared to 4.7% in 2008 (table 16). Barring Afghanistan, a country highly dependent on foreign aid, India achieved the highest growth

TABLE 16. Rate of economic growth and inflation in South and South-West Asian economies, 2008 to 2010

(Percentages)

	Real GDP growth			Inflation[a]		
	2008	2009[b]	2010[c]	2008	2009[b]	2010[c]
South and South-West Asia[d,e]	**4.7**	**2.9**	**6.1**	**11.5**	**11.2**	**8.4**
Afghanistan	3.4	15.1	7.6	26.8	−10.0	8.4
Bangladesh	6.2	5.9	6.0	9.9	6.7	6.0
Bhutan	5.0	5.7	6.6	6.3	7.2	8.4
India	6.7	7.2	8.3	9.1	11.9	7.5
Iran (Islamic Republic of)	3.3	2.0	5.0	25.5	16.0	15.0
Maldives	5.8	−2.6	2.1	12.3	8.5	6.0
Nepal	5.3	4.7	3.5	7.7	13.2	7.5
Pakistan	4.1	2.0	3.2	12.0	20.8	12.0
Sri Lanka	6.0	3.5	6.0	22.6	3.4	8.6
Turkey	0.9	−6.0	3.0	10.4	6.3	7.2

Notes: [a] Changes in the consumer price index.

[b] Estimates.

[c] Forecasts (as of 15 April 2010).

[d] Calculations are based on GDP figures at market prices in United States dollars in 2007 (at 2000 prices) used as weights to calculate the subregional growth rates.

[e] The estimates and forecasts for countries relate to fiscal years defined as follows: fiscal year 1 April 2008 to 31 March 2009 for India; 21 March 2008 to 20 March 2009 for the Islamic Republic of Iran; 1 July 2007 to 30 June 2008 for Bangladesh and Pakistan; 16 July 2007 to 15 July 2008 for Nepal are 2008.

Sources: ESCAP calculations based on national sources; ESCAP estimates; and IMF, *Afghanistan National Development Strategy: First Annual Report* (2008-09), IMF Country Report No. 09/319, November 2009.

rate at 7.2% in 2009. Growth contracted in only two countries: Maldives and Turkey.

Economic growth slows but less than in other subregions

In Afghanistan, economic activity is dominated by security considerations. The economy rests primarily on agriculture and is vulnerable to weather conditions. GDP growth in 2008 was 3.4% but is expected to have been 15.1% in 2009, owing to improved weather and a good harvest. The large fluctuations in GDP growth underline the inherent vulnerability of the economy to weather conditions. Growth will also benefit from investment in construction, much of it linked to donor-led development projects. The economy depends heavily on foreign aid, much of it outside the Government budget. If overseas development assistance could be delivered through the Government in greater amounts,

programme coordination, ownership and accountability could be enhanced. For that purpose governance and the capacity of Government institutions would need to be improved to administer aid-funded projects.

In Bangladesh, GDP growth was 6.2% in 2008 and decelerated only slightly to 5.9% in 2009. Growth was underpinned by good performance in agriculture, which accounts directly for some 20% of GDP and employs more than half the labour force. The slowdown in industrial growth mainly resulted from export decline for most of the items other than apparels and textiles. The exports of apparels continued to grow despite the crisis because of the focus of Bangladesh on the lower ends of the market that were relatively less affected from the downturn. Growth in overseas workers' remittances helped in sustaining domestic demand.

GDP growth in Bhutan peaked at nearly 21.4% in 2007 with the completion of the Tala hydropower project in 2007, but returned to a more normal level of 5.0% in 2008 and 5.7% in 2009. In the coming years growth in the economy will be underpinned by three more hydropower projects.

India achieved one of the world's highest growth rates

India felt the crisis after a period of high growth momentum that had reached an annual average of 8.8% over the previous five years. In 2008, growth was 7.7% during the first half of the fiscal year, but fell to 5.8% in the second half (October 2008 to March 2009). Even so, at 6.7% India achieved one of the world's highest growth rates in 2008. While the economy largely sustained the momentum of the previous five years, both external and domestic demand were affected by the crisis. There was a slowdown in the services sector, in domestic private consumption, in investment demand and in manufacturing output.

By the beginning of the third quarter of 2009, despite the uncertain global macroeconomic scenario, domestic and external financing conditions showed signs of improving and the business outlook turned positive, signalling a revival of industrial activity. From August to November 2009 industrial output grew in double digits, while GDP growth during the second quarter of the fiscal year 2009 (July to September 2009) was 7.9%. According to the preliminary estimates, GDP grew by 7.2% for the full fiscal year 2009. This recovery is remarkable given the fact that the agriculture output declined by 0.2% due to poor weather conditions as a result of delayed and sub-normal monsoon. Both the industrial and services sectors grew by over 8%.

The Islamic Republic of Iran is the net oil exporter and the country remains highly dependent on oil revenues that provide over 80% of Government revenue. As a result of reduced oil prices and declining output, GDP growth plummeted from 3.3% in 2008 to 2.0% in 2009. That will impede the Government's plans for an expansionary fiscal policy, which in turn will affect the rate of private consumption and investment. The hydrocarbons industry will continue to suffer from a lack of foreign investment, and as refining capacity remains underdeveloped, despite petrol rationing, the country will rely increasingly on fuel imports. A drought in early 2009 was expected to lead to a rise in imports of wheat and other agricultural produce. The new five-year development plan (2010 to 2015) sets an ambitious 8% target for annual GDP growth that will not be easy to achieve.

Having grown by 7.2% in 2007 and 5.8% in 2008, the economy of Maldives is expected to have contracted by 2.6% in 2009, largely because of a significant decline in tourist arrivals. In addition, problems with external financing have held up capital projects for resort development and other major projects, causing a sharp decline in construction.

Despite the recent political fragility in Nepal on top of the global economic crisis, the macroeconomic situation remains broadly stable. GDP growth was 5.3% in 2008 and fell only slightly in 2009 to 4.7%. Some of the fall reflects adverse weather, since agricultural output, which accounts for around one third of GDP and which had grown by 4.7% in 2008, grew by only 2.2% in 2009. The non-agricultural sector was constrained by severe electricity shortages and difficult industrial relations and strikes that delayed the movement of goods and prevented people from getting to work. In recent years the services sector has, however, grown steadily and accounts for around half of GDP.

In Pakistan, GDP growth fell from 4.1% in 2008 to 2.0% in 2009. The economy has been affected not just by the global economic crisis but also by the declining security situation and intensification of conflict linked to terrorism. Industry, especially large-scale manufacturing, suffered the worst of all sectors from the drop in international demand, while also having to cope with acute shortages of electricity. Improved performance of the service sector offset it to some extent, growing 3.6% in 2009, as well as a rebound in agriculture which benefited from a bumper wheat crop. While consumer spending remained strong, gross fixed capital formation, which had expanded by 3.8% in 2008, contracted by 6.9% in 2009.

The end of the internal conflict in Sri Lanka should raise confidence among consumers and businesses

---

GDP growth in Sri Lanka fell from 6.0% in 2008 to 3.5% in 2009, corresponding to slower growth in the industrial and services sectors and falling exports. The end of the internal conflict in May 2009 should raise confidence among consumers and businesses. Much of the economic impetus will come from developing areas affected by conflict and resettling internally displaced persons. A boost in agricultural output in the north and east of the country, higher rural incomes and increased private consumption can be expected.

Turkey is strongly linked with the crisis-hit economies of the developed world and thus felt the full force of the crisis as it contracted by 6.0% in 2009. GDP growth started to contract in the last quarter of 2008, which dampened growth at barely 0.9% in 2008. That reflected a sharp decline in exports which affected domestic production, as well as much greater difficulties in foreign financing. However, imports fell even more, owing to low energy prices and the slowdown in economic activity. As a result, the current account deficit shrank from around 6.0% of GDP in 2007 and 2008 to 2.1% in 2009 – which will help ease external financing pressure.

Inflation is key policy concern

High inflation continues to be a serious problem in several countries of the subregion, rising rapidly to double digits or close to that in 2008 (table 16). Despite the deceleration in 2009, rates remained high compared with other subregions.

In India, consumer prices, particularly of food, remain stubbornly high and the consumer price index (for industrial workers) rose to about 9.0% in 2008 (table 16). Inflationary pressures continued into 2009, largely resulting from the poor monsoon with adverse impact on food supplies, firming up of global commodity prices and the Government expansionary fiscal stance. Inflation as measured by the consumer price index was around 12.0% in 2009. A faster increase in food prices has become a cause of concern.

In Pakistan, inflation rose sharply from 12% in 2008 to 20.8% in 2009 mainly because of food price increases. The Government increased the wheat support price by more than 50%, which pushed up retail prices of wheat and wheat flour across the country. It also phased out subsidies on petroleum products. To contain inflation, the Government has been cutting spending and attempting to improve the supply and distribution of essential commodities. Inflation is projected to decline in 2010 although it will remain in double digits. Upward pressures will remain high, particularly if higher oil prices, electricity tariff increases, higher wages, and fiscal expansion come to bear. A more active monetary policy might be needed to manage inflationary pressures.

A more active monetary policy might be needed to manage inflationary pressures

---

Faster reduction in inflation occurred in Bangladesh and Sri Lanka. In Bangladesh, lower world food and fuel prices drove inflation down to 6.7% in 2009 from 9.9% in 2008. Food inflation decelerated even more sharply from 12.3% in 2008 to 7.2% in 2009 supported by higher rice and wheat harvests. Non-food inflation has been comparatively lower and remained relatively stable. Inflation in Sri Lanka, after reaching a high of 28% on a year-on-year basis in June 2008, decelerated sharply to less than 1.0% in September 2009, owing to restrictive monetary policy efforts, favourable domestic supply conditions and significantly lower global commodity prices. On average inflation in 2009 was estimated at 3.4%.

Inflation in Bhutan and Nepal is linked to inflation in India due to the fixed rates of exchange of their currencies with the Indian rupee. Inflation in Nepal reached 13.2% in 2009. It was driven by a 16.5% spike in the cost of food and beverages, which account for a 53.2% weight in the consumer price index.

In the Islamic Republic of Iran, annual inflation declined from 25.5% in 2008 to 16.0% in 2009, owing to a sharp drop in international oil and non-oil commodity prices. With fiscal policy likely to remain expansionary, albeit not to the extent it was in previous years, concerns over inflation will persist in the coming years. The adoption of a tighter financial policies stance, which has been expansionary and procyclical, will be needed. Even though expansionary fiscal and monetary policies have brought about some short-term gains in production and employment, the high and persistent inflation that they generate can undermine long-term growth and adversely affect the poor.

Given the sharp economic slowdown in Turkey and much lower international commodity prices, consumer price inflation decreased to 6.3% in 2009 from 10.4% in 2008. The decreasing inflationary pressure enabled the central bank to implement growth-supporting monetary policy without deviating from the main objective of price stability.

Trade declines sharply but workers' remittances stay strong

Before the onset of global economic crisis, high oil prices had created severe problems for the balance of payments position of some countries. However, during the global crisis, both exports and imports slowed down and helped contain trade and current account deficits. Furthermore, workers' remittances have been rising sharply. They account for a substantial share of GDP, particularly in least developed countries, and provide current account support. A major part of remittances inflows originates from oil-rich Gulf Cooperation Countries. While there were some concerns that large-scale layoffs could happen if the recent financial problems experienced in Dubai spread, past experience shows that remittances from those countries are resilient, even during volatile oil price periods. Many of those countries have heavily invested in developing their infrastructure as a long-term development strategy, for which funding is available from large reserves accumulated over the years. Therefore, large-scale lay off of migrant workers seems unlikely even though rate of growth of remittances has declined.

In India, the balance of payments came under pressure in 2008, when the current account deficit widened to 2.4% of GDP in 2008. Furthermore, net capital inflows fell to $9.1 billion in 2008 as compared with net capital inflows of $108 billion in 2007, reflecting the unstable nature of those flows. Both exports and imports fell in 2009 but workers remittances remained strong. The current account deficit further widened to 3.3% of GDP for the first nine months of fiscal year 2009.

Similarly, Pakistan endured a decline in exports of 6.0% in 2009, while imports contracted at a much faster rate of 11%. Combined with a strong growth momentum in workers' remittances of 20%, reaching a total of $7.8 billion, the current account deficit in 2008 of 8.4% of GDP was reduced to 5.3% of GDP in 2009. The global economic slowdown and political and security uncertainties resulted, however, in slackening of capital inflows with reduced FDI inflows, higher portfolio outflows, lower disbursements of loan and higher amortization payments.

In Bangladesh, the balance of payments strengthened considerably in 2009 with a current account surplus of 1.0% of GDP. Imports growth decelerated markedly from 26.1% in 2008 to 4.1% in 2009 after the onset of the global financial crisis and lower demand for capital and intermediate goods. Lower food and fuel import prices and a good harvest also played a role. The apparel and textile industries continued to expand because Bangladesh largely produces for the lower end of the market which was less affected by the downturn.

Total exports grew at 15.8% in 2008 and 10.3% in 2009 which, when compared with the double-digit declines experienced by major exporting countries of the region, clearly shows that Bangladesh has become more competitive than other Asian and Pacific economies in the exports of those products. At the same time overseas workers' remittances increased 22% in 2009, to $9.7 billion, being almost 11% of GDP and lending further support to the current account balance. The Bangladeshi taka remained relatively stable.

In Nepal, due to the continued growth of remittances, the current account and balance of payments remain in surplus despite large merchandise trade deficit. Workers' remittances increased by 24.2% to $2.7 billion in 2009. For-eign exchange reserves also went up by 15.8% to $3.6 billion in mid-July 2009 as compared with reserves one year earlier.

In Sri Lanka, relatively lower oil prices, a sharp decline in imports, a steady flow of remittances, and continued flexibility in the exchange rate allowed the current account deficit to recover from 9.0% of GDP in 2008 to around 0.3% of GDP in 2009. Exports are estimated to have fallen by 12.2% and imports by 29.5%, while workers' remittances increased by 14.1% in 2009. In contrast, in the Maldives, the current account deficit has become unsustainably high through a fall in tourism inflows and exports. A decrease in the current account deficit is estimated from 51.4% of GDP in 2008 to 25.1% of GDP in 2009 as the global outlook improves.

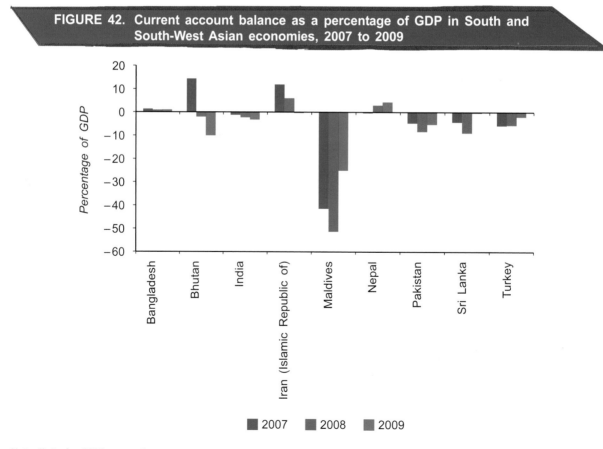

FIGURE 42. Current account balance as a percentage of GDP in South and South-West Asian economies, 2007 to 2009

Note: Data for 2009 are estimates.
Sources: ESCAP, based on national sources and ESCAP estimates.

The Islamic Republic of Iran, being a net exporter of oil, suffered sharp contraction in its exports in 2009 owing to lower oil prices and demand. Imports also fell but at a slower rate as economic activity moderated in the country. As a result, the trade surplus fell in 2009 and the current account registered a small deficit, after a large surplus in the previous year.

In Turkey, imports declined more rapidly than exports. The contraction in imports stemmed partly from decline in energy prices and partly from the slowdown in economic activity. The current account deficit is expected to shrink to 2.1% of GDP in 2009 from just under 6.0% of GDP in 2007 and 2008. The smaller deficit will help to ease external financing pressure as the global credit squeeze has made international financing more difficult and more costly than in the recent past.

With regard to the exchange rate against the United States dollar in 2009, the Indian rupee depreciated in the beginning of the year but in subsequent months appreciated. The Sri Lankan rupee followed a similar course but could not regain lost ground and ended the year slightly lower. The Pakistani rupee consistently depreciated over the year. The Bangladeshi taka showed the greatest stability over the year.

Policy responses

As for all other subregions of Asia and the Pacific, Governments in this subregion used expansionary fiscal and monetary policies to counter the negative fallout of the global slowdown and moderate the decline in growth. On the fiscal side, although budget deficits were already high prior to the global crisis, Governments had little choice but to run up higher deficits as a means of countercyclical stabilization. Moving forward, it is important that governments in the subregion prepare a clear roadmap of fiscal consolidation to be implemented at the earliest. This is important to anchor long run expectations about interest rates and private sector investments.

A clear roadmap of fiscal consolidation needed

Central banks showed much more willingness to implement a range of monetary-easing and liquidity-enhancing measures including reduction in the cash reserve ratio, the statutory liquidity ratio and key policy rates in support of expansionary fiscal policies. Looking ahead, and as inflationary pressures increase, there are signs that monetary policy has started to tighten. The Reserve Bank of India in January 2010 raised the cash reserve ratio by 0.75% to 5.75% and in March 2010 policy interest rates were raised by 25 basis points, pushing the repo rate up to 5%. It was part of a fine balancing act between containing inflationary pressures and supporting the domestic economy as the global recovery process remains weak.

Acceleration in expansionary fiscal policy

The Government of India introduced a large fiscal stimulus package to boost domestic demand and contain the adverse impact of the global economic crisis. Fiscal stimulus was in the form of tax relief to boost demand, and increased expenditure on public projects to create employment and public assets. The Government renewed its efforts to increase infrastructure investments in telecommunications, power generation, airports, ports, roads and railways, besides expansion of the National Rural Employment Guarantee Scheme (box 5) as a part of fiscal stimulus in 2009 budget. The fiscal stimulus also included write-off of agricultural loans, revision of salaries of Government staff (undertaken in 2008 and 2009). Fiscal stimulus spending over 2008 and 2009 is estimated at the equivalent of 7.1% of GDP. As a result, the budget deficit increased from 2.6% GDP in 2007 to 5.9% of GDP in 2008 and is estimated to rise to 6.5% of GDP in 2009 (figure 43). The budget for the fiscal year 2010 attempted to address the challenge of fiscal consolidation in the face of growing public debt by raising revenues and containing unproductive expenditure. As a result, budget deficit is expected to come down to 5.5% of GDP in 2010.

BOX 5. Indian National Rural Employment Guarantee Scheme

In 2005, through the National Rural Employment Act, the Government of India launched a bold, innovative scheme to provide employment to the rural poor: the National Rural Employment Guarantee Scheme. It provides guaranteed employment at minimum wage for 100 days each year to every rural household whose adult members volunteer to do unskilled manual work.[a] At least one third of the beneficiaries must be women.

In any poverty reduction programme the most difficult task is to identify the poor. In this case the programme is self targeting since the non-poor are not usually attracted by hard manual work at minimum wages. People interested in the scheme are issued registration cards and can apply for a minimum of 14 days' continuous work either to the local Government or the programme officer. They will be offered work, if possible within a 5-kilometre radius or, if farther away, are entitled to a transport allowance and some extra living expenses. If applicants are not offered work within 15 days they are paid an unemployment allowance.

The scheme operates on a huge scale. During fiscal year 2008/2009 it provided more than 1 billion person-days of employment for 45 million people.[b] For fiscal year 2009/2010 the Government has allocated 391 billion rupees, being more than $8 billion. Most of the financial resources are provided by central Government, but implementation and management are largely through State and local Governments that identify public works projects. The Government has been providing training to all the functionaries involved. This decentralized participatory management system helps improve delivery and public accountability. It can also be monitored centrally since details on the progress and outcomes of the scheme are available on the Internet, allowing higher-level Government officials, if necessary, to take remedial action.

The scheme has many advantages. Besides providing employment to the rural poor, it also helps address the causes of chronic poverty like drought, deforestation and soil erosion, through public works projects in water conservation and harvesting, afforestation, rural connectivity, and construction and repair of embankments for flood control. It promotes an inclusive form of financial development since, in order to protect poor workers from being cheated, payments are made through bank or post office accounts. Long distance to available banks and post offices in some rural areas can be a serious problem; in such cases mobile counters of banks/post offices can be provided.[c]

Initial evidence suggests that the programme is achieving its objectives in providing income security for the poor, achieving high participation of women and marginalized groups, stemming distress migration, increasing access to markets and services and regenerating national resources. Such a scheme could be replicated in many developing countries.

Notes:
[a] Government of India, *National Rural Employment Guarantee Act,* available from http://india.gov.in/sectors/rural/national_rural.php (accessed 11 Jan. 2010).
[b] Government of India, *The Mahatma Gandhi National Rural Employment Guarantee Act,* "Employment generated during the year 2008-2009", available from http://164.100.12.7/netnrega/writereaddata/citizen_out/DemRegister_0809.html (accessed 11 Jan. 2010).
[c] Mehrotra, Santosh, "NREG two years on: where do we go from here?", *Economic and Political Weekly,* Vol. 43, No. 31, Mumbai, India, 2 Aug. 2008.

Yet another challenge for the economy is to manage portfolio capital inflows, mainly foreign institutional investments that contribute to bubbles in capital markets and put upward pressure on exchange rates. The Bombay Stock Exchange Sensitive Index (SENSEX) appreciated by more than 100% between early in March 2009 and the end of 2009 as foreign institutional investment flows returned to the capital markets. The Indian rupee appreciated by around 6% in 2009.

In Pakistan, fiscal deficit has been rising in recent years, standing at 7.6% of GDP in 2008. In November 2008, the Government of Pakistan signed a $7.6 billion, 23-month Stand-By Arrangement with the IMF to support the country's stabilization programme and help the country remedy balance of payments difficulties. Fiscal performance improved substantially in 2009 due to more stringent fiscal policy. The budget deficit came down to 5.2% of GDP. While performance on the revenue side was not very encouraging,

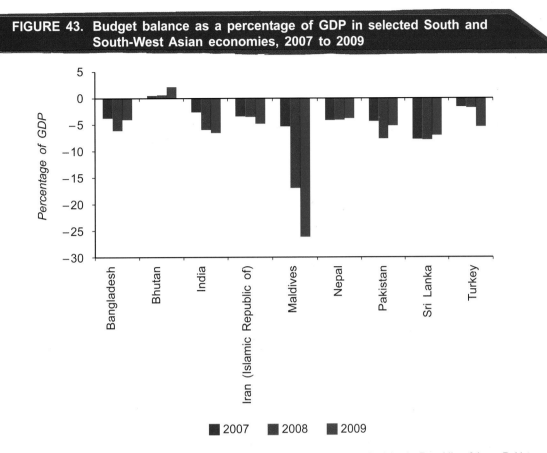

FIGURE 43. Budget balance as a percentage of GDP in selected South and South-West Asian economies, 2007 to 2009

■ 2007   ■ 2008   ■ 2009

Notes: Data for 2009 are estimates. Budget balance excludes grants for Bangladesh, Islamic Republic of Iran, Pakistan and Sri Lanka.
Sources: ESCAP, based on national sources; ADB, *Key Indicators for Asia and the Pacific 2009* (Manila, 2009), available from www.adb.org/Documents/Books/Key_Indicators/2009/default.asp (accessed 9 Nov. 2009); and ESCAP estimates.

the fiscal improvement in 2009 was largely based on reduction in oil subsidies and development spending which is likely to impinge on the medium-term growth rate. The Government needs to improve the tax base and raise the very low tax-to-GDP ratio in order to reduce the fiscal deficit to sustainable levels.[77] The tax burden can be made more equitable by spreading it across different sectors of the economy, particularly services and agriculture.

In Bangladesh, the budget deficit was contained at 4.0% of GDP in 2009, partly due to under-

implementation of its development budget. In Sri Lanka, with the return of peace to the country, the budget deficit is expected to continue to come down; in 2009, to 7% of GDP, from 7.8% of GDP in 2008. The Government signed a 20-month Stand-By Arrangement with IMF of about $2.6 billion to support the country's economic reform programme and rebuild international reserves. To contain its budget deficit, the Government introduced several measures to enhance revenues and rationalize current expenditures. As revenue measures usually take time to yield results, the Government's adjustment pro-

---

[77]   State Bank of Pakistan, *Annual Report 2008-2009* (Vol. I), available from www.sbp.org.pk/reports/annual/arFY09/qtr-index-eng-09.htm.

gramme in 2009 relied more on expenditure restraint, while ensuring protection of vulnerable groups. The highest priority is being given to the reconstruction and development of the previously war-torn areas and resettlement of internally displaced persons. Economic stimulus measures could lead to sustained long-term growth through appropriate economic reforms, including restructuring of public-sector enterprises.[78]

The budget deficit in Maldives has remained high in recent years, rising to 26.1% of GDP in 2009 from 16.9% of GDP in 2008. In December 2009, IMF approved blended financing arrangements amounting to about $92.5 million spread over 3 years. The financing is designed to support the Government's policy programme aimed at addressing the adverse impact of the global economic crisis and restoring macroeconomic stability and fiscal sustainability.

In Nepal, the budget deficit fell to 3.8% of GDP in 2009 from 4.1% in 2008 owing to strong revenue growth and below-target spending. The ratio of revenue mobilization to GDP grew to 14.8% in 2009 in comparison with the ratio of 13.2% in 2008 because of encouraging growth in revenue collection.

Due to large oil revenues, the Government of the Islamic Republic of Iran has been following an expansionary fiscal policy. For sharing the benefits of oil revenues with the people, the fiscal system incorporates huge explicit and implicit subsidies. Energy prices including prices of petroleum products and electricity remain highly subsidized. The agricultural sector and food imports are also subsidized. Government is in the process of reforming and overhauling the subsidy system by gradually phasing it out in favour of a new targeted welfare system. Poor families are to receive cash grants and basic services such as healthcare.

In response to the crisis, the Government in Turkey cut some taxes and boosted certain expenditures, equivalent to 0.8% of GDP in 2008 and 1.6% in 2009. It also relaxed monetary policy to make credit cheaper and more available. As a consequence and with the loss of revenue from economic contraction, the budget deficit widened from 1.8% of GDP in 2008 to 5.4% of GDP in 2009. The financial sector remained relatively stable, having benefited from major restructuring and improved regulation and supervision following the 2001 financial crisis. Consumer price inflation fell in 2009, which enabled the central bank to implement a growth-supporting monetary policy while maintaining price stability. As aggregate demand recovers, however, inflation could rise.

Outlook and policy challenges

As the global outlook improves, the subregion should resume rapid economic growth. It is forecast to grow at 6.1% in 2010 with stronger linkages with other fast-growing Asian and Pacific developing economies supporting its growth. Some countries are already developing new partnerships for trade and investment relations that will combine into an Asian community of trading nations and a node of economic growth.

Growth improves but downside risks persist

Most countries are projecting stronger growth in 2010: for example, 8.3% in India and 6.0% in Sri Lanka and Bangladesh. In India, the structural growth impulses of the economy remain strong, given the high domestic savings rate, sound financial system and a macroeconomic policy environment supportive of growth. With a revival in investment and private consumption, growth in exports and strong expansion in industrial production in recent months, growth in GDP is projected to accelerate in 2010. The improved security situation in Sri Lanka should benefit all major sectors of the economy, particularly tourism and agriculture, while investment is likely to expand strongly in 2010 as companies prepare for a period of accelerated

---

[78]   Institute of Policy Studies of Sri Lanka, *Sri Lanka State of the Economy 2009,* Colombo, 2009.

growth in domestic demand. Renewed foreign investor interest in the tourism sector holds promise.

Higher growth in Pakistan is also projected, on the assumption of improved security situation, relaxation of fiscal policy and some respite from electricity shortages. The anticipated recovery is expected to be supported by the restocking of inventories and a small recovery in exports as the incipient recovery in major economies gather pace. Large-scale manufacturing sector which contracted in 2009 is projected to register positive growth in 2010.

In Bangladesh, as external demand picks up, growth in crisis-hit sectors of manufacturing may follow, while remittances will continue to support the economy and domestic demand.

In Nepal, the Government target of 5.5% GDP growth in 2010 will be supported by strong private consumption and an expansionary fiscal budget, but may be constrained due to delayed monsoon and poor weather conditions. GDP growth in 2010 is expected to be around 3.5%.

For Maldives, a positive GDP growth is forecast in 2010 along with some recovery in the world economy.

With projected increase in oil prices, the economy of Islamic Republic of Iran should also experience higher growth.

For Turkey, moderate growth of 3.0% is projected in 2010, driven by improved domestic demand as the main European export markets are expected to remain weak and no major boost from external demand is expected.

This growth outlook is subject to downside risks linked to uncertainties that the global economy faces. Rising oil prices could also push up inflation and lead to higher budget and current-account deficits. Bad weather could damage

harvests; the subregion will always be prone to floods, earthquakes and other natural disasters. There are also security risks: internal conflicts and terrorist attacks can undermine consumer and investor confidence. Across the subregion, in the face of rising international food and fuel prices and the return of capital flows, Governments may struggle to manage price and exchange rate stability without compromising economic growth.

Accelerating economic growth is crucial to bring down poverty levels

Looking beyond 2010, accelerating economic growth is crucial to bring down poverty levels. The challenge will be how to make growth more inclusive by spreading its benefits to larger segments of the population. More resources should be devoted to provision of basic services such as education, health, sanitation and housing particularly for those belonging to lower income groups. Targeted programmes for the benefit of the poor in the broader framework of social protection should also be a priority.

Finally, the inadequacies of physical infrastructure remain a key constraint holding back the potential of economic growth. Of particular concern is electricity shortage in Pakistan and Nepal, where disruptions in the supply of electricity are compromising growth. Huge investments are needed to enhance capacity of electricity generation. At the same time, renovation of transmission and distribution lines is necessary to minimize electricity losses. Potentials of trade in electricity among countries of the subregion should be explored and subregional cooperation in electricity generation and distribution should be promoted to overcome electricity shortages.[79]

---

[79]   Research and Information System for Developing Countries (RIS), *South Asia Development and Cooperation Report 2008* (Oxford University Press, New Delhi, 2008).

Generally, the year 2010 presents complex issues for policymakers as they seek to manage price and exchange rate stability without compromising growth momentum, in the face of rising international food and fuel prices and return of capital flows.

SOUTH-EAST ASIA

In South-East Asia the global crisis overturned prevailing economic logic. Previously, the large export-driven industrial base had been seen almost entirely as a source of strength. But as the financial crisis cut export demand from major markets, the dependence on trade was revealed also as a source of vulnerability. Export dependence (defined as the ratio of exports to GDP) rose from less than 50% in the mid-1990s to over 70% by 2007. Openness (defined as the ratio of imports and exports to GDP) is also high with ratios for Singapore, Thailand, Malaysia, and Viet Nam reaching 362%, 161%, 130% and 160%, respectively. Those ratios are significantly higher than those for the two largest Asian developing economies: China at 60% and India at 40%.

Moreover, that trade is still highly concentrated. While the subregion has to some extent diversified its export destinations, its biggest markets are still the developed economies. And even when there has been a rise in intraregional trade, it is largely based on interlocking production networks whose output, channelled through China as a production hub, is ultimately destined for the developed countries.

The fall in external demand notwithstanding, the economies in the subregion have enough policy levers to weather the crisis. As the following section will point out, many economies in the region are poised for a faster recovery, than what was initially expected.

Impact of the crisis

In contrast to the 1997 Asian financial crisis, the genesis of the current global economic crisis occurred outside of South-East Asia. The subregion was largely spared the institutional failures that saddled the United States and European financial systems. Clearly, the lessons from the Asian crisis were not lost on policymakers as bank lending practices, regulations and supervision have been tightened over the years. Rather, the shock this time around was transmitted via the trade channel. South-East Asian economic growth thus slowed down significantly from 4% in 2008 to 0.6% in 2009, although there were differences among countries.

Economic contraction

The national economies of Malaysia, Singapore and Thailand all contracted in 2009. The Philippines managed to keep growth positive, but experienced a dramatic deceleration. The economies of Indonesia and Viet Nam, on the other hand, though also undergoing a slowdown, did not contract to the same extent. Two least developed countries, Timor-Leste and Lao People's Democratic Republic, grew the fastest in the subregion (table 17).

The variations are due to many factors, including domestic problems of varying intensity. Nevertheless, overall, some patterns across countries emerge. The worst-affected countries all had shares of exports to GDP that exceeded 60%, with the European Union and United States accounting for relatively large shares of exports. The country most exposed to trade shock is Cambodia, with close to 80% of total exports bound for the United States or Europe. Singapore and Malaysia, with exports accounting for more than 100% of GDP, are quite exposed to trade shock as well (figure 44).

Another factor that played a role was the composition of exports. Countries with a high share of export products based on regional production networking and outsourcing arrangements, such as apparel, machinery, electronics and motor vehicles, were more exposed to perturbations in global trade. The extent of exposure is illustrated in figure 45. The highest concentration for those sectors is in the Philippines at around 70%; the proportions are also high in Singa-

TABLE 17. Rate of economic growth and inflation in South-East Asian economies, 2008 to 2010

(Percentages)

	Real GDP growth			Inflation[a]		
	2008	2009[b]	2010[c]	2008	2009[b]	2010[c]
South-East Asia[d]	**4.0**	**0.6**	**5.1**	**8.6**	**2.1**	**4.1**
Brunei Darussalam	−1.9	−0.5	0.6	2.7	1.2	1.2
Cambodia	6.7	0.0	4.0	25.0	−0.8	5.0
Indonesia	6.1	4.5	5.5	10.1	4.6	5.3
Lao People's Democratic Republic (the)	7.9	5.4	6.0	7.6	0.2	5.0
Malaysia	4.6	−1.7	5.0	5.4	0.6	2.0
Myanmar	2.0	2.0	3.1	26.8	6.6	10.4
Philippines (the)	3.8	0.9	3.5	9.3	3.3	4.7
Singapore	1.1	−2.0	7.0	6.5	0.6	2.3
Thailand	2.5	−2.3	4.0	5.5	−0.8	3.5
Timor-Leste[e]	12.8	7.4	7.5	7.6	1.3	4.0
Viet Nam	6.2	5.3	5.8	23.1	7.0	10.3

Notes: [a] Changes in the consumer price index.
     [b] Estimates.
     [c] Forecasts (as of 15 April 2010).
     [d] Subregional calculations based on GDP figures at market prices in United States dollars in 2007 (at 2000 prices) used as weights to calculate the subregional growth rates.
     [e] Refer to real non-oil GDP growth (excluding locally paid compensation of United Nations peacekeeping mission staff).
Sources: ESCAP calculations based on national sources; IMF, *International Financial Statistics (IFS) Online Service*, available from www.imfstatistics.org/imf/; ADB, *Key Indicators for Asia and the Pacific 2009* (Manila, 2009); CEIC Data Company Ltd., available from http://ceicdata.com/; and ESCAP estimates.

FIGURE 44. Combined share of United States and European Union purchases of merchandise exports of selected South-East Asian economies, 2006 to 2007 and 2008

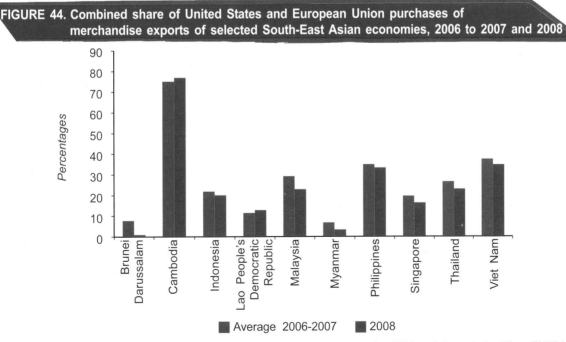

Note: Average 2006-2007 = average of (exports to US + EU15)/total exports for 2006 and (exports to US + EU15)/total exports for 2007. EU15 denotes the 15 original members of the European Union.
Source: IMF, *Direction of Trade Statistics* database, available from www2.imfstatistics.org/DOT/ (accessed 5 Feb. 2010).

pore, Malaysia and Thailand. The main Indonesian exports, on the other hand, are oil and other primary goods. As figure 45 shows, in all those economies the proportion has been declining as a result of a drop in demand for such goods, particularly electronics.

Rebound gathers momentum. Tracking economic performance on a quarterly basis tells the most about the extent of the crisis, its evolution and adjustment processes that Governments put in place. After all, recessionary forces struck South-East Asia only in the middle of 2008. Annual averages thus mask the depth of the crisis. Table 18 indicates a general improvement towards the middle of 2009, with the prospects of a V-shaped recovery gaining ground.

To some extent such rebound appears quick because some economies were starting from a low base. In addition, events in some senses were working in the favour of the subregion. First, perhaps largely unappreciated, was the benefit of a credible and timely early warning. By being able to observe the implosion of the

financial markets in the United States and Europe, in the wake of the subprime crisis in 2007 that triggered the banking crisis and the collapse of Lehman Brothers, a major investment bank in the United States, policymakers could anticipate a massive incoming trade shock. That gave them enough time to counteract the expected deflationary forces with appropriate expansionary macroeconomic policies. Unlike the 1997 Asian financial crisis, this crisis did not take the region by surprise.

Unlike the 1997 Asian financial crisis, this crisis did not take the region by surprise

Second, the subregion had, by and large, sound macroeconomic fundamentals. Until the second quarter of 2008 exports were still increasing and inflation, although high in the first half of

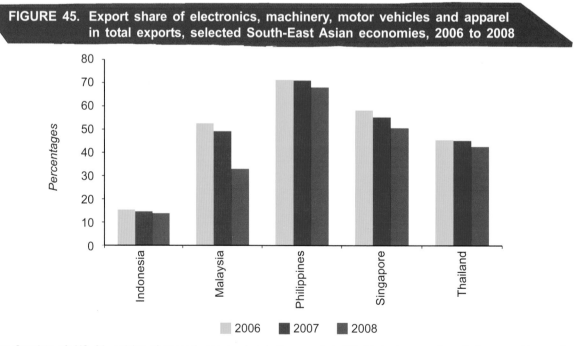

FIGURE 45. Export share of electronics, machinery, motor vehicles and apparel in total exports, selected South-East Asian economies, 2006 to 2008

Notes: Consists of: HS 61, articles of apparel, accessories, knit or crochet; HS 84 nuclear reactors, boilers, machinery, etc; HS 85, electrical, electronic equipment; HS 87, vehicles other than railway, tramway.
Source: UN COMTRADE database, available from http://comtrade.un.org/db/dqQuickQuery.aspx (accessed 5 Feb. 2010).

TABLE 18. Percentage changes of real GDP of major South-East Asian economies, year-on-year, 2007 to 2009

		Indonesia	Malaysia	Philippines	Singapore	Thailand	Viet Nam
2007	Q1	6.1	5.4	6.9	7.7	4.6	7.7
	Q2	6.7	5.6	8.3	9.0	4.5	8.0
	Q3	6.7	6.5	6.8	10.0	5.3	8.7
	Q4	5.8	7.2	6.3	6.2	5.3	9.1
2008	Q1	6.2	7.4	3.9	7.3	6.4	7.5
	Q2	6.3	6.6	4.2	2.8	5.2	5.8
	Q3	6.2	4.8	4.6	0.1	2.9	6.5
	Q4	5.3	0.1	2.9	−4.2	−4.2	5.4
2009	Q1	4.5	−6.2	0.6	−9.4	−7.1	3.1
	Q2	4.1	−3.9	0.8	−3.1	−4.9	4.4
	Q3	4.2	−1.2	0.4	0.6	−2.7	5.2
	Q4	5.4	4.5	1.8	4.0	5.8	7.7

Source: ESCAP calculations based on data from CEIC Data Company Ltd., available from http://ceicdata.com/ (accessed 9 Mar. 2010).

the year, subsequently fell. Again in contrast to the period prior to the Asian financial crisis of 2007, Governments had, in varying degree, maintained prudent public finances. They had kept external debt at manageable levels and built up sufficient reserves to cover contingent capital outflows. Hence, the economies in the subregion could stand up to the scrutiny of international speculators.

Third, as a result of reforms in the aftermath of the Asian crisis, many countries had stable financial systems. Banks were still reasonably profitable and most economies had relatively few non-performing loans. In 2008, non-performing loan ratios were under 6% in Indonesia, Malaysia, the Philippines and Thailand, compared with 1998 figures of 49% for Indonesia and 45% for Thailand. Bank capital adequacy ratios also exceeded the prudent threshold: in 2008; they were in double digits in Indonesia, Malaysia, the Philippines, Singapore and Thailand. So when Governments started to prime the fiscal pumps, the financial infrastructure was in place to support that.

Fourth, Governments that had not been running high deficits had the resources to support their responses. They could adopt vigorous countercyclical policies. Since inflation was mod-

erate they also had room for expansionary monetary policies.

When the crisis came, the stage was set for Governments to design, prepare and execute the necessary policies. As they did so, and the crisis unfolded, the economic outlook in the subregion changed.

Performances vary widely

Indonesia has weathered the global slump better than its South-East Asian neighbours. With a population of 226 million, Indonesia has a large domestic market base. Exports account for only 27% of GDP, compared with 185% of GDP in Singapore at the other extreme. Also, the share of electronics, machineries and other manufactured exports, whose demand collapsed as the crisis unfolded in 2008, is rather small, while only one fifth of its exports go to the United States and European market. Furthermore the share in its exports of the combined markets of India and China, two of the fastest-growing economies in the region, in its exports is increasing.

The subregion is home to two small oil-producing States: Brunei Darussalam and Timor-Leste. Because 70% of its GDP comes from oil, the economy of Brunei Darussalam proved to be less exposed to the crisis via the non-oil trade and investment channels. Nevertheless, export income fell with the global oil price late in 2008. Investment income from overseas assets is also likely to have declined. As a result the GDP contracted in 2008.

When Governments started to prime the fiscal pumps, the financial infrastructure was in place to support that

---

Similarly, most of the Timorese GDP is related to oil: its oil GDP is five times greater than its non-oil GDP, so much will depend on the oil price outlook for 2010. In 2008, the non-oil GDP grew by 13%, partly because it started from a low base.

The Philippines, despite a trade profile that is heavily vulnerable to shocks, has just barely been able to withstand the global downturn, partly as a result of services exports, such as business process outsourcing, and more importantly the large flows of foreign exchange through remittances, which in 2008 were $16.4 billion or 13% of GDP. Remittances grew by 5% in 2009, contrary to expectations. They account for around 10% of GDP and have reached a record level of $17 billion. Among the mitigating factors is the wide geographical dispersion of overseas Filipino workers, and the mix of skills and positions held in overseas jobs market, many of which are in health care, a crisis-neutral sector.

The large stimulus package introduced in Singapore, which includes a sizeable construction component, should contribute to future growth. Trade is also likely to resume faster than initially anticipated, given the recovery in the electronics trade, and estimates of growth have therefore been revised sharply upwards.

In Viet Nam, growth has exhibited a sharp V-shape. In 2008, it grew at a brisk 6.2%, with inflation hitting 23%; combined with a current account deficit running at 11.9% of GDP, fears of overheating were raised. In January of 2009, as a result of the crisis, exports fell by more than 20%. The Government responded with an aggressive fiscal and monetary policy, and growth in 2009 reached 5.3% year-on-year. The State Bank of Viet Nam devalued the dong by around 5% in late November 2009, and a further 3% in February 2010, given the strains in the balance of payment deficits.

Growth in 2009 in Lao People's Democratic Republic proved brisk. This is partly as a result of higher metal prices, especially gold, which has attracted investment from China, Thailand and Viet Nam. The economy also received a boost as a result of pay increases for public servants as well as increased public investment on infrastructure for the 2009 South-East Asian Games. Lao People's Democratic Republic should also expect a rise in exports to China, but the prospects for other major markets are less sanguine: demand from Thailand, for example, may fall, especially since some of this is for goods re-exported to third countries.

At the onset of the global crisis, Malaysia suffered a deep contraction in its export-oriented manufacturing sector combined with a significant outflow in portfolio capital. Confidence was undermined and weakened investment spending leading to a negative growth rate in 2009. To counteract the fall in external demand, the authorities mounted two fiscal stimulus packages, while monetary authorities supported pump-priming activities by easing the cash reserve requirement and lowering policy interest rates. As a result, consumption increased and stabilized a decelerating economy towards the second half of 2009.

Thai exports have a large share of crisis-sensitive manufactures like electronics and machineries. Its service sector depends significantly on tourism which is very income elastic and was hit hard by the global recession and continuing political tensions. In the first half of 2009, the Thai GDP fell by 6%, the largest drop in the subregion. To boost the anaemic demand, the Government delivered two stimulus packages supported by expansionary monetary policy. However, they were insufficient to offset the severe contraction in the first half of 2009, as GDP fell by 2.3% for the whole of 2009 although a turnaround in the fourth quarter of 2009 was observed.

Cambodia is the only least-developed country in the region whose economy is not expected to experience any economic growth in 2009. Trade accounts for around half of GDP and is heavily oriented to crisis-affected developed countries. In the first half of 2008, exports of garments dropped by as much as 25% and tourism receipts also fell. The authorities responded with fiscal loosening. The country could be faced with a fiscal deficit along with an upsurge in inflation. On the other hand, Cambodia tends to export garments to niche markets so if demand in these revives quicker than anticipated there could be a rapid turnaround in growth.

The GDP growth of Myanmar weakened in 2008 owing to feeble external demand and to the destruction caused by cyclone Nargis. The agricultural sector still felt the lingering effects of the cyclone in 2009, dampening domestic demand. The largest export item is natural gas whose price has fallen and, given the drop in both internal and external demand, growth in 2009 was likely to be flat. Myanmar was also affected by the downturn in its biggest export market, Thailand, although that was partially offset by the robust growth of its second biggest market, India.

Policy responses

With sufficient warning, the Governments of the subregion were able to proceed with timely and aggressive fiscal policies to boost domestic spending. The packages varied considerably – in terms of size, elements, targeted sectors and criteria – depending on national priorities, fiscal space and institutional structures of decision-making and disbursement. Indonesia, for example, utilized income tax cuts in its fiscal package. Singapore offered some support for consumption, but opted for spending more on investment and on training as well as offering guarantees on loans for working capital. Viet Nam also offered support for credit but did so through a temporary interest rate subsidy of around 4% on certain bank loans.

Some patterns can be discerned across countries. First, the more aggressive responses came from the countries hardest hit by the

trade shock. Thailand introduced a package worth 17% of GDP. Malaysia offered one worth 9% of GDP. Both cases involved two tranches. The Singaporean package was also large: 8% of GDP. Indonesia and the Philippines, on the other hand, being less affected, had programmes worth less than 5% of GDP.

The more aggressive responses came from the countries hardest hit by the trade shock

---

Second, a number of Governments based their stimulus package on pragmatic considerations such as speed of disbursement. They often frontloaded budget items in the first half of the fiscal year while also producing supplemental budgets in order to disburse funds quickly. The Philippines, for instance, prioritized such easily implemented projects as road repairs, irrigation facilities and hospitals, while also planning more complex infrastructure programmes that would require longer lead times. Thailand, similarly, first embarked on a short-term stimulus package to support consumption spending with transfer payments and cash handouts, particularly to the poor and senior citizens, before unveiling a second package which involved major public investment.

Third, nearly every stimulus package involved some expenditure on infrastructure. Malaysia, for example, under its first, $2-billion package, combined small-scale infrastructure projects, such as upgrading roads, hospitals and schools with investment in strategic industries including broadband. The "Stronger Thailand for 2012" package, which spans 2010 to 2012, aims to bolster competitiveness and encourage private investment by investing in mass transit, energy, water resources, healthcare and housing. In the Lao People's Democratic Republic, the Government spent on infrastructure in preparation of the South-East Asian Games, which helped stoke demand. Viet Nam and Indonesia also announced programmes that combined spending on infrastructure with programmes for poverty reduction. Directing the fiscal stimulus packages at infrastructure has a number of advantages – not only stimulating demand for many supplying industries, but also generating employment. And since some economies are constrained by poor infrastructure this should in the longer term enhance competitiveness.

Fourth, unlike the United States, the countries in this subregion did not need to bail out many specific companies or financial institutions. The financial systems in South-East Asia have been relatively sound, and no systemically significant corporations needed rescuing.

More than half of the fiscal stimulus packages were implemented in the first half of 2009, but a number of economies embarked on a second round shortly thereafter. For example, Malaysia announced a package worth around 9% of GDP over two years. It includes increasing guarantee funds, tax incentives and other forms of assist-

ance to the private sector. The second Thai package is spread over three years. The increased spending, coupled with lower tax revenues, will put pressure on fiscal balances. The projected 2009 budget positions across the subregion are shown in figure 46.

Across the subregion, most central banks, unencumbered by concerns about inflation, have pursued expansionary policies. For example, the Bank of Viet Nam, which had already made five policy rate cuts in the second half of 2008, cut the base rate again by 150 basis points in 2009 which, on a year-to-date basis, represented a cut of 700 basis points, from 14% in October 2008 to a low of 7%. Other countries in the subregion also cut their rates, though more slowly.

In some economies, despite the fall in central bank policy rates, there are concerns that bank lending rates may be "sticky" downwards. With inflation low, real interest rates thus become

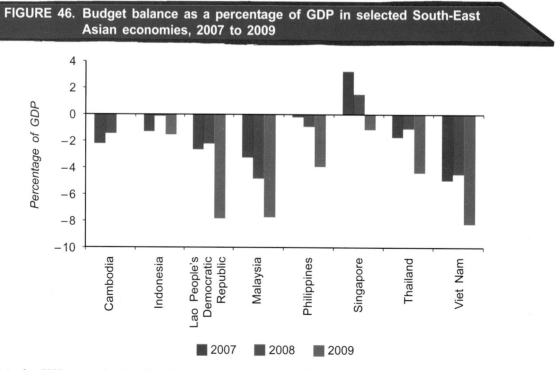

FIGURE 46. Budget balance as a percentage of GDP in selected South-East Asian economies, 2007 to 2009

■ 2007 ■ 2008 ■ 2009

Notes: Data for 2009 are estimates. Budget balance excludes grants for Cambodia, Indonesia, Malaysia, Singapore and Thailand.
Sources: ESCAP, based on national sources; ADB, *Key Indicators for Asia and the Pacific 2009* (Manila, 2009), available from www.adb.org/Documents/Books/Key_Indicators/2009/default.asp (accessed 9 Nov. 2009); and CEIC Data Company Ltd., available from http://ceicdata.com/ (accessed 25 Feb. 2010).

high. A further concern is that creating credit too rapidly will stoke inflation and create asset bubbles. In response, and in a departure from the overall monetary trend of the subregion, the State Bank of Viet Nam in late November 2009 increased its policy base rate from 7% to 8% and devalued the reference rate for its currency to the United States dollar by 5%. Viet Nam, as of January 2010, has an inflation rate of over 7%, which is high relative to the past six months. With the possible exception of Viet Nam, the inflation outlook for most of the subregion appears benign. A few economies such as Thailand and Cambodia, for instance, had a deflationary environment for most of 2009. Early in 2010, however, inflation started to pick up in Malaysia, Thailand and Viet Nam. Timor-Leste, on the other hand, has a firm inflation anchor due to its "dollarization".

Early in March 2010, the Malaysian monetary authorities raised interest rates by 25 basis points, from 2.00% to 2.25%, marking Malaysia

as one of the first economies to reign in an expansive monetary policy in 2010. The tightening was regarded as fairly mild, however, and not expected to threaten economic recovery.

External sector

For the economies of the subregion, the drop in exports could have put a strain on the current account balance had it not been accompanied by a sharp fall in imports. The decline in imports was due partly to a reduction in domestic consumption and investment but also reflected a drop in the demand for intermediate inputs for exported items – especially in parts and components for electronic goods that tend to respond more rapidly to perturbations in demand. As a consequence, current accounts generally remained positive and in some cases actually improved (figure 47). The exceptions were Cambodia and Viet Nam which are expected to have negative balances.

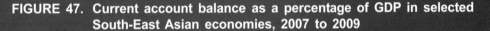

FIGURE 47. **Current account balance as a percentage of GDP in selected South-East Asian economies, 2007 to 2009**

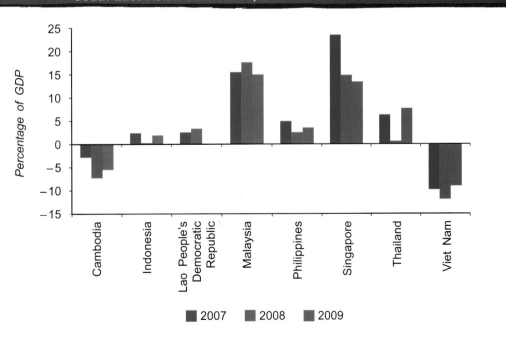

Note: Data for 2009 are estimates.
Sources: ESCAP calculations based on national sources; IMF, *International Financial Statistics* (CD-ROM) (Washington, D.C.: Oct. 2009); and ESCAP estimates.

A substantial proportion of imports comes from within the subregion – during the first three quarters of 2009, intraregional imports actually increased at the expense of those from the United States and Japan (tables 19 and 20). China, likewise, has become a more important source.

Periods of economic contraction often provoke protectionism. In South-East Asia some Governments have become involved in trade remedy cases and other forms of contingency protection, but generally they have shown restraint and did not systematically increase tariffs. On the contrary, they have locked in further liberalization commitments by negotiating preferential trade agreements – seven agreements involving South-East Asian economies came into force in 2008 and 2009.

A V-shaped pattern has followed in capital flows. In the latter part of 2008 there was some capital flight, mostly flows of portfolio investment. However, as Governments took measures to stabilize their economies, international investors became more confident in regional equity markets and the capital promptly returned.

Towards the second half of 2009, trade and capital flows combined to put upward pressure on exchange rates. Economies had performed better than expected, which bolstered investor confidence in the financial and equity markets – and in turn created additional expectations of currency appreciation (figure 48). Indeed, comparing average exchange rates between December 2009 and December 2008, the Indonesian rupiah appreciated against the dollar by close to 16%, while the Malaysian ringgit,

TABLE 19. Import growth by ASEAN economies, by source, 2008 and 2009, in percentages

	2008	2008 Q1-3	2009 Q1-3
ASEAN	22.7	35.1	−20.4
China	18.2	27.7	−17.7
EU	13.1	20.9	−22.5
Japan	14.3	21.7	−23.6
US	16.0	22.4	−28.9
Others	37.8	53.7	−30.1
World	24.1	35.4	−24.7

Source: IMF, *Direction of Trade Statistics* database, available from www2.imfstatistics.org/DOT/ (accessed 5 Feb. 2010).

TABLE 20. Percentage shares of imports by ASEAN economies, by source, 2004 to 2008, in percentages

	2004	2007	2008	2008 Q1-3	2009 Q1-3
ASEAN	23.9	24.7	24.4	24.8	26.2
China	9.5	12.5	11.9	11.8	12.9
EU	11.2	10.8	9.8	9.8	10.1
Japan	15.1	11.7	10.8	10.5	10.7
US	11.2	9.6	9.0	8.8	8.3
Others	29.1	30.6	34.0	34.3	31.8
World	100.0	100.0	100.0	100.0	100.0

Source: IMF, *Direction of Trade Statistics* database, available from www2.imfstatistics.org/DOT/ (accessed 5 Feb. 2010).

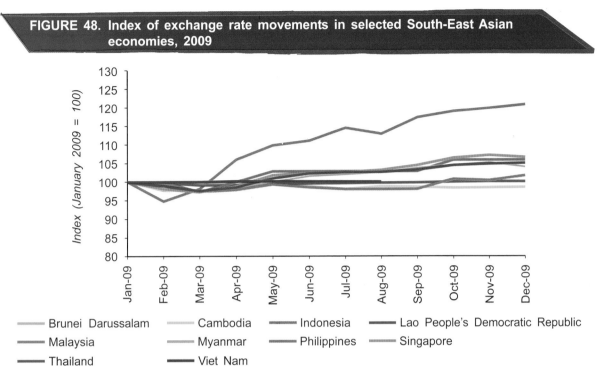

FIGURE 48. Index of exchange rate movements in selected South-East Asian economies, 2009

Legend:
— Brunei Darussalam   — Cambodia   — Indonesia   — Lao People's Democratic Republic
— Malaysia   — Myanmar   — Philippines   ⋯ Singapore
— Thailand   — Viet Nam

Note: A positive trend represents appreciation and vice versa.
Sources: ESCAP calculations based on data from CEIC Data Company Ltd., available from http://ceicdata.com/ (accessed 25 Feb. 2010); and IMF, *International Financial Statistics (IFS) Online Service,* available from www.imfstatistics.org/imf/ (accessed 9 Mar. 2010 for Brunei Darussalam, Cambodia, Lao People's Democratic Republic, Myanmar and Viet Nam).

Singaporean dollar and Thailand baht appreciated by around 5%.

Exports could become less competitive as a result, especially when the Chinese yuan has effectively been depreciating in tandem with the falling United States dollar. In these circumstances Governments could either let their currencies continue to rise, or allow international reserves to accumulate. Most have chosen the latter course and added to a growing pool of foreign reserves (table 21). An exception is the State Bank of Viet Nam which, in November 2009, in response to the strains on the balance of payments, devalued the dong by around 5%. In February 2010, the Vietnamese dong was further devalued by 3% in an effort to reduce a widening trade deficit and stabilize the foreign exchange market. The move puts additional competitive strain on the exports of other ASEAN economies and could increase pressures for competitive devaluation. However, the impact of the two rounds of devaluation of the

Vietnamese dong on the competitiveness of other ASEAN exporters is not likely be very significant because headline inflation (a cost factor) in Viet Nam as of January 2010 at 7.62% is higher than the other economies in the subregion. In addition, most economies in the subregion have positive current account balances, which ameliorates pressures on currency devaluation. For those reasons, the devaluation of the dong is not expected to spark a round of massive competitive devaluation in the subregion.

Prospects

Despite facing the full force of the global financial crisis, the economies of South-East Asia were thus fairly resilient and policymakers were generally able to respond effectively. Nevertheless, the subregion remains structurally dependent on trade with the developed countries. The IMF, for example, projects a 5.8% growth in the volume of world trade in goods and services for

TABLE 21. Foreign exchange reserves minus gold, selected South-East Asian economies, 2009, in billions of United States dollars

	Indonesia	Malaysia	Philippines	Singapore	Thailand
Dec-07	55.0	101.0	30.2	163.0	85.2
Dec-08	49.6	91.1	33.2	174.2	108.7
Jan-09	48.8	90.9	34.7	167.1	108.2
Mar-09	52.7	87.4	34.5	166.3	113.7
Jun-09	55.4	91.2	34.8	173.2	118.3
Sep-09	60.0	94.8	37.5	182.0	129.1
Dec-09	63.1[a]	95.4	38.5[a]	188.9[a]	135.5

Note: [a] Data refer to November 2009.

Source: ESCAP, based on data from IMF, *International Financial Statistics (IFS) Online Service*, available from www.imfstatistics.org/imf/ (accessed 17 Feb. 2010).

2010.[80] Moreover, global capital is again flowing to the subregion and equity markets are exceptionally buoyant. Malaysia and Thailand should also see benefits from succeeding tranches of their stimulus packages. The subregion is thus forecast to grow by 5.1% in 2010.

South-East Asia should therefore see a rebound towards the end of 2009. During 2010 some countries that depend heavily on trade should see positive growth: Malaysia, 5.0%; Singapore, 7.0%; and Thailand, 4.0%. Growth should be even stronger in Indonesia, at 5.5%, and Viet Nam, at 5.8%. With large domestic markets, those commodity-rich countries were able to weather the 2009 recessional forces and should lead the recovery in 2010.

Cambodia is expected to resume economic growth by 4.0% on the back of an improving market for its main exports, while the Lao People's Democratic Republic should continue to grow quite rapidly, by 6%. The Philippines expects a boost in consumption demand during 2010 from election spending and continued remittance flows. Timorese non-oil GDP, on the other hand, is expected to expand by 7.5% in 2010. Brunei is expected to grow by 0.6%.

As spending from the stimulus programmes winds down, economic prospects will rely on resurgence of the private sector. Nevertheless, infrastructure projects can be expected to continue beyond 2010, with their largest impact in developing countries where they will not only provide employment but help address infrastructure weaknesses that impede growth.

South-East Asian economies will want to look elsewhere for fresh sources of economic growth

The increase in spending is inevitably putting a strain on public finances, so policymakers will want to induce more private spending on consumption and investment. They could use the opportunity to review the investment climate and introduce further reforms, particularly those linked to improving governance. With the recovery still tentative, careful judgement about the pace and timing of the exit strategy will be required.

Since traditional markets in the developed countries have softened, South-East Asian economies will want to look elsewhere for fresh sources of economic growth – especially to

---

[80] IMF, *World Economic Outlook Update: A Policy-driven Multispeed Recovery* (Washington, D.C.: 26 January 2010); available from www.imf.org/external/pubs/ft/weo/2010/update/01/index.htm (accessed 16 Mar. 2010).

exploit the potential for trade with the wider Asian and Pacific region. They need not decouple from traditional markets but rather accelerate regional integration and pursue more aggressive trade and investment liberalization policies. Within their economies, they will also want to make growth more inclusive. That will lead to more equitable development as well as develop stronger markets for high-value-added products.

BOX 6. The changing direction of ASEAN trade

Exports of the member countries of the Association of South East Asian Nations (ASEAN) contracted severely in the first three quarters of 2009. Intra-ASEAN trade was hit particularly hard, declining by 26.4%. ASEAN exports to China also fell, by 17%. Chinese import demand for ASEAN products fell by less than that of the rest of the world. (table 22). Will the crisis encourage a shift in the direction of trade? Table 23 shows that the shares of intra-ASEAN trade and ASEAN trade to China have risen at the expense of the traditional markets. The ASEAN-China Free Trade Agreement, which entered into effect on January 1, 2010, is expected to intensify trading relations further. The trade share analysis does not differentiate between effects of exchange rate movements and those of cost competitiveness. Although the trade situation is very fluid and the profile could easily change, the analysis highlights the emerging Chinese role as a trade partner in the subregion.

TABLE 22. ASEAN export growth, 2008 and 2009, in percentages

	2008	2008 Q1-3	2009 Q1-3
ASEAN	16.0	28.7	−26.4
China	12.2	24.9	−17.1
EU	6.9	12.7	−27.3
Japan	20.5	25.9	−31.8
US	-1.9	1.8	−23.0
Others	21.8	32.3	−20.5
World	14.5	23.7	−24.0

Source: IMF, *Direction of Trade Statistics* database, available from www2.imfstatistics.org/DOT/ (accessed 5 Feb. 2010).

TABLE 23. Percentage shares of ASEAN exporters in destination markets, in selected years

	2004	2007	2008	2008Q1-3	2009Q1-3
ASEAN	24.9	25.2	25.6	25.9	25.1
China	7.3	9.2	9.0	9.2	10.1
EU	13.8	12.6	11.7	11.7	11.2
Japan	11.8	10.3	10.8	10.5	9.4
US	15.0	12.4	10.6	10.4	10.6
Others	27.3	30.3	32.2	32.2	33.7
World	100.0	100.0	100.0	100.0	100.0

Source: IMF, *Direction of Trade Statistics* database, available from www2.imfstatistics.org/DOT/ (accessed 5 Feb. 2010).

"The challenge ahead of us is, how to replace these crisis response policies with structural policies that will correct global imbalances and promote sustainable, inclusive growth not just in the recovery phase, but beyond"

**Susilo Bambang Yudhoyono
President of Indonesia**

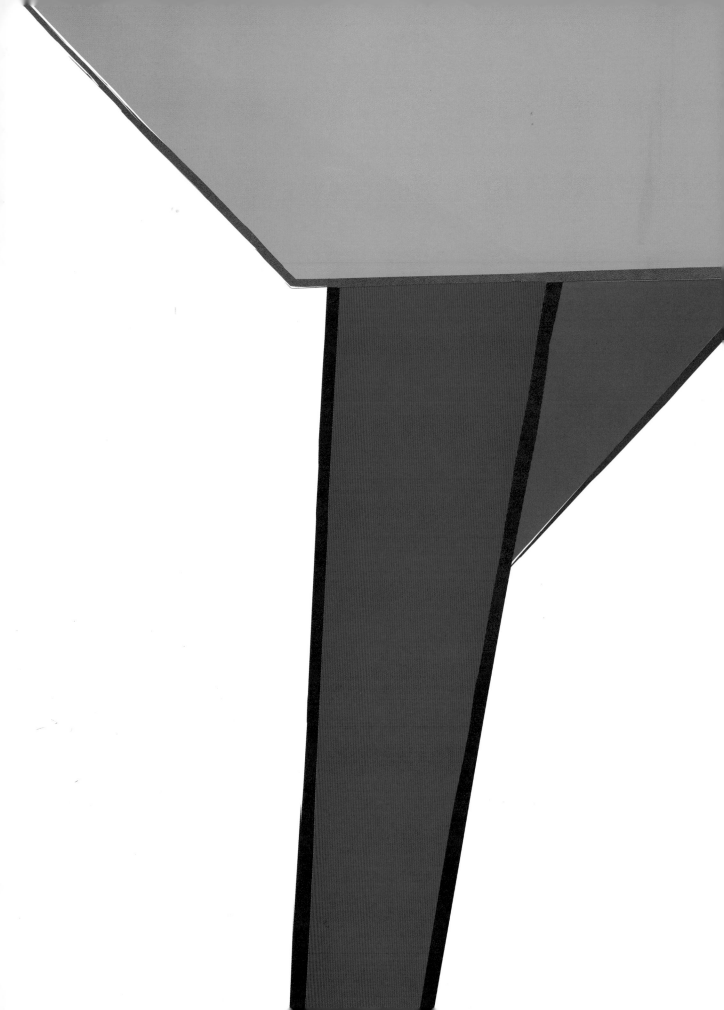

MULTIPLE IMBALANCES AND DEVELOPMENT GAPS AS NEW ENGINES OF GROWTH 3

The analysis in previous chapters has shown how national Governments have responded with timely, unprecedented fiscal stimulus packages and expansionary monetary policy that have helped in reviving growth in most Asian and Pacific economies. However, those packages must be seen essentially as short-term responses to an external shock. They cannot continue forever to sustain the growth momentum because of constraints of fiscal space and their potential to stoke inflationary tendencies. Consensus is growing on the need for a new growth paradigm. As argued by the APEC leaders at their November 2009 Summit in Singapore, the advanced economies are unlikely to go back to "growth as usual" and "trade as usual" scenarios.[81] As seen in chapter 1, even with a recovery, the import demand in the advanced countries is unlikely to revive to pre-crisis levels because of the compulsions to restrain debt-fuelled consumption and reduce levels of public debt in order to unwind global imbalances. Asian and Pacific countries need to find new sources of demand to sustain their dynamism beyond the stimulus packages to make up for the considerable loss of demand in the advanced countries. They will need to "rebalance" their economies in favour of greater domestic and regional consumption. In the search for new impulses for growth, this chapter investigates the different imbalances and development gaps, for the effort to close them could help in generating additional aggregate demand.

Asia and the Pacific, home to 4.1 billion people who comprise more than 60% of the world's population, has distinguished itself as the fastest-growing region in the world, especially since 1990. In particular, the region's developing economies[82] grew at an average annual rate of 5.3% between 1970 and 2008, which largely exceeds the growth rates of other developing and developed regions (figure 49). As a result of its dynamism, the region has made remarkable progress on a number of fronts, including poverty reduction and technological advances that will see people living longer, healthier and more interconnected lives than ever before.

---

[81] See the 2009 Leaders' Declaration of the 17th APEC Economic Leaders' Meeting, "Sustaining growth, connecting the region", Singapore, 14-15 November 2009. Available from www.apec.org/apec/leaders__declarations/2009.html (accessed 14 Apr. 2010).

[82] The developing economies of Asia and the Pacific are all the economies in the region with the exceptions of Australia, Japan and New Zealand.

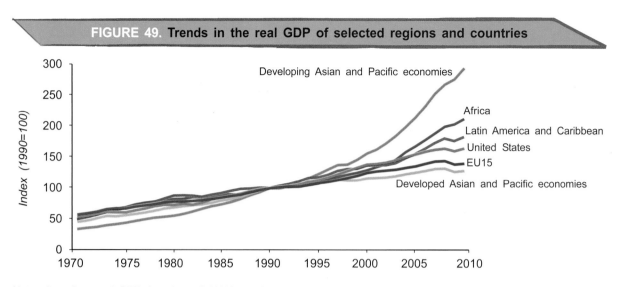

FIGURE 49. Trends in the real GDP of selected regions and countries

Notes: Based on real GDP (at prices of 1990) in US dollars; 2009 estimates; 2010 forecasts (as of 27 Jan. 2010); GDP of North and Central Asian countries (included in ESCAP developing countries) before 1990 estimated according to their shares in the former USSR's GDP in 1990.

Sources: ESCAP based on data from United Nations Statistics Division, *National Accounts Main Aggregates Database;* IMF, *World Economic Outlook,* January 2010 update; and ESCAP estimates.

The region's achievements have been punctuated by two major global crises that brought steadily worsening insecurity: the food and fuel price crisis of 2008 and the global financial crisis of 2008 and 2009. The crises have exposed global and regional structural imbalances that threaten the sustainability of the region's economic growth and dynamism. The threats to economic growth posed by persistent increases in fuel and food prices were examined in the previous edition of this *Survey*.[83] This chapter extends the analysis by focusing on three major imbalances that have characterized the process of economic growth in Asia and the Pacific:

- Macroeconomic imbalances
- Social imbalances and development gaps
- Ecological imbalances.

The macroeconomic imbalances are global in nature, being reflected in the large trade and current account surpluses of Asian and Pacific countries vis-à-vis the United States and other

Western developed countries. The imbalances were not entirely detrimental to the region. Firstly, the United States and other Western countries increased their importance as motors for the region's economic growth by providing expanding markets for Asian and Pacific exports. Secondly, the region's large current account surpluses resulted in a sizeable accumulation of foreign exchange reserves, which reached $4.9 trillion as of June 2009. Those reserves protected the region from the risk of collapsing exchange rates – as during the Asian financial crisis of 1997 – that could have made the region substantially more vulnerable to contagion from the current global financial crisis.

The perpetuation and deepening of the global macroeconomic imbalances into the medium term is very unlikely, however. With the external debt of the United States more than doubling, from $6.7 trillion as of September 2003 to $13.7 trillion as of September 2009,[84] and its budget deficit reaching close to 10% of GDP in 2009, a

[83] ESCAP, *Economic and Social Survey 2009.*
[84] United States Department of the Treasury, U.S. Gross External Debt Statistics, www.treas.gov/tic/external-debt.shtml (accessed 20 Feb. 2010).

macroeconomic adjustment of its economy is expected.[85] As a result, import demand from the United States is not expected to play the buoyant role it did in the past decade. Asia and the Pacific will need to reduce its trade and current-account surpluses and ignite new motors of growth to compensate for the anticipated reduction in dynamism of its traditional export markets.

Despite the region's accelerating growth, social imbalances are pervasive, with close to 1 billion people living under $1.25 per day poverty line. The large number of poor reflects standards of

living that are still relatively low in the region. As figure 50 shows, the PPP-adjusted real GDP per capita[86] of Asian and Pacific developing countries (excluding North and Central Asia) was approximately $5,000 in 2008 or about half the world average. The figure also shows that those countries made remarkable progress after the 1970s, when their real per capita GDP was only $1,000 or half that of Africa. Although the number of poor dropped very significantly – by around 600 million between 1990 and the mid-2000s – most of the drop was concentrated in a few countries, while the number of poor increased in others.

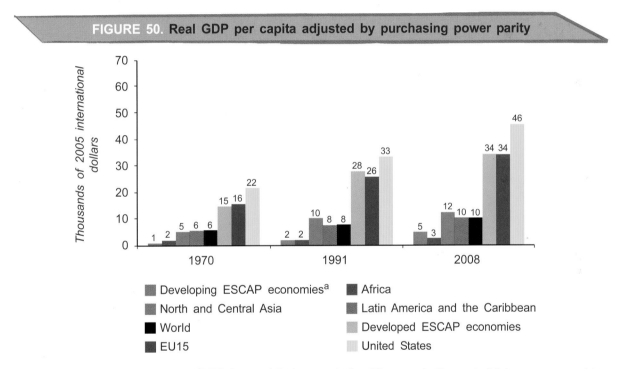

FIGURE 50. Real GDP per capita adjusted by purchasing power parity

Legend:
- Developing ESCAP economies[a]
- North and Central Asia
- World
- EU15
- Africa
- Latin America and the Caribbean
- Developed ESCAP economies
- United States

Notes: (a) Purchasing power parity (PPP) is a tool that accounts for differences in the cost of living across countries. It is the amount of a certain basket of basic goods which can be bought in a given country with the money it produces. The best-known and most-used PPP exchange rate is the Geary-Khamis dollar (the "international dollar").

(b) Based on real GDP at 1990 prices expressed in international dollars of 2005; GDP of North and Central Asian countries in 1970 estimated according to their shares in GDP of the former USSR in 1990.

[a] Excluding North and Central Asia.

Sources: ESCAP based on data from United Nations Statistics Division, *National Accounts Main Aggregates Database;* United Nations Population Division, *World Population Prospects;* and World Bank, *World Development Indicators Database,* 15 September 2009 update.

---

[85] The United States Congressional Budget Office projects deficits to decrease in coming years, from 9.2% of the GDP in 2010 to 6.5% in 2011, 4.1% in 2011, and 3.2% in 2012. See Congressional Budget Office, Budget Projections, www.cbo.gov/budget/budproj.shtml (accessed 20 Feb. 2010).

[86] See notes to figure 50 for an explanation of purchasing power parity (PPP).

Reducing poverty and making the fruits of economic prosperity available for the population at large is not only a moral imperative but is the ultimate purpose of economic development. In the case of the Asia-Pacific region, the sheer number of poor represents a potential market larger than the European Union and the United States combined. If social and infrastructural investments in the region contribute to providing employment and business opportunities for the poor, their additional demand has the potential for not only preserving the dynamism of the region's growth but also providing a growth engine for the global economy.

Import demand from the United States is not expected to play the buoyant role it did in the past decade

The ecological imbalances are reflected in the degradation of key natural resources such as forests and freshwater, in unsustainable uses of energy and in fast growth of carbon emissions. Although the impacts of those imbalances are not immediately apparent, they pose formidable challenges to the sustainability of economic growth into the long run. Forests, for instance, offer a natural protection from landslides, floods and soil depletion which lead to desertification and lower agricultural yields. Agricultural yields are also suffering as a result of the increased frequency of droughts and other extreme weather events associated with climate change. Thus, as the demand for food grows in tandem with the population, measures need to be taken to protect the natural capital. Investing in R&D and rural infrastructure is also necessary in order to increase agricultural yields.

Besides its critical role in supporting the long-run sustainability of economic growth of the region, addressing the ecological imbalances could also provide an additional motor for growth and help alleviate poverty. For instance, promoting investments in renewable energy and in technologies to improve energy efficiency could create opportunities for innovations, businesses and employment in promising "new economy" industries. The preservation of natural resources could lead to the generation of "green jobs". Moreover, because the poor are more likely to live in ecologically vulnerable areas and depend on the availability of natural resources to make a living, addressing the ecological imbalances of growth in Asia and the Pacific would make a substantial contribution to the objective of reducing poverty.

Asia-Pacific's poor constitute a potential market larger than the European Union and the United States. If social and infrastructural investments in the region create employment and business opportunities for them, their demand for goods and services can not only preserve the region's dynamism but also provide a growth engine to the world

In sum, sustaining economic growth in the Asia-Pacific region beyond the current recovery calls for addressing fundamental macroeconomic, social and ecological imbalances. As anticipated above and explained in greater detail in the rest of the chapter, there are important synergies across policies that address each of the imbalances. The best option for the region would be an integrated approach that takes into account the impacts of policy measures on the three imbalances and gives the highest priority to those policies that simultaneously address more than one imbalance.

MACROECONOMIC IMBALANCES

Prior to the global financial crisis that began in 2008, the world economy was characterized by record large trade and current account imbalances among major trading partners. The United States current account deficit increased moderately from 1991 to 1997, reaching 1.7% of the GDP in 1997; after that year it soared to

4.3% of GDP in 2000 and 6% of the GDP in 2005. In contrast, five Asian and Pacific economies (China, Japan, Malaysia, the Russian Federation and Singapore) have experienced soaring current account surpluses, especially since 2001 (figure 51). As a percentage of their joint GDP, their current account surpluses increased from 2.7% in 2001 to 5.7% in 2005 and 7.7% in 2007. Both phenomena are related, as the United States is an important destination for Asian and Pacific exports. Furthermore, in the absence of a well-developed regional financial architecture, Asian and Pacific countries have been investing the bulk of their foreign exchange reserves in the United States Treasury bills, thereby assisting the United States to continue increasing its current account deficits.

The growing global imbalances have helped the Asia-Pacific region especially the East and South-East Asian countries. An increasingly buoyant United States market opened further possibilities for exporters and contributed to the recovery of the economies hardest hit by the Asian financial crisis of 1997. Figure 52 shows that net exports of goods and services increased substantially their share in long-term real GDP growth in East and South-East Asia after that year.[87] In the case of East Asia, the share of net exports in GDP growth reached a peak of 25% for the 15-year period between 1993 and 2008. As East Asia grew at an annual average rate of 7.7% during that period, as much as 2 full percentage points of annual growth were accounted for by the increase in net exports of goods and services.

Net exports also supported growth in South-East Asia after the Asian financial crisis had caused the GDP in the subregion to drop 8.6%

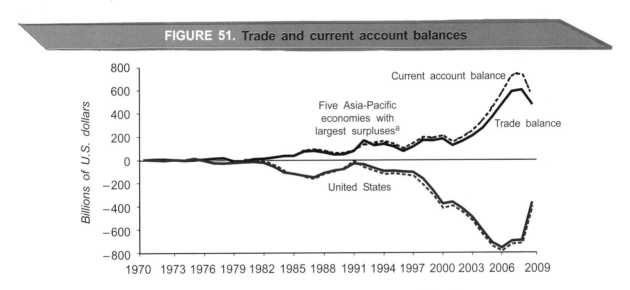

FIGURE 51. Trade and current account balances

Notes: Data for Russian Federation since 1990; current account data since 1980; 2009 estimate.
    [a] China, Russian Federation, Japan, Singapore and Malaysia.
Sources: ESCAP based on data from United Nations Statistics Division, *National Accounts Main Aggregates Database,* U.S. Census Bureau, *Foreign Trade Statistics, Historical Series,* and Economist Intelligence Unit, *Country Database* (accessed 5 Feb. 2010).

---

[87]   From the macroeconomics identity *GDP = C + G + I + NE,* where C is private consumption, G is public consumption, I is gross fixed capital formation, and NE is net exports, we can write
    $\Delta GDP/GDP \equiv (\Delta C/C)^*(C/GDP) + (\Delta G/G)^*(G/GDP) + (\Delta I/I)^*(I/GDP) + (\Delta NE/NE)^*(NE/GDP)$. We define the share of net exports in long-term GDP growth as $100[(\Delta NE/NE)^*(NE/GDP)]/(\Delta GDP/GDP)$, where $\Delta x \equiv x_t - x_{t-15}$ is the change in the value of variable x between year $t - 15$ and year t.

in 1998 from the previous year. During that dramatic adjustment process, imports contracted by 13%, resulting in a jump of net exports to 8.2% of the GDP, compared to -1.3% the year before. As a result, the share of net exports in long-term GDP growth jumped from 1% in 1997 to 18% in 1998, staying roughly at that level until 2009.

Not all the subregions of Asia and the Pacific experienced boosts in growth through increases in net exports. In the case of South Asia, also shown in figure 52, the share of net exports in GDP growth was negative throughout the period considered in that figure. Between 1998 and 2002, it increased from -8% to -1%, but after that year it decreased substantially as a result of a deterioration of the trade balance. Therefore, the macroeconomic imbalances have not only been growing at the global level but also between subregions of Asia and the Pacific.

The figure also shows that the share of net exports in long-term annual real GDP growth in the United States – a major market for Asian and Pacific exporters – dropped from -4% in 1997 to a low of -19% in 2005 and 2006. Since

the onset of the subprime mortgage crisis in 2007, the negative share started to shrink and is estimated to have reached -9% in 2009.

For the heavily export-oriented economies of Asia and the Pacific, the downside risk of relying so heavily on net exports – their vulnerability to adverse shocks affecting export markets – became evident with the onset of the global financial crisis of 2008. As shown in figure 51, the adjustment of the United States current account deficit was well underway by 2009 – as was the adjustment of the current account surpluses of the leading Asian and Pacific surplus economies. As a result of the adjustment process, net exports started to decrease its share in long-term economic growth in East Asia (figure 52).

Besides boosting growth, another important consequence of the growing trade surpluses of the Asia-Pacific region has been the accumulation of substantial amounts of foreign exchange reserves. By July 2008, shortly before the onset of the global financial crisis, the region held a total of $4.8 trillion, 43% higher than only 18 months earlier. When the crisis hit, many countries used part of their reserves to stabilize their

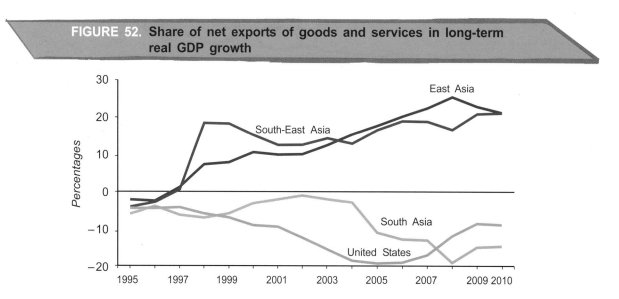

FIGURE 52. Share of net exports of goods and services in long-term real GDP growth

Notes: 2009 estimates; 2010 forecasts; East Asia: China; Hong Kong, China; Republic of Korea; and Taiwan Province of China. South-East Asia: Cambodia, Indonesia, Malaysia, Philippines, Singapore, Thailand, and Viet Nam. South Asia: Bangladesh, India, Pakistan, and Sri Lanka.
Sources: ESCAP based on data from United Nations Statistics Division, *National Accounts Main Aggregates Database* and Economist Intelligence Unit, *Country Data* (accessed 5 Feb. 2010).

exchange rates. Between July 2008 and February 2009 countries in the region, including India, Malaysia, the Republic of Korea, the Russian Federation and Sri Lanka, lost 19% or more of their reserves for that reason. However, in February 2009 the financial crisis started to ease and reserves increased again in Asia and the Pacific, reaching $4.9 trillion by June 2009.

Overall, the huge accumulation of foreign exchange reserves has allowed Asian and Pacific countries to weather the global financial storm without suffering major disruptions to their exchange rates, in contrast with the experience of the Asian financial crisis of 1997. That experience and the procyclical conditionalities of IMF emergency loans at that time are often extolled as a major motivation for countries in the region to accumulate reserves and self-insure against future crises. While self-insurance has paid off, it is clearly not the best solution. Alternatives for protecting exchange-rate stability in the region are discussed below.

Sources of imbalances

Trade imbalances reflect underlying changes in the levels of production and aggregate demand. From the macroeconomic identity $GDP \equiv C+G+I+NE$, and the definition of gross domestic saving, $S \equiv GDP - (C + G)$, it follows that $NE \equiv S - I$. Thus trade surpluses can be driven by increases in savings (or increases in consumption), decreases in investment or a combination of the two. Figures 53 and 54 show the shares in long-term economic growth of gross fixed investment and total consumption to assess the relative importance of those factors in explaining the growing trade surpluses of selected subregions.[88] Data for the United States are included for comparison.

As shown in figure 53, a decrease in investment played a major role in South-East Asia. The share of gross fixed investment in long-term GDP growth dropped from 41% in 1995 to 17% in 1998, revealing that the adjustment

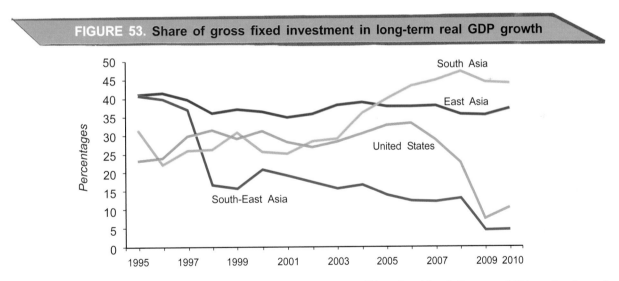

FIGURE 53. Share of gross fixed investment in long-term real GDP growth

Notes: 2009 estimates; 2010 forecasts; East Asia: China; Hong Kong, China; Republic of Korea; and Taiwan Province of China. South-East Asia: Cambodia, Indonesia, Malaysia, Philippines, Singapore, Thailand, and Viet Nam. South Asia: Bangladesh, India, Pakistan, and Sri Lanka.
Sources: ESCAP based on data from United Nations Statistics Division, *National Accounts Main Aggregates Database* and Economist Intelligence Unit, *Country Data* (accessed 5 Feb. 2010).

---

[88] These shares are defined, respectively, as $100[(\Delta I/I)^*(I/GDP)]/(\Delta GDP/GDP)$ and $100[(\Delta(C+G)/(C+G))^*((C+G)/GDP)]/(\Delta GDP/GDP)$, where $\Delta x \equiv x_t - x_{t-15}$ is the change in the value of variable x between year $t - 15$ and year t.

process during the Asian financial crisis fell overwhelmingly on investment.[89] Similar evidence for Malaysia, Thailand and Singapore after 1997 reported by the Asian Development Bank can be interpreted as a correction of overinvestment before the crisis.[90] A similar correction is currently underway in the United States, where the share of investment in GDP growth increased from 23% in 1995 to 31% in 1997 and a peak of 33% in 2005 and 2006, before dropping sharply to 9% in 2009. Figure 53 also shows the share of investment in long-term GDP growth to have been large and stable in East Asia, at around 38%, and fast-increasing in South Asia, where it rose from 29% in 2003 to 47% in 2008.

Figure 54 shows that the share of consumption in long-term GDP growth in the United States increased from 74% in 1998 to 86% in 2007. In East Asia, by contrast, it decreased steadily from 61% in 1996 to 46% in 2008. In South Asia it also decreased, from 71% in 1998 to 60% in

2006, increasing slightly thereafter. In South-East Asia the share of consumption in long-term GDP growth increased from 60% in 1996 to 68% in 2004 and has remained relatively stable since then. In East Asia higher gross domestic saving is estimated to have accounted for 58% of the increase in the share of net exports in GDP growth between 1996 and 2007.

In summary, the analysis suggests that the large trade deficits of the United States were driven both by increases in investment and decreases in saving, and that the brunt of the adjustment of the surpluses during the crisis so far has fallen on investment. In South-East Asia a large drop in investment after the Asian crisis of 1997 played a key role in the growth of trade surpluses. The opposite is true for East Asia. Although that subregion did experience a small drop in the share of investment in GDP growth in the immediate aftermath of the 1997 Asian financial crisis, that share stabilized afterwards, in contrast with the steady decline in the share

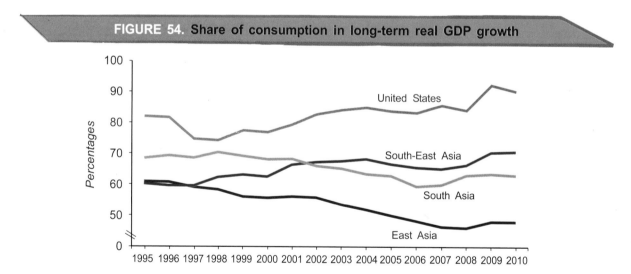

FIGURE 54. Share of consumption in long-term real GDP growth

Notes: 2009 estimates; 2010 forecasts; East Asia: China; Hong Kong, China; Republic of Korea; and Taiwan Province of China. South-East Asia: Cambodia, Indonesia, Malaysia, Philippines, Singapore, Thailand, and Viet Nam. South Asia: Bangladesh, India, Pakistan, and Sri Lanka.
Sources: ESCAP based on data from United Nations Statistics Division, *National Accounts Main Aggregates Database* and Economist Intelligence Unit, *Country Data* (accessed 5 Feb. 2010).

---

[89] Gross investment dropped from an average of 36% of the GDP between 1994 and 1997 to 23% between 1998 and 2001, and remained at about 22% afterwards.
[90] ADB, *Asian Development Outlook 2009: Rebalancing Asia's Growth* (Manila: 2009).

of consumption. Thus, the "savings glut" explanation for the increasing trade surpluses seems to apply only for East Asia.

The "savings glut" explanation for the increasing trade surpluses seems to apply only for East Asia

---

The analysis above is based on shares of aggregate demand components in GDP growth, which are not accurate measures of contributions to GDP growth. However, box 7 assesses its sensitivity to alternative computation methods and finds that its conclusions remain the same: Exports increased their contribution to GDP growth significantly between two periods, 1982 to 1997 and 1992 to 2007, especially in East and South-East Asia. The contribution of domestic demand

components to GDP growth dropped across subregions, although with some differences. East Asia was characterized mostly by a decreased contribution of consumption (or increase in saving), while South-East Asia by a decrease in the contribution of investment. Box 7 also shows that the contribution of consumption to GDP growth decreased considerably in South Asia, while the contribution of investment increased.

Perhaps the most unsettling aspect of the global imbalances discussed in this section is the anomaly of capital flowing from Asian and Pacific developing countries to finance consumption and investment in rich countries such as the United States. Such a flow is the opposite of what conventional economic theory would dictate on the grounds of the higher rates of return to capital in developing countries.[91] The absence of a well-developed regional financial architecture has impeded the productive deployment of those resources within the region, or in subregions

---

BOX 7. Sensitivity of the results to alternative methods to compute the contribution of aggregate demand components to GDP growth

Shares of aggregate demand components, such as gross domestic investment, in GDP growth are not accurate measures of contributions to GDP growth because they do not take into account the imports needed to satisfy such demand. Shares of aggregate demand in GDP growth are also difficult to compare across countries, for smaller and more open economies tend to satisfy a larger share of their consumption, investment and exports through imports.

An alternative to using shares in GDP growth, the "traditional" method is to subtract from each demand component the imports required for its production. Technical details of the "import-adjusted" method are provided in annex I. The implementation of the import-adjusted method requires estimates of the import intensity of each component of consumption, investment and exports. For lack of empirical data on import intensities for developing countries, two alternative assumptions are used for the intensities: that (a) they are equal across expenditure components; and (b) they are similar to empirical data for the European Union. As explained in annex I, that assumption that each of those components has identical import intensities leads to underestimates of the contribution of consumption to GDP growth and overestimates of the contribution of exports to GDP growth. Using European Union import intensities is not entirely satisfactory either, but the main purpose of the exercise is to compare the robustness of the results across various estimation methods.

(Continued on next page)

---

[91]   During the period, the region received net private capital inflows in the form of foreign direct investment and portfolio investment. Those funds were, however, transferred out of the region as central banks chose to invest their foreign exchange reserves outside the region, rather than inside it.

BOX 7. *(continued)*

Table 24 compares estimates of the contributions to GDP growth of consumption, investment and exports using the traditional method and two variants of the import-adjusted method. The traditional method computes net exports, X – M, rather than exports X alone; in this case, table 24 includes a computation of the share of exports in GDP growth for comparison with the import-adjusted method. Notice that the shares of consumption, investment and exports to GDP growth in the traditional method cannot be compared across countries or regions because they add up to more than 100%, but they nevertheless can be compared across time for the same region. The latter is also true for the import-adjusted method, allowing us to check to what extent changes over time in contributions to growth of different expenditure components are similar within regions even when different computation methods are used.

Regardless of differences in the estimates according to the method employed, the results are consistent. In the three subregions included in the table, the contribution of exports to GDP growth increased quite significantly between the period 1982 to 1997 and 1992 to 2007. The increase was highest in East Asia, where exports increased its contribution to GDP growth between 18 and 20% points (using the two variants of the import-adjusted method). The contribution of exports to GDP growth increased between 13 and 17% points in South-East Asia, and between 7 and 10% points in South Asia. The contribution of consumption to GDP growth decreased some 16 to 20% points in South Asia and 14 to 15% points in East Asia, while it increased 2 to 5% points in South-East Asia. Finally, the contribution of gross fixed investment to GDP growth increased 7 to 10% points in South Asia, but it decreased between 4 and 5% points in East Asia and 17% points in South-East Asia.

Overall, the import-adjusted method seems to provide more accurate estimates of the contribution of expenditure components to GDP growth. Therefore, furthering cooperation across national statistical offices to improve the collection of data on import intensities in Asia and the Pacific is a worthwhile undertaking that could help improve the accuracy of estimates of the contribution of demand components to GDP growth in the region.

TABLE 24. **Contributions of consumption, investment and exports to GDP growth**

		Traditional method		Import-adjusted method (equal import intensities)		Import-adjusted method (EU import intensities)	
		1982-1997	1992-2007	1982-1997	1992-2007	1982-1997	1992-2007
East Asia	C	59	44	42	27	49	35
	I	40	35	29	24	28	24
	X	50	80	29	49	23	41
South-East Asia	C	61	68	36	38	46	51
	I	38	13	22	5	22	5
	X	78	129	41	58	31	44
South Asia	C	78	65	64	44	67	51
	I	29	49	24	35	23	32
	X	15	29	12	22	10	17

Notes: East Asia: China; Hong Kong, China; Republic of Korea; and Taiwan Province of China. South-East Asia: Cambodia, Indonesia, Malaysia, Philippines, Singapore, Thailand, and Viet Nam. South Asia: Bangladesh, India, Pakistan, and Sri Lanka.
Sources: ESCAP based on data from United Nations Statistics Division, *National Accounts Main Aggregates Database;* and Kranendonk and Verbruggen (2008).

running growing current account deficits. In fact, the Asian-Pacific accumulated foreign exchange reserves represent roughly one third of the regional GDP. If productively deployed, they could boost regional development and contribute toward eliminating poverty and hunger.

SOCIO-ECONOMIC IMBALANCES AND DEVELOPMENT GAPS

Poverty reduction: remarkable but uneven

As a consequence of the fast economic growth and increase in standards of living, developing countries in Asia and the Pacific made significant progress in reducing poverty. Fifteen countries representing 93% of the population had their headcount poverty rates[92] reduced from 52.1% around 1990 to 25.2% in the mid-2000s (table 25). Cuts in poverty rates were sharpest in China, Indonesia, Viet Nam and Thailand, and in only one of the countries shown in the table, Turkey, did the poverty rate increase over the period.

The total number of poor in the 15 countries shown in table 25 was also reduced significantly to 596 million, from 1,493 million circa 1990 and 897 in the mid-2000s. Almost all of the

TABLE 25. Poverty reduction between 1990 and the mid-2000s

Country	Period	Headcount poverty rates (per cent)		Number of Poor (millions)			Percentage of total poverty reduction
		Initial	Final	Initial	Final	Poverty reduction	
Bangladesh	1992-2005	66.8	49.6	80.4	76.0	4.4	0.7
Cambodia	1994-2004	48.6	40.2	5.4	5.5	−0.1	0.0
China (rural)	1990-2005	74.1	26.1	614.2	204.2	409.9	68.8
China (urban)	1990-2005	23.4	1.7	73.2	9.1	64.1	10.8
India (rural)	1988-2005	55.6	43.8	344.5	353.3	−8.9	−1.5
India (urban)	1988-2005	47.5	36.2	98.1	117.3	−19.2	−3.2
Indonesia (rural)	1987-2005	70.5	24.0	85.7	27.3	58.3	9.8
Indonesia (urban)	1987-2005	62.0	18.7	29.0	19.7	9.3	1.6
Iran (Islamic Republic of)	1990-2005	3.9	1.5	2.2	1.0	1.2	0.2
Kazakhstan	1996-2003	5.0	3.1	0.8	0.5	0.3	0.1
Lao People's Democratic Republic	1992-2002	55.7	44.0	2.5	2.5	0.0	0.0
Pakistan	1991-2005	64.7	22.6	76.7	37.5	39.2	6.6
Philippines	1988-2006	30.5	22.6	18.1	19.7	−1.6	−0.3
Russian Federation	1993-2005	2.8	0.2	4.2	0.2	4.0	0.7
Sri Lanka	1985-2002	20.0	14.0	3.2	2.7	0.6	0.1
Thailand	1988-2004	17.2	0.4	9.5	0.3	9.2	1.5
Turkey	1987-2005	1.3	2.7	0.7	1.9	−1.2	−0.2
Viet Nam	1993-2006	63.7	21.5	44.7	18.2	26.5	4.4
Median		48.0	22.0				
Weighted average		52.1	25.2				
Total (15 countries)				1 492.9	896.9	596.0	100.0

Notes: Population weights used to compute weighted averages; the 15 countries included in the table represent 93% of the population of Asian and Pacific developing economies; poor defined as individuals consuming less than $1.25 (adjusted by PPP) per day.
Sources: ESCAP based on data from World Bank, *PovcalNet Database;* and United Nations Population Division, *World Population Prospects.*

---

[92]   The headcount poverty rate is defined as the percentage of a country's population living in households with consumption or income per person below the $1.25 dollar per day poverty line (expressed in international dollars of 2005). See notes to figure 50.

reduction took place in just a few countries, of which China represented 79.5% and Indonesia 11.4%. In other countries, such as Cambodia, India, the Lao People's Democratic Republic and the Philippines, the cuts in poverty rates were insufficient to reduce the total number of poor; India had 28 million more poor in 2005 than in 1988.

Figure 55 shows paths of poverty rates and GDPs per capita in selected countries. All those paths are downward-sloping, showing that the poverty rate decreases as the GDP per capita increases. However, the rate of poverty reduction per unit of increase in the per capita GDP varies across countries. In some cases, such as Bangladesh, Viet Nam, and Indonesia, the slope has been rather steep, but in others, such as the Philippines and Sri Lanka, the slope has been flatter. Notice that Indonesia is the only country in the chart in which the per capita GDP declined and poverty increased between

two survey years. This occurred between 1997 and 2000, which encompasses a dramatic 13% decline in this country's GDP in 1998 as a result of the Asian financial crisis. In any event, the figure suggests that economic growth is an important factor in reducing poverty, but not the only factor.[93]

Poverty-inequality-household consumption nexus

Rising inequality can adversely affect the speed of poverty reduction with growth. Table 26 shows that the Gini coefficient increased between 1990 and the mid-2000s in 9 of 15 countries examined; the increase was higher in urban than in rural areas. In addition, the poverty rates considered in table 25 are defined on the basis of monthly per-capita household consumption data obtained from household surveys, whose evolution over time differs from that of

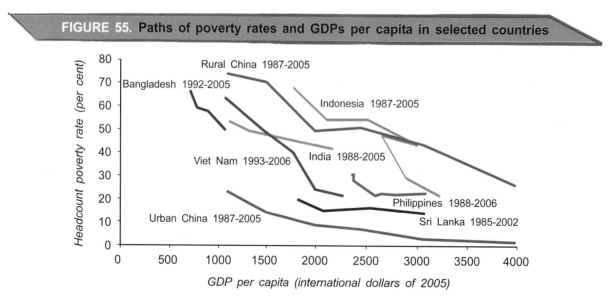

FIGURE 55. Paths of poverty rates and GDPs per capita in selected countries

Note: Poverty rates for India and Indonesia computed as weighted averages of rural and urban poverty rates using urbanization rates as weights.
Sources: ESCAP based on data from World Bank, *PovcalNet Database;* United Nations Statistics Division, *National Accounts Main Aggregates Database;* United Nations Population Division, *World Population Prospects;* and World Bank, *World Development Indicators Database,* 15 September 2009 update.

---

[93] As is clear from figure 55, decrease in poverty is faster at low levels of GDP per capita. That is to be expected given the usual shape of income distribution functions. See Suryanarayana, M. H., "Pro-poor growth: Illusions of marriage and divorce?", Working Paper No. WP-2008-006, Indira Gandhi Institute of Development Research (Mumbai: 2008).

each country's per-capita GDP.[94] Table 26 shows that in all but three countries the rate of GDP growth exceeded the rate of growth of per-capita household consumption during the period considered. The three exceptions were the Philippines, where both grew at the same rate, urban Indonesia and Pakistan, where average household consumption grew faster than per capita GDP. On the other hand, the rate of growth of household consumption was zero or

TABLE 26. Inequality and household consumption growth between 1990 and the mid-2000s

Country	Gini Coefficient (per cent)		Average Annual Growth Rate (per cent)		Counterfactual additional poverty reduction (in millions)	
	Initial	Final	Household consumption per capita	GDP per capita	No change in inequality	Household consumption grew at an additional 1% per year[a]
Bangladesh	26.2	31.0	2.2	3.2	6.5	9.5
Cambodia	38.3	41.9	1.9	5.2	0.4	0.7
China (rural)	30.6	35.9	5.1	9.1	36.3	54.5
China (urban)	25.6	34.8	7.0		9.1[b]	9.1[b]
India (rural)	30.1	30.5	0.9	4.0	2.3	66.3
India (urban)	35.6	37.6	1.2		5.8	26.6
Indonesia (rural)	27.7	29.5	3.3	3.4	1.8	0.0
Indonesia (urban)	32.8	39.9	4.6		6.6	0.0
Iran (Islamic Republic of)	43.6	38.3	−0.2	2.9	−3.3	1.0[b]
Kazakhstan	35.3	33.9	−0.3	6.9	−0.2	0.5[b]
Lao People's Democratic Republic	30.4	32.6	1.7	3.9	0.1	0.3
Pakistan	33.2	31.2	3.9	1.7	−3.0	0.0
Philippines	40.6	44.0	1.6	1.6	2.6	0.0
Russian Federation	48.3	37.5	0.0	2.0	−13.6	0.2[b]
Sri Lanka	32.5	41.1	1.9	3.2	1.4	1.6
Thailand	43.8	42.5	3.7	4.4	−0.8	0.0
Turkey	43.6	43.2	0.5	2.2	−0.2	1.9[b]
Viet Nam	35.7	37.8	5.7	6.0	1.6	0.0
Median	34.3	37.6	1.9	3.2		
Weighted average	32.2	34.8	3.3	6.0		
Total (15 countries)					53.4	172.0

Notes: Population weights used to compute weighted averages; the periods considered for each country are the same as those of table 25; see footnote 98 in the text for details on the computation of the counterfactuals shown in the last two columns of the table.

[a] Applied only to countries where the annual average rate of GDP growth exceeded the rate of growth of household consumption by 1% or more.

[b] Enough poverty reduction to drive the poverty rate to zero.

Sources: ESCAP based on data from World Bank, *PovcalNet Database;* United Nations Statistics Division, *National Accounts Main Aggregates Database;* and United Nations Population Division, *World Population Prospects.*

---

94   See the World Bank PovcalNet database for details on the data; available from http://iresearch.worldbank.org/ PovcalNet/povcalSvy.html.

negative in three countries: the Islamic Republic of Iran, Kazakhstan and the Russian Federation.

Differences between rates of growth of the per capita GDP based on national accounts, and rates of growth of household consumption based on household surveys have been observed in a wide cross-section of countries and can be explained in several ways.[95] They are of great significance because household consumption is a more informative measure of economic well-being than GDP. According to the recent report of the Commission on the Measurement of Economic Performance and Social Progress, "While it is informative to track the performance of economies as whole, trends in citizens' material living standards are better followed through measures of household income and consumption. Indeed, the available national accounts data shows that in a number of OECD countries real household income has grown quite differently from real GDP, and typically at a lower rate".[96]

The divergence between per capita GDP and per-capita household consumption is further illustrated in figure 56, which shows weighted averages of the two variables for the 15 countries in tables 25 and 26. The figure shows that per capita GDP doubled between 1990 and the mid-2000s, while per-capita household consumption increased by only 50%. To be sure, those weighted averages are influenced by the weight of the two largest countries in the region, China and India. However, an alternative calculation shows that the median per-capita household consumption for the 15 countries increased 20 percentage points less than the median GDP (58% against 78%), which is still a significant difference. The discrepancy in the evolution of both variables was recently noted by the ADB, which considers it a major reason for the growing current account surpluses of the developing Asian and Pacific economies over the last 10 years.[97]

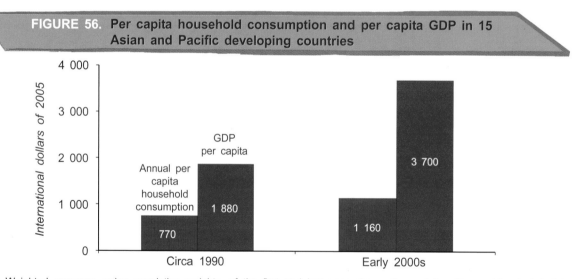

FIGURE 56. Per capita household consumption and per capita GDP in 15 Asian and Pacific developing countries

Note: Weighted averages, using population weights, of the first and last year observations of the 15 countries included in tables 25 and 26; average annual household consumption in China, India and Indonesia computed as weighted averages of rural and urban average annual household consumption using urbanization rates as weights.
Sources: ESCAP based on data from World Bank, *PovcalNet Database;* United Nations Statistics Division, *National Accounts Main Aggregates Database;* United Nations Population Division, *World Population Prospects;* and World Bank, *World Development Indicators Database,* 15 September 2009 update.

---

[95]   Ravallion, Martin, "Measuring aggregate welfare in developing countries: How well do national accounts and surveys agree?", *The Review of Economics and Statistics,* vol. 85, No. 3.

[96]   Stiglitz, Joseph E., Amartya Sen and Jean-Paul Fitoussi, *Report by the Commission on the Measurement of Economic Performance and Social Progress;* available from www.stiglitz-sen-fitoussi.fr/documents/rapport_anglais.pdf.

[97]   ADB, *Asian Development Outlook 2009: Rebalancing Asia's Growth.*

To assess the relative importance of rising in-equality and slow growth in per-capita house-hold consumption on the speed of poverty re-duction, the additional reduction in the number of poor under two "counterfactual" scenarios was estimated: (a) no change in inequality and (b) an additional 1% growth in per-capita house-hold consumption in districts where the differ-ence between the rate of growth of per capita GDP and per-capita household consumption has been 1% or more.[98] The results are shown in the last two columns of table 26. If the Gini coefficient had not changed from its values of around 1990, poverty would have been reduced by an additional 53.5 million people, 9% more than the poverty reduction of 611 million that actually took place. Notice that under that coun-terfactual scenario, China's urban poverty rate would have been driven to zero by 2005, com-pared to its actual value of 1.7%.

Although the total number of poor dropped by almost 600 million between 1990 and the mid-2000s, almost all of this drop was accounted for by a few countries

---

The additional reduction in poverty is more than three times larger under the second counterfac-tual scenario of an extra 1% increase in per-capita household consumption. In that case, poverty in the Asia and the Pacific would have dropped by an additional 172 million, 93 million of which would be attributable to India alone. Under this alternative scenario, the poverty rates of urban China, the Islamic Republic of Iran, Kazakhstan, the Russian Federation and Turkey would have been driven to zero by the mid-2000s.

All in all, headcount poverty rates were reduced remarkably in the developing economies of Asia

and the Pacific, consistently with the region's high rates of GDP growth. However, the reduc-tion in the number of poor was uneven, with few countries especially China accounting for bulk of it. The two main factors that slowed down the rate of poverty reduction have been rising inequality and a significantly slower rate of growth of per-capita household consumption compared to that of per capita GDP. The latter factor is related to the declining share of con-sumption in GDP growth identified in the section on macroeconomic imbalances.

Poverty and multiple deprivations

The above analysis employs headcount poverty rates because they provide a simple summary measure of the extent of poverty in a given country at a particular point in time. The state of poverty is characterized by multiple depriva-tions, however, that are not adequately captured in a simple summary measure. In order to complement the analysis, the rest of this section explores the relationship between poverty rates and selected characteristics of poverty in the areas of employment security, nutrition, educa-tion and access to sanitary infrastructure, meas-ured by selected indicators taken from the Mil-lennium Development Goals database.

Figure 57 shows a positive relationship between headcount poverty rates and the share in total level of employment of own-account and con-tributing family workers, a common measure of informal employment. Work in the informal sec-tor is not subject to labour safety and regula-tions on hours of work, dismissal rules, mater-nity benefits, minimum wages, employers' liabil-ity in case of employment-related injury caused to workers, and employers' contributions to so-cial insurance schemes such as pension plans or unemployment insurance. Informal workers are highly vulnerable to various sorts of economy-wide and idiosyncratic risks. In the figure, the countries with the highest headcount poverty rates (Bangladesh, Cambodia, the Lao

---

[98] For the computation of these counterfactuals we estimated the following regression based on data for the districts included in tables 25 and 26: $H_{it} = 213.6 - 49.02*\log(C_{it}) + 0.88* G_{it}$, N = 83, R^2 = 0.88.
$$(-5.76) \qquad (3.09)$$

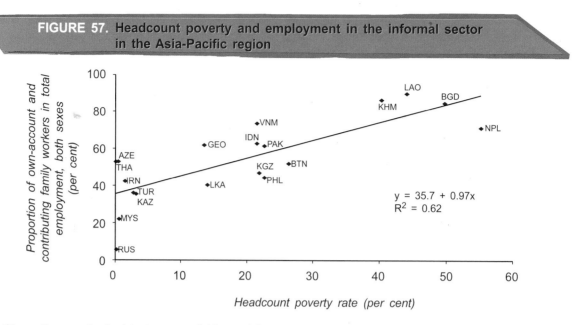

FIGURE 57. Headcount poverty and employment in the informal sector in the Asia-Pacific region

$$y = 35.7 + 0.97x$$
$$R^2 = 0.62$$

Note: Observations are for the latest years available as of September 2009.
Sources: ESCAP based on data from World Bank, *PovcalNet Database* and United Nations Statistics Division, *Millennium Development Goals Database.*

People's Democratic Republic and Nepal) have between 72% and 90% of their workers employed in the informal sector. In countries with intermediate poverty rates, such as Sri Lanka and Viet Nam, the participation of workers in the informal sector ranges between 43% and 74%. Finally, in countries with low poverty rates, participation in the informal sector ranges more widely, from 6% in the Russian Federation to 53% in Azerbaijan and Thailand.

Figure 58 shows that there is a positive relationship between headcount poverty rates and the share of underweight children, a key indicator of child malnutrition. As expected, countries with high headcount poverty rates have also high rates of underweight children, ranging from 36% in Cambodia to 49% in Timor-Leste. The main exception in this group is Uzbekistan, which despite its high poverty rate (46%) has only 5% of its children underweight. Other transition economies such as Armenia, Georgia, Kyrgyzstan, Kazakhstan and the Russian Federation are also characterized by low rates of underweight children. Notice that in contrast with the participation of workers in the informal sector, countries with low poverty rates are also

characterized by consistently low rates of underweight children.

Figure 59 shows a negative relationship between headcount poverty rates and the primary education survival rate, defined as the percentage of a cohort of students who enter the first grade of primary school that complete the last grade of primary school, regardless of repetition. Successful completion of primary school is of critical importance for the acquisition of basic literary and numerical skills. The figure shows that in the case of the high-poverty countries, this indicator ranges between 55% for Cambodia and 66% for India. Uzbekistan, as well as other countries formerly part of the Union of Soviet Socialist Republics, is again the exception to the rule. Similar conclusions are obtained from figure 60, which shows a negative relationship between poverty rates and access to improved sanitation.

In sum, while the headcount poverty rate does not capture the multiple deprivations of poverty, it is nevertheless associated with indicators of some of those deprivations. Countries with high poverty rates tend to have high rates of under-

FIGURE 58. Headcount poverty and underweight children in the Asia-Pacific region

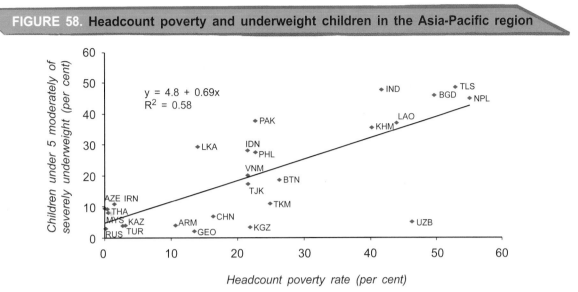

Note: Observations are for the latest years available as of September 2009.
Sources: ESCAP based on data from World Bank, *PovcalNet Database* and United Nations Statistics Division, *Millennium Development Goals Database.*

FIGURE 59. Headcount poverty and primary education survival rate in the Asia-Pacific region

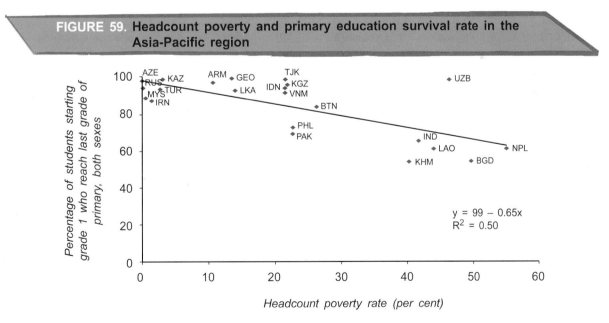

Note: Observations are for the latest years available as of September 2009.
Sources: ESCAP based on data from World Bank, *PovcalNet Database;* and United Nations Statistics Division, *Millennium Development Goals Database.*

FIGURE 60. Headcount poverty and access to improved sanitation in the Asia-Pacific region

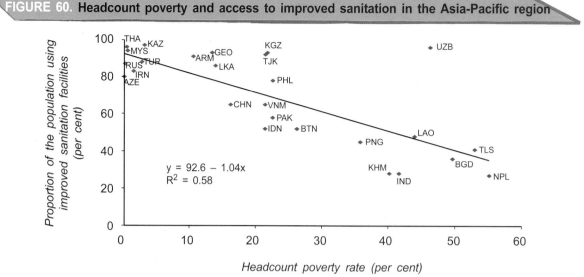

Note: Observations are for the latest years available as of September 2009.
Sources: ESCAP based on data from World Bank, *PovcalNet Database* and United Nations Statistics Division, *Millennium Development Goals Database.*

weight children, low primary school survival rates, high rates of employment in the informal sector and low access to improved sanitation facilities. However, an important message of figures 57 to 60 is that while the correlation between poverty rates and the various indicators examined is high, it is not by any means absolute. For many countries social indicators are better than would be expected according to their headcount poverty rates. Thus the data suggest that it is possible, through the implementation of appropriate policies, to improve the social conditions of the population regardless of a country's poverty rate.

To be sure, improving the provision of basic social services and developing effective social protection systems are costly and require strong political commitment. The data indicate that much remains to be done in this regard in Asia and the Pacific. The average public spending in education in the region during 2005 was 3.4% of GDP, below the world average of 4.7%.[99] Moreover,

spending levels have been lower in low-income economies and least developed countries (2.5%) – those that need it the most – compared with high-income economies (3.9%). In some subregions, such as South and South-West Asia and North and Central Asia, spending has dropped during the first half of the 2000s. Regarding health services, a large share of health expenditures in the region is funded out-of-pocket, limiting access of poor individuals to basic services.[100] A related concern is the low coverage rates of social protection programmes, particularly in health-care assistance, labour market programmes, assistance to persons living with disabilities and access to microcredit by the poor.[101] But on a positive note, existing levels of poverty and other deprivations provide substantial headroom for increasing aggregate demand in the Asia-Pacific region. Therefore, poverty reduction must occupy a central place in the economic development strategy designed to sustain Asian dynamism in the coming years.

---

[99] ESCAP, *Economic and Social Survey 2008.*
[100] ESCAP, *Development of Health Systems in the Context of Enhancing Economic Growth towards Achieving the Millennium Development Goals in Asia and the Pacific,* Sales No. E.07.II.F.12 (Bangkok: 2007).
[101] ESCAP, *Economic and Social Survey 2009;* and ESCAP, ADB and UNDP, *Achieving the Millennium Development Goals.*

Infrastructure and other development gaps

While the Asia-Pacific region has made impressive progress in reducing the number of poor, this progress has been uneven across countries. And the observed relationship between headcount poverty rates and selected Millennium Development Goals indicators suggests that progress in reaching those goals must have been uneven as well. The following section summarizes gaps across Asian and Pacific subregions in the achievement of the Millennium Development Goals, together with a preliminary examination of gaps in infrastructural development across countries in the region.

The availability and quality of infrastructure hold great significance for economic development. As public goods, the availability of quality infrastructural facilities assists in "crowding in" private investments by reducing the magnitude of required investments. In other words, physical infrastructure contributes to economic growth through "multipliers" of investment, employment, output, income and ancillary development. The role of physical infrastructure in fostering economic development and integration has been supported by extensive empirical literature.[102] Thus, closing the infrastructural development gaps across the region appears to be a necessary condition for inclusive and balanced regional development.

As far as the Millennium Development Goals are concerned there is considerable variation across subregions and country groupings.[103] Table 27 shows that among the subregions, the greatest progress has been in South-East Asia, which has already achieved 11 out of the 21 assessed indicators and is on track for another four. Next come the North and Central-Asian countries which, as a group, have already achieved nine of the indicators.

The Asia-Pacific region includes the world's two most populous countries – China and India – so the region's overall achievement on poverty and other indicators is swayed by their performance. Table 27 shows that the performance of Asia and the Pacific excluding China and India on some indicators has been worse than for the region as a whole: it has progressed only slowly in ensuring primary enrolment, and regressed on HIV prevalence. On the other hand, this group of smaller countries has done better on gender parity in secondary educational attainment on which it is an early achiever. Starting from a low base on many Millennium Development Goal indicators, South Asia has made good progress on eight indicators, but is progressing only slowly on many others. Given the weight of India in subregional aggregates, it may be useful to consider "South Asia without India". That grouping is on track for poverty, but progressing slowly on primary enrolment and the provision of clean water supplies and regressing in HIV prevalence and forest cover.

The Pacific Island countries have been less successful – regressing or making no progress in 11 indicators and advancing only slowly in another two, those for infant and under-five mortality. Excluding Papua New Guinea, the Pacific island countries are early achievers in gender equality. The 14 least developed countries in Asia and the Pacific have made slow or no progress on most indicators – performing well only on gender equality in primary and secondary education and on reducing the prevalence of HIV and TB.

The existence of infrastructure gaps in the region has received less attention in recent times than gaps in the achievement of the Millennium Development Goals, partly because of the large number of existing indicators of different aspects of infrastructure that make comparisons

---

[102] See the following references for discussion: Aschauer, David Alan, "Is public expenditure productive?", *Journal of Monetary Economics,* vol. 23, No. 2 (March 1989), pp. 177-200; Easterly, William, and Sergio Rebelo, "Fiscal policy and economic growth: An empirical investigation", *Journal of Monetary Economics,* vol. 32, No. 3 (December 1993), pp. 417-458; Gramlich, Edward M., "Infrastructure investment: A review essay", *Journal of Economic Literature,* vol. 32, No. 3 (1994), pp. 1176-1196; World Bank, *World Development Report 1994: Infrastructure for Development* (New York: Oxford University Press, 1994).

[103] ESCAP, *Supportive Financial System and Green Growth for Achieving the Millennium Development Goals in the Asia-Pacific Region:* Theme Study 2010.

TABLE 27. Country groups on and off track for the Millenium Development Goals

Goal	1		2			3			4		5		6			7					
	$1.25/day poverty	Underweight children	Primary enrolment	Reaching last grade	Primary completion	Gender primary	Gender secondary	Gender tertiary	Under-5 mortality	Infant mortality	Antenatal care, at least once	Births by Skilled Professional	HIV prevalence	TB incidence	TB prevalence	Forest cover	Protected area	CO$_2$ emissions	ODP substance consumption	Water, total	Sanitation, total
Asia-Pacific	▲	■	▲	■	■	●	▲	●	■	■	■	■	●	●	●	▼	●	▼	●	●	■
Excluding China and India	▲	■	■	■	■	●	●	●	■	■	■	■	▼	●	●	▼	●	▼	●	▲	■
South-East Asia	●	▲	▲	■	●	●	●	●	▲	■	■	■	●	●	●	▼	●	▼	●	●	▲
South Asia	■	■	▲	■	■	●	▲	●	■	■	■	■	●	●	●	●	●	▼	●	●	■
Excluding India	▲	■	■	■	■	●	▲	▲	■	■	■	■	▼	●	●	●	●	▼	●	■	■
Pacific islands				▼		▼	▼	▼	■	■	▼	▼	▼	●	●	▼	●	▼	●	▼	▼
Excluding Papua New Guinea			▼	▼	▼	●	●	●	■	■		■		●	●	▼	●	●	●	▼	▼
North and Central Asia	▼	▲	●	●	●	●	●	●	●	●		■		▲	▼	▼	●	▼	●	▲	●
Excluding Russian Federation	▼	●	●	●	●	●	●	●	●	●	▲	▲	▼	▼	▼	▼	●	▼	●	▲	■
LDCs Asia-Pacific	■	■	■	■		●	●	●	■	■	■	■	●	●	●	▼	●	▼	●	■	■

● Early achiever   ▲ On track   ■ Slow   ▼ Regressing/No progress

Source: ESCAP/ADB/UNDP (2010), p. 10.

across countries difficult.[104] For instance, a country may be well developed in road infrastructure but may have poor telecommunication or information infrastructure. Hence, neither a measure of road transport infrastructure or of telecommunication infrastructure would adequately capture the overall quality or availability of infrastructure. A single comprehensive indicator of infrastructural development would be desirable. To get a sense of the infrastructural development gaps in Asia and the Pacific, one such composite measure capturing aspects of transport infrastructure (roads, railways and air transport density), ICT infrastructure (telephone and internet density), energy availability (intensity of energy use) and banking infrastructure (bank branches density) is proposed here. The composite measure represents an average of all the eight unit-free indicators following the methodology of the UNDP human development index. (See annex II for methodological details.)

The patterns that emerge from the composite indicator as summarized in figure 61 suggest that high-income and upper-middle-income countries such as. Singapore; Japan; New

---

[104] The many indicators include some related to transportation facilities such as road networks, ports and airports; and some about communication infrastructure covering telecommunication networks, information infrastructure and energy availability, among others.

FIGURE 61. Infrastructure composite scores in Asia and the Pacific, 2007

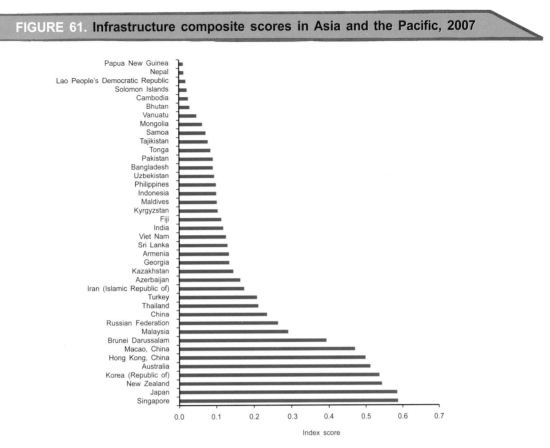

Source: ESCAP calculations as indicated in Annex II.

Zealand; the Republic of Korea; Australia; Brunei Darussalam; Hong Kong, China; and Macao, China have reached a very high level of infrastructural development, holding the top eight positions. On the other end of the spectrum, the least developed countries, small island economies and landlocked developing countries such as Papua New Guinea, Nepal, the Lao People's Democratic Republic, Solomon Islands, Cambodia, Bhutan, Vanuatu and Mongolia, among others have very wide gaps in the levels of infrastructural development remaining to be closed. Other developing countries occupy the middle positions with significant gaps remaining to be closed.[105]

Closing the infrastructural development gaps across the region appears to be a necessary condition for inclusive and balanced regional development

The resource requirements for bridging or even narrowing those gaps are substantial. A recent study estimated that the Asia-Pacific regional infrastructure needs for the decade beginning in 2010 to be of the order of nearly $8 trillion ($5.4 trillion for new capacity and $2.6 trillion for

---

[105] Such a composite index of infrastructure also can be used to see if the gaps are widening over time or closing.

replacement of old infrastructure).[106] The investment needs are on the order of $800 billion per year of which much remains unfunded under current arrangements.

Narrowing the development gaps in Asia and the Pacific including poverty reduction and achievement of other Millennium Development Goals and infrastructural gaps provides valuable opportunities for augmenting aggregate demand while making the pattern of development more balanced and inclusive.

GROWING ECOLOGICAL IMBALANCES

Rapid economic growth and modernization has put huge pressure on the natural capital of many countries in the region, depleting key natural resources such as freshwater and forests. Market failures are largely to blame, reflected in imperfect information on the value of goods and services provided by the natural environment, a misalignment between the social and private costs involved, and shortcomings in the governance of natural resources.

The decline in the natural resource base is particularly worrisome in Asia and the Pacific because of the region's high population density and low per-capita access to critical resources such as water and energy. Furthermore, the economic impacts of the declining natural capital base are likely to fall disproportionately on the poor, many of whom live on ecologically vulnerable areas and depend on the availability of natural resources to make a living.

Figure 62 shows the net increase or loss in forest area between 1990 and 2005 for 28 Asian and

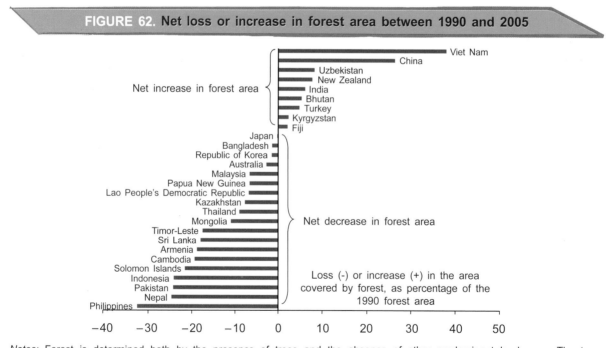

FIGURE 62. Net loss or increase in forest area between 1990 and 2005

Notes: Forest is determined both by the presence of trees and the absence of other predominant land uses. The trees should reach a minimum height of 5 metres (m) in situ. Areas under reforestation that have not yet reached but are expected to reach a canopy cover of 10% and a tree height of 5 m are included, as are temporarily unstocked areas, resulting from human intervention or natural causes, which are expected to regenerate.
Source: ESCAP, based on data from United Nations Statistical Division, *Millennium Development Goals Database*.

---

[106] ADB and Asian Development Bank Institute, *Infrastructure for a Seamless Asia* (Tokyo: 2009), p. 167; available from www.adbi.org/intal/intalcdi/PE/2009/03979.pdf.

Pacific countries for which data are available. In 19 of them the forest area was reduced during that period at an average rate of loss of 1% per annum.[107] The annual average rate of decrease in forest area was highest for the Philippines (2.6%), Nepal (1.9%), Pakistan and Indonesia (1.8%), and the Solomon Islands (1.6%). On other hand, 9 countries experienced an increase in their forest area between 1990 and 2005 at an average rate of 0.7% per annum. The annual average rate of increase in forest area was highest in China (1.6%) and Viet Nam (2.2%).

The loss of forest area has several adverse effects on the environment. When trees are cut, burned or left to decay to convert forest areas to agricultural and other uses, their stored carbon is released into the atmosphere, adding to carbon emissions from burning fossil fuels. Tropical forest clearing accounts for roughly 20% of the annual anthropogenic carbon emissions.[108]

Forests also provide critical ecosystem services for economies and societies. For instance, the loss of forest area increases the likelihood of landslides, floods and soil depletion of vital mineral nutrients, making it less able to sustain agricultural production and leading to desertification. Deforestation also causes severe damage to natural ecosystems that provide life-supporting services such as water purification and waste decomposition.

The supply of freshwater resources provided by nature is another essential ecosystem service that faces multiple threats related to climate change, land-use change and expanding demand for water. Figure 63 shows that the rate of use of freshwater resources varies substantially across countries in the region. According to the latest data available, it ranges from less than 10% in Malaysia, the Russian Federation, Indo-

nesia, Georgia and Viet Nam to close to 100% or higher in Turkmenistan and Uzbekistan. Other countries with elevated water-use rates include Tajikistan and Pakistan (75%), Islamic Republic of Iran (68%) and Kyrgyzstan (49%). In the cases of the Islamic Republic of Iran and Pakistan, the percentage of water resources withdrawn has been increasing over time. While still at relatively moderate levels, percentages increased significantly between 1990 and 2000 in China, India and Sri Lanka, raising the risk of water stress in those countries.

While the increasing demand for water is the main reason for those trends, an additional cause for concern is the uncertain impact on freshwater resources of the loss of mass being experienced by most world glaciers.[109] In the short- to medium-run, such a loss could cause an increased frequency of floods; over the long-run, it could lead to water shortages in important river systems of the world that bring water to billions of people.

Forest and hydrological systems are vulnerable to climate change, and the loss of forests in turn increases vulnerability to drought and a host of natural disasters that are occurring with increased frequency and intensity. Therefore, the sustainable management of both forests and water systems is important not only for the preservation of critical sources of natural capital but also for adapting to extreme events and disasters. However, while adaptation to climate change constitutes a major focus of the scientific community and policymakers in the region, the need to take steps towards the mitigation of climate change has been moving up the policy agenda.

Because of their very fast economic growth, Asian and Pacific developing economies have been increasing their emissions of carbon diox-

---

[107] That figure for the annual rate of loss was derived from the forest area lost between 1990 and 2005 divided by the forest area in 1990 and expressed as an annual rate.

[108] Intergovernmental Panel on Climate Change, *Climate Change 2007: the Physical Science Basis – Summary for Policymakers* (Geneva: 2007); available from www.aaas.org/news/press_room/climate_change/media/4th_spm2 feb07.pdf.

[109] Dyurgerov, Mark B., and Mark F. Meier, "Glaciers and the changing earth system: A 2004 snapshot", Occasional Paper No. 58, Institute of Arctic and Alpine Research (University of Colorado, 2005).

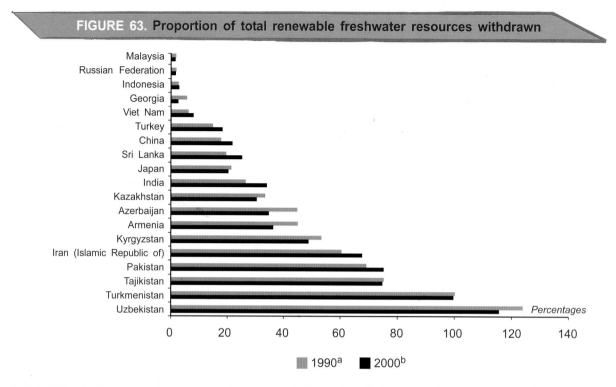

FIGURE 63. Proportion of total renewable freshwater resources withdrawn

■ 1990a ■ 2000b

Notes: Total volume of groundwater and surface water withdrawn from their sources for human use in the agricultural, domestic and industrial sectors expressed as a percentage of the total volume of water available annually through the hydrological cycle.

a 1995 for Islamic Republic of Iran.
b 2005 for Armenia, Azerbaijan, Georgia, Islamic Republic of Iran and Turkey.
Source: ESCAP based on data from United Nations Statistical Division, *Millennium Development Goals Database.*

ide rapidly. In 2006 China became the country with the highest level of emissions (table 28). However, on a per-capita basis, the carbon emissions of China, India and other developing countries in the region are still substantially lower than those of the developed countries. Because the developing countries are still industrializing and developing their infrastructure, their shares in the global cumulative emissions are also considerably lower than those of the developed countries. The developing countries are concerned about potential trade-offs between stringent emission-reduction commitments and their aspirations to industrialize, reduce poverty and raise standards of living to levels similar to those of the developed countries. As a result,

international negotiations on how to share the costs of addressing climate change issues have been extraordinarily complex and contentious; as evidenced at the United Nations Climate Change Conference in Copenhagen in December 2009.[110]

And yet, many countries of the region are adopting a forward-looking perspective and taking actions that seek to redress the imbalance between the supply and demand for ecosystem services. A consensus is starting to emerge in the region that an inclusive approach to development also needs to address the substantial challenges involved in maintaining the integrity of resources on which especially the poor de-

---

[110] For a more detailed discussion refer to UN-DESA, *World Economic and Social Survey 2009: Promoting Development, Saving the Planet.*

TABLE 28. Carbon dioxide emissions from selected major economies

	Share of global CO_2 emissions in 2006		Annual average growth rate of CO_2 emissions 1992-2006	Per capita CO_2 emissions in 2006		Share of global cumulative CO_2 emissions 1840-2006
	Per cent	Rank	Per cent	Mt^a	Rank	Per cent
1) Asia-Pacific economies						
Australia	1.4	(13)	1.6	19.3	(8)	1.1
China	21.8	(1)	6.2	4.7	(65)	8.1
India	4.7	(4)	4.8	1.2	(120)	2.4
Indonesia	1.3	(15)	3.6	1.6	(109)	0.6
Iran (Islamic Republic of)	1.7	(10)	4.6	6.7	(47)	0.8
Japan	4.4	(5)	0.5	9.8	(27)	3.6
Republic of Korea	1.8	(9)	3.7	10.8	(23)	0.8
Russian Federation	5.7	(3)	−2.0	11.3	(19)	8.0
2) Other economies						
Canada	1.9	(7)	1.1	16.8	(9)	2.0
Germany	3.0	(6)	−1.0	10.2	(27)	6.7
United Kingdom	1.9	(8)	−0.2	9.0	(32)	5.9
United States	20.3	(2)	1.2	19.3	(7)	27.8

Note: [a] Metric tons of CO_2.
Sources: ESCAP, based on United Nations (2009, table 1.3, p. 9) and data from United Nations Statistics Division, *Millennium Development Goals Database;* Marland, Boden and Andres (2008); and World Resources Institute, *Climate Analysis Indicators Tool* (CAIT) Version 7.0, http://cait.wri.org/.

pend, for example by keeping freshwater use within sustainable levels, restoring water quality in rivers, protecting the ecological services of forests and adapting to climate change. Consequently, in response to the global financial crisis, some ESCAP member countries have allocated a high proportion of green investments in their fiscal stimulus packages.[111] In addition, countries such as China, the Republic of Korea, and India have made high-level commitments to building environmental sustainability into economic growth and to promote international cooperation mechanisms to fight climate change. The Chinese Premier, Wen Jiabao, has stated: "All nations should continue to find common ground, bridge differences and strengthen cooperation to crack the hard issues facing human existence and development, and benefit the generations to come."[112]

A key to addressing the region's ecological imbalances will be the implementation of broadly understood technological innovations that will reduce the adverse impacts of production and consumption activities on the environment, as well as unsustainable pressures on natural resources. The promotion and adoption of such innovations is possible, but requires a societal consensus about their benefits, as well as strong Government support and international co-

[111] Bernard, Steve, and others, "The greenest bail-out?", *Financial Times,* 2 Mar. 2009; available from www.ft.com/cms/s/0/cc207678-0738-11de-9294-000077b07658.html?nclick_check=1.

[112] Xinhua News Agency, "Chinese premier, UN chief discuss climate change", *China View,* Window on China sec., 30 Dec. 2009; available from http://news.xinhuanet.com/english/2009-12/30/content_12730059.htm.

operation. Past experience suggests that economic incentives have encouraged the emergence of such societal consensus and Government support.

It should be pointed out that least developed countries, landlocked developing countries and small island developing States – which are disproportionately vulnerable to the consequences of climate change – do not have the financial resources and expertise to develop new technologies. A number of international agreements, notably the United Nations Framework Convention on Climate Change (UNFCCC), recognize those constraints by stressing that developed countries need to support developing countries according to the principle of common but differentiated responsibilities. Developed countries are thereby committed to supporting developing countries financially and through transfer of technology so that they can diversify their production into higher value-added and less pollution-intensive manufacturing and service industries, through the use of environmentally sound technologies and know-how. To date, much remains to be done, not only in terms of providing financing to developing countries on preferable terms, but also in enhancing "green" market access opportunities for developing countries.

A consensus is starting to emerge in the region about the need to keep freshwater use within sustainable levels, restore water quality in rivers, protect the ecological services of forests, and adapt to climate change

In their search for new sources of growth in the aftermath of the crisis, Asian and Pacific countries might pay attention to opportunities that may exist in environmentally sound processes and technologies through appropriate public interventions, international support and regional cooperation. Concurrently, as key developing countries move ahead in their development aspirations and in their capacity to generate tech-

nological innovations, the prospects for South-South technical and financial cooperation in that area appear promising.

LINKAGES BETWEEN THE THREE IMBALANCES

Figure 64 presents a schematic view of the production process. It shows three uses of GDP -investments, net exports and consumption, and four production inputs: capital, including that derived from natural resources, technology, and labour. The figure also shows an externality related to environmental degradation. Finally, the figure makes clear that production alone is insufficient to achieve the objective of poverty reduction, which is shown as linked to employment and availability of consumption goods and services. This figure illustrates the macroeconomic imbalances of the growth process in Asia and the Pacific discussed in this chapter.

To sustain economic growth over the long run, the Asia-Pacific region needs to address its macroeconomic, social and ecological imbalances in an integrated manner: policies that address simultaneously more than one imbalance should be given the highest priority

The links between elements in the figure are depicted as colour-coded arrows to highlight the three imbalances, as well as elements of the current growth strategy that have delivered, on average, positive development results. The blue arrows highlight key elements of Asian and Pacific growth strategy that have contributed to the region's high rates of economic growth over the past 40 years. They include high investment rates leading to a fast accumulation of capital which, combined with an abundant supply of

FIGURE 64. A schematic view of the three imbalances

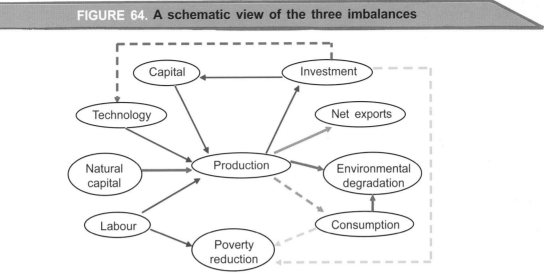

Source: ESCAP.

labour, have facilitated dramatic expansion of production. The expansion of employment, also a key contributor to the fast rate of GDP growth, has provided earning opportunities that have helped to lift millions out of poverty.

Addressing the imbalances means a weakening of some links shown and strengthening of others. Dotted arrows, linking production with consumption, denote that the link is weak and that it should be strengthened. The social imbalances are highlighted with yellow arrows. They are associated with the significantly slower growth rates of per-capita household consumption compared to per capita GDP and with insufficient levels of investment in the provision of basic social services and the development of social protection systems. The links between consumption and investment in poverty reduc-

tion are depicted with dotted arrows, indicating that they are weaker than desirable.

The ecological imbalances are highlighted with green arrows. Production activities involve both (a) the overuse of natural resources, reflected in losses of forest area and increasing risks of water stress in some countries; and (b) the emission of carbon dioxide from burning fossil fuels as well as from high carbon-emitting consumption activities. To address those imbalances, policies should be devised to weaken the links depicted by the green arrows. In addition, a strong investment programme in technological innovations to improve energy efficiency and develop alternative sources of energy will be required, combined with a clear commitment by developed countries to support the reduction of financial and technological gaps in the region.

Annex I

Import-adjusted method to compute the contribution of aggregate demand components to GDP growth

Assume that the production of consumption, investment and exports requires an identical proportion of imported goods and services, or import intensity, *m*. Under this assumption we can express the GDP identity $GDP \equiv C + G + I + X - M$ as

$$GDP \equiv C + G + I + X - mGDP, \text{ or}$$

$$GDP \equiv \frac{1}{1+m} (C + G + I + X), \text{ or}$$

$$GDP \equiv \left(1 - \frac{m}{1+m}\right)(C + G + I + X).$$

Thus, to implement the decomposition it is necessary to subtract $\left(\dfrac{m}{1+m}\right)C$ from private consumption, $\left(\dfrac{m}{1+m}\right)G$ from government consumption, $\left(\dfrac{m}{1+m}\right)I$ from investment and $\left(\dfrac{m}{1+m}\right)X$ from exports and proceed with the usual growth decomposition.

While the assumption of identical import intensities is useful as a first approximation, it underestimate the contribution of consumption to GDP growth because private and government consumption typically have smaller import content than investments and exports. By the same token, this assumption will overestimates the contributions of investment and exports to GDP growth.

An alternative approach is to take into account empirical data on import intensities. Although such data are not easily available in Asia and Pacific countries, it is possible to explore up to what extent the results sensitive to the assumption of equal import intensities by using on import intensities observed in other areas of the world. The accompanying table presents data on import intensity from a selection of European countries.

The European data show consistently that the import intensities of both private and Government consumption are clearly below the average, while those of exports are clearly above the average. Although there is some variation across countries, the data suggest the presumption that using identical import intensities will bias downward the contribution of consumption to GDP growth and bias upward the contribution of exports to GDP growth. In the table in the text we apply the import-adjusted method using both identical import intensities and the median import intensities of the countries shown in the accompanying table.

To implement this alternative method, decompose imports as

$$0.7\alpha C + 0.3\alpha G + 1.1\alpha I + 1.5\alpha X = M$$

where α is obtained as $\alpha = \dfrac{m}{1+m}$.[a] It is thus necessary to subtract $0.7\left(\dfrac{m}{1+m}\right)C$ from private consumption, $0.3\left(\dfrac{m}{1+m}\right)G$ from government consumption, $1.1\left(\dfrac{m}{1+m}\right)I$ from investment and $1.5\left(\dfrac{m}{1+m}\right)X$ from exports before proceeding with the usual growth decomposition.

---

[a] The coefficients 0.7, 0.3, 1.1, and 1.5 are the medians in the bottom line of the table below. Notice that $\alpha (C + G + I + X) = M$. Thus $\alpha (GDP + M) = M$ and $\alpha = \dfrac{M}{GDP + M} = \dfrac{m}{1+m}$.

Import intensities of selected European countries, 2005

	C	G	I	X	Total
1) In per cent					
Belgium	32	10	48	62	45
France	18	8	26	45	23
Germany	22	9	33	42	28
Italy	19	8	31	26	20
Netherlands	27	12	41	60	42
Spain	16	8	23	65	27
2) Ratio to total					
Belgium	0.7	0.2	1.1	1.4	1.0
France	0.8	0.3	1.1	2.0	1.0
Germany	0.8	0.3	1.2	1.5	1.0
Italy	1.0	0.4	1.6	1.3	1.0
Netherlands	0.6	0.3	1.0	1.4	1.0
Spain	0.6	0.3	0.9	2.4	1.0
Medians	0.7	0.3	1.1	1.5	1.0

Source: ESCAP based on data from Kranendonk and Verbruggen (2008).

Annex II

The composite measure of infrastructure development is based on 8 physical infrastructure indicators covering 40 ESCAP member countries in the region for 2007. It is a summary measure and it measures the average achievement of a country. The aspects of infrastructure covered in the construction of the composite index and their measurements are as follows:

Transport infrastructure: There could be several aspects of transport infrastructure such as availability of roads, railways, air transport and ports. In view of the availability of comparable indicators, we have employed following five indicators for capturing the availability of transport infrastructure: (i) Air transport is captured by passengers carried per 10,000 population and air freight million ton-km, (ii) Road infrastructure by the length of roads network per 1000 sq. km. of geographical area, (iii) Railway infrastructure by length of railway lines per 1000 sq. km. of geographical area.

ICT infrastructure: The availability of ICT infrastructure is captured with the help of "teledensity" and availability of Internet captured by total number of telephones (mobiles and fixed line) per 100 population and Internet users per 100 inhabitants respectively.

Energy availability: Energy availability is captured by intensity of electric power consumption (kWh) per inhabitant.

Banking infrastructure: Captured by number of banks per 100,000 population.

Data sources include *World Development Indicators* (World Bank), *Statistical Yearbook for Asia and the Pacific* (ESCAP), and *Key Indicators for Asia and the Pacific* (Asian Development Bank).

We follow the United Nations Development Program's (UNDP) Human Development Index (HDI) methodology while indexing the physical infrastructure development.[a] In general, to transform a raw variable, say x, into a unit-free index of a development dimension x between 0 and 1 (which allows different indices to be added together), we use following formula:

$$\text{Dimension}_x = \frac{x - \min(x)}{\max(x) - \min(x)}$$

where *min* and *max(x)* are the lowest and highest values the variable *x* can attain, respectively.

The composite index was calculated as a simple average of all the unit free indicators.

---

[a]   For concept and methodology, see the example in Sudhir Anand and Amartya Sen, *Sustainable Human Development: Concepts and Priorities,* (UNDP, 1994).

"We...need to remain vigilant and active to ensure that our policies and economic reforms strongly support the enabling environment for economic growth. In addition, we have to pay special attention to our social protection policies to ensure that our poor, our children and our women, who are the most vulnerable, are not left behind"

Edward Natapei
Prime Minister of Vanuatu

A REGIONAL POLICY AGENDA FOR REGAINING THE DYNAMISM

4

Trillions of dollars accumulated in foreign exchange reserves during the decade that preceded the global crisis, as net exports, became a key element supporting GDP growth in Asia and the Pacific.[113] As this *Survey* describes in the previous chapter, those reserves were mostly invested in treasury bonds issued by developed countries outside the region, which in turn fed debt-driven consumption abroad. With the advent of the first worldwide recession since the 1930s and the enormous debt burden accumulated by developed-country Governments, a return to business as usual seems unlikely. There is little likelihood that even a recovery in major developed economies could rekindle the pre-crisis, export-led growth trend for the region.[114]

Asian and Pacific countries therefore need to find new sources of domestic and regional demand to make up for weakened Western demand for their exports, to help sustain their dynamism and allow for a gradual unwinding of global imbalances. Part of the solution could be to develop a more consumer-centric economy in the region — one in which rising consumption is increasingly fed by production from within the region. By allocating financial capital more efficiently within the region, more jobs could be generated and the benefits of economic growth could be spread more equitably, in turn stimulating increases in private consumption.

---

[113] While not all subregions of Asia and the Pacific experienced a disproportionately large contribution of net exports to economic growth over the past decade, private consumption has generally diminished, at least up to the onset of the global financial crisis of 2008.

[114] The President of the United States Mr. Barack Obama stated on 9 May 2009: "The long-term deficit and debt that we have accumulated is unsustainable. We can't keep on just borrowing from China or borrowing from other countries... [A]t some point they're just going to get tired of buying our debt. And when that happens, we will really have to raise interest rates to be able to borrow..." [Reuters, "Obama says U.S. can't keep borrowing from China", 14 May 2009, available from www.reuters.com/article/politicsNews/idUSTRE54D58Q20090514.

Corrections in the large socio-economic and ecological imbalances in the region could provide much headroom for generating new aggregate demand, as this *Survey* discusses in the preceding chapter. With nearly 1 billion people in poverty and wide gaps in infrastructure and lifestyles, opportunities could be developed to augment aggregate demand through private consumption and investment. Critical for regaining the region's dynamism are policy measures taken at national and regional levels that can reduce poverty and facilitate more inclusive economic growth. Similarly, greener "new-economy" industries and businesses based on energy- and material-saving innovations could also be sources of growth, providing more affordable products for consumption by the poor while promoting environmental sustainability. Therefore, inclusive and sustainable growth is not only desirable but also a necessary condition for regaining the dynamism of the Asia-Pacific region in the aftermath of the global economic crisis.

Asia-Pacific needs to find new sources of domestic and regional demand to help sustain its dynamism and contribute to the gradual unwinding of global imbalances

The present chapter outlines a policy agenda for the region at the national and regional levels that could help unleash latent domestic and regional demand and address the macroeconomic, social and ecological imbalances described in chapter 3 in an integrated manner.

REDRESSING SOCIO-ECONOMIC AND ENVIRONMENTAL IMBALANCES FOR EXPANDING DOMESTIC CONSUMPTION

With over 950 million poor as of 2005, the challenge of reducing poverty in Asian and Pacific countries remains formidable and should be assigned the highest policy priority. Poverty reduction also has the potential to enhance domestic consumption by adding hundreds of millions of new consumers to the mainstream. The skyrocketing food and fuel prices of 2008 and subsequent global financial crisis were stark reminders that poverty can suddenly increase during turbulent times, wiping out hard-won gains. In the context of poverty reduction, measures such as strengthening social protection, focusing on agriculture and rural development and enhancing financial inclusiveness could help in expanding the domestic base of demand while addressing socio-economic imbalances.

Strengthening social protection

Addressing the social imbalances of the region calls for two different, but equally important, policy goals: (a) to redouble efforts to reduce entrenched poverty and deprivation; and (b) to protect the population at large from the risk of falling into poverty as a result of various hazards, including adverse economic shocks, natural disasters, illness, disability and other circumstances. Both goals can be addressed through broadly understood policies that provide social protection in times of adversity and reduce unacceptable levels of deprivation.[115] Such social protection policies should be concerned with developing short-term safety nets, preventing increases in deprivation, and promoting better chances of individual development.[116]

---

[115] Kannan, K. P., "Social security in a globalizing world", *International Social Security Review,* Vol. 60, Nos. 2-3, 2007, pp. 19-37.

[116] Guhan, S., "Social security options for developing countries", *International Labour Review,* Vol. 133, No. 1, 1994, pp. 35-54.

Social protection systems are key to attaining a more inclusive development process. They can serve as automatic stabilizers during periods of crisis by providing additional income to the poor and helping maintain their food intake and access to education and health services. In non-crisis times they can help support domestic demand by reducing the need for precautionary saving against catastrophic out-of-pocket expenses in coping with medical or other emergencies. Some types of social protection measures are particularly relevant for tackling crisis situations as they can provide quick relief to the poor in the short-term.[117] Among them are (a) employment generation measures; (b) cash transfers programmes – conditional or unconditional; (c) targeted social services, such as feeding programmes and health and education programmes that focus on benefits for women and girls; and (d) expansion of microcredit schemes to impoverished groups and localities.

Many of those programmes have the nature of social assistance and social services. The stimulus packages in the region contain many such measures for crisis relief. For example, the stimulus package in India includes an expansion of the National Rural Employment Guarantee Scheme. The Indonesian package emphasizes labour-intensive infrastructure projects. Stimulus packages in the Philippines and Thailand include social security benefits and cash transfers to the poor, while subsidies for health, education and social services in general find a major place in the stimulus packages of China, Singapore, Thailand and Hong Kong, China. Easing the availability of financing for affected groups such as women and small entrepreneurs has been a feature of the Indian and Thai packages. To be effective in relieving crises, social protection measures should be able to target the affected people and provide enough benefits to overcome crisis impacts.

Despite their usefulness in attaining an inclusive development process and in minimizing adverse impacts of economic crises, the coverage of social protection programmes in the Asian and Pacific region is among the lowest in the world. Most of the poorer developing countries lack institutionalized welfare systems. They may have a variety of social protection measures but their programmes may not be sufficiently funded, coherent or extensive to protect vulnerable populations. The fragmented social safety nets that do exist are generally biased towards the formal sector, leaving many people without basic services and rights. For instance, social insurance tends to reach only a small proportion of the workforce – generally government workers and some of those employed in the formal sector – which in India, for example, represents less than one tenth of the total workforce.

The coverage of social protection programmes in the Asian and Pacific region is among the lowest in the world

Across the region, people working in the informal economy do not generally benefit from social safety nets. ESCAP has estimated that across Asia and the Pacific only 20% of the unemployed and underemployed have access to labour market programmes for unemployment benefits, training or public welfare, including work-for-food programmes.[118] Only 30% of the elderly receive pensions and only 20% of the regional population has access to health-care assistance – making out-of-pocket medical expenses in Asia and the Pacific among the highest in the world.[119] Even in China social insurance has been largely restricted to urban

---

[117]   This discussion draws on ESCAP, ADB and UNDP, *Achieving the Millennium Development Goals,* pp. 60-66.

[118]   ESCAP, *Economic and Social Survey 2009,* p. 64.

[119]   "In some countries in the region, more than 60% of money spent on health care comes from the patient's pocket. By contrast, in Germany an average of just 13% of all medical expenses are borne by the patient, with the rest covered by social health insurance or by the Government". (WHO, Regional Office for the Western Pacific, "Governments not spending enough on health", press release, 3 Mar. 2010; available from www.wpro.who.int/media_centre/press_releases/pr20100303.htm).

populations, although the Government has made a concerted effort to extend it to migrants and the rural population. In South Asian countries only 8% of the population is covered by healthcare programmes, compared to 20% for the Asia-Pacific region in general.

Social protection systems can be strengthened in several ways. While systems vary across countries for many reasons, a minimum floor of social security benefits for all citizens should include (a) guaranteed universal access to essential health services; (b) guaranteed income security for all children through family and/or child benefits; (c) guaranteed access to basic means-tested or self-targeted social assistance for the poor and the unemployed; and (d) guaranteed income security through basic pensions for people in old age and people living with disabilities.[120]

Several Asian and Pacific countries provide examples of ambitious social security programmes. In 2001 Thailand took the historic step of legislating full population coverage in health care by introducing a universal health-care scheme, popularly referred to as the "30-baht Scheme" from the amount initially stipulated as a co-payment. Any Thai citizen not already covered by the social security health insurance scheme or the Civil Servants' Medical Benefit Scheme enjoy full access to health services provided by designated district-based networks of providers -health centres, district hospitals and cooperating provincial hospitals. The eligible population must register with the networks to obtain a free insurance card. The initial 30 baht co-payment – a little less than $1 – for each outpatient visit or hospital admission has been abolished and medications on prescription are also free of charge.[121] Evaluations suggest that the Scheme has succeeded in making the coverage of health-care services near-universal and in significantly reducing household out-of-pocket medical expenditures, thus demonstrating that universal health-care is achievable in a lower middle-income country.[122]

Another important type of social protection in Asia and the Pacific consists of public works programmes aimed at reducing poverty. The National Rural Employment Guarantee Act (NREGA) of India provides a legal guarantee of 100 days of employment every year for adult members of any rural household willing to do unskilled manual work at the statutory minimum wage, as discussed in chapter 2. The central Government funds the cost of wages, 75% of the cost of materials, and part of the administrative expenses; the remaining costs are funded by State Governments. Participants in NREGA work in projects such as water conservation, flood control, irrigation and land development. The programme has many benefits, including the reduction of distress migration, employment generation in the most distressed areas, and improvements in the natural resource base for poor communities. Acknowledging the potential of gender discrimination, the Act mandates equality in wage payments of men and women and the availability of childcare at the work site. At least one third of NREGA beneficiaries must be women and women must be represented in the management and monitoring of the programme as well as in its social audit. Where work is to be performed beyond 5 km of their residences, women should be given preference to work nearer to their residence and members of the same household should be allowed to work at the same work site. Finally, by recognizing a single person as a household, NREGA enables widows and other single women to access the programme. Recent data shows an average female participation rate in the programme of 49.7%, with 22 of 32 states exceeding the mandated rate of one third.[123]

---

[120] ESCAP, *Economic and Social Survey 2009,* p. 65.

[121] ESCAP, ADB and UNDP, *Achieving* the *Millennium Development Goals,* p. 61.

[122] Damrongplasit, Kannika, "Thailand's universal coverage system and preliminary evaluation of its success", presentation at Freeman Spogli Institute for International Studies, Stanford University, 15 Oct. 2009; available from http://iis-db.stanford.edu/evnts/5747/presentation_Kannika.pdf.

[123] Data were obtained for fiscal year 2008/09 from the NREGA website, http://nrega.nic.in/writereaddata/mpr_out/nregampr_0809.html (accessed 17 Mar. 2010). (See also India, Ministry of Rural Development, 2008a).

A novel approach to social protection is the use of conditional cash transfers. An example is given by Pantawid Pamilyang Pilipino Program ("4Ps") of the Philippines, which provides poor households with 500 pesos a month for their health needs and a 300-peso educational subsidy for each child up to age 14. Poor families can get the educational subsidy for a maximum of three children. In return, beneficiaries are required to comply with the following conditions: (a) pregnant women must receive prenatal care, childbirth must be attended by a skilled or trained person, and mothers must receive postnatal care; (b) children 0 to 5 years of age must have regular health check-ups and vaccinations; and (c) children 6 to 14 must attend school at least 85% of the time. Failure to comply with those conditions could mean losing the subsidy. School principals and the municipal health officers are tasked to monitor compliance. The rationale for the conditions is to create incentives for the recipients to invest in their own human capital. Such investments should give them, especially the children, a better chance to exit poverty permanently in the long term.

A promising policy framework for the implementation of broad social protection policies in the region is given by the 2004 Social Charter of the South Asia Association for Regional Cooperation (SAARC). The charter emphasizes the importance of the objective of reducing poverty in South Asia to (a) ensure that "every member of society is enabled to satisfy basic human needs and to realize his or her personal dignity, safety and creativity" and (b) support economic growth. In order to achieve the goal, the Charter highlights the need for enshrining rights of access to basic social services in national laws:

> States Parties agree that access to basic education, adequate housing, safe drinking water and sanitation, and primary health-care should be guaranteed in legislation, executive and administrative provisions...[124]

To be sure, guaranteeing universal access to all those basic services is expensive. A key concern of many low-income developing countries is the implications for fiscal balances, especially because of current budgetary strains. But given the low coverage of social safety net programmes, public expenditures should be reprioritized so that such programmes can be adequately financed. The reallocation of spending can be an important source of financing for an enhanced safety net package. Moreover, significant efficiency gains within the existing safety net system can be realized, under the right set of reforms, allowing countries to consolidate small programmes, which might be unable to reach satisfactory economies of scale individually.

Policies that generate income opportunities and improve access to basic social services in rural areas are essential in reducing poverty and rural-urban imbalances

---

A "green revolution" for food security and poverty reduction

Poverty in Asia and the Pacific remains predominantly a rural phenomenon. Up to 80% of the poor in China, India and Indonesia – 585 million out of 731 million – lived in rural areas in 2005 (table 25, chapter 3). Policies that promote the generation of jobs, increase income opportunities in rural areas, and improve access to basic social services are essential in reducing poverty and rural-urban imbalances. Because the rural poor derive most of their income from agricultural activities,[125] policies to facilitate the access of smallholder producers to land, agricultural inputs, extension services, fi-

---

[124] SAARC, *Social charter,* available from http://www.saarc-sec.org/main.php?id=13.

[125] Davis, Benjamin, and others, "Rural income generating activities: a cross country comparison", ESA Working Paper No. 07-16 (Rome: FAO, 2007); available from ftp://ftp.fao.org/docrep/fao/010/ah853e/ah853e.pdf.

nance and markets could significantly contribute to reducing rural poverty, decreasing distress migration to the cities – and thereby urban poverty – and increasing the supply of food. Moreover, vibrant agricultural communities are likely to attract other economic activities, contributing to the creation of non-farm business and employment opportunities.[126]

Besides the critical roles of agriculture and rural development in poverty reduction, two other considerations make them key priorities for investment and promotion policies for the medium-to long-term.

Firstly, the spikes in food commodity prices of 2007 and 2008, while abated by the global financial crisis during 2009, are not expected to be a fluke. The episode of high food prices reflected structural, long-run factors, as described in the *Survey 2009,* which were considerably attenuated but not eliminated as a result of the sharp contraction in economic activity that took place in 2009. Those factors included

the dramatic increase in crude oil prices, record low levels of world cereal stocks, rapid growth in the world GDP, expansion of the biofuel production, enhanced speculative activity in commodities, and a long-term decline in investment in agriculture that led to a drop in the rate of growth of yields.

Food prices moderated significantly in 2009 with respect to 2008 (figure 65). The FAO food price index dropped 36% between June 2008 and February 2009, not surprisingly in light of a sharp world recession and the dramatic drop in the price of crude oil during the second half of 2008. However, food prices started to climb back up, increasing 25% between February 2009 and January 2010. More dramatically, the price of crude oil – which had dropped 70% between July and December of 2008 – increased by as much as 91% between December 2008 and January 2010. Given the high correlation between food and crude oil prices from the 2000s, those trends – which are depicted in trend lines in figure 65 – are worrisome.[127]

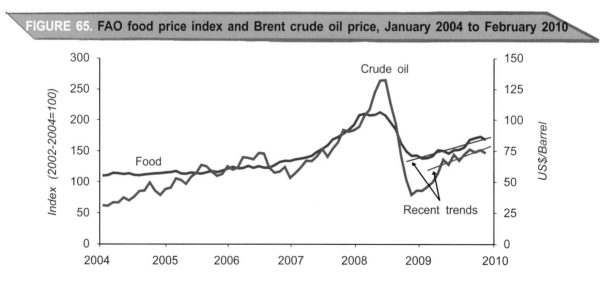

FIGURE 65. **FAO food price index and Brent crude oil price, January 2004 to February 2010**

Sources: ESCAP based on data FAO, World Food Situation, http://www.fao.org/worldfoodsituation/FoodPricesIndex/en/ and United States Energy Information Administration, available from http://tonto.eia.doe.gov/dnav/pet/hist/rbrteM.htm (accessed 10 Mar. 2010).

---

[126] Anriquez, Gustavo, and Kostas Stamoulis, "Rural development and poverty reduction: is agriculture still the key?", ESA Working Paper No. 07-02 (Rome: FAO. 2007); available from ftp://ftp.fao.org/docrep/fao/010/ah885e/ah885e.pdf.

[127] The correlation coefficient between the FAO index and the Brent crude oil price, using monthly observations between January 2000 and January 2010 is r=0.93.

Secondly, by 2050 the population of Asia and the Pacific is expected to increase by one and a half billion people and the demand for food and feed is expected to double from current levels. However, according to current trends in yields, it is projected that the region's supply of grains by 2050 will fall considerably short of matching that increase in demand.[128] Therefore, investing in agriculture with the objective of increasing its yields must be a top priority for the region. Achieving that objective is even more critical in the face of unpredictable, but increasingly more common, extreme weather events such as prolonged dry periods or heavy rainfall spells that are known to reduce crop yields and cause extensive crop losses.[129] Moreover, by some accounts, if current warming trends continue, the yields of major food crops in tropical countries could decrease by 20% to 30%.[130]

In past publications ESCAP has suggested specific policy recommendations to achieve those goals.[131] Here we highlight the need for the "second green revolution". While the Green Revolution of the last century achieved significant yield increases in the Asia-Pacific region, it brought concomitant problems from its high inputs of irrigation, chemical fertilizers, pesticides and insecticides, and its excessive energy use. As Asian and Pacific economies rebalance, a second green revolution is needed that can move agriculture from high chemical and water inputs to knowledge-intensive and sustainable agriculture. The second green revolution should integrate the region's unique traditional knowledge with advances in science and agricultural engineering, including plant genetics, plant pathology and information and communication technology. The approach should emphasize ecological sustainability with integrated pest and soil fertility management, minimum tillage and drip irrigation. A knowledge-intensive agriculture commends itself also on the grounds of environmental resilience and social inclusiveness as it attempts to return power to the producer – the farmer, especially women farmers.

To foster the second green revolution, Governments should focus on the right factor inputs; namely,

➢ assets such as land, tools, machinery and renewable water and energy resources.

➢ efficient credit allocation through the promotion of financial inclusiveness.

➢ knowledge generation through publicly funded agricultural research and development together with agricultural extension services, to rapidly transfer and diffuse knowledge from the laboratory to the field.

➢ information and communication technology applicable to farming.

Furthermore, risk management and social protection systems, such as crop insurance and improved crop transport and storage systems, besides efficient rural infrastructure, need to be provided.

The institutions that could provide critical help for farmers include those supporting extension education, post-harvest processing, credit and marketing, and communication connectivity including mobile phones. Farmers need them for help in meeting international standards, especially in food safety. One reason why the benefits of higher food prices have not accrued to farmers in many Asian and Pacific developing countries is that institutions that allow farmers to take advantage of the higher food prices in the international market were not in place. Wherever institutions existed, farmers have reaped benefit; Viet Nam is a case in point where small farmers have benefited from high international prices of rice by accessing export markets.

[128] International Water Management Institute and FAO, *Revitalizing Asia's Irrigation: To Sustainably Meet Tomorrow's Food Needs* (Colombo: 2009); available from www.fao.org/nr/water/docs/Revitalizing_Asias_Irrigation.pdf.

[129] Lansigan, Felino P., "Coping with climate variability and change in rice production systems in the Philippines" in *Rice is Life: Scientific Perspectives for the 21st Century,* K. Toriyama, K.L. Heong and B. Hardy, eds. (Manila: International Rice Research Institute, 2009), pp. 542-545.

[130] *Science Daily,* "Dramatic changes in agriculture needed as the world warms and grows", 12 Feb. 2010; available from http://www. sciencedaily.com/releases/2010/02/100211141140.htm.

[131] ESCAP, *Economic and Social Survey 2008;* and ESCAP, *Sustainable Agriculture and Food Security.*

A key element here would be a system that could help small farms benefit from economies of scale in marketing and assist them in meeting international standards. That role used to be played by parastatals, howsoever inefficiently, many of which were dismantled as a part of liberalization, privatization and deregulation policies under structural adjustment programmes. To provide for such needs, community-based organizations such as the self-help groups in India, the grass-roots non-governmental organizations (NGOs) and farmers' organizations in the Philippines such as the Indigenous Multi-Purpose Cooperative (IMPCI), Namitpitan Bulo Farmers Associations Inc. (NBFAI), Bado Dangwa Federation of Association and Cooperatives (BDFCO) and Pide Aguid Fidilisan Multi-Purpose Cooperative (PAFMPCI) are showing that they can do better than the erstwhile quasi-government agencies, if promoted and nurtured in an enabling environment.

The system of institutes of the Consultative Group on International Agricultural Research (CGIAR) have a key role in generating new knowledge and technology in agriculture and putting it in the public domain, where it is available to national agricultural research systems for adaptation to their geoclimatic conditions. Those institutes include the International Rice Research Institute (IRRI) in Los Baños, Philippines and the International Crop Research Institute for Semi-Arid Tropics (ICRISAT) in Hyderabad, India, among others. They should be enabled by the international community to play a similar role along with such institutions as the Centre for Alleviation of Poverty through Secondary Crops' Development in Asia and the Pacific (CAPSA) and Asian and Pacific Centre for Agricultural Engineering and Machinery (APCAEM) of ESCAP.

One recent success story in agricultural transformation based on knowledge through international cooperation is the New Rice for Africa (NERICA) programme of the West African Rice Development Association (WARDA; renamed the Africa Rice Center). In 1994 NERICA developed a new rice variety combining the best traits of African and Asian rice varieties. As a major collaborative project, it involved institutions in 17 African countries and the CGIAR with support from the Japanese Government and other multilateral donors. As a result of the growing demand for NERICA rice, cultivated areas are being extended to 210,000 hectares in West and Central Africa, exposing more than 1.7 million African farmers to the new crop and associated technologies. African rice production has increased to 744,000 tons per year with savings of $88 million in rice imports.[132] South-South and "triangular" cooperation are ought to play an equally important role in fostering the second green revolution in Asia and the Pacific.

"Green growth": new green industries as engines of growth

Today's challenges of combining developmental aspirations with sustainability are even starker than before. Widespread environmental degradation and extreme weather events such as more frequent and stronger tropical storms in the Pacific and Indian oceans, record droughts and more frequent flash floods, have made the Asia-Pacific region particularly crisis-prone. The poor bear a disproportionate burden of the adaptation costs. The new weather patterns are the result of divergent global growth and rising inequality that has built up over many decades, as the quest for development and prosperity particularly of the advanced economies has produced the bulk of greenhouse gases. Developing countries are deeply concerned that theirs is an environmentally constrained world, where their efforts to catch up in growth and economic convergence may be seriously limited.

ESCAP promotes the "Green Growth" approach that emphasizes environmentally sustainable economic progress to foster low-carbon, socially inclusive development. Among the pillars of

---

[132] Kumar, Nagesh, "South-South and triangular cooperation in Asia-Pacific: towards a new paradigm in development cooperation", UNESCAP Working Paper WP/09/05 (Bangkok: ESCAP, 2009); available from www.unescap.org/pdd/publications/workingpaper/wp_09_05.pdf.

Green Growth are sustainable consumption and production, greening of businesses and markets, sustainable infrastructure, green tax and budget reforms and investment in natural capital, as endorsed by the Fifth Ministerial Conference on Environment and Development in 2005.[133] Even though no one size may fit all, the movement of developing countries towards environmentally sustainable consumption and production could be facilitated by the following policy measures.

Industrial policies – strategic collaborations between the private sector and the Government to uncover and remove obstacles to the adoption of new technologies or the adaptation of existing technologies to local contexts – have a critical role to play in the promotion of investments in environmentally friendly technologies

First is the case for gearing industrial policy to promote investment in environmentally friendly technologies and products. Such investments are critical, particularly during the early phases of development and deployment of new technologies. Green technologies need to be sustained until they take root. They also need complementary investments along the entire supply chain. Industrial policies – understood as strategic collaboration between the private sector and the Government, aimed at uncovering and removing obstacles to the adoption of new technologies or

the adaptation of existing technologies to local contexts – have a critical role to play. The rationale for public intervention here is that action to promote innovation has great social value but is poorly remunerated.[134] Action for innovation might not take place at all without Government support. Moreover, in the case of environmentally friendly technologies, innovation is critical as local conditions differ from one region to another and from one country to another. Government support that permits experimentation and knowledge-sharing could bring substantial sharing of benefits and saving of resources, at the same time nurturing new frontiers of economic growth within the region. Government support for innovation in developing countries may be all the more critical in view of barriers to entry in relevant fields from competitive corporations that are themselves protected by intellectual patent regimes and other restrictive practices.

Government support should cover the development and commercialization of environmentally friendly technologies that lead to affordable products and improve the wellbeing of the poor and rural populations. Rural solar electric systems for homes, popularized by Grameen Shakti in Bangladesh (box 8), is one such technology.[135] The Governments of Japan, China, India and the Republic of Korea, among others, have adopted measures to support development of such innovations as a part of their national action plans on climate change.[136] China has become a top investor in clean energy, with investments soaring by more than 50% in 2009 to reach $34.6 billion; far ahead of the second largest investor, the United States, at $18.6 billion. The Chinese Government has set some of the world's most ambitious targets

---

[133] See ESCAP, *Greening Growth in Asia and the Pacific,* Sales No. E.09.II.F.6, available from www.unescap.org/esd/ environment/publications/gg_asia_pacific/GreeningGrowth.pdf; and *Navigating Out of the Crisis,* ST/ESCAP/2538, available from www.unescap.org/tid/publication/tipub2538.pdf.

[134] "If the entrepreneur fails in his venture, he bears the full cost of his failure. If he is successful, he has to share the value of his discovery with other producers who can follow his example and flock into the new activity". (Rodrik, Dani, "Industrial policy for the twenty-first century", CEPR Discussion Paper DP4767, Centre for Economic Policy Research; available from www.cepr.org/pubs/dps/DP4767.asp).

[135] "Grameen Shakti to launch solar power system in Dhaka, cities", *Bangladesh Economic News,* 26 June 2009; http://bangladesheconomy.wordpress.com/2009/06/26/grameen-shakti-to-launch-solar-power-system-in-dhaka-cities/; "Bangladesh decides to use solar power to save energy", *Bermana,* 5 Nov. 2009, http://www.bernama.com/ bernama /v5/newsworld.php?id=452797.

[136] ESCAP, *Economic and Social Survey 2009,* p. 80.

BOX 8. Pro-poor investments in renewable energy and beyond

Grameen Shakti, a not-for-profit subsidiary of the Grameen Bank established in 1996, had financed and installed about 220,000 home solar systems in rural Bangladesh by March 2009, providing electricity to more than 2 million people.[a] The systems include a rooftop solar photovoltaic panel, a battery and the required electronics, and cost between $350 and $400 each. Customers generally pay 10 to 15% as down payment and the rest in monthly instalments for three years. The system should last them 20 years. The panel provides enough electricity to power a few lights, a black-and-white TV and a cell phone.[b] While that level of electricity use sounds modest, it is crucial for the close to 70% of Bangladeshi households that are not connected to the national grid, and rely on kerosene for lighting.

Solar home systems have greatly benefited entire communities not just individual households, providing for lighting in rural clinics and schools, and the elimination of the adverse health consequences of kerosene smoke. Solar home systems have also extended opening hours for rural businesses and led to the creation of new job opportunities for solar and electronic technicians. In order to support the new demand, Grameen Shakti has trained over 1,000 female technicians on renewable energy technologies through its Grameen Technology Center Program.[c] Grameen Shakti has also started expanding its operations to Dhaka and other major urban centres with packages that are more powerful to cater to the requirements of urban consumers, but are also more expensive.

[a] Grameen Shakti website, "Programs at a glance," www.gshakti.org/glance.html.
[b] Gunthier, Marc (2009), "Grameen Shakti brings sustainable development closer to reality", GreenBiz.com, 21 Jan, www.greenbiz.com/blog/2009/01/21/grameen-shakti-brings-sustainable-development-closer-reality-bangladesh.
[c] Grameen Shakti website, "Creating 100,000 green women entrepreneurs", www.gshakti.org/ green-women.html.

in renewable energy use, notably wind and solar alternatives.[137] Likewise, the Government of Republic of Korea plans to spend $84 billion over five years to develop environmentally friendly industries and use them as a growth engine for the wider economy. That level of investment represents 2% of GDP per year. Through that plan the Republic of Korea expects to transform itself into one of the world's seven strongest nations in terms of energy efficiency and green technology by 2020.[138]

Secondly, strategically framed regulations and incentives, and taxes, can facilitate the adoption of environmentally sound practices and technologies. For instance, Governments worldwide promote energy conservation through taxes on fuels, personal vehicles and high parking charges while subsidizing public transport systems. Sometimes regulations and standards are adopted to promote environmentally friendly practices and products. Cases in point are standards of energy efficiency indicated on electric appliances, or of emissions imposed on vehicles, or decrees requiring compliance with new norms. In New Delhi, for example, conversion of the entire fleet of public transport to a cleaner fuel, compressed natural gas (CNG), led to significant improvement in air quality. Evidence that high energy prices encourage energy conservation has sparked discussion about phase-out of fuel subsidies. The G-20 summit meeting at Pittsburgh in September 2009 endorsed phasing out of fuel subsidies, together with provision of essential energy serv-

[137] The Pew Charitable Trusts, *Who's Winning the Clean Energy Race? Growth, Competition, and Opportunity in the World's Largest Economies* (Washington, D. C.: 2010); available from www.pewglobalwarning.org/cleanenergyeconomy/index.html.
[138] Agence France Press, "SKorea unveils massive plan for green growth", *France24,* 6 July 2009; available from http://mobile.france24.com/en/node/4895801.

ices for those in need through the use of targeted cash transfers, among other appropriate mechanisms.[139]

Thirdly, an important condition for ensuring environmental sustainability in developing countries is to the availability of environmentally sound technologies. The United Nations Framework Convention on Climate Change (UNFCCC) provides for the commitment of developed countries to support developing countries, through transfer of technology according to the principle of common but differentiated responsibilities.[140] The bulk of the technology in the field is protected by intellectual property rights, such as patents that tend to be dominated by corporations based in developed countries. For instance, four fifths of all renewable energy patents granted from 2000 to 2004 are owned by the European Union, the United States and Japan (the "Group of 3", or G-3); moreover, their share in motor-vehicle abatement technologies is as high as 95%.[141] Such a high concentration of patent ownership by private corporations based in a few developed countries affects the access of developing countries to relevant technologies.

Although transfer and dissemination of technology is an explicit objective of the Agreement on Trade-Related Aspects of Intellectual Property Rights (TRIPs Agreement),[142] which provides for measures to prevent practices that adversely affect international transfer of technology,[143] the Agreement leaves the provisions for transfer of technology quite vague. The conditions, norms and practices for facilitating transfers of environmentally friendly technologies need to be defined. A review of the Agreement could address the important issue of transfer of technology and conditions under which technologically less advanced countries could seek transfer of technology from patent owners. Developing countries can fully use the flexibilities provided in the TRIPs Agreement, including provisions for compulsory licensing in their own patent legislation in order to safeguard themselves from possible abuses of monopoly power by patent owners as provided by TRIPs.[144] Discussions leading to the recognition of public health related exceptions showed some flexibility in interpreting what constitutes 'exigent circumstances' opening the door to potential use of these exceptions in the climate change context.[145]

Alternative mechanisms to facilitate access of developing countries to new technologies have been suggested, such as technology pools in the public domain, dedicated multilateral funding mechanisms for supporting innovative activity in developing countries, and formation of R&D alliances involving developing country enterprises.[146]

Fourthly, the UNFCCC also provides for financial support from developed countries to aid adaptation efforts of developing countries. Multi-

[139] The leaders of the Group of 20 endorsed the objective of phasing out fuel subsidies in September 2009. They also recognized "the importance of providing those in need with essential energy services, including through the use of targeted cash transfers and other appropriate mechanisms". See Juliet Eilperin, "G20 leaders agree to phase out fossil fuel subsidies", *Washington Post,* 25 Sept. 2009.

[140] UNFCCC, "Draft Decision -/CP.15", 18 Dec. 2009, available from http://unfccc.int/resource/docs/2009/cop15/eng/l07.pdf. [old 143].

[141] United Nations, DESA, *World Economic and Social Survey 2009: Promoting Development, Saving the Planet,* Sales No. E.09.II.C.1, p. 128; available from www.un.org/esa/policy/wess/wess2009files/wess09/wess2009.pdf.

[142] Article 7 of the TRIPs Agreement; see Annex 1C of the Marrakesh Agreement Establishing the World Trade Organization, signed in Marrakesh, Morocco on 15 Apr. 1994; available from www.wto.org/english/tratop_e/trips_e/t_agm0_e.htm.

[143] Ibid., Article 8.

[144] Ibid., Article 31.

[145] United Nations, DESA, *World Survey 2009,* p. 131.

[146] Ibid., chapter V.

lateral agencies such as the World Bank group, the Global Environment Facility (GEF) and individual Governments have initiated action in that regard. Despite their efforts there is a staggering difference between the sheer size of resources necessary for adaptation, which has been estimated in the range of $50 billion to $100 billion per year (and of which about half would be needed in developing countries), and the amount actually mobilized and available, which is about $154 million.[147] The United Nations Climate Change Conference in Copenhagen in December 2009 recognized that scaled-up, additional and adequate funding, as well as improved access, should be provided to developing countries to support enhanced action on mitigation. The collective commitment by developed countries to provide new resources approached $30 billion for the years from 2010 to 2012. Developed countries also committed themselves to jointly mobilizing $100 billion a year by 2020 to address the needs of developing countries.[148]

Finally, valuable opportunities present themselves for sharing development experiences and best practices among the developing countries in the area of sustainable consumption and production. Developing countries in the region have demonstrated their capability in work on biofuels, solar and wind power and waste management, among others, that could be valuable for others and could be fruitfully shared. ESCAP, for example, has helped cities in Bangladesh, Pakistan, Sri Lanka and Viet Nam in managing solid waste by replicating an initiative of Waste Concern, a Bangladeshi NGO, using decentralized treatment plants.[149]

Enhancing financial inclusiveness

Patently, a well-functioning financial system is crucial to economic growth. Inclusive financial systems could likewise assist in poverty alleviation. From the perspective of the poor, an inclusive financial system would offer options for accessing financial products and services. This could include obtaining savings, credit and insurance on favourable terms and conditions and accessing payments services for undertaking transactions and remittances in a secure and cost-effective manner. Robust evidence from several ESCAP member countries shows that poor households with access to financial services can improve their economic well-being, while they invest in children's education, and enjoy better nutrition and health status, than similar households without such access. Furthermore, women of such households have been found to increase their role in decision-making, contributing to improve the welfare of children.

The poor are typically excluded from accessing core services offered by the formal financial sector such as savings, credit, insurance and payments

Unfortunately, across most developing countries of Asia and the Pacific, financial services are used by only a small proportion of the population. Only in a handful of countries do more than half the households have access to formal financial services. The vast majority of the population in most of those countries, especially the poor and those slightly above the poverty line, are typically excluded from accessing the core services offered by the formal financial sector, such as savings, credit, insurance and payments. Most countries have far to go in order to achieve financial inclusiveness.

---

[147] Ibid., pp. 93 onward; see also Khor, Martin, "Copenhagen: key issues facing developing countries", South Centre Climate Policy Brief; available from www.southcentre.org/index.php?option=com_content&task=view&id=1130&Itemid=1.

[148] Copenhagen Accord, paragraph 8: UNFCCC, "Draft Decision".

[149] ESCAP, *Economic and Social Survey 2009*, p. 83.

Barriers to financial access exist on both the demand side and supply side. The demand-side factors are primarily the capacity of potential clients to deal with banks, including their literacy levels, income, occupation and the appropriateness of the services and products on offer. On the supply side the factors include the perception of banks about the profitability and risks involved in dealing with poor customers and the cost of dealing with a large number of clients carrying out very small transactions. Moreover, the banking system is fraught with several built-in biases such as the location and business hours of banks, costs, and cultural prejudices of banking staff that prevent the poor and women from accessing banking services.

Most countries typically have a range of financial institutions, among which commercial banks are central to the financial system. Commercial banks have historically had only limited success in reaching out to the poor. Capital markets (equity and bond markets) by their nature have a very limited role in achieving financial inclusiveness as they cater to investment needs of relatively larger enterprises. Others such as development finance institutions and microfinance institutions have had relatively more success at reaching out to the poor and to the small and microenterprises. Furthermore, public and technology-enabled networks such as post offices, telecommunications companies and the Internet also hold potential for bringing forth financial inclusiveness.

To promote inclusive banking, Governments should foster efficient and fair banking with safety features such as a well-defined lender of last resort, a deposit insurance agency, safe cash remittance and transit facilities, and an institutional mechanism to deal with distressed banks. An inclusive banking policy should go hand in hand with development projects and provision of other services to the poor such as health and education, so that they can equip themselves to make use of banking services.

The regulatory environment should aim to encourage a diversity of financial service providers who can increase the options available to the poor. Policymakers should ensure that fewer entry barriers exist for new institutions, as in a tiered system of banking, while allowing sound existing institutions to develop appropriate banking services. Flexibility in terms of ownership regulations and reduced capital requirements should be the norm for service providers that reach out to the poor. Tax incentives could also be provided to encourage more inclusive microfinance-type lending, by commercial banks. Concurrently, the Government might also encourage widespread use of information and communications technologies to provide "branchless banking" services to the poor in villages and in remote areas through innovative partnerships with NGOs, microfinance institutions, post offices, telecommunications companies and other local entities such as village shopkeepers. A new range of products and services to help the poor improve their livelihood can be provided such as mobile banking services, microsavings, microcredit, microrepayment, microremittances and microinsurance.[150].

Governments could aim to improve the banking architecture by establishing institutions that facilitate financial inclusiveness such as credit bureaus and credit guarantee funds for microfinance activities. The regulatory environment could be improved with accounting and audit standards for microfinance institutions and other potential new entrants for financial inclusiveness. Governments might also undertake large-scale financial literacy campaigns to equip the poor to benefit from financial inclusiveness. Banks could be encouraged to offer convenient branches along transportation routes and provide mobile banks, on vans, boats or other appropriate vehicles, to extend their reach to the poor and in remote areas.

---

[150]   ESCAP, "Theme Study" for the Sixty-sixth Commission Session (forthcoming).

Enhanced access of the excluded poor through microfinance and microinsurance, among other means, may protect them against the vulnerabilities that they face and assist them in exploiting opportunities for self-employment. Many successful experiments in Asia and the Pacific are enhancing financial inclusiveness. The scope is wide for sharing the best practices for everyone's benefit.

EXPANDING DEMAND THROUGH COOPERATION

Some might say that the policy recommendations discussed above would be more feasible in certain countries than in others because of the heterogeneity of the Asia-Pacific region. Larger countries, especially those with high savings and overall prudent macroeconomic objectives, are much more likely to be able to rebalance growth strategies to enhance the domestic consumption of the poor than are smaller countries. Similarly, countries with more developed and technically advanced economies have a higher potential for innovating and adapting green technologies that are likely to be in high demand in future. Smaller and less developed countries are less likely to be able to implement such policies on their own. Those countries did not exhibit the same resilience during the crisis and went into recession. At the same time, vast opportunities remain untapped in those countries. Benefits could be garnered from the markets and dynamism of their larger and more advanced counterparts. In turn, their comparative advantages to bring enhanced efficiencies to regional supply chains would benefit the larger and more advanced countries in a mutually supportive manner. Action needs to be taken to unlock those potential developments.

The case has been made for Asian and Pacific countries to embark on a new development paradigm whose strategic goal is to become a more integrated and competitive matrix which can generate its own rapid growth that is inclusive and sustainable.

Boosting regional economic integration has become an imperative: the region needs to find new sources of economic growth from within

Boosting regional economic integration has become an imperative: the region needs to find new sources of economic growth from within. To date the connections with Europe and North America have been better than with each other. Until the global recession hit, that pattern served the region well. Historical, political and topographical reasons have played their part – the orientation of maritime transport networks, for example, has been directed towards the major seaports which in turn provided connections onward to Europe, North America and elsewhere. Furthermore, the emergence of new countries since the Second World War has engendered non-physical barriers, such as regulatory controls, at new borders where previously transport networks had been relatively well connected. The physical and non-physical barriers to trade and transport have significantly increased the costs of moving goods across borders, which in turn has induced reductions in the volumes of intra- and inter-regional overland trade. In the financial sphere the case is no different: massive savings in the region had to be invested in low-interest debt of the United States and other developed countries (albeit to a lesser extent in the latter) because of the relatively less developed state of regional financial architecture, despite the huge investment needs of the region. There are serious institutional, market and policy obstacles to channelling those savings to more profitable and socially desirable investments within the region. Large investment opportunities with higher returns are available in the region, but first the issues of availability of finance, its costs, overall risk perceptions and enabling conditions for wider public-private partnerships must be addressed.

In sum, obstacles at the regional level persist. The deficiencies are part of existing development gaps. They cover a wide spectrum of constraints in the institutional and physical infrastructure as well as existing policy obstacles. Addressing the deficiencies should be delayed no longer because the benefits of economic integration need to be spread among low-income economies and the vast swathes of poor people who remain far behind – living on less than $1.25 per day. The future of the region depends on narrowing those gaps.

The remaining pages of this *Survey* focus on identifying opportunities and proposing the regional actions that Governments, regional organizations such as the Association of Southeast Asian Nations (ASEAN) and SAARC, and institutions such as ESCAP and ADB could facilitate in reforming the policy agenda. Four elements are presented here that could leverage complementarities across the region and lay the foundations for an inclusive and sustainable path for development.

Evolving a broader framework for economic integration

Asia and the Pacific have lagged behind other regions in exploiting the potential of regional economic integration – Europe, North America, South America and Africa have all established some form of customs unions and even monetary unions.

Cooperation in the Asia-Pacific region is fostered by such groups as ASEAN in South-East Asia, SAARC in South Asia and the Bay of Bengal Initiative for Multi-Sectoral Technical and Economic Cooperation (BIMSTEC) in South and South-East Asia that promote regional trading and investment arrangements. Among them ASEAN is the most advanced in economic cooperation with plans of forming an ASEAN Economic Community by 2015. Besides deepening economic integration between member countries, ASEAN is bringing together six large Asian and Pacific economies as partners (Japan, China, the Republic of Korea, India, Australia and New Zealand) and negotiating "ASEAN+1" free-trade agreements with them. The interaction has also encouraged many other bilateral free-trade agreements among ASEAN and its

partners or among the partners themselves, resulting is an Asian "noodle bowl" phenomenon. Other trade arrangements are developing, such as the Asia-Pacific Trade Agreement (APTA) under ESCAP auspices, that brings together Bangladesh, India, Sri Lanka, China, the Republic of Korea and the Lao People's Democratic Republic, with Mongolia among others, showing interest. Functional groupings such as the Asian Cooperation Dialogue (ACD) promote regional cooperation in specific sectors.

Despite the complex network of political groupings, Asian and Pacific leaders have articulated a vision through various fora, of a unified economic space that would evolve over time. Moving from vision to action requires identifying an approach whereby all perceive that the economic and social benefits override geopolitical sensitivities.

With growth poles such as China and India along with economic powerhouses like Japan, a unified Asia-Pacific market has the potential to emerge as a centre of gravity in the world economy

With growth poles such as China and India along with economic powerhouses like Japan, a unified Asia-Pacific market has the potential to emerge as a centre of gravity in the world economy. Two proposals are helping to broaden the regional arrangements driven by ASEAN: (1) an East Asia free-trade agreement (EAFTA) that would ally ASEAN+3 countries and is being considered in the ASEAN+3 summit framework; and (2) a comprehensive economic partnership of East Asia (CEPEA) that would cover a free-trade agreement, trade facilitation and economic cooperation and would combine ASEAN with its partners Australia, China, Japan, India, New Zealand and the Republic of Korea in the East Asia Summit (EAS) framework. At their last meeting in Hua Hin, Thailand, in October 2009, the EAS leaders examined the EAFTA and

CEPEA proposals.[151] Independent simulation studies using general equilibrium models show that EAFTA and CEPEA hold significant welfare gains for their member countries. Higher welfare gains were reported for CEPEA compared with alternative options, probably because of synergies brought by additional members such as India, Australia and New Zealand and indeed the larger market.[152] In the wake of the current crisis, steps towards formation of a unified market and broadening of economic cooperation should be expedited.

Developing regional transportation networks and improving trade facilitation

Intercountry transport and infrastructural issues are increasingly the focus of attention; in particular, removing regulatory barriers to trade and transport and improving the efficiency of trans-port operations. Intraregional transport networks are being formalized, intercountry transport is being upgraded, missing links are being constructed, trade facilitation agreements are being formulated and implemented, and transport logistics are improving.

After decades in negotiation, the ESCAP Intergovernmental Agreement on the Asian Highway Network and the ESCAP Intergovernmental Agreement on the Trans-Asian Railway Network entered into force in 2005 and 2009, respectively (figure 66). While agreements are important elements in increasing regional connectivity, much remains to be done in actually building the infrastructure. The magnitude of investment in physical infrastructure required to realize such transport connectivity is huge. An ESCAP study found that in a list of 121 high-priority projects in 25 countries to develop sections of Asian

FIGURE 66. Asian Highway and Trans-Asian Railway Networks

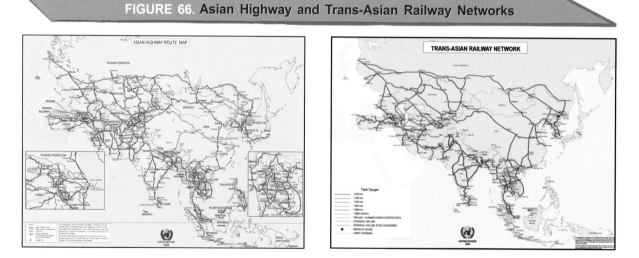

Source: ESCAP.

[151] Chairman's Statement of the 4th East Asia Summit, Cha-am, Thailand, 25 October 2009; available from www.aseansec.org/23609.htm.

[152] Kawai, Masahiro, and Ganeshan Wignaraja, "ASEAN+3 or ASEAN+6: which way forward?", ADB Institute Discussion Paper No. 77 (Tokyo: 2007), available from www.adbi.org/files/dp77.asean.3.asean.6.pdf; and Kumar, Nagesh, "Towards broader regional cooperation in Asia", RIS Discussion Paper.(Colombo: Asia-Pacific Trade and Investment Initiative, 2007), available from www.ris.org.in/tbrcia.pdf.

Highway routes, member States were already investing or had committed to invest $25 billion. However, the study found that an additional $18 billion was necessary in upgrading and improving 26,000 km of the existing Highway. For the Trans-Asian Railway, similar levels of investment need to be budgeted to build the missing links, upgrade existing routes and, most significantly, ensure interoperability across borders.

Trade procedures involved in moving goods from the factory to the closest seaport take an average of over 60 days in landlocked countries

Without sound legal and regulatory bases for vehicles, goods and people to cross borders and transit countries, no international traffic can move along the infrastructure. Decades of policy focus in many countries on trade with developed countries that transits seaports and airports has resulted in neglect of trade issues with land borders. Slow and costly processes, formalities and procedures hinder movement of goods. That translates into a big disadvantage, particularly for landlocked countries where trade procedures involved in moving goods from the factory to the closest seaport take an average of over 60 days, nearly twice the average for Asian and Pacific developing countries and 10 times more than in Singapore. The complex procedures increase transactional costs and create opportunities for rent-seeking that discourage cross-border trade. Ultimately, the considerable welfare loss on account of trade transaction costs and time delays may wipe out the benefits of trade liberalization in the region. In addition, physical and regulatory barriers to trade are an obstacle for the development of border areas.

Even before the entry into force of the network Agreements, member countries have considered "essential that Governments take a leading role in more effectively integrating the different forms of transport in order to develop sustainable intermodal transport systems that deliver efficient domestic transport services and at the same time provide access to international markets and wider hinterlands".[153] The value of setting a long-term vision for an international, integrated, intermodal transport system in Asia and the Pacific has been recognized by successive Ministerial Conferences. The development of such an integrated system requires intermodal transfer points where goods, containers or vehicles can be trans-shipped onto the most economical and energy-efficient mode of transport for specific segments of their movement from origin to destination. The transfer points connecting different inland transportation modes like highways, railways or waterways are known as "dry ports".

Dry ports are equipped to transfer goods, containers and vehicles between modes. They have customs clearance facilities that give them a similar status to seaports or international airports. They may also provide facilities for product grading, sorting and packaging. The areas surrounding dry ports may develop into special economic zones that provide opportunities to act as growth poles in the deeper hinterland. In a number of countries and country groups in the region, the concept of the transport corridor is being adopted. Examples include the domestic Mumbai-New Delhi corridor in India; the North-South, East-West and other corridors of the Greater Mekong Subregion (GMS);[154] and the six Central Asia Regional Economic Cooperation Corridors (CAREC).[155] Economic corridors linking dry ports can become valuable means of inclusive growth that spread economic activity to the hinterland and bring new investment and employment opportunities to impoverished regions, while reducing pressure on the coastal areas.

---

[153] Seoul Declaration on Infrastructure Development in Asia And The Pacific, adopted at the Ministerial Conference on Infrastructure held at Seoul from 12 to 17 November 2001, E/ESCAP/MCI(2)/Rep., 6 December 2001.

[154] GMS comprises Cambodia, China (Yunnan Province and Guangxi Zhuang Autonomous Region), the Lao People's Democratic Republic, Myanmar, Thailand, and Viet Nam.

[155] CAREC comprises Afghanistan, Azerbaijan, China, Kazakhstan, Kyrgyzstan, Mongolia, Tajikistan and Uzbekistan.

Trade and transport facilitation is the other side of the connectivity coin. Facilitation at land borders has taken second priority to issues of trade with developed countries that transits seaports and airports. The problems usually result from complicated, lengthy and frequently changing procedures and documentation, different requirements in different countries, duplicated inspections, and high charges. In some countries, traded goods have to be trans-loaded near border crossings because trucks of some countries are not permitted to cross borders or only permitted to travel a short distance in other countries.

Too often has trade facilitation been narrowly interpreted as the modernization of customs clearance and technical controls at the border. Actually such procedures account for less than one fifth of the time needed to move goods from factory to ship. The most time is taken in preparation of documents required for imports and exports, because of the large number of agencies and organizations involved[156] that deal with trade, transport, customs, immigration, security, health, veterinary and phytosanitary issues, and produce quality, as well as the private sector. Its very multiplicity increases the difficulty in identifying and addressing bottlenecks in documentation processes across entire international trade and transport chains. A more comprehensive approach to trade facilitation adopted in many countries focuses on enhancing coordination and collaboration between the official agencies involved as well as between those agencies and the providers of transportation, logistics, conformity assessment and financial services. The Republic of Korea, for example, has implemented an electronic "single-window" system that links users with more than 60 Government and private-sector organizations.

Efficiency levels vary greatly in the mix of trade and transport facilitation in the region. Singapore and Hong Kong, China rank among the best performers in the world where export procedures take 6 days or less to complete and cost less than $650 per container on average; in comparison, the same job in the G-7 countries might take 10 days and cost $1,124. However, the region is also home to some of the worst performers whose export procedures consume more than 75 days on average and cost over $3,000. On average, export procedures in Asian and Pacific developing countries take more than 3 times longer to complete than in G-7 countries. The huge difference stems partly from the volume of documents required in completing import and export procedures. Asian and Pacific firms also face trading costs that are on average 17% higher than those in the G-7 countries.

ASEAN leaders recognize the region's potential to flourish as a hub, at the crossroads of an economically vibrant region bounded by India to the west, China, Japan and the Republic of Korea in the northeast; and Australia and New Zealand in the south. At its Summit in October 2009, ASEAN established the High-Level Task Force together with ADB, ESCAP and the Economic Research Institute for ASEAN and East Asia (ERIA) to study ASEAN's internal and external connectivity and to develop an ASEAN master plan on regional connectivity.[157]

The imperative to strengthen regional connectivity assumes new relevance as the value of regional synergies and sources of demand emerges in the aftermath of the global crisis. Streamlining the flow of goods and services across the region, as well as exploiting the potential of investments in developing physical infrastructure, serves one of the key strategies for recovery: augmenting the aggregate demand. Governments need to identify the gaps in the Asian Highway and TransAsian Railway networks, prioritize them and act to develop them, besides strengthening the trade and transport facilitation at the borders.

---

[156] Examples include health authorities, agencies and service providers involved in ensuring conformity with product standards prevailing in the destination country, port authorities, banks and immigration services.

[157] See ASEAN Leaders' Statement on ASEAN Connectivity, Cha-am, Hua Hin, Thailand, 24 October 2009.

Strengthening connectivity through information and communications technology (ICT)

Although the world had reached unprecedented levels of ICT penetration by the end of 2008, with over 4 billion mobile cellular subscriptions, 1.3 billion fixed telephone lines and close to one quarter of the world's population using the Internet, major imbalances across and within countries remained.[158] In all economies mobile phone use has increased tremendously, facilitating the expansion of markets, business and public services. On average, the Asia-Pacific region has over 50 mobile subscribers per 100 persons, but access to mobile communication ranges widely in the region from as low as 0.8 subscribers per 100 persons in Myanmar and Kiribati to 177 in Macao, China. The digital divide is even starker regarding access to Internet services. In 2008, there were 78 Internet users per 100 persons in the Republic of Korea, 69 in Japan, 67 in Singapore and 63 in Malaysia, compared with only 0.5 in Cambodia, 0.3 in Bangladesh and 0.1 in Myanmar and Timor-Leste. Broadband subscribers in the region are still few: about 4 subscribers per 100 persons and an average of only 0.02 for least-developed countries.

The extent to which a country connects with the region and the rest of the world can be gauged by its available international bandwidth, which varies enormously by country. Low bandwidth further limits the extension of Internet use since many developing countries rely on content and applications from overseas. A number of initia-

tives are under way to increase bandwidth capacity available to Asian and Pacific countries, such as the recently concluded Asia-America Gateway Cable System which links the United States with several South-East Asian countries,[159] and initiatives to reutilize underused cables, especially first-generation fibre-optic cables that connect underserved Pacific islands developing countries with global telecommunications networks.[160]

In parallel with increasing external connectivity is a push by Governments to share or expand backbone infrastructure, in many cases through regional ICT cooperation. One such example is the Greater Mekong Subregion Information Superhighway project; it reached an important milestone recently in inaugurating a fibre-optic network with a transmission speed of 620 Mbps and construction and upgrades of stations along the route, linking Cambodia, the Lao People's Democratic Republic, Myanmar, Viet Nam, Thailand and Yunnan Province of China.[161]

Besides facilitating the expansion of markets and business opportunities, ICT connectivity can play a role in bringing social and economic benefits and in poverty reduction. For instance, the South Asia Subregion Economic Cooperation (SASEC) Information Highway project for India, Bangladesh, Nepal and Bhutan aims to set up village networks that are expected to expand broadband wireless connectivity to rural communities and improve their access to services such as telemedicine, distance learning, and e-government services.[162]

ICT connectivity can also play a key role in connecting remote communities and providing

[158] International Telecommunications Union, *Trends in Telecommunication Reform 2009: Hands-on or Hands-off? Stimulating Growth through Effective ICT Regulation,* 10th ed. (Geneva: 2009); available from www.itu.int/publ/D-REG-TTR.11-2009/en.

[159] Othman, Azlan, "Tests completed on Asia-America gateway", *Brudirect.com,* 11 Nov. 2009; available from www.brudirect.com/index.php/2009111110259/Local-News/tests-completed-on-asia-america-gateway.html.

[160] ESCAP, *Enhancing Pacific Connectivity: the Current Situation, Opportunities for Progress,* Sales No. E.08.II.F.14 (Bangkok: 2008); available from www.unescap.org/idd/Pubs/st_escap_2472.pdf.

[161] Xinhua News Agency, "Cambodia, China complete phase 1 of GMS Information Highway Project", *People's Daily Online,* 15 July 2009; available from http://english.people.com.cn/90001/90776/90883/6701499.html.

[162] *iGovernment,* "Four South Asian countries to set up info-highway", New Delhi, 16 October 2007; available from www.igovernment.in/site/four-south-asian-countries-to-set-up-info-highway/.

them with access to educational services. For instance, the University of the South Pacific network links 14 campuses in 12 countries (Cook Islands, Fiji, Kiribati, the Marshall Islands, Nauru, Niue, Solomon Islands, Tokelau, Tonga, Tuvalu, Vanuatu and Samoa) through satellite-based ICT, providing audio- and video-conferencing, e-curricula, e-learning materials and Internet services.[163]

Countries are committed to intraregional connectivity to enhance regional integration and economic growth in the near future. For instance, the ASEAN ICT Master Plan 2010-2015 will reinforce the role of ICT for ASEAN integration. Their initiatives will also lead into still undeveloped potential for ICT: supporting early-warning systems for disaster-preparedness with emergency procedures and response activities (box 9).

BOX 9. Connectivity for improved disaster preparedness, response and management

In the first half of 2009, Asia and the Pacific saw 40 disasters that killed more than 1,000 people and affected 5.9 million other lives. The economic damages were estimated at more than $1,500 million.[a] In September 2009, the region experienced multiple disasters over a brief time. Typhoon Ketsana hit the Philippines, Viet Nam, Cambodia and the Lao People's Democratic Republic. A tsunami struck Samoa, American Samoa and Tonga. Two massive earthquakes rocked Sumatra, followed by devastating typhoons the next month that affected South-East Asian countries. All those disasters eroded social and economic development efforts leading toward achieving the Millennium Development Goals.

Despite rapid expansion in telecommunication connectivity, ICT tools have not been fully used to reduce the impact of disasters. Capacity is insufficient for analysing and interpreting data for evidence-based policymaking and decision-making. Access to telecommunication networks is limited during disasters. The challenges underline the need for Asian and Pacific countries to enhance regional connectivity and jointly address disaster preparedness, response and management that builds on the strengths of each country.

The ASEAN Agreement on Disaster Management and Emergency Response (AADMER) is an exemplary mechanism. The first of its kind in the world, AADMER is a regional agreement that legally binds ASEAN member States together to promote regional cooperation and collaboration in reducing disaster losses and intensifying joint emergency response to disasters in the ASEAN region. AADMER provides for disaster risk identification, monitoring and early warning, prevention and mitigation, preparedness and response, rehabilitation, technical cooperation and research, mechanisms for coordination, and simplified customs and immigration procedures. AADMER also supports the establishment of the ASEAN Coordinating Centre for Humanitarian Assistance for operational coordination of disaster management activities under the ASEAN Agreement. AADMER entered into force at the end of 2009.

Asian and Pacific countries could also leverage ICT resources and services that are available regionally and globally by joining cooperative mechanisms and capacity-building programmes for disaster risk management being promoted by ESCAP, such as the Regional Space Applications Programme for Sustainable Development and the Sentinel Asia project, as well as the United Nations Platform for Space-based Information for Disaster Management and Emergency Response being executed by the United Nations Office for Outer Space Affairs. Tsunami-prone countries can seek support from sources such as the ESCAP Trust Fund for Tsunami, Disaster and Climate Preparedness in strengthening their multi-hazard capacities and creating a regional early warning system for tsunami and other hazards.

[a] CRED, November 2009.

---

[163] The University of the South Pacific, "USP – an introduction"; available from www.usp.ac.fj/index.php?id=usp_introduction.

Developing financial architecture for crisis prevention and narrowing the gaps

The crisis has revealed the glaring lack of financial tools available at regional level, beyond those in the hands of Governments. While some countries had built up sufficient reserves to protect their balance of payments, less fortunate countries had no recourse to regional sources of assistance given the dearth of monetary and financial cooperation. The Asian Clearing Union, for example, has few members, remains focused on the settlement of payments on trade transactions among members, and does not deal with exchange-rate stability. The Asian Bond Fund, another regional initiative, remains small in scale and cannot yet serve as a credible and cost-effective source of financing. The Chiang Mai Initiative (CMI) of ASEAN+3 (APT), the clearest example of a regional financial cooperation scheme, remains insufficiently developed as a first source of assistance; some members found alternative sources of support as discussed in chapter 1. The crisis also highlighted how the lack of well-developed regional financial architecture prevented efficient intermediation between the region's expanding foreign exchange reserves and its substantial unmet investment needs, thus leaving the central banks no option but to invest their reserves in United States Treasury bills and equivalent securities in the West that earn poor, if not negative, returns in real terms. In the aftermath of the crisis and need for augmenting aggregate demand in the region, the function of regional intermediation acquires a degree of criticality. Besides crisis prevention and intermediation between savings and investment in the region, a regional financial architecture could also be instrumental in exchange-rate coordination and in evolving a regional perspective and coordinated voice for reform of international financial architecture.

Enhanced regional cooperation should not be regarded as an alternative to full participation in global economic relations, but rather a comple-

ment, for filling in the gaps and putting in place building blocks for multilateral cooperation at the global level. That was clearly recognized in the Outcome Document of the United Nations Conference on World Financial and Economic Crisis and Its Impact (2009):[164]

> Given the sensitivity of regional and subregional institutions to the specific needs of their constituencies, we note the value of regional and subregional cooperation efforts in meeting the challenges of the global economic crisis and we encourage enhanced regional and subregional cooperation, for example, through regional and subregional development banks, commercial and reserve currency arrangements, and other regional initiatives, as contributions to the multilateral response to the current crisis and to improved resilience to potential future crises.

Some of the elements needed for policy reform action are discussed below.

Crisis prevention and management

For effective prevention of systemic crises, a regional crisis fund should include as many countries of the region as possible. The quantum of funds should be sufficient for the fund to act as the lender of first recourse in the event of macroeconomic or balance-of-payment difficulty. The fund should ideally include support for domestic financial sectors in its remit, in addition to balance-of-payments support to Governments, to enable assistance to banks as was undertaken by Governments in the United States and Europe during the current crisis. The fund would require a physical infrastructure with well-qualified staff to engage in monitoring of emerging trends prior to and during crises, as well as design of the terms associated with the support provided to Governments in the region. Availability of a well-endowed regional crisis-

---

[164]   United Nations Conference on the World Financial and Economic Crisis and Its Impact on Development, "The world financial and economic crisis and its impact on development: Report of the Secretary-General", A/CONF.214/4, 24-26 June 2009.

response facility could reduce pressure on Governments to build large foreign-exchange reserves for protecting their economies against speculative attacks and liquidity crises.

The crisis has provided a window of opportunity for creating an effective regional crisis-response fund. Although the opportunity became available right after the 1997 crisis, the relatively rapid return of economic growth resulted in a loss of policy urgency. The multilateralization of the APT CMI reserves pool in its present form could evolve into a truly effective first line of defence for the region, if its geographical coverage, size and functions were expanded. As long ago as the eighth APT Finance Ministers' Meeting in Istanbul in May 2005, there was an agreement to re-evaluate the process, including the possibility of regionalizing the arrangements.[165] There was agreement on looking into developing a collective mechanism to activate the swaps. The need to improve on the extent of regional dialogue and surveillance was also recognized, and to link them more closely and effectively with the CMI. Progress on those issues was slight until recently. At the APT Finance Ministers' Meeting in Bali, Indonesia in May 2009, the APT countries reached an agreement to transform the existing bilateral arrangements into a regional foreign reserve pool of $120 billion to "address short-term liquidity difficulties in the region and to supplement the existing international financial arrangements".[166] The CMI multilateralization (CMIM) came into effect on 24 March 2010.

The "Plus-Three" countries of China, Japan and the Republic of Korea are committed to funding 80%, to the pool while the 10 ASEAN members will share the remaining 20%. Of that amount, Japan will contribute $38.4 billion to the pool, as will China (in conjunction with Hong Kong, China). Japan has also extended $60 billion

worth of yen-denominated swap facilities separately. The Republic of Korea will contribute $19.2 billion. Within ASEAN, Indonesia, Malaysia, Thailand and Singapore will each contribute $4.77 billion and the Philippines will give $3.68 billion. Other details remain unclear, though the same conditions as with the CMI remain (i. e., 20% unrestricted borrowing and 80% balance only with IMF conditionalities). Importantly, the regional economies have agreed to create a stronger regional surveillance system in conjunction with the ADB and the ASEAN Secretariat "to monitor and analyze regional economies and support CMIM decision-making".[167] Presumably if and when this surveillance system is effectively established, the 20% of reserve that can be tapped without IMF conditionality will be increased.

Availability of a well-endowed regional crisis-response facility could reduce pressure on Governments to build large foreign-exchange reserves

Since the region holds reserves of almost $5 trillion, the proposed reserve fund has the potential for significant expansion over time. Expansion of membership to include key countries such as India also needs to be resolved if the CMIM is to evolve into a truly regional reserve pool. The pool could involve three tiers of liquidity. The first tier would be CMIM-owned reserves, which offer the highest degree of liquidity and have zero conditionality; however, that would be costly. The second tier would consist of all the countries' own reserves placed with the regional pool. The third tier would be con-

[165] ASEAN, Joint Ministerial Statement of the 8th ASEAN+3 Finance Ministers' Meeting, Istanbul, Turkey, 4 May 2005, available at http://www.aseansec.org/17448.htm.

[166] ASEAN, Joint Media Statement of the 12th ASEAN+3 Finance Ministers' Meeting, Bali, Indonesia, 3 May 2009; available from: http://www.aseansec.org/22536.htm.

[167] Ibid., paragraph 9.

ventional IMF lending via its various facilities.[168] With such a structure the degree of liquidity could be inversely related to the degree of conditionality. Such a regional reserve or insurance pool would help supplement the ongoing restructured/new IMF lending facilities to fortify the regional economies against future financial crises.

Effective deepening of regional monetary integration will not happen until there is considerable strengthening of the regional surveillance mechanism with well-worked-out surveillance and policy conditionality. The announcement of strengthening of surveillance alongside the creation of the CMIM is therefore an important step. Nonetheless, surveillance in itself is insufficient if it lacks enforcement capacity that would enable implementation of remedial action for member countries that might be running unsustainable policies.

There is the equally hard issue of what such a regional liquidity arrangement implies for exchange-rate coordination. Countries with relatively stable fixed exchange rates would require somewhat greater reserves in managing their currencies and/or pursue much more disciplined domestic economic policies, while countries running more flexible regimes could potentially cause or be faced with competitiveness pressures in the near term vis-à-vis the others, if their currencies were to appreciate or depreciate sharply.

Regional funding of development gaps

The crisis has exposed the need for regional cooperation in funding action to close development gaps in an effort to augment aggregate demand while fostering balanced and sustainable development. The region's stock of foreign exchange reserves becomes particularly important if funding from foreign sources, through official assistance and the private sector, is likely to be curtailed by resource constraints in the developed world in the aftermath of the crisis. To exploit the full potential of financial cooperation, financing regional integration and development, countries need to strike a collective balance between, on the one hand, emerging investment opportunities especially in regional public goods and, on the other, rising foreign-exchange reserves.

Until the crisis struck, the lack of depth in regional capital markets, and resulting perceptions of risks and costs, drove regional funds to investments in developed countries. Far greater emphasis must be given to integrating regional equity markets and fostering the development of local-currency bond markets at the regional level. Intraregional investment in local currency bonds has remained small because of excessive legal and institutional impediments, as well as the lack of investment information.[169] The Asian Bond Market Initiative (ABMI),[170] intended to foster growth of local currency bond markets, has moved slowly as countries have remained preoccupied with addressing issues of harmonization of rules and regulations. The ABMI has not spurred private investment as much as hoped because transparency in its investment targets and fund performance is lacking. Nevertheless an excessive emphasis on growing capital markets in the region may increase the risk of financial instability for economies by opening themselves more to speculation. In sum, the crisis makes a persuasive case for a return to fundamentals to ensure stability through greater use of the banking system, combined with effective regulations, to recycle regional savings into regional investments.

---

[168] Rajan, R., and R. Siregar, "Centralized reserve pooling for the ASEAN+3 (APT) countries", in *Monetary and Financial Integration in East Asia,* vol. 1, *The Way Ahead* (Manila: ADB; United Kingdom: Palgrave McMillan; 2004), pp. 33-34.

[169] Arner, Douglas, Paul Lejot, and S. Ghon Rhee, *Impediments to Cross-border Investments in Asian Bonds* (Singapore: Institute of Southeast Asian Studies, 2005), chap. 4, pp. 21-50.

[170] For general information, see ADB presentation, available from www.adbi.org/conf-seminar-papers/2005/06/17/1167.asean.abmi.presentation/.

One of the clearest alternative uses for some portion of these assets, both for domestic development and for increasing regional integration, lies in funding for the massive infrastructural needs across Asia and the Pacific. ESCAP has been at the forefront of analysis regarding that issue for some years.[171] Recent estimates indicate that the region needs an annual investment of more than $800 billion in transport, energy, water and telecommunications, with an annual shortfall of more than $200 billion.[172] A regional financial architecture can develop the capacity to facilitate intermediation between the region's foreign exchange reserves and the growing unmet investment requirements. The objective is to narrow the development gaps in the region while augmenting the aggregate demand. The architecture could include an infrastructure development fund managed by a regional institution. Mobilizing just 5% of the region's reserves – currently at nearly $5 trillion – would provide start-up capital of nearly $250 billion for the fund. It would be able to mobilize additional funds, as and when required, by issue of bonds to the central banks of the region to enable them to park their foreign-exchange reserves. By co-financing viable projects along with other sources, such an architecture could expedite investments in infrastructural development, especially in cross-border connectivity linking poorer parts of the Asia-Pacific region with regional growth centres.

In sum, reserve pooling may be directed towards the twin goals of crisis management and development finance, to enhance management of both roles in an integrated manner.

Trade finance

Another area in crisis management that lends itself to regional cooperation is trade finance. In the 1997 crisis, trade finance to the region seized up, although that was linked to perceptions of increased riskiness of domestic banks. Seizing up of trade finance in the current crisis, however, was not due to shortcomings of domestic banks but to generalized global unwillingness to lend between banks. The perceived risks involved in financing trade during the crisis could be considered a form of market failure. Hence, Governments could have a role to play in mitigating the harm in a future crisis from the paucity of trade finance. For instance, they could provide export credit insurance and guarantees as a way of lowering the commercial risk in financing trade.[173] Such countries as India, Indonesia and Thailand have already taken such actions. Since trade finance risks are shared among partners in different countries, regional collaboration has a role to play in this area. Asia and the Pacific remains the only developing region in the world without its own trade finance institution.

A new regional financial architecture could facilitate the intermediation between the region's foreign exchange reserves and unmet investment requirements to narrow development gaps

---

Regional exchange rate stability

Another pressing policy gap at the regional level which has been brought into relief by the crisis is the lack of mechanisms for exchange rate cooperation. During the economic recovery phase the pressure on countries to maintain exchange rate competitiveness in order not to impair the revival of exports will increase. Without cooperation the risk is that competitive devaluation may be instigated which may not yield

---

[171] ESCAP, *Enhancing Regional Cooperation in Infrastructure Development Including That Related to Disaster Management,* Sales No. E.06.II.F.13, ST/ESCAP/2408 (New York: United Nations; Bangkok: 2006).

[172] ADB and ADBI, *Infrastructure for a Seamless Asia* (Tokyo: 2009).

[173] ESCAP, *Economic and Social Survey 2009,* p. 35.

net benefits in the quantity of exports and instead result in lower domestic export receipts because of exchange-rate losses for each country.

Diverse exchange-rate arrangements exist in the region whose inherent incompatibility becomes evident especially in times of instability. At one extreme are independently floating currencies such as those of Japan, the Republic of Korea and the Philippines. At the other is Hong Kong, China which has a currency board operating an explicit peg to the United States dollar. In between are the tightly managed pegs of China and Malaysia and the relatively more flexible regimes of Thailand, India and Singapore. During large swings of the dollar, a high degree of instability ensues in Asian exchange rates (table 29).

As intraregional trade is expected to grow in future, it needs a currency management system that facilitates trade and macroeconomic stability vis-à-vis intraregional and extraregional trading partners. A possible approach for the region might be a basket parity relative to a number of reserve currencies, a band and a crawl of the exchange rate (a "BBC" regime). A basket of three reserve currencies could be targeted, instead of the dollar alone, with a common set of

weights determined on the basis of regional trade shares. Each country would announce a central parity vis-à-vis the basket and commit to keeping it within a unilaterally chosen band. There would be no restrictions over the choice of the exchange rate regime by individual countries; that is, each country would be free to choose its own regime with respect to the common basket. Here too, as with the dollar peg, changes among reserve currencies would not affect intraregional exchange rates: in other words, if each participant stabilized its currency vis-à-vis a common basket of reserve currencies, they would also stabilize against each other. The common basket peg would have the advantage of enhancing stability of effective exchange rates.

The BBC regime combines flexibility with stability. It allows the currency to fluctuate within a relatively narrow range while the central parity is shifted in response to changes in the underlying fundamentals and large, durable shocks. Such an approach has the potential to produce relatively stable intraregional currency values for an initial subgroup of participating countries that possess similar trade baskets, such as the major developing economies of East Asia. Required supporting arrangements, which would not be serious impediments, would include

TABLE 29. Regional currency swings during the crisis

	Dollar rates			Yuan rates		
	Boom	Bust	Recovery	Boom	Bust	Recovery
Chinese yuan	9.3	10.7	0.1	–	–	–
Indian rupee	19.2	−16.6	5.4	9.0	−26.2	5.4
Indonesian rupiah	−2.7	−20.0	20.2	−11.0	−27.7	20.0
Malaysian ringgit	10.0	−4.5	4.5	0.6	−13.8	4.5
Philippine peso	17.9	−3.0	−2.0	7.9	−12.4	−2.0
Singapore dollar	14.7	0.3	6.9	4.9	−9.5	6.8
S. Korean won	28.8	−33.5	20.9	17.8	−40.0	20.7
Taiwan dollar	5.9	−2.7	6.2	−3.2	−12.1	6.2
Thai baht	43.4	−14.3	6.3	30.9	−22.6	6.3

Note: Boom defined as January 2003 to July 2007, Bust as from August 2007 to February 2009, and Recovery as from March 2009 to September 2009.
Table adapted from Akyuz, 2009, "Capital Flows and Macroeconomic Management: National and Regional Policy Options, Presentation by Yilmaz Akyuz at ESCAP Regional Expert Group Meeting, 7-8 October 2008, Singapore".

greater intraregional capital-account openness and access to intraregional reserves by the basket of reserve currencies.[174]

For regional cooperation in exchange rates to be effective in supporting exports, all major exporting economies of the region would need to be included

---

For regional cooperation in exchange rates to be effective in supporting exports, all major exporting economies of the region would need to be included. China's return in the post-crisis period to its earlier managed-float system, would be a great help in supporting the recovery of Asia-Pacific exporting economies. During the crisis China maintained a relatively fixed exchange rate to ensure stability for its economy when capital flows were excessively volatile. Furthermore, China's return to the band system would help in promoting intraregional trade by further encouraging the economy's shift to a more consumption-led economy. Such a development would boost China as a source of final goods demand for exporting economies, besides assisting in macroeconomic management. It would also help the yuan gradually emerge as a regional and eventually global reserve currency. Such a trend could be critically important for the region in coming years as it looks within itself for sources of final demand to replace the curtailed post-crisis spending power of developed economies.

Management of capital flows

The potential for exchange-rate cooperation extends to the critical issue of managing ex-change-rate vulnerability to short-term capital in-flows. The frequency and magnitude of financial crises have given renewed and unprecedented vigour to proponents of restraining cross-border capital movements. The discussion of capital controls is highly complex with no definitive policy conclusion to date.

Restraints on capital movement may be divided into controls on capital account transactions per se ("capital controls") and controls on foreign currency transactions ("exchange con-trols"). Four key features of curbs on capital movement are whether they are (a) comprehen-sive or selective; (b) meant to be temporary or permanent; (c) imposed on outflows or inflows; and (d) direct/administrative or price-based.

In view of relatively robust recovery in Asia and the Pacific, the concern is that the huge volume of liquidity in developed countries from loose monetary policy will flow to the region in the form of short-term capital seeking good returns. Besides being highly volatile, such flows tend to put pressure on exchange rates of the host economies, as discussed in Chapter 1. Hence, debate on the relevance of measures to moder-ate such inflows is increasing. Numerous mechanisms for managing capital inflows could be considered, ranging from administrative measures such as introducing deposit require-ments on capital inflows, to market-based in-struments such as levying financial transaction taxes on inflows, including taxes that vary with the maturity period of the capital inflow or which are countercyclical; to "throw some sand in the well-greased wheels" of international markets, in the words of economist James Tobin who first proposed it.[175] Attention is being renewed to arrangements such as the Chilean unremuner-ated reserve requirements (URR) or *Encaje,* which appears to have been helpful in manag-

---

[174] Reference regarding the proposal and analysis in the preceding paragraphs is made to Akyuz, Yilmaz, "Exchange rate management, growth and stability: national and regional policy options in Asia", Policy Paper Series (Colombo: UNDP Regional Centre for Asia Pacific, 2009); available from www2.undprcc.lk/resource_centre/pub_pdfs/P1115.pdf.

[175] Tobin, James, "A proposal for international monetary reform", *Eastern Economic Journal,* vol. 4, Nos. 3-4, pp. 153-159.

ing capital surges when it was in place in the 1990s,[176] as well as Malaysian adoption of capital controls following the 1997 crisis.

Notwithstanding the merits and demerits of various options, the appropriate level at which to enact such controls must be considered. Since the first entrant tends to be affected adversely in a "prisoner's dilemma" type of situation, such measures yield optimal results when applied globally. Following an extensive debate on the relevance of such a tax to moderating the volatility of capital flows internationally,[177] the IMF was asked by the G-20 to examine the proposal. Besides moderating the volatility of flows, it has been argued that such taxes can generate valuable revenue for funding global public goods such as poverty reduction and other Millennium Development Goals. Given the scale of daily financial transactions, it has been estimated that even a very small tax can yield substantial revenue. In case a global consensus fails to emerge, Asian and Pacific countries can consider imposing such taxes regionally or even individually to moderate the instability caused by short-term capital flows, as Brazil has done recently. The IMF now acknowledges that controls on foreign capital in emerging economies can be part of the policy options available to Governments to counter the potentially negative economic and financial effects of sudden surges in capital.[178]

Evolving a regional perspective on reform of international financial architecture

The international community has addressed the reform agenda through a number of fora. Perhaps the most visible has been the emergence of G-20 as the premier forum on global economic policy coordination, including global financial and regulatory issues. The G-20 super-

sedes the G-8 and signals the systemic importance of major emerging countries in the Asia-Pacific region, with the accession of China, India, Turkey, Indonesia, the Republic of Korea and Australia to membership; besides Japan and the Russian Federation, already part of the G-8. Furthermore, the G-20 established the Financial Stability Board at the London Summit in April 2009 with members from the central banks and other financial regulatory agencies of all G-20 member Governments of the Asia-Pacific region. Notably, the membership of its predecessor the Financial Stability Forum included a single Asian country, Japan.

The Pittsburgh G-20 meeting held in September 2009 made further progress in strengthening cooperation in macroeconomic policies and giving a more influential agenda-setting role to major developing economies of Asia and the Pacific. An important reform undertaken there was establishment of a peer review mechanism of the economic policy framework of G-20 countries; for the first time, developing country members had the opportunity to review developed countries' policies and thus contribute to the transparency of regulatory policies and accountability of systemically important countries. Leaders also committed to a shift in the IMF quota share to emerging market and developing countries of at least 7%, although that has not yet come into force. Finally, in the short term, leaders pledged that fiscal stimulus of developed countries should not end prematurely as such an action would hurt developing nations the most.

In general, the region has acquired an increasingly important voice through the representation of its major economies at the global policymaking table. The enhanced role also places increased responsibility on those major economies. Regulatory regimes, financial and

---

[176] Bird, Graham, and Ramkishen S. Rajan, "Does FDI guarantee stability of international capital flows? Evidence from Malaysia", Centre for International Economic Studies Discussion Paper No. 0044 (South Australia: Adelaide University, 2000); available from www.adelaide.edu.au/cies/papers/0044.pdf.

[177] Heaney, Vince, "Tobin tax talk not without merit", *Financial Times,* 21 Dec. 2009, p. 24; available from www.ft.com/cms/s/0/06a8cade-ecc6-11de-8070-00144feab49a.html.

[178] Ostry, Jonathan D., and others, "Capital inflows: the role of controls", IMF Staff Position Note SPN/10/04, 19 Feb. 2010, p. 15; available from www.imf.org/external/pubs/ft/spn/2010/spn1004.pdf.

non-financial institutions and policymaking organs will all be subjected to more stringent performance and reporting requirements. Furthermore, those economies must deal with the expectations of other developing countries that are not part of the G-20 but expect progress in resolving shortcomings that continue to persist.

For example, reform of IMF conditionalities and other policies have not been tackled in sufficient scope. Some developing countries are asking for a new approach in removing conditionalities that could have procyclical effects.[179] In their view it would be more helpful for the IMF to focus on providing sufficient funds to support exchange rates while countries pursue expansionary policies to restart growth. Likewise, for economic crises a framework for debt standstills and cancellations should be worked out, to obviate the need for simultaneously dealing with debt repayments. Progress remains sketchy on other fronts, including the issue of how best to reduce the scale of financial trading, possibly through a global tax on financial transactions (a "Tobin" tax) to moderate the volatility as discussed above and the design of a new global reserve currency system. Overall, under the G-20 process, the structure of the current financial system has remained fundamentally unchanged. But at the same time the level of risk in the global financial system has grown, as the concentration of systemically important banks engaged in unregulated activities increased along with the bailouts given to them.

The list of drawbacks emphasizes that no one process can bring lasting change. Major drawbacks of the G-20 process include its limitation on membership and lack of a legal institutional structure, raising questions about its enforcement capacity.

Global cooperation on the future financial architecture needs to proceed in parallel tracks, so that countries that have been left out of the G-20 process can voice their views. The majority of the world's people who have been left out are from developing countries that are most dependent on globalization and yet are most at risk from its deficiencies. For that reason, in providing analysis and technical support and in building consensus through policy dialogues, the United Nations has an important complementary role. The United Nations Conference on the World Financial and Economic Crisis and Its Impact on Development was held in New York from 23-24 June 2009, preceded by the Commission of Experts of the President of the General Assembly on the Reform of International Monetary and Financial System; nearly all United Nations members could thus gather and devise a uniquely inclusive and comprehensive agenda for action.

The Conference was able to highlight the challenges faced by developing countries, especially the poorer ones. The meeting emphasized the plight of developing countries with the sudden reversal of private capital flows, large and volatile movements in exchange rates, falling revenues and reduced fiscal space for taking corrective measures. It called for a coordinated and comprehensive global response to focus on restoration of the flow of development finance without unwarranted conditionalities and on debt relief to developing countries for "fostering an inclusive, green and sustainable recovery"; among many other measures.

The Asia-Pacific region needs to formulate a position on the issues emerging around reform of the international monetary and financial architecture to promote stability and minimize the risk of future financial crisis. Debate continues on the relevance of a "Tobin tax" to moderate volatility and on curbing excessive risk-taking of financial institutions by restricting bank bonuses and introducing bank taxes. Debate also continues on diversifying currency reserves from the United States dollar to other currencies or to a

---

[179] A recent study has found that 31 of 41 IMF loan agreements with developing countries involved procyclical macroeconomic policies (Weisbrot, Mark, and others, *IMF-supported Macroeconomic Policies and the World Recession: a Look at Forty-One Borrowing Countries* [Washington, D. C.: Center for Economic and Policy Research, 2009], p. 4; available from www.cepr.net/documents/publications/imf-2009-10.pdf).

basket of currencies along the lines of the IMF Special Drawing Rights (SDRs). China has proposed the development of a transnational reserve currency system, based on a basket of the world's major currencies, similar to the current SDR scheme but with the basket of SDR currencies being expanded from the dollar, pound, euro and yen to include other Asian currencies.[180] The Russian Federation has also supported the idea of using an expanded basket of currencies as the basis for a global reserve system, with a similar expansion in the mix to include other currencies.[181] The Russian Federation and China have taken practical measures to support the increased use of SDRs as an additional reserve currency. For example, in the IMF sale of $150 billion of SDR bonds in July, China purchased $50 billion and the Russian Federation $10 billion, in effect diversifying their reserves from dollars to the basket of SDR currencies.

With 53 member States and 9 associate members, ESCAP could coordinate a common and inclusive Asian and Pacific voice that could contribute in building reform in the global financial architecture. ESCAP has provided a forum for the purpose: at its high-level policy dialogue in Dhaka from 18 to 20 January 2010, finance ministers and other senior officials of Asian and Pacific least developed countries produced a regional review of the Brussels Programme of Action on Least Developed Countries in which they raised their concerns about financing for development and sought representation at the newly established Financial Stability Board established by the G-20.

The development of regional financial architecture may help Asian and the Pacific countries in coordinating their views for a position in the discussion on international monetary reform and financial architecture. It may also help the region avoid disruptions in the flow of development finance and preserve macroeconomic stability. The aim is to resume the pre-crisis trajectory of regional growth and pursue the agenda of inclusive and sustainable development.

---

[180] Zhao Xiaochuan, "Reform the international monetary system" speech by the Governor of the People's Bank of China, 23 Mar. 2009; available from www.gov.cn/english/detail.asp?col=6500&id=178.

[181] Embassy of the Russian Federation in the Kingdom of Norway, President of Russia Dmitry Medvedev's address to St. Petersburg International Economic Forum, plenary session, 5 Jun. 2009; available from www.norway.mid.ru/news_fp/news_fp_124_eng.html.

"As a region, we must build upon our collective strengths if we are not only to recover from the present crisis, but build the foundations for a more inclusive and sustainable society for all peoples of Asia-Pacific"

Noeleen Heyzer
Under-Secretary-General of the United Nations and
Executive Secretary of the United Nations
Economic and Social Commission
for Asia and the Pacific

REFERENCES AND FURTHER READINGS

Abella, Manolo and Geoffrey Ducanes (2009). The effect of the global economic crisis on Asian migrant workers and Governments' responses. Technical Note. Bangkok: ILO Regional Office for Asia and the Pacific. Available from www.ilo.org/wcmsp5/groups/public/---asia/---ro-bangkok/documents/ meetingdocument/wcms_101731.pdf.

Agence France Press (2009a). SKorea unveils massive plan for green growth. *France24,* 6 July. Available from http://mobile.france24.com/en/node/4895801.

_____ (2009b). Global crisis hits African investment: UN. *News on African Politics,* 18 September. Available from www.africanpoliticsinfo.com/article/674708/?k=j83s12y12h94s27k02.

Ahmed, Mushir (2009). Grameen Shakti to launch solar power system in Dhaka, cities. *Bangladesh Economic News,* 26 June. Available from http://bangladesheconomy.wordpress.com/2009/06/26/grameen-shakti-to-launch-solar-power-system-in-dhaka-cities/.

Akyüz, Yilmaz (2008). *The Current Global Financial Crisis and Asian Developing Countries.* ESCAP Series on Inclusive and Sustainable Development No. 2. Bangkok. Available from www.unescap.org/pdd/publications/escap_series/ESCAP_ISD2_Akyuz_full.pdf.

_____ (2009). *Exchange Rate Management, Growth, and Stability: National and Regional Policy Options in Asia.* Colombo: UNDP Regional Centre for Asia Pacific. Available from www2.undprcc.lk/resource_centre/pub_pdfs/P1115.pdf.

_____ (2010). Global economic prospects: the recession may be over but where next? South Centre Research Paper 26. Available from www.southcentre.org/index.php?option=com_content&view=article&id=1250: global-economic-prospects-the-recession-may-be-over-but-where-next&catid=142:global-financial-and-economic-crisis&Itemid=67&lang=en.

Anand, Sudhir, and Amartya K. Sen (1994a). Human development index: methodology and measurement. Human Development Report Office Occasional Papers. New York: UNDP. Available from http://economics.ouls.ox.ac.uk/12469/1/HDI_methodology.pdf.

_____ (1994b). Sustainable human development: concepts and priorities. UNDP Human Development Report Office. Available from http://hdr.undp.org/docs/publications/ocational_papers/Oc8a.htm.

Anriquez, Gustavo, and Kostas Stamoulis (2007). Rural development and poverty reduction: is agriculture still the key? ESA Working Paper No. 07-02. Rome: FAO. Available from ftp://ftp.fao.org/docrep/fao/010/ah885e/ah885e.pdf.

Arner, Douglas, Paul Lejot and S. Ghon Rhee (2005). *Impediments to Cross-border Investments in Asian Bonds.* Singapore: Institute of Southeast Asian Studies.

Aschauer, David Alan (1989). Is public expenditure productive? *Journal of Monetary Economics,* vol. 23, No. 2 (March), pp. 177-200.

Asia-Pacific Economic Cooperation (2009). *2009 Leaders' Declaration: A new growth paradigm for a connected Asia-Pacific in the 21st century.* Statement by APEC Leaders. Singapore, 14-15 Nov. Available from www.apec.org/apec/leaders__declarations/2009/aelm_growthparadigm.html.

Asia-Pacific Research and Training Network on Trade (ARTNeT; 2009). APTIAD Interactive Trade Indicators. Available from www.unescap.org/tid/artnet/artnet_app/iti_aptiad.aspx.

Asian Development Bank (2008a). The US financial crisis, global financial turmoil, and developing Asia: is the era of high growth at an end? ADB Economics Working Paper Series, No. 139. Manila.

_____ (2008b). *Emerging Asia Regionalism: a Partnership for Shared Prosperity.* Manila. Available from www.aric.adb.org/emergingasianregionalism.

_____ (2009a). *Asian Development Outlook 2009: Rebalancing Asia's Growth.* Manila. Available from www.adb.org/Documents/Books/ADO/2009/.

_____ (2009b). *Asian Development Outlook 2009 Update: Broadening Openness for a Resilient Asia.* Manila. Available from www.adb.org/Documents/Books/ADO/2009/update/default.asp.

_____ (2009c). *Key Indicators for Asia and the Pacific 2009.* Manila. Available from www.adb.org/Documents/ Books/Key_Indicators/2009/default.asp.

_____ (2009d). *Pacific Economic Monitor,* No. 3 (November). Available from www.adb.org/Documents/Reports/ PacMonitor/pem-issue03.asp.

_____ (2010a). Central Asia Regional Economic Cooperation (CAREC). Available from www.adb.org/carec/ about.asp.

_____ (2010b). *Pacific Economic Monitor,* No. 4 (February). Available from www.adb.org/Documents/Reports/ PacMonitor/pem-issue04.asp.

_____ , Asia Regional Integration Center (2009a). *Asia Economic Monitor* (July). Available from http:// aric.adb.org/pdf/aem/jul09/Jul_AEM_complete.pdf.

_____ , Asia Regional Integration Center (2009b). *Asia Economic Monitor* (December). Available from http:// aric.adb.org/pdf/aem/dec09/Dec_AEM_complete.pdf.

_____ and Asian Development Bank Institute (2009). *Infrastructure for a Seamless Asia.* Tokyo: ADBI. Available from www.iadb.org/intal/intalcdi/PE/2009/03979.pdf.

Association of Southeast Asian Nations (2005). The Joint Ministerial Statement of the 8th ASEAN+3 Finance Ministers' Meeting, Istanbul, Turkey, 4 May. Available from www.aseansec.org/17448.htm.

_____ (2009a). The Joint Media Statement of the 12th ASEAN+3 Finance Ministers' Meeting, Bali, Indonesia, 3 May. Available from www.aseansec.org/22536.htm.

_____ (2009b). Chairman's statement, the 10th ASEAN Plus Three Foreign Ministers Meeting, 22 July 2009, Phuket, Thailand. Available from www.aseansec.org/PR-42AMM-Chairman-Statement-ASEAN+3.pdf.

_____ (2009c). ASEAN Leaders' Statement on ASEAN Connectivity, Cha-am, Hua Hin, Thailand, 24 October. Available from www.aseansec.org/23573.htm.

_____ (2009d). Chairman's Statement of the 4th East Asia Summit, Cha-am, Hua Hin, Thailand, 25 October. Available from www.aseansec.org/23609.htm.

_____ (2009e). The Establishment of the Chiang Mai Initiative Multilateralization. Joint press release, 28 December. Available from www.mof.go.jp/english/if/091228press_release.pdf.

Athukorala, P-C., and N. Yamashita (2006). Production fragmentation and trade integration: East Asia in a global context. *North American Journal of Economics and Finance,* vol. 17, No. 3 (December).

Awad, Ibrahim (2009). *The Global Economic Crisis and Migration Workers: Impact and Response.* Geneva: ILO. Available from www.ilo.org/wcmsp5/groups/public/---ed_dialogue/---actrav/documents/publication/ wcms_112967.pdf.

Ban Ki-Moon (2009). If not now, when? *Daily News* (Egypt), 4 July. Available from www.un.org/sg/article Full.asp?TID=103&Type=Op-Ed.

Bergsten, C. Fred, and Yung Chul Park (2002). Toward creating a regional monetary arrangement in East Asia. Research Paper 50. Tokyo: ADB Institute. Available from www.adbi.org/files/2002.12.rps50.regional. monetary.pdf.

BERNAMA (2009). Bangladesh decides to use solar power to save electricity. *BERNAMA.com*, Malaysian National News Agency, 5 November. Available from www.bernama.com/bernama/v5/newsworld.php?id= 452797.

Bernard, Steve, and others (2009). The greenest bail-out? *Financial Times, 2* March. Available from www.ft.com/cms/s/0/cc207678-0738-11de-9294-000077b07658.html?nclick_check=1.

Bird, Graham, and Ramkishen S. Rajan (2000). Financial crises and the composition of international capital flows: does FDI guarantee stability? CIES Discussion Paper No. 0044. South Australia: Centre for International Economic Studies, Adelaide University. Available from www.adelaide.edu.au/cies/papers/ 0044.pdf.

_____ (2002). The evolving Asian financial architecture. Essays in International Economics No. 226. Princeton: International Economics Section, Princeton University.

Caliari, Aldo (2009). The financial crisis and trade in Asia: towards an integrated response in Asia. Proceedings from the ESCAP Regional High-Level Workshop on Strengthening the Response to the Global Financial Crisis in Asia-Pacific: The Role of Monetary, Fiscal and External Debt Policies. Dhaka, Bangladesh, 27-30 July.

Canning, David (1998). A database of world stocks of infrastructure. *World Bank Economic Review,* vol. 12, No. 3, pp. 529-547. Available from http://wber.oxfordjournals.org/cgi/issue_pdf/frontmatter_pdf/12/3.pdf.

CEIC Data Company Ltd. (2010). Global Database. Available from www.ceicdata.com/.

Chang-mock, Shin (2009). Korea focus: retrospect on Korean economy in 2009. CEO Information No. 736. Seoul: Samsung Economic Research Institute. Available from www.koreafocus.or.kr/design2/layout/ content_print.asp?group_id=102863.

Chatani, Kazutoshi, and Kee Beom Kim (2009). Labour and social trends in Indonesia 2009: recovery and beyond through decent work. Jakarta: ILO. Available from www.ilo.org/jakarta/whatwedo/publications/lang- -en/docName--WCMS_119134/index.htm.

Chauffour, Jean-Pierre, and Thomas Farole (2009). *Trade finance in crisis: market adjustment or market failure?* Policy Research Working Paper 5003. Washington, D.C.: World Bank. Available from www-wds. worldbank.org/external/default/WDSContentServer/IW3P/IB/2009/07/20/000158349_20090720085356/Ren- dered/PDF/WPS5003.pdf.

China Daily (2009). Russia, China hold similar positions on financial reform. 31 March. Available from www.chinadaily.com.cn/china/g20/2009-03/31/content_7633245.htm.

_____ (2010). Real estate prices rise at record pace. China sect., Economy, Beijing, 11 March. Available from www.chinadaily.com.cn/china/2010-03/11/content_9570137.htm.

Coady, David, and others (2006). The magnitude and distribution of fuel subsidies: evidence from Bolivia, Ghana, Jordan, Mali, and Sri Lanka. IMF Working Paper No. WP/06/247. Available from www.imf.org/ external/pubs/ft/wp/2006/wp06247.pdf.

Cookson, Robert (2009). East Asia debt market 'underdeveloped'. *Financial Times,* 15 September. Available from www.ft.com/cms/s/0/95b0bbce-a225-11de-9caa-00144feabdc0.html.

Damrongplasit, Kannika (2009). Thailand's universal coverage system and preliminary evaluation of its success. Presentation at Freeman Spogli Institute for International Studies, Stanford University, 15 October. Available from http://iis-db.stanford.edu/evnts/5747/presentation_ Kannika.pdf.

Davis, Benjamin, and others (2007). Rural income-generating activities: a cross-country comparison. ESA Working Paper No. 07-16. Rome: FAO. Available from ftp://ftp.fao.org/docrep/fao/010/ah853e/ah853e.pdf.

Dean, J., K.C. Fung and Z. Wang (2008). How vertically specialized is Chinese trade? BOFIT Discussion Papers 31/2008. Bank of Finland, Institute for Economies in Transition. Available from www.bof.fi/NR/rdonlyres/0F367D7B-DA85-4D13-8788-9E2EF25DFBCB/0/dp3108.pdf.

Dyurgerov, Mark B., and Mark F. Meier (2005). Glaciers and the changing earth system: a 2004 snapshot. Occasional Paper No. 58. Institute of Arctic and Alpine Research, University of Colorado. Available from http://instaar.colorado.edu/other/download/OP58_dyurgerov_meier.pdf.

Easterly, William, and Rebelo, Sergio (1993). Fiscal policy and economic growth: an empirical investigation. *Journal of Monetary Economics,* vol. 32, No. 3 (December), pp. 417-58.

Economic Times (2009). India's June FDI up 8% in June at $2.58 billion. 20 August. Available from http://economictimes.indiatimes.com/news/economy/indicators/Indias-June-FDI-up-8-at-258-billion/articleshow/4913044.cms.

Economist Intelligence Unit, Country Analysis and Forecasts (2009, 2010). *EIU CountryData.* Accessible at http://countryanalysis.eiu.com/.

Eichengreen, B. (2003). *Capital flows and crisis.* Cambridge, MA: MIT Press.

_____ (2006). The parallel-currency approach to Asian monetary integration. *American Economic Review,* vol. 96, No. 2.

Eilperin, Juliet (2009). G20 leaders agree to phase out fossil fuel subsidies. *Washington Post,* 25 Sept. Available from www.washingtonpost.com/wp-dyn/content/article/2009/09/25/AR200909250 2453.html.

Emirates Business 24-7 (2009). Domestic growth may help India's outward FDI. Available from www.business24-7.ae/opinion/analysis/domestic-growth-may-help-india-s-outward-fdi-2009-08-19-1.30387.

Epstein, Gerald (2009). *Should financial flows be regulated? Yes.* DESA Working Paper No. 77, ST/ESA/2009/DWP/77. New York: United Nations. Available from www.un.org/esa/desa/papers/2009/wp77_2009.pdf.

Fitoussi, Jean-Paul, and Joseph Stiglitz (2009). The ways out of the crisis and the building of a more cohesive world. Documents de Travail N° 2009-17. Observatoire Francais des Conjonctures Economiques (OFCE). Available from http://econpapers.repec.org/RePEc:fce:doctra:0917.

Fix, M., and others (2009). *Migration and the global recession.* Policy Research Working Paper 5015. Washington, D.C.: Migration Policy Institute. Available from www.migrationpolicy.org/pubs/MPI-BBCreport-Sept09.pdf.

Food and Agriculture Organization of the United Nations (2009, 2010). *World Food Situation: Food Price Indices.* Available from www.fao.org/worldfoodsituation/FoodPricesIndex/en.

Freund, Caroline (2009). *The trade response to global downturns: historical evidence.* Policy Research Working Paper 5015. Washington, D.C.: World Bank. Available from www-wds.worldbank.org/external/default/WDS ContentServer/IW3P/IB/2009/08/06/000158349_20090806152233/Rendered/PDF/WPS5015.pdf.

Goldstein, Morris, and Daniel Xie (2009). *The impact of the financial crisis on emerging Asia.* Peterson Institute Working Paper Series WP09-11. Washington, D.C.: Peterson Institute for International Economics. Available from http://ideas.repec.org/s/iie/wpaper.html.

Grameen Shakti (2009a). Creating 100000 (one hundred thousands) green women entrepreneurs. In Solar Energy Development Programme by Grameen Shakti. Renewable Energy & Environmental Information Network. Available from www.reein.org/solar/gs/index.htm.

_____ (2009b). Programs at a glance. Available from www.gshakti.org/index.php/programs-at-a-glance.html.

Greater Mekong Subregion (2010). Available from www.adb.org/GMS/.

_____ , Environment Operations Center (2010). GMS Core Environment Programme. Available from www.gms-eoc.org/CEP/CEP.aspx.

Griffith-Jones, S., and J. A. Ocampo (2009). *The financial crisis and its impact on developing countries.* Working Paper No.53. Brasilia: International Policy Centre for Inclusive Growth. Available from www.ipc-undp.org/pub/IPCWorkingPaper53.pdf.

Gubert, Flore, and Christophe J. Nordman (2009). *The Future of International Migration to OECD Countries.* Paris: OECD.

Guhan, S. (1994). Social security options for developing countries. *International Labour Review,* vol. 133, No. 1.

Gunther, Marc (2009). Grameen Shakti brings sustainable development closer to reality in Bangladesh. GreenBiz.com, 21 January. Available from www.greenbiz.com/blog/2009/01/21/grameen-shakti-brings-sustainable-development-closer-reality-bangladesh.

Hausmann, Ricardo, Jason Hwang and Dani Rodrik (2005). *What you export matters.* NBER Working Paper No. 11905. Cambridge, MA: National Bureau of Economic Research. Available from www.nber.org/papers/w11905.

Heaney, Vince (2009). Tobin tax talk not without merit. *Financial Times,* 21 December, p.24. Available at www.ft.com/cms/s/0/06a8cade-ecc6-11de-8070-00144feab49a.html; and from www.offshoreannouncements.com/LatestNews/ArticleInformation/tabid/129/articleid/YpNQ6EmPbCUcV2Hwwrm-ow/Default.aspx.

Heyzer, Noeleen (2009). Keynote speech: Innovative government, innovation on the road to economic recovery. Singapore, 3 December. Available from www.unescap.org/oes/statements/ST20091203-Innovative-Government.pdf.

_____ and M. Khor (1999). Globalization and the way forward. Development Outreach "Speaker's Corner". Washington, D.C.: World Bank. http://devoutreach.com/summer99/Globalizationandthe WayForward/tabid/819/Default.aspx.

Hong Kong Special Administrative Region Government (2009). The 2009-10 Policy Address: Breaking new ground together. October.

Huynh, P., S. Kapsos, K. B. Kim and G. Sziraczki (forthcoming). Impacts of the current global economic crisis on Asia's labour market. ADBI Discussion Paper. Tokyo: Asian Development Bank Institute.

iGovernment (2007). Four South Asian countries to set up info-highway. New Delhi, 16 October. Available from www.igovernment.in/site/four-south-asian-countries-to-set-up-info-highway/.

India (2008). NREGA Implementation Status Report for the Financial Year 2008-2009. Available from http://nrega.nic.in/writereaddata/mpr_out/nregampr_0809.html.

_____ , Ministry of Finance (2010). *Economic Survey 2009-2010.* Available from http://indiabudget.nic.in/es2009-10/esmain.htm.

_____ , Ministry of Rural Development (2008). *The National Rural Employment Guarantee Act 2005 (NREGA): Operational Guidelines 2008*. 3rd ed. New Delhi: Department of Rural Development. Available from http://nrega.nic.in/Nrega_guidelinesEng.pdf.

Institute of Policy Studies of Sri Lanka (2009). *Sri Lanka: State of the Economy 2009*. Colombo: IPS.

Intergovernmental Panel on Climate Change (2007). Climate change 2007: the physical science basis – summary for policymakers. Geneva: IPCC. Available from www.aaas.org/news/press_room/climate_change/media/4th_spm2feb07.pdf.

International Labour Organization (2009a). *Key Indicators of the Labour Market (KILM)*, 6th ed. Economic and Labour Market Analysis Department. Available at http://kilm.ilo.org/KILMnetBeta/default2.asp.

_____ (2009b). *Protecting People, Promoting Jobs: A Survey of Country Employment and Social Protection Policy Responses to the Global Economic Crisis*. ILO Report to the G20 Leaders' Summit. Pittsburgh, 24-25 September.

_____ , Economic and Labour Market Analysis Department (2009). Trends Econometric Models. (See www.ilo.org/empelm/what/projects/lang--en/WCMS_114246/index.htm.)

International Monetary Fund (2009a). *Regional Economic Outlook: Asia and the Pacific – Global Crisis: the Asian Context*. World Economic and Financial Surveys. Washington, D.C. Available from www.imf.org/external/pubs/ft/reo/2009/APD/ENG/areo0509.htm.

_____ (2009b). *Asia and the Pacific: Building a Sustained Recovery*. World Economic and Financial Surveys: Regional Economic Outlook (October). Washington, D.C. Available from www.imf.org/external/pubs/ft/reo/2009/apd/eng/areo1009.pdf.

_____ (2009c). Bangladesh: 2009 Article IV Consultation – Preliminary conclusions of the IMF Mission. Available from www.imf.org/external/np/ms/2009/102909.htm.

_____ (2009d). Bhutan: 2009 Article IV Consultation – Staff report; Staff supplement; and Public information notice on the Executive Board discussion. IMF Country Report No. 09/334. Washington, D.C.

_____ (2009e). Democratic Republic of Timor-Leste: 2009 Article IV Consultation – Staff report; Public information notice on the Executive Board discussion; and Statement by the Executive Director for the Democratic Republic of Timor-Leste. IMF Country Report No. 09/219. Washington, D.C.

_____ (2009f). Georgia: 2009 Article IV Consultation and Second Review under the Stand-by Arrangement – Staff report; Press release and public information notice on the Executive Board discussion; and Statement by the Executive Director for Georgia. IMF Country Report No. 09/127. Washington, D.C.

_____ (2009g). International Financial Statistics. IFS Database and Browser on CD-ROM. Washington, D.C.

_____ (2009h). Kyrgyz Republic: 2009 Article IV Consultation and First Review under the 18-month Arrangement under the Exogenous Shocks Facility – Staff report; Staff supplement; Public information notice and press release on the Executive Board discussion; and Statement by the Executive director for the Kyrgyz Republic. IMF Country Report No. 09/209. Washington, D.C.: IMF.

_____ (2009i). Mongolia: First Review under the Stand-by Arrangement – Staff report; Press release on the Executive Board discussion; and Statement by the Executive Director for Mongolia. IMF Country Report No. 09/254. Washington, D.C.: IMF.

_____ (2009j). Public information notice: IMF Executive Board concludes 2009 Article IV Consultations. *IMF News*. Available from www.imf.org/external/news/default.aspx?pn.

_____ (2009k). Republic of Kazakhstan: 2009 Article IV Consultation – Staff report; Staff statement; Public information notice on the Executive Board discussion. IMF Country Report No. 09/300. Washington, D.C.

_____ (2009l). Russian Federation: 2009 Article IV Consultation – Staff report; Staff statement; Public information notice on the Executive Board discussion. IMF Country Report No. 09/246. Washington, D.C.

_____ (2009m). World Economic and Financial Surveys: World Economic Outlook Database (October 2009). Washington, D.C. Available from www.imf.org/external/pubs/ft/weo/2009/02/weodata/index.aspx.

_____ (2009n). *World Economic Outlook: Sustaining the Recovery* (October 2009). World Economic and Financial Surveys. Washington, D.C. Available from www.imf.org/external/pubs/ft/weo/2009/02/pdf/text.pdf.

_____ (2010a). International Financial Statistics (IFS) Online Service. Available from www.imfstatistics.org/imf/.

_____ (2010b). Direction of Trade Statistics database. Available from www2.imfstatistics.org/DOT/.

_____ (2010c). *World Economic Outlook Update: A Policy-driven, Multispeed Recovery,* 26 January. Available from www.imf.org/external/pubs/ft/weo/2010/update/01/index.htm.

International Organization for Migration (2009). The impact of the global economic crisis on migrants and migration. IOM Policy Brief. Available from www.egypt.iom.int/Doc/IOM%20Policy%20Brief%20Financial%20Crisis.pdf.

International Telecommunications Union (2009). *Trends in Telecommunication Reform 2009: Hands-on or Hands-off? – Stimulating Growth through Effective ICT Regulation.* 10th ed. Geneva. Available from www.itu.int/publ/D-REG-TTR.11-2009/en.

International Water Management Institute and Food and Agriculture Organization of the United Nations (2009). *Revitalizing Asia's irrigation: to sustainably meet tomorrow's food needs.* Colombo: IWMI-FAO. Available from www.fao.org/nr/water/docs/Revitalizing_Asias_Irrigation.pdf.

Interstate Statistical Committee of the Commonwealth of Independent States (2009). Statistics. Available from www.cisstat.com/eng/index.htm.

Ito, Takatoshi (2006). A case for a coordinated basket for Asian countries. In *A Basket Currency for Asia.* Takatoshi Ito, ed. Ch. 6, pp. 124-141. London: Routledge.

Jomo, Kwame Sundaram (2010). Financing for Development and the MDGs, presentation at the Fourth High-Level Dialogue of the UNGA on Financing for Development, 24 March, available at www.un.org/esa/ffd/hld/HLD2010/presentation_jomo.pdf.

Kabeer, Naila (2009). *Social protection in South Asia: a review.* Brighton: Centre for Social Protection, Institute of Development Studies. Available from www.ids.ac.uk/index.cfm?objectid=4A452CF9-E522-F732-EEF7B977C1F90545.

Kannan, K. P. (2007). Social security in a globalizing world. *International Social Security Review,* vol. 60, No. 2-3. Available from http://papers.ssrn.com/sol3/papers.cfm?abstract_id=996144##.

Kawai, Masahiro, and Ganeshan Wignaraja (2007). ASEAN+3 or ASEAN+6: which way forward? ADB Institute Discussion Paper No. 77. Tokyo: Asian Development Bank Institute. Available from www.adbi.org/files/dp77.asean.3.asean.6.pdf.

Khan, Ashfaque H. (2009). Role of remittances. *The News International,* Pakistan, 8 September. Available from www.thenews.com.pk/editorial_detail.asp?id=197238.

Khor, Martin (2009a). Trade: protectionism on the rise hits developing countries hardest. TWN Info Service on WTO and Trade Issues (Feb09/09), 11 February. Available from www.twnside.org.sg/title2/wto.info/2009/twninfo20090208.htm.

_____ , (2009b). Copenhagen: key issues facing developing countries. South Centre Climate Policy Brief. Available from www.southcentre.org/index.php?option=com_content&task=view&id=1130& Itemid=1.

Kim, Kee Beom, and others (2009). Impacts of the current global economic crisis on Asia's labour markets. Presentation at the Labour Market in the People's Republic of China and Its Adjustment to Global Financial Crisis, Tokyo, 18-19 June. Available from www.adbi.org/conf-seminar-papers/2009/07/17/3221. impact.gec.asia.labour.markets/.

Knowles, J.C., E. M. Pernia and M. Racelis (1999). Social consequences of the financial crisis in Asia: the deeper crisis. EDRC Briefing Notes No.16. Manila: ADB. Available from http://aric.adb.org/pdf/edrcbn/edrcbn17.pdf.

Kose, M. A., and others (2006). *Financial globalization: a reappraisal.* NBER Working Paper No.12484. Cambridge, MA: National Bureau of Economic Research. Available from www.brookings.edu/~/media/Files/rc/papers/2006/08globaleconomics_rogoff/20060823.pdf.

Kranendonk, Henk, and Johan Verbruggen (2008). *Decomposition of GDP growth in European countries: different methods tell different stories.* CPB Document No. 158. The Hague: CPB Netherlands Bureau of Economic Policy Analysis. Available from www.cpb.nl/eng/pub/cpbreeksen/document/158/doc158.pdf.

Krugman, Paul (2009). Oil speculation. *The New York Times,* Opinion sect., 8 July. Available from http://krugman.blogs.nytimes.com/2009/07/08/oil-speculation/.

Kumar, Nagesh (2007). *Towards broader regional cooperation in Asia.* UNDP/RCC Discussion Paper. Colombo: Asia-Pacific Trade and Investment Initiative. Available from www2.undprcc.lk/resource_centre/pub_pdfs/P1059.pdf.

_____ (2009). *South-South and triangular cooperation in Asia-Pacific: towards a new paradigm in development cooperation.* UNESCAP Working Paper WP/09/05. Available from www.unescap.org/pdd/publications/workingpaper/wp_09_05.pdf.

_____ and Prabir De (2008). *East Asian infrastructure development in a comparative global perspective: an analysis of RIS infrastructure index.* RIS Discussion Papers RIS-DP # 135. New Delhi: RIS. Available from http://www.ris.org.in/dp135_pap.pdf.

Kwon, Huck-Ju (2007). *Transforming the developmental welfare states in East Asia.* DESA Working Paper No. 40. ST/ESA/2007/DWP/40. New York: United Nations. Available from www.un.org/esa/desa/papers/2007/wp40_2007.pdf.

Lansigan, Felino P. (2005). Coping with climate variability and change in rice production systems in the Philippines. In *Rice is Life: Scientific Perspectives for the 21st Century.* K. Toriyama, K. L. Heong and B. Hardy, eds. Pp.542-545. Manila: International Rice Research Institute.

Macao Special Administrative Region Government (2009). *Monthly Bulletin of Statistics,* August. Available from www.dsec.gov.mo/Statistic/General/MonthlyBulletinOfStatistics.aspx?lang=en-US.

Marland, G., T. A. Boden and R. J. Andres (2008). Global, regional, and national CO2 emission estimates from fossil fuel burning, cement production, and gas flaring, 1751-2002. Carbon Dioxide Information Analysis Center, Numeric Data Package. CDIAC_NDP-030. Available from http://cdiac.ornl.gov/ndps/ndp030.html.

Najib Tun Razak (2009). Sixth Annual Kuala Lumpur Islamic Finance Forum, speech. Kuala Lumpur: Office of the Prime Minister of Malaysia, 3 November. Available from www.pmo.gov.my/?menu=speech&news_id=173&page=1676&speech_cat=2.

Newfarmer, Richard (2009). The financial crisis, trade and effects on women. Presentation made at Women Leading Change: Traction for Change, Geneva, 4 March. Available from www.intracen.org/womenandtrade/documents/Newfarmer_Women_and_Trade_March_4_ 2009.pdf.

Obstfeld, M., J. C. Shambaugh and A. M. Taylor (2008). *Financial stability, the trilemma, and international reserves.* NBER Working Paper 14217. Cambridge, MA: National Bureau of Economic Research.

Ocampo, José Antonio (2007). *The instability and inequities of the global reserve system.* DESA Working Paper No. 59. New York: United Nations. Available from www.un.org/esa/desa/papers/2007/wp59_2007.pdf.

Organisation for Economic Co-operation and Development (2008). *OECD Economic Surveys: Korea.* Paris.

_____ (2009a). *OECD Economic Outlook,* No.86 (November 2009). Paris.

_____ (2009b). *OECD Economic Surveys:* Japan. Paris.

_____ (2009c). *OECD Employment Outlook 2009: Tackling the Jobs Crisis.* Paris.

_____ (2009d). *OECD in Figures 2009.* Paris.

_____ (2009e). *OECD Regions at a Glance 2009.* Paris.

_____ (2010). Harmonised unemployment rates. News release, January. Paris.

Ostry, Jonathan D., and others (2010). Capital inflows: the role of controls. IMF Staff Position Note SPN/10/04. Available from www.imf.org/external/pubs/ft/spn/2010/spn1004.pdf.

Othman, Azlan (2009). Tests completed on Asia-America gateway. *Brudirect.com,* 11 November. Available from www.brudirect.com/index.php/2009111110259/Local-News/tests-completed-on-asia-america-gateway.html.

Panetta, F., and others (2009). *An assesment of financial sector rescue programmes.* BIS Paper No. 48. Basel: Bank for International Settlements. Available from www.bis.org/publ/bppdf/bispap48.pdf.

Papua New Guinea (2009, 2010). *National Budget.* Vol. 1, November.

_____ , National Statistical Office (2009). Arrival and departure historical releases archive. Available from www.nso.gov.pg/Tourism/tourism.htm.

Persaud, Avinash (2009). We should put sand in the wheels of the market. *Financial Times,* Opinion sect., 27 August. Available from www.ft.com/cms/s/0/08523a6a-934c-11de-b146-00144feabdc0.html.

Pew Charitable Trusts (2010). *Who's Winning the Clean Energy Race? Growth, Competition and Opportunity in the World's Largest Economies.* G-20 Clean Energy Factbook. Washington, D.C.: The Pew Charitable Trusts. Available from www.pewglobalwarming.org/cleanenergyeconomy/pdf/PewG-20Report.pdf.

Philippine Information Agency (2009). Gov't earmarks P1-B for Fil-Expat Livelihood Support Fund, PGMA tells OFWs in Riyadh. Press release, 5 February. Available from www.pia.gov.ph/?m=12&sec=reader&rp=1&fi=p090205.htm&no=8&date=.

Pilling, David (2009). Mixed signals from Asia's animal spirits. *Financial Times,* 14 May. Available from www.ft.com/cms/s/0/2ba14cd2-3fef-11de-9ced-00144feabdc0.html.

Poon, Terence (2009). Foreign direct investment in China continues to slide. *Wall Street Journal,* Asia ed., Economy sect. (online), 18 August. Available from http://online.wsj.com/article/SB12504778199693 5959.html?KEYWORDS=%22foreign+direct+investment+in+china+continues+to+slide%22.

Rajan, Ramkishen, and Reza Siregar (2004). Centralized reserve pooling for the ASEAN+3 (APT) countries. In *Monetary and Financial Integration in East Asia;* vol. 1: *The Way Ahead.* Manila: Asian Development Bank; United Kingdom: Palgrave Macmillan.

Ratha, Dilip, Sanket Mohapatra and Ani Silwal (2009). Migration and remittance trends 2009: a better-than-expected outcome so far, but significant risks ahead. Migration and Development Brief 11. Washington, D.C.: World Bank.

Ravallion, Martin (2003). Measuring aggregate welfare in developing countries: how well do national accounts and surveys agree? *The Review of Economics and Statistics,* vol. 85, No. 3.

Reinhart, Carmen M., and Kenneth S. Rogoff (2009). The aftermath of financial crises. *American Economic Review,* vol. 99, No. 2. Also publ. as NBER Working Paper No. 14656. Available from www.nber.org/ papers/w14656.

_____ , and Vincent R. Reinhart (2009). Capital flow bonanzas: an encompassing view of the past and present. In *NBER International Seminar in Macroeconomics 2008.* Jeffrey Frankel and Christopher Pissarides, eds. Chicago: National Bureau of Economic Research.

Republic of the Fiji Islands (2009). Economic and fiscal update: supplement to the 2010 budget address – Strengthening the foundations for economic growth and prosperity. Suva: Ministry of Finance and National Planning. Available from www.mfnp.gov.fj/Documents/2010_Budget_Supplement.pdf.

_____ , Fiji Island Bureau of Statistics (2009a). Visitor arrivals April 2009. Available from www.statsfiji.gov.fj/.

_____ , (2009b). Visitor arrivals statistics. Available from www.statsfiji.gov.fj/Tourism/Visitor_Arrivals.htm.

Republic of Korea, Ministry of Foreign Affairs and Trade (2009). Joint Statement of the ASEAN-Republic of Korea Commemorative Summit. Available from http://asean.korea.net/News/NewsView.asp?board_ no=20876.

Research and Information System for Developing Countries (2008). *South Asia Development and Cooperation Report 2008.* New Delhi: Oxford University Press.

Reserve Bank of Australia (2009). Statement of Monetary Policy. 6 November. Sydney: RBA. Available from www.rba.gov.au/publications/smp/2009/nov/html/index.html.

Reuters (2009). "Obama says U.S. can't keep borrowing from China", 14 May. Available from www.reuters.com/ article/politicsNews/idUSTRE54D58Q20090514.

Rodrik, Dani (2004). Industrial policy for the twenty-first century. CEPR Discussion Paper DP4767. London: Centre for Economic Policy Research. Available from www.cepr.org/pubs/dps/DP4767.asp.

_____ (2006). The social cost of foreign exchange reserves. *International Economic Journal,* vol. 20, No. 3 (September). Also publ. as NBER Working Paper No. 11952, January. Available from www.nber.org/ papers/w11952.

_____ (2009). *Growth after the Crisis.* Cambridge, MA: Commission on Growth and Development. Available from www.growthcommission.org/storage/cgdev/documents/financial_crisis/rodrikafterthecrisis.pdf.

_____ and Arvind Subramanian (2009). *Why did financial globalization disappoint?* IMF Staff Papers 56, pp.112-138. Washington, D.C.: IMF. Available from www.fringer.org/wp-content/writings/rodrik-paper.pdf.

Rosen, Daniel H., and Thilo Hanemann (2009). China's changing outbound foreign direct investment profile: drivers and policy implications. Policy Brief No. PB09-14. Washington, D.C.: Peterson Institute for International Economics. Available from www.iie.com/publications/pb/pb09-14.pdf.

Russian Federation, Embassy of the Russian Federation in the Kingdom of Norway (2009). President of Russia Dmitry Medvedev's Address to St. Petersburg International Economic Forum, Plenary Session, 5 June. Available from www.norway.mid.ru/news_fp/news_fp_124_eng.html.

Sakakibara, Eisuke (2003). Asian cooperation and the end of Pax Americana. In *Financial Stability and Growth in Emerging Economies: The Role of the Financial Sector.* Jan Joost Teunissen and Mark Teunissen, eds., pp:227-240. The Hague: FONDAD. Available from www.fondad.org/product_books/pdf_download/8/Fondad-Stability-BookComplete.pdf.

Samoa, Ministry of Finance (2009). *Quarterly Economic Review,* No. 45 (April-June). Available from www.mof.gov.ws/uploads/quarterly_economic_review_iss_45.pdf.

Scrase, Ivan, and others (2009). Climate policy is energy policy. In *Energy for the future: A new agenda.* Ivan Scrase and Gordon MacKerron, eds. United Kingdom: Palgrave.

Shanghai Daily (2009). Concern over property prices. China.org.cn, 29 September. Available from www.china.org.cn/business/2009-09/29/content_18627727.htm.

Sim, William, and Nipa Piboontanasawat (2009). South Korea, China, Japan agree on currency swaps for stability. *Bloomberg.com,* 12 December. Available from www.bloomberg.com/apps/news?pid=20601089&sid=aMtclSyeEF8E.

Singh, Manmohan (2009). PM's remarks at the G-20 meeting at Pittsburgh: Plenary Session. Pittsburgh, 25 September. India: Prime Minister's Office. Available from http://pmindia.nic.in/speech/content.asp?id=823.

Solomon Islands, National Statistics Office (2009a). Migration and tourism. Available from www.spc.int/prism/Country/SB/Stats/Migration%20and%20Tourism/Tour-Index.htm.

_____ , (2009b). Visitor arrival – June Quarter 2007. Available from www.spc.int/prism/Country/SB/Stats.

Soubbotina, Tatyana P. (2004). *Beyond Economic Growth: an Introduction to Sustainable Development.* 2nd ed. Washington, D.C.: World Bank/IBRD.

South Asian Association for Regional Cooperation (2004). *Social Charter.* Kathmandu: SAARC. Available from www.saarc-sec.org/main.php?id=13.

Speck, Stefan (2008). Possibilities of environmental fiscal reform in developing countries. Paper for presentation at Bank Indonesia Annual International Seminar, Macroeconomic Impact of Climate Change: Opportunities and Challenges, Bali, 1-2 August. Available from www.bi.go.id/NR/rdonlyres/57BF6537-1BEA-4D42-B476-209DC56F11DA/14255/StefanSpeckdoc.pdf.

State Bank of Pakistan. *Annual Report 2008-2009* (Vol. I). Karachi. Available from www.sbp.org.pk/reports/annual/arFY09/qtr-index-eng-09.htm.

Stiglitz, Joseph E. (2010). *Risk and global economic architecture: why full financial integration may be undesirable.* NBER Working Papers No 15718. Cambridge, MA: National Bureau of Economic Research. Available from www.nber.org/papers/w15718.pdf.

_____ , Amartya Sen and Jean-Paul Fitoussi (2009). *Report by the Commission on the Measurement of Economic Performance and Social Progress.* Available from www.stiglitz-sen-fitoussi.fr/documents/rapport_anglais.pdf.

Sudarshan, Ratna M. (2009). Examining India's National Regional Employment Guarantee Act: its impact and women's participation. Social Protection in Asia Working Paper. New Delhi: Institute of Social Studies Trust. Available from www.socialprotectionasia.org/pdf/ISST-SPA-WP05.pdf.

Suryanarayana, M. H. (2008). Pro-poor growth: illusions of marriage and divorce? Working Paper No. WP-2008-006. Mumbai: Indira Gandhi Institute of Development Research. Available from www.igidr.ac.in/pdf/publication/WP-2008-006.pdf.

Sziraczki, Gyorgy, Phu Huynh and Steven Kapsos (2009). The global economic crisis: labour market impacts and policies for recovery in Asia. ILO Asia-Pacific Working Paper Series. Geneva: ILO. Available from www.ilo.org/wcmsp5/groups/public/---asia/---ro-bangkok/documents/publication/wcms_110095.pdf.

Tang, Anne (2009). Hu expounds China's views on sustainable development. GOV.cn, 15 November. Available from http://english.gov.cn/2009-11/15/content_1465068.htm.

Thailand, National Economic and Social Development Board (2009). Economic outlook: Thai economic performance in Q2 and outlook for 2009. Press release, 24 August. Available from www.nesdb.go.th/Portals/0/eco_datas/economic/eco_state/2_52/Press%20Eng%20Q2-2009.pdf.

The Hindu Business Line (2009). Overseas borrowing gets easier for India Inc. Chennai, India, 31 July. Available from www.thehindubusinessline.com/2009/07/31/stories/2009073151870100.htm.

Tobin, James (1978). A proposal for international monetary reform. *Eastern Economic Journal,* vol. 4, Nos. 3-4, pp. 153-159. Available from http://econpapers.repec.org/article/eejeeconj/v_3a4_3ay_3a1978_3ai_3a3-4_3ap_3a153-159.htm.

Tong, Beretitenti Anote (2010). Closing of Pacific High-Level Dialogue to Review Progress with Implementation of the Mauritius Strategy Statement; by the President of Kiribati, 9 February.

Tonga, Department of Statistics (2009). Key statistics. Available from www.spc.int/prism/Country/TO/stats/.

United Kingdom, The Financial Services Authority (2009). *The Turner Review: a Regulatory Response to the Global Banking Crisis.* London. Available from www.fsa.gov.uk/pubs/other/turner_review.pdf.

United Nations (2009a). *Report of the Commission of Experts of the President of the United Nations General Assembly on Reforms of the International Monetary and Financial System.* New York. Available from www.un.org/ga/econcrisissummit/docs/FinalReport_CoE.pdf.

_____ (2009b). *World Economic and Social Survey 2009: Promoting Development, Saving the Planet.* Sales No. E.09.II.C.1. Available from www.un.org/esa/policy/wess/wess2009files/wess09/wess2009.pdf.

_____ (2009c). Draft outcome document of the Conference on the World Financial and Economic Crisis and Its Impact on Development. A/CONF.214/3. Available from www.unglobalcompact.org/docs/about_the_gc/government_support/A-CONF-214-3.pdf.

_____ (2009d). Forests: the green and REDD of climate change. UN-DESA Policy Brief No. 16, April. Department of Economic and Social Affairs. Available from www.un.org/esa/policy/policybriefs/policybrief16.pdf.

_____ (2010). *World Economic Situation and Prospects 2010.* Sales No. E.10.II.C.2. Available from www.un.org/esa/policy/wess/wesp.html.

_____ , Statistics Division (2009). United Nations Commodity Trade Statistics Database. Available from http://comtrade.un.org/db/dqQuickQuery.aspx.

_____ , (2010a). National Accounts Main Aggregates Database. Available from http://unstats.un.org/unsd/snaama/Introduction.asp.

_____ , (2010b). Millennium Development Goals Indicators. Available from http://mdgs.un.org/unsd/mdg/Data.aspx.

United Nations Conference on Trade and Development (2003). *Trade and Development Report 2003: Capital Accumulation, Growth and Structural Change.* Sales No. E.03.II.D.7.

_____ (2009a). *Trade and Development Report, 2009: Responding to the Global Crisis Climate Change Mitigation and Development.* Sales No. E.09.II.D.16.

_____ (2009b). *World Investment Report 2009: Transnational Corporations, Agricultural Production and Development.* Sales No. E.09.II.D.15. Available from www.unctad.org/en/docs/wir2009_en.pdf.

United Nations Conference on the World Financial and Economic Crisis and Its Impact on Development (2009). The world financial and economic crisis and its impact on development: Report of the Secretary-General. New York, 24-26 June. A/CONF.214/4.

United Nations, Economic and Social Commission for Asia and the Pacific (2002). *Seoul Declaration on Infrastructure Development in Asia and the Pacific: Regional Action Programme Phase II (2002-2006).* Ministerial Conference on Infrastructure, Seoul, 12-17 November 2001. Available from www.unescap.org/TTDW/Publications/TPTS_pubs/Seoul_Declaration.pdf.

_____ (2007a). *Development of Health Systems in the Context of Enhancing Economic Growth towards Achieving the Millennium Development Goals in Asia and the Pacific.* Sales No. E.07.II.F.12. Available from www.unescap.org/publications/detail.asp?id=1209.

_____ (2007b). *Trade Statistics in Policymaking: A Handbook of Commonly Used Trade Indices and Indicators.* Sales No. E.07.II.F.21.

_____ (2008a). *Economic and Social Survey of Asia and the Pacific 2008: Sustaining Growth and Sharing Prosperity.* Sales No. E.08.II.F.7. Available from www.unescap.org/survey2008/download/01_Survey_2008.pdf.

_____ (2008b). *Enhancing Pacific Connectivity: the Current Situation, Opportunities for Progress.* Sales No. E.08.II.F.14. Available from www.unescap.org/idd/Pubs/st_escap_2472.pdf.

_____ (2008c). *Greening Growth in Asia and the Pacific.* Sales No. E.09.II.F.6. Available from www.unescap.org/esd/environment/publications/gg_asia_pacific/GreeningGrowth.pdf.

_____ (2009a). *Asia-Pacific Trade and Investment Report: Trade-led Recovery and Beyond.* Sales No. E.09.II.F.19.

_____ (2009b). *Economic and Social Survey of Asia and the Pacific 2009: Addressing Triple Threats to Development.* Sales No. E.09.II.F.11. Available from www.unescap.org/pdd/publications/survey2009/download/Survey2009.pdf.

_____ (2009c). Green growth capacity development programme: Map to green growth in Asia and the Pacific. Brochure. Available from www.greengrowth.org/capacity_building/Download/GG_capacity_development/Green_Growth_Capacity_Development_Brochure-resized.pdf.

_____ (2009d). *Economic and Social Survey of Asia and the Pacific 2009: Year-end Update.* Available from www.unescap.org/pdd/publications/yearend2009/yearend2009.pdf.

_____ (2009e). *Navigating Out of the Crisis: A Trade-led Recovery – A practical guide for trade policymakers in Asia and the Pacific.* ST/ESCAP/2538. Available from www.unescap.org/tid/publication/tipub2538.pdf.

_____ (2009f). *Statistical Yearbook for Asia and the Pacific 2008.* Sales No. E.09.II.F.1. Available from www.unescap.org/stat/data/syb2008/ESCAP-SYB2008.pdf.

_____ (2009g). Strengthening social protection systems in Asia and the Pacific in the aftermath of the global financial crisis. Macroeconomic Policy Brief, No. 3. Available from www.unescap.org/pdd/publications/ me_brief/mepb_3.pdf.

_____ (2009h). *Sustainable Agriculture and Food Security in Asia and the Pacific.* Sales No. E.09.II.F.12. Available from www.unhcr.org/refworld/pdfid/49f589db2.pdf.

_____ (forthcoming). Supportive financial system and green growth for achieving the Millennium Development Goals in the Asia-Pacific region. Preliminary document available from www.unescap.org/pdd/calendar/ EGM_themestudy_2010/outline.pdf.

_____ , Asian Development Bank and the United Nations Development Programme (2010). *Asia Pacific Regional Report 2009/10: Achieving the Millennium Development Goals in an Era of Global Uncertainty.* Sales No. E.10.II.F.10. Available from www.mdgasiapacific.org/regional-report-2009-10.

United Nations Environment Programme (2009). Global green New Deal – an update for the G20 Pittsburgh Summit. Available from www.unep.org/pdf/G20_policy_brief_Final.pdf.

United Nations Framework Convention on Climate Change (2009). Copenhagen Accord. Draft Decision -/15, 18 Dec. 2009. Draft document available from http://unfccc.int/files/meetings/cop_15/application/pdf/cop15_ cph_auv.pdf.

United Nations Population Fund (2009). Asia and the Pacific at a glance. Available from http://asiapacific. unfpa.org/public/cache/offonce/pid/3948;jsessionid=FACFF872B3A5C9C7E10AC03E32E3FB8F.

United States (2010). *Economic Report of the President.* Washington, D.C.: United States Government Printing Office. Available from www.gpoaccess.gov/eop/2010/2010_erp.pdf.

_____ , Bureau of Economic Affairs (2009). Gross domestic product: third quarter 2009 (advance estimate). Press release, 29 Oct. Available from www.bea.gov/newsreleases/national/gdp/gdpnewsrelease.htm.

_____ , Census Bureau (2010). Foreign Trade: Historical Series. Available from www.census.gov/foreign-trade/ statistics/historical/.

_____ , Congressional Budget Office (2010). Budget Projections. Available from www.cbo.gov/budget/budproj. shtml.

_____ , Department of the Treasury (2010). Treasury International Capital System: U.S. Gross External Debt Statistics. Available from www.treas.gov/tic/external-debt.shtml.

_____ , Energy Information Administration. Petroleum Navigator. Available from http://tonto.eia.doe.gov/dnav/pet/ hist/LeafHandler.ashx?n=PET&s=rbrte&f=M.

_____ , Federal Reserve (2009). Federal Reserve Statistical Release, 7 December. Available from www. federalreserve.gov/releases/g19/20091207/.

_____ , (2009). Minutes of the Federal Open Market Committee, 3-4 November. Available from www. federalreserve.gov/monetarypolicy/files/fomcminutes20091104.pdf.

The University of the South Pacific (2009). USP – an introduction. Available from www.usp.ac.fj/index.php? id=usp_introduction.

Vanuatu, National Statistics Office (2009). Tourism statistics. Available from www.spc.int/prism/country/vu/stats/ TOURISM/tourism-index.htm.

Viet Nam, General Department of Vietnam Customs (2009). February exports up 25.1%. Vietnam Customs, News and Events. Available from www.customs.gov.vn/English/Lists/News/ViewDetails.aspx?ID=31.

Weisbrot, Mark, and others (2009). IMF-supported macroeconomic policies and the world recession: a look at forty-one borrowing countries. Washington, D.C.: Center for Economic and Policy Research. Available from www.cepr.net/documents/publications/imf-2009-10.pdf.

Wijnholds, J. Onno de Beaufort, and Arend Kapteyn (2001). Reserve Adequacy in Emerging Market Economies. IMF Working Paper WP/01/143. Washington, D.C.: IMF. Available from www.imf.org/external/pubs/ft/wp/2001/wp01143.pdf.

Williamson, John (2005). A currency basket for East Asia, not just China. Policy Briefs in International Economics, No. PB05-1 (August). Washington, D.C.: Peterson Institute for International Economics. Available from www.iie.com/publications/pb/pb05-1.pdf.

World Bank (1994). *World Development Report 1994: Infrastructure for Development.* New York: Oxford University Press.

_____ (2008). *World Development Report 2009: Reshaping Economic Geography.* Washington, D.C. Available from http://econ.worldbank.org/WBSITE/EXTERNAL/EXTDEC/EXTRESEARCH/EXTWDRS/EXTWDR20090,,contentMDK:21955654~pagePK:64167689~piPK:64167673~theSitePK:4231059,00.html.

_____ (2009a). *Doing Business 2010: Reforming through Difficult Times – Comparing Regulation in 183 Countries.* Washington, D. C.: World Bank and International Finance Corporation; United Kingdom: Palgrave Macmillan. Available from www.doingbusiness.org/documents/fullreport/2010/DB10-full-report.pdf.

_____ (2009b). East Asia update November 2009 – video interview with Ivailo Izvorski. Available from http://web.worldbank.org/WBSITE/EXTERNAL/COUNTRIES/EASTASIAPACIFICEXT/0,,contentMDK:22375721~pagePK:146736~piPK:146830~theSitePK:226301,00.html.

_____ (2009c). Transforming the rebound into recovery, East Asia and Pacific update. Cityscape Intelligence: Breaking News, 4 November. Washington D. C. Available from www.cityscapeintelligence.com/world-bank-online-east-asia.

_____ (2010a). PovcalNet. Available from http://iresearch.worldbank.org/PovcalNet/povcalSvy.html.

_____ (2010b). World Development Indicators Online. Available from http://ddp-ext.worldbank.org/ext/DDPQQ/member.do?method=getMembers&userid=1&queryId=6.

World Health Organization, Regional Office for the Western Pacific (2010). Governments not spending enough on health. Press releases, 3 March. Available from www.wpro.who.int/media_centre/press_releases/pr20100303.htm.

World Resources Institute. Climate Analysis Indicators Tool (CAIT) Version 7.0. Available from http://cait.wri.org/.

World Trade Organization (1994). Agreement on Trade-Related Aspects of Intellectual Property Rights. Available from http://www.wto.org/english/tratop_e/trips_e/t_agm0_e.htm.

_____ (2009). Report to the TPRB from the Director-General on the financial and economic crisis and trade-related developments. WT/TPR/OV/W/2. Available from www.wto.org/english/news_e/news09_e/tpr_13jul09_dg_report_e.doc.

Xinhua News Agency (2009a). 20 million jobless migrant workers return home. *China View,* Window on China sect., 2 February. Available from http://news.xinhuanet.com/english/2009-02/02/content_10750749.htm.

_____ (2009b). Cambodia, China complete phase 1 of GMS Information Highway Project. *People's Daily Online,* 15 July. Available from http://english.people.com.cn/90001/90776/90883/6701499.html.

_____ (2009c). Chinese premier, UN chief discuss climate change. *China View,* Window on China sect., 30 December. Available from http://news.xinhuanet.com/english/2009-12/30/content_12730059.htm.

Yap, Josef T. (2009). Impact of the global financial and economic crisis on the Philippines: a rapid assessment. Bangkok and Geneva: International Labour Organization. Available from www.ilo.org/wcmsp5/groups/public/---asia/---ro-bangkok/documents/meetingdocument/wcms_101595.pdf.

Zhou, Xiaochuan (2009). Reform the international monetary system. Speech by the Governor, 23 March. People's Bank of China. Available from www.pbc.gov.cn/english/detail.asp?col=6500&id=178.

STATISTICAL ANNEX

List of tables

Page

1. Real gross domestic product growth rates 196

2. Gross domestic savings rates 197

3. Gross domestic investment rates 198

4. Inflation rates 199

5. Budget balance 200

6. Current account balance 201

7. Change in money supply 202

8. Merchandise export growth rates 203

9. Merchandise import growth rates 204

10. Inward foreign direct investment 205

11. Official development assistance and workers' remittances 206

12. International migration 207

13. Primary, secondary and tertiary education 208

14. Poverty and malnutrition 209

15. Unemployment rate by gender and age group 210

Table 1. Real gross domestic product growth rates

(Percentages)

	1998	1999	2000	2001	2002	2003	2004	2005	2006	2007	2008	2009
East and North-East Asia	0.1	3.2	5.3	2.7	3.5	4.1	5.3	4.7	5.2	5.8	2.1	−1.1
China	7.8	7.6	8.4	8.3	9.1	10.0	10.1	10.4	11.6	13.0	9.0	8.7
Democratic People's Republic of Korea	−1.1	6.2	1.3	3.7	1.2	1.8	2.2	3.8	−1.1	−2.3	3.7	..
Hong Kong, China	−6.0	2.6	8.0	0.5	1.8	3.0	8.5	7.1	7.0	6.4	2.4	−1.9
Japan	−2.0	−0.1	2.9	0.2	0.3	1.4	2.7	1.9	2.0	2.4	−1.2	−5.2
Macao, China	−4.6	−2.4	5.7	2.9	10.1	14.2	27.3	6.9	16.5	26.0	12.9	1.3
Mongolia	3.5	3.2	1.1	0.9	4.7	7.0	10.6	7.3	8.6	10.2	8.9	0.5
Republic of Korea	−6.9	9.5	8.5	4.0	7.2	2.8	4.7	4.0	5.1	5.1	2.2	0.2
Russian Federation	−5.3	6.4	10.0	5.1	4.7	7.3	7.2	6.4	7.7	8.1	5.6	−7.9
North and Central Asia	−3.8	6.1	9.6	5.9	5.3	7.5	7.5	7.4	8.8	8.9	5.8	−5.8
Armenia	7.3	3.3	5.9	9.6	13.2	14.0	10.5	13.9	13.2	13.8	6.8	−14.4
Azerbaijan	10.0	7.4	11.1	9.9	10.6	11.2	10.2	26.4	34.5	25.0	10.8	9.3
Georgia	3.1	2.9	1.8	4.8	5.5	11.1	5.9	9.6	9.4	12.3	2.1	−4.0
Kazakhstan	−1.9	2.7	9.8	13.5	9.8	9.3	9.6	9.7	10.7	8.9	3.3	1.0
Kyrgyzstan	2.1	3.7	5.4	5.3	0.0	7.0	7.0	−0.2	3.1	8.5	7.6	2.3
Russian Federation	−5.3	6.4	10.0	5.1	4.7	7.3	7.2	6.4	7.7	8.1	5.6	−7.9
Tajikistan	5.3	3.7	8.3	9.6	10.8	11.0	10.3	6.7	7.0	7.8	7.9	3.4
Turkmenistan	7.1	16.5	5.5	4.3	0.3	3.3	5.0	13.0	11.4	11.6	9.8	6.1
Uzbekistan	4.3	4.3	3.8	4.2	4.0	4.4	7.7	7.0	7.3	9.5	9.0	8.1
Oceania	4.5	4.3	3.2	2.6	4.0	3.4	3.7	3.2	2.7	4.6	2.0	1.0
Australia	5.0	4.3	3.2	2.6	3.9	3.2	3.6	3.2	2.7	4.8	2.3	1.2
Cook Islands	−0.8	2.7	13.9	4.9	2.6	8.2	4.3	0.0	0.7	1.3	−1.2	−0.1
Fiji	1.3	8.8	−1.6	1.9	3.2	1.0	5.5	0.6	1.9	−0.5	−0.1	−2.5
Kiribati	15.2	−1.2	7.6	−5.1	6.1	2.3	2.2	0.0	3.2	−0.5	3.4	1.5
Marshall Islands	−3.6	−2.9	5.1	2.7	3.8	3.4	5.6	2.0	2.4	3.3	−2.0	0.5
Micronesia (Federated States of)	5.5	−2.1	4.7	0.1	0.9	2.9	−3.3	−0.6	−2.3	−3.1	−1.0	0.5
New Zealand	0.8	4.7	3.8	2.4	4.7	4.9	4.5	3.1	2.3	3.1	−0.5	−0.5
Palau	2.0	−5.4	0.3	1.3	−3.5	−1.3	6.0	5.9	4.8	2.1	−1.0	−3.0
Papua New Guinea	4.7	1.9	−2.5	−0.1	2.0	4.4	0.6	3.9	2.3	7.2	6.7	4.5
Samoa	2.4	2.2	3.3	8.2	3.2	4.8	4.8	5.4	1.0	6.4	−4.9	−0.8
Solomon Islands	3.2	−1.6	−14.2	−8.0	−2.8	6.5	4.9	5.4	6.9	10.7	6.9	0.4
Tonga	3.5	2.3	5.4	7.2	1.4	3.4	2.6	−3.0	0.8	−3.2	1.2	0.4
Tuvalu	10.5	2.4	−12.8	13.2	5.5	4.0	4.0	2.0	1.0	2.0	1.5	1.0
Vanuatu	4.3	−3.2	2.7	−2.6	−7.4	3.2	5.5	6.5	7.4	6.8	6.6	3.0
South and South-West Asia	4.9	3.4	5.1	2.3	4.7	7.1	7.6	8.6	8.2	7.5	4.7	2.9
Afghanistan	..	..	..	−3.5	81.1	14.3	9.4	14.5	11.2	16.2	3.4	15.1
Bangladesh	5.2	4.9	6.0	5.3	4.4	5.3	6.3	6.0	6.6	6.4	6.2	5.9
Bhutan	5.8	7.7	7.2	6.8	10.9	7.2	6.8	6.5	6.3	21.4	5.0	5.7
India	6.7	6.4	4.4	5.8	3.8	8.5	7.5	9.5	9.7	9.2	6.7	7.2
Iran (Islamic Republic of)	1.6	2.8	5.1	3.3	7.5	6.8	4.8	5.7	6.2	6.9	3.3	2.0
Maldives	9.8	7.2	4.8	3.5	6.5	8.5	9.5	−4.6	18.0	7.2	5.8	−2.6
Nepal	3.2	4.3	6.0	5.4	0.1	3.9	4.7	3.1	3.7	3.3	5.3	4.7
Pakistan	3.5	4.2	3.9	2.0	3.1	4.7	7.5	9.0	5.8	6.8	4.1	2.0
Sri Lanka	4.8	4.3	6.0	−1.4	4.0	6.0	5.4	6.2	7.7	6.8	6.0	3.5
Turkey	3.1	−3.4	6.8	−5.7	6.2	5.3	9.4	8.4	6.9	4.7	0.9	−6.0
South-East Asia	−6.9	4.1	6.6	1.9	4.9	5.5	6.6	5.8	6.1	6.5	4.0	0.6
Brunei Darussalam	−0.6	3.1	2.8	2.7	3.9	2.9	0.5	0.4	4.4	0.2	−1.9	−0.5
Cambodia	5.0	12.6	8.4	7.7	7.0	8.5	10.3	13.2	10.8	10.2	6.7	0.0
Indonesia	−13.1	0.8	4.9	3.6	4.5	4.8	5.0	5.7	5.5	6.3	6.1	4.5
Lao People's Democratic Republic	4.0	7.3	5.8	5.7	5.9	5.8	6.9	7.3	8.3	7.9	7.9	5.4
Malaysia	−7.4	6.1	8.9	0.5	5.4	5.8	6.8	5.3	5.8	6.2	4.6	−1.7
Myanmar	5.8	10.9	13.7	11.3	12.0	13.8	13.6	13.6	12.7	5.5	2.0	2.0
Philippines	−0.6	3.4	6.0	1.8	4.4	4.9	6.4	5.0	5.4	7.1	3.8	0.9
Singapore	−1.4	7.2	10.1	−2.4	4.1	3.8	9.3	7.3	8.4	7.8	1.1	−2.0
Thailand	−10.5	4.4	4.8	2.2	5.3	7.1	6.3	4.6	5.2	4.9	2.5	−2.3
Timor-Leste	−2.1	−35.5	13.7	16.5	2.4	0.1	4.2	6.2	−5.8	8.4	12.8	7.4
Viet Nam	5.8	4.8	6.8	6.9	7.1	7.3	7.8	8.4	8.2	8.5	6.2	5.3
Memorandum items:												
Developing ESCAP economies	2.5	6.0	7.1	4.5	6.7	7.1	8.1	8.0	8.7	9.1	5.7	4.0
(excluding China and India)	−2.8	4.5	6.8	1.0	5.5	4.5	6.6	5.8	6.0	6.0	2.7	−0.6
Developed ESCAP economies	−1.4	0.3	2.9	0.4	0.6	1.6	2.8	2.0	2.1	2.6	−0.9	−4.6
Pacific island economies	3.5	3.3	−1.9	0.6	1.8	3.7	2.5	3.0	2.4	4.6	3.8	1.9

Notes: Figures for 2009 are estimates. Data and estimates for countries relate to fiscal years defined as follows: 2008 refers to fiscal year
India: 1 April 2008-31 March 2009;
Islamic Republic of Iran: 21 March 2008-20 March 2009;
Bangladesh, Pakistan: 1 July 2007-30 June 2008;
Nepal: 16 July 2007-15 July 2008.
The term "developing ESCAP economies" refers to developing Asian and Pacific economies, excluding those of North and Central Asia.
The term "developed ESCAP economies" refers to Australia, Japan and New Zealand.

Sources: ESCAP, based on national sources; International Monetary Fund, *International Financial Statistics* databases (Washington, D.C.,
September 2009); ADB, *Key Indicators for Asia and the Pacific 2009* (Manila, 2009); CEIC Data Company Limited; and the website of the
Interstate Statistical Committee of the Commonwealth of Independent States (www.cisstat.com), 22 March 2010; and ESCAP estimates.

Table 2. Gross domestic savings rates

(Percentage of GDP)

	1998	1999	2000	2001	2002	2003	2004	2005	2006	2007	2008	2009
East and North-East Asia												
China	38.9	38.0	38.0	39.0	40.4	43.0	45.6	46.6	47.8	49.9	50.4	50.8
Hong Kong, China	29.4	30.1	32.0	29.8	31.1	31.2	30.7	33.0	33.1	31.8	31.2	30.2
Japan	27.6	26.2	26.4	24.3	23.6	23.8	24.0	24.6	24.2	23.9	23.6	20.6
Macao, China	46.5	42.9	47.4	47.9	51.6	56.7	63.5	63.5	67.2	70.5	70.1	..
Mongolia	14.3	14.6	10.4	5.7	3.4	12.2	19.5	32.0	39.8	37.2	35.7	..
Republic of Korea	37.9	35.8	33.3	31.3	30.7	32.2	34.1	32.3	31.0	30.9	30.3	29.0
Russian Federation	21.6	31.9	38.7	34.6	30.8	32.1	33.1	33.7	34.0	34.2	34.6	30.0
North and Central Asia												
Armenia	−11.2	−8.3	−8.9	−4.8	0.9	6.5	7.4	14.0	17.7	18.7	17.9	16.1
Azerbaijan	4.8	8.6	20.4	24.9	24.7	27.6	31.3	47.5	54.4	56.9	56.2	57.0
Georgia	6.5	7.4	9.9	15.9	15.3	16.7	15.3	15.7	6.7	8.4	2.6	1.7
Kazakhstan	15.9	16.0	26.0	28.7	33.8	34.3	34.9	38.9	44.1	43.8	47.5	39.4
Kyrgyzstan	−6.1	3.2	14.3	17.7	13.8	5.3	5.8	−2.1	−13.1	−4.6	−10.8	−1.8
Russian Federation	21.6	31.9	38.7	34.6	30.8	32.1	33.1	33.7	34.0	34.2	34.6	30.0
Tajikistan	6.3	15.9	9.3	−0.5	3.2	3.0	3.3	−12.0	−20.5	−23.8	−21.5	−18.1
Turkmenistan	7.3	12.3	49.3	36.2	43.2	31.1	25.2	40.2	..	..	..	..
Uzbekistan	19.9	17.3	19.4	20.0	21.8	26.9	31.9	32.7	33.9	29.5	28.9	..
Oceania												
Australia	23.2	22.6	23.1	22.4	23.1	23.0	23.5	23.9	25.5	26.3	28.1	28.3
Cook Islands	14.8	20.2	21.8	26.7	24.0	21.4	18.1	25.0	21.5	..	..	..
Fiji	30.7	22.4	12.2	8.1	17.3	13.6	2.5	1.5	−4.5	0.6	..	..
Kiribati	4.2	−0.6	2.8	2.1	1.4	2.1	1.9	1.8	1.9	..	..	..
New Zealand	20.6	21.5	23.2	24.7	24.1	23.8	24.0	22.8	22.0	22.9	21.3	20.4
Papua New Guinea	22.6	13.2	38.8	36.0	27.9	35.7	31.0	35.9	36.1	35.9	35.4	34.2
Samoa	−6.5	−13.0	−9.2	−14.1	−14.5	−14.0	−14.1	−14.0	−13.9	..	..	..
Solomon Islands	−9.7	−0.2	−7.9	−12.7	−5.5	4.1	0.0	−6.8	−6.5	−5.5	−10.2	..
Tonga	−17.2	−10.2	−9.4	−22.6	−25.5	−24.3	−18.4	−24.9	−26.4	−31.4	−38.9	..
Tuvalu	..	..	..	..	..	..	..	..	..	..	..	..
Vanuatu	22.4	19.2	19.3	17.9	9.4	12.7	16.4	20.2	23.8	24.9	..	..
South and South-West Asia												
Bangladesh	17.4	17.7	17.9	18.0	18.2	18.6	19.5	20.0	20.2	20.4	20.3	20.0
Bhutan	22.9	22.5	23.3	40.9	39.7	39.1	36.0	27.7	38.6	37.2	..	..
India	22.3	24.8	23.7	23.5	26.3	29.8	31.7	34.2	35.7	37.7	33.9	34.5
Iran (Islamic Republic of)	25.5	25.4	26.8	38.4	38.5	38.6	39.6	39.3	37.7	38.1	41.3	..
Maldives	46.7	44.2	44.2	44.9	46.3	49.1	46.2	..	..	..	..	..
Nepal	12.8	12.6	14.1	11.7	9.5	8.6	11.7	11.6	9.0	9.9	11.2	8.0
Pakistan	16.7	14.0	16.0	15.9	16.5	17.3	17.6	15.2	14.1	15.4	11.5	11.2
Sri Lanka	19.6	18.0	15.2	16.1	15.5	15.6	15.9	17.2	17.0	17.6	16.2	15.6
Turkey	23.3	19.3	17.8	19.2	19.2	16.6	16.8	16.5	17.1	16.5	16.4	14.7
South-East Asia												
Brunei Darussalam	29.9	36.9	49.4	44.3	47.2	48.6	51.4	59.1	62.1	59.1	..	..
Cambodia	2.3	7.6	8.1	11.6	8.5	9.1	8.5	9.9	13.8	16.1	30.3	..
Indonesia	26.5	19.5	31.8	31.5	25.1	23.7	24.9	27.5	28.7	28.1	30.6	30.5
Lao People's Democratic Republic	14.8	16.4	15.1	15.4	17.9	17.0	18.2	17.3	18.7	22.3	27.0	..
Malaysia	48.7	47.4	46.1	41.8	42.0	42.5	43.4	42.8	43.2	42.0	42.2	36.7
Myanmar	11.8	13.0	12.3	11.5	10.2	11.0	12.3	13.3	13.8	13.6	14.5	14.9
Philippines	12.4	14.3	17.3	17.1	19.1	19.7	21.2	21.0	20.1	20.8	19.2	16.0
Singapore	53.0	49.0	47.4	44.2	40.5	43.6	47.1	48.8	50.3	52.4	50.0	45.5
Thailand	34.8	32.5	32.5	31.4	31.7	32.0	31.7	30.9	32.4	34.1	33.2	30.6
Viet Nam	21.5	24.6	27.1	28.8	28.7	27.4	28.5	30.3	30.6	29.2	26.6	27.2

Notes: Figures for 2009 are estimates. Data for Islamic Republic of Iran, the Lao People's Democratic Republic and Nepal are based on national sources. Data for the Islamic Republic of Iran refer to gross national savings. Data for Cook Islands, Kiribati and Samoa are calculated on the basis of United Nations Statistics Division databases.

Source: ESCAP, based on ADB, *Key Indicators for Asia and the Pacific 2009* (Manila, 2009) with updates and estimates from national sources.

Table 3. Gross domestic investment rates

(Percentage of GDP)

	1998	1999	2000	2001	2002	2003	2004	2005	2006	2007	2008	2009
East and North-East Asia												
China	37.1	36.7	35.1	36.3	37.9	41.2	43.3	44.0	44.5	43.1	44.4	43.8
Hong Kong, China	28.9	24.8	27.5	25.3	22.8	21.9	21.8	20.6	21.7	20.9	20.4	18.9
Japan	26.3	24.8	25.4	24.8	23.1	22.8	23.0	23.6	23.8	24.1	23.5	20.3
Macao, China	17.7	17.7	11.6	10.3	11.0	14.6	17.0	27.5	35.4	36.8	29.2	..
Mongolia	35.2	37.0	36.2	36.1	39.6	35.5	34.5	37.0	35.1	40.2	38.6	..
Republic of Korea	25.0	29.1	30.6	29.3	29.1	30.0	29.9	29.7	29.6	29.4	31.4	25.5
Russian Federation	15.0	14.8	18.7	21.9	20.0	20.8	20.9	20.1	21.3	24.6	25.3	23.3
North and Central Asia												
Armenia	19.1	18.4	18.6	19.8	21.7	24.3	24.9	30.5	35.9	37.2	39.9	39.5
Azerbaijan	33.4	26.5	20.7	20.7	34.6	53.2	58.0	41.5	29.9	21.5	20.2	19.0
Georgia	27.2	26.5	26.6	30.3	28.5	31.3	31.9	33.5	30.9	32.1	27.0	27.1
Kazakhstan	15.8	17.8	18.1	26.9	27.3	25.7	26.3	31.0	33.9	35.5	28.0	32.3
Kyrgyzstan	15.4	18.0	20.0	18.0	17.6	11.8	14.5	16.4	24.2	26.6	24.8	21.4
Russian Federation	15.0	14.8	18.7	21.9	20.0	20.8	20.9	20.1	21.3	24.6	25.3	23.3
Tajikistan	15.4	17.3	9.4	9.7	9.4	10.0	12.2	11.6	16.0	24.6	17.4	..
Turkmenistan	45.5	39.7	34.7	31.7	27.6	25.4	23.1	22.9	23.8	23.3	..	..
Uzbekistan	20.9	17.1	19.6	21.1	21.2	20.8	23.9	23.0	22.3	19.9	..	..
Pacific island economies												
Australia	23.9	24.8	25.1	22.1	22.9	25.0	26.1	26.4	27.0	27.5	28.7	28.1
Cook Islands	18.4	17.2	16.8	15.8	16.4	16.9	17.6	16.7	16.9	17.7	..	..
Fiji	28.2	22.8	17.3	16.1	19.7	22.0	19.2	19.4	16.2	17.1	..	..
Kiribati	42.5	44.9	43.2	43.5	43.9	43.5	43.6	43.7	43.6	..	..	..
New Zealand	20.3	22.3	21.6	22.3	22.2	23.5	24.8	24.8	23.7	24.1	23.2	19.0
Papua New Guinea	17.9	16.1	21.9	23.0	25.0	21.4	21.4	17.5	15.7	15.1	15.9	17.6
Samoa	14.0	14.1	14.2	14.3	13.1	12.3	11.2	10.4	9.8	9.1	8.7	..
Solomon Islands	6.8	6.2	6.6	6.8	5.4	9.4	11.4	13.8	14.6	18.9	17.8	..
Tonga	19.0	20.2	19.4	18.0	19.7	18.4	19.4	19.8	17.6	16.1	17.6	..
Tuvalu	54.9	57.9	54.7	55.8	56.1	55.6	55.8	55.8	55.7	..	..	..
Vanuatu	17.7	20.3	22.2	20.0	21.1	19.4	21.2	21.5	23.9	25.8	..	..
South and South-West Asia												
Bangladesh	21.6	22.2	23.0	23.1	23.2	23.4	24.0	24.5	24.7	24.5	24.2	24.2
Bhutan	35.7	39.7	47.3	59.2	59.2	56.8	62.0	51.2	46.9	38.9	..	..
India	23.3	25.9	24.3	22.8	25.2	27.6	32.1	35.5	36.9	39.1	36.5	36.5
Iran (Islamic Republic of)	24.7	26.0	27.1	32.6	33.9	35.1	35.7	35.8	35.0	34.4	36.8	37.6
Maldives	30.1	33.6	26.3	28.1	25.5	27.1	35.0	53.5	..	..	..	..
Nepal	23.1	19.0	22.6	22.3	20.2	21.4	24.5	26.5	26.9	28.1	31.8	29.7
Pakistan	17.7	15.6	17.2	17.0	16.6	16.8	16.6	19.1	22.1	22.5	22.0	19.7
Sri Lanka	25.4	25.6	25.4	22.2	22.0	21.6	24.7	26.1	27.4	27.3	27.1	25.5
Turkey	22.1	19.1	20.8	15.1	17.6	17.6	19.4	20.0	22.1	22.2	21.8	16.1
South-East Asia												
Brunei Darussalam	33.8	21.4	13.1	14.4	21.3	15.1	13.5	11.4	10.4	12.9	11.6	..
Cambodia	11.8	16.7	16.9	18.5	18.1	20.1	16.2	18.5	20.6	20.8	23.7	22.5
Indonesia	16.8	11.4	22.2	22.0	21.4	25.6	24.1	25.1	25.4	24.9	27.8	27.4
Lao People's Democratic Republic	24.9	22.7	20.5	21.0	24.0	21.4	21.1	17.5	21.4	22.0	24.0	..
Malaysia	26.7	22.4	26.9	24.4	24.8	22.8	23.0	20.0	20.5	21.7	19.1	13.8
Myanmar	12.4	13.4	12.4	11.6	10.1	11.0	12.2	13.2	13.8	13.5	14.4	14.9
Philippines	20.3	18.8	21.2	19.0	17.7	16.8	16.8	14.6	14.5	15.4	15.2	14.8
Singapore	32.3	32.0	32.5	26.0	23.7	16.0	21.8	20.2	20.1	20.7	30.9	28.9
Thailand	20.4	20.5	22.8	24.1	23.8	25.0	26.8	31.4	28.4	26.6	28.8	21.3
Viet Nam	29.0	27.6	29.6	31.2	33.2	35.4	35.5	35.6	36.8	43.1	41.1	41.9

Notes: Figures for 2009 are estimates. Data for Cambodia, Islamic Republic of Iran and the Lao People's Democratic Republic are based on national sources.

Data for Cook Islands, Kiribati, Samoa, and Tuvalu are calculated based on United Nations Statistics Division databases.

Sources: ESCAP, based on ADB, *Key Indicators for Asia and the Pacific 2009* (Manila, 2009) with updates and estimates from national sources.

Table 4. Inflation rates

(Percentages)

	1998	1999	2000	2001	2002	2003	2004	2005	2006	2007	2008	2009
East and North-East Asia	2.1	3.4	0.7	0.9	0.1	0.9	1.8	1.2	1.2	2.0	3.5	−0.3
China	−0.8	−1.4	0.3	0.7	−0.8	1.1	3.9	1.8	1.5	4.8	5.9	−0.7
Hong Kong, China	2.8	−4.0	−3.8	−1.6	−3.0	−2.5	−0.4	0.9	2.1	2.0	4.3	0.5
Japan	0.7	−0.3	−0.7	−0.8	−0.9	−0.3	0.0	−0.3	0.2	0.1	1.4	−1.4
Macao, China	0.2	−3.2	−1.6	−2.0	−2.6	−1.6	1.0	4.5	5.2	5.6	8.6	1.2
Mongolia	9.4	7.5	11.6	6.2	0.9	5.2	8.3	12.8	4.8	9.6	28.0	7.0
Republic of Korea	7.5	0.8	2.3	4.1	2.8	3.5	3.6	2.8	2.2	2.5	4.7	2.8
Russian Federation	27.7	85.7	20.8	21.5	15.8	13.7	10.9	12.7	9.7	9.0	14.1	11.7
North and Central Asia	24.8	72.3	19.3	19.7	14.8	12.4	10.1	11.9	9.7	9.5	14.4	10.7
Armenia	8.7	0.7	−0.8	3.1	1.1	4.8	7.0	0.6	2.9	4.4	9.0	3.4
Azerbaijan	−0.8	−8.5	1.8	1.5	2.8	2.1	6.8	10.0	8.3	16.7	20.8	1.5
Georgia	3.6	19.1	4.0	4.7	5.6	4.8	5.7	8.2	9.2	9.2	10.0	1.7
Kazakhstan	7.1	8.3	13.2	8.4	5.9	6.4	6.9	7.6	8.6	10.8	17.0	7.3
Kyrgyzstan	10.4	36.0	18.7	6.9	2.1	3.1	4.1	4.4	5.6	10.2	24.5	6.8
Russian Federation	27.7	85.7	20.8	21.5	15.8	13.7	10.9	12.7	9.7	9.0	14.1	11.7
Tajikistan	43.0	26.0	24.0	36.5	10.2	17.1	6.8	7.8	11.9	21.5	20.4	6.4
Turkmenistan	16.8	23.5	8.0	11.6	8.8	5.6	5.9	10.7	8.2	6.3	13.0	10.0
Uzbekistan	29.0	29.1	25.0	27.3	27.3	11.6	6.6	10.0	14.2	12.3	12.7	8.0
Oceania	1.0	1.4	4.3	4.2	3.0	2.8	2.3	2.7	3.5	2.3	4.4	1.9
Australia	0.9	1.5	4.5	4.4	3.0	2.8	2.3	2.7	3.5	2.3	4.4	1.8
Cook Islands	0.7	1.3	3.2	8.7	3.4	2.0	0.9	2.5	3.4	2.5	7.8	6.5
Fiji	5.9	2.0	1.1	4.3	0.8	4.2	2.8	2.4	2.5	4.8	7.7	3.7
Kiribati	4.3	0.6	0.9	7.0	1.6	2.6	−1.9	−0.5	−0.2	3.7	18.6	6.6
Marshall Islands	2.2	1.7	1.6	1.7	1.3	−2.8	2.2	4.4	4.3	3.1	17.5	9.6
Micronesia (Federated States of)	..	..	2.2	0.5	−0.1	0.1	2.3	4.3	4.4	3.6	6.8	2.9
Nauru	..	..	..	..	..	..	2.3	2.7	3.5	2.3	4.5	1.8
New Zealand	1.3	−0.1	2.6	2.6	2.7	1.8	2.3	3.0	3.4	2.4	4.0	2.1
Palau	..	..	..	−1.8	−1.3	0.9	5.0	3.9	4.5	3.2	12.0	5.2
Papua New Guinea	13.6	14.9	15.6	9.3	11.8	14.7	2.1	1.8	2.4	0.9	10.6	6.9
Samoa	5.4	0.3	0.9	4.7	8.1	0.1	16.3	1.9	3.8	5.5	11.5	6.1
Solomon Islands	12.3	8.0	7.1	7.7	9.3	10.0	7.1	7.4	11.2	7.7	17.2	8.0
Tonga	3.3	4.5	6.2	8.3	10.4	11.6	11.0	8.3	6.4	5.9	10.4	1.6
Tuvalu	0.6	4.0	1.3	1.3	8.0	3.3	2.8	3.2	3.8	2.2	5.3	3.8
Vanuatu	3.2	3.1	2.1	3.5	2.1	1.1	3.2	1.2	2.0	3.9	4.8	4.5
South and South-West Asia	30.8	21.4	17.4	17.2	15.5	10.3	6.4	6.7	8.3	8.4	11.5	11.2
Afghanistan	..	..	..	..	..	24.1	13.2	12.3	5.1	13.0	26.8	−10.0
Bangladesh	9.0	7.0	2.8	1.9	2.8	4.4	5.8	6.5	7.2	7.2	9.9	6.7
Bhutan	10.6	6.8	4.0	3.4	2.5	2.1	4.6	5.3	5.0	5.2	6.3	7.2
India	13.2	4.7	4.0	3.8	4.3	3.8	3.8	4.4	6.7	6.2	9.1	11.9
Iran (Islamic Republic of)	18.1	20.1	12.6	11.4	15.8	15.6	15.2	12.1	13.6	18.4	25.5	16.0
Maldives	−1.4	3.0	−1.2	0.7	0.9	−2.9	6.4	3.3	3.5	7.4	12.3	8.5
Nepal	8.3	11.4	3.4	2.4	2.9	4.8	4.0	4.5	8.0	6.4	7.7	13.2
Pakistan	7.8	5.7	3.6	4.4	3.5	3.1	4.6	9.3	7.9	7.8	12.0	20.8
Sri Lanka	9.4	4.7	6.2	14.2	9.6	6.3	9.0	11.0	10.0	15.8	22.6	3.4
Turkey	84.7	64.9	54.9	54.4	45.1	25.3	8.6	8.2	9.6	8.8	10.4	6.3
South-East Asia	21.0	7.7	2.4	4.9	4.6	3.3	4.1	5.9	6.7	3.9	8.6	2.1
Brunei Darussalam	−0.4	−0.1	1.2	0.6	−2.3	0.3	0.9	1.1	0.2	0.3	2.7	1.2
Cambodia	14.8	4.0	−0.8	−0.6	3.2	1.2	3.9	6.3	6.1	7.7	25.0	−0.8
Indonesia	58.5	20.5	3.7	11.5	11.9	6.6	6.2	10.5	13.1	6.3	10.1	4.6
Lao People's Democratic Republic	91.0	128.4	25.1	7.8	10.6	15.5	10.5	7.2	6.8	4.5	7.6	0.2
Malaysia	5.3	2.7	1.5	1.4	1.8	1.0	1.5	3.0	3.6	2.0	5.4	0.6
Myanmar	51.5	18.4	−0.1	21.1	57.0	36.6	4.5	9.4	20.0	35.0	26.8	6.5
Philippines	9.3	5.9	4.0	6.8	3.0	3.5	6.0	7.7	6.3	2.8	9.3	3.3
Singapore	−0.3	0.0	1.4	1.0	−0.4	0.5	1.7	0.5	1.0	2.1	6.6	0.6
Thailand	8.1	0.3	1.6	1.6	0.6	1.8	2.8	4.5	4.6	2.2	5.5	−0.8
Timor-Leste	..	..	63.6	3.6	4.7	7.2	3.2	1.8	4.1	8.9	7.6	1.3
Viet Nam	7.3	4.1	−1.7	−0.4	3.8	3.2	7.8	8.3	7.4	8.3	23.1	7.0
Memorandum items:												
Developing ESCAP economies	11.3	6.1	4.9	5.6	4.4	3.7	4.2	3.7	4.0	5.0	7.3	3.1
(excluding China and India)	20.5	12.5	9.0	10.1	8.5	5.9	4.5	5.1	5.2	4.8	8.0	3.8
Developed ESCAP economies	0.7	−0.1	−0.3	−0.3	−0.5	0.0	0.2	0.0	0.6	0.3	1.7	−1.1
Pacific island developing economies	10.1	9.6	9.8	7.5	8.1	10.3	3.5	2.3	3.1	2.7	10.1	6.3

Notes: Figures for 2009 are estimates. The data and estimates for countries relate to fiscal years defined as follows: 2008 refers to fiscal year
India: 1 April 2008-31 March 2009;
Islamic Republic of Iran: 21 March 2008-20 March 2009;
Bangladesh, Pakistan: 1 July 2007-30 June 2008;
Nepal: 16 July 2007-15 July 2008.
The term "developing ESCAP economies" refers to developing Asian and Pacific economies, excluding those of North and Central Asia.
The term "developed ESCAP economies" refers to Australia, Japan and New Zealand.
Data for the following countries (Brunei darussalam, Cook Islands, Micronesia, Nauru, Palau and Tuvalu) are based on *ADB, Key Indicators for Asia and the Pacific 2009*.
Consumer price inflation for the following countries are for a given city or group of consumers: Cambodia is for Phnom Penh, India's data refer to the industrial workers index, Nepal is for national urban consumers, Sri Lanka is for Colombo, and Timor-Leste is for Dili.

Sources: ESCAP, based on national sources; International Monetary Fund, *International Financial Statistics* databases (Washington, D.C., September 2009), and *World Economic Outlook Databases* (Washington, D.C., October 2009); ADB, *Key Indicators for Asia and the Pacific 2009* (Manila, 2009); CEIC Data Company Limited; and the website of the Interstate Statistical Committee of the Commonwealth of Independent States (www.cisstat.com), 22 March 2010 and ESCAP estimates.

Table 5. Budget balance

(Percentage of GDP)

	1998	1999	2000	2001	2002	2003	2004	2005	2006	2007	2008	2009
East and North-East Asia												
China	−2.4	−3.0	−2.8	−2.5	−2.6	−2.2	−1.3	−1.2	−0.8	0.6	−0.4	−3.8
Hong Kong, China	−1.8	0.8	−0.6	−4.9	−4.8	−3.2	1.7	1.0	4.0	7.7	−0.3	−2.4
Japan	−10.6	−7.3	−6.4	−5.9	−6.7	−6.7	−5.2	−6.2	−1.0	−2.6	−2.7	−7.4
Mongolia	−14.3	−11.6	−7.7	−4.5	−5.8	−3.7	−1.8	2.6	3.3	2.9	−5.0	−6.0
Republic of Korea	−3.9	−2.5	1.1	1.1	3.1	1.0	0.6	0.4	0.4	3.5	1.2	−4.0
Russian Federation	−4.8	−1.2	2.4	3.1	1.7	2.4	4.8	7.5	7.5	5.4	4.1	−5.9
North and Central Asia												
Armenia	−3.8	−5.2	−4.9	−4.3	−2.6	−1.3	−1.7	−1.9	−1.5	−1.5	−1.2	−6.6
Azerbaijan	−1.8	−2.4	−1.0	−0.4	−0.5	−5.1	−2.6	−2.3	−4.6	−5.5	−6.1	−8.2
Georgia	−6.2	−6.7	−3.7	−1.8	−3.7	−2.9	−3.2	−1.1	−3.0	−4.7	−6.3	−8.9
Kazakhstan	−3.9	−3.5	−0.1	−0.4	−0.3	−0.9	−0.3	0.6	0.8	−1.7	−2.1	−3.1
Kyrgyzstan	−3.0	−2.0	−2.2	0.4	−1.0	−0.8	−0.5	0.2	−0.2	0.1	0.8	−1.5
Russian Federation	−4.8	−1.2	2.4	3.1	1.7	2.4	4.8	7.5	7.5	5.4	4.1	−5.9
Tajikistan	−2.7	−2.4	−5.7	−3.1	−2.4	−1.8	−2.4	0.2	0.8	1.6	1.0	−0.5
Turkmenistan	−2.6	0.0	−0.3	0.6	0.2	−1.4	0.5	0.9	6.0	4.5	3.2	−2.0
Uzbekistan	−3.4	−1.7	−1.0	−1.0	−1.5	0.6	1.2	2.9	3.8	2.7	1.5	0.1
Oceania												
Australia	−0.3	0.6	1.9	0.9	−0.4	0.7	0.7	1.4	1.7	1.6	1.9	−2.7
Cook Islands	−2.5	−2.4	−1.8	1.3	−4.2	−0.8	−1.0	2.1	2.1	3.6	3.7	..
Fiji	5.0	−0.3	−3.2	−6.5	−5.7	−5.8	−3.1	−3.4	−2.8	−1.7	0.5	−2.5
Kiribati	70.2	37.5	42.7	10.1	3.8	9.9	12.3	7.7	12.0	37.9	..	..
New Zealand	0.4	0.1	2.1	2.0	3.9	4.2	4.4	5.4	6.3	5.3	−1.3	−4.9
Papua New Guinea	−1.8	−2.4	−2.0	−3.4	−3.8	−0.9	1.7	0.1	3.2	2.6	−2.2	−0.4
Samoa	2.0	0.3	−0.7	−2.2	−2.0	−0.6	−0.8	0.3	0.3	1.1	−3.3	..
Solomon Islands	3.0	5.0	−0.6	−7.4	−20.2	−5.8	4.9	−0.9	−3.9	0.5	0.0	..
Tonga	−2.4	−0.2	−0.4	−1.5	−1.4	−3.1	0.9	2.4	1.5	1.4	2.0	1.3
Tuvalu	19.1	−3.5	−2.2	−45.7	33.7	−33.3	−14.7	−7.4	18.7	−14.3	7.2	4.6
Vanuatu	−9.4	−1.5	−7.0	−3.7	−2.2	−1.8	0.9	2.0	0.4	0.3	2.3	0.7
South and South-West Asia												
Bangladesh	−3.4	−4.6	−6.1	−5.2	−4.7	−4.2	−4.2	−4.4	−3.9	−3.7	−6.1	−4.0
Bhutan	0.9	−1.7	−3.8	−10.6	−4.6	−9.8	1.8	−6.6	−0.8	0.6	0.7	2.2
India	−5.1	−5.4	−5.7	−6.2	−5.9	−4.5	−3.9	−4.0	−3.3	−2.6	−5.9	−6.5
Iran (Islamic Republic of)	−2.2	−0.2	−0.2	−0.4	−4.1	−3.4	−3.0	−3.7	−7.2	−3.4	−3.5	−4.8
Maldives	−1.9	−4.1	−4.4	−4.7	−4.9	−3.4	−1.6	−10.9	−6.9	−5.3	−16.9	−26.1
Nepal	−5.5	−4.9	−4.3	−5.5	−5.0	−3.3	−2.9	−3.1	−3.8	−4.1	−4.1	−3.8
Pakistan	−7.6	−6.1	−5.4	−4.3	−4.2	−3.6	−2.4	−3.3	−4.3	−4.4	−7.6	−5.2
Sri Lanka	−8.9	−7.3	−9.7	−10.6	−8.6	−7.7	−7.9	−8.4	−8.0	−7.7	−7.8	−7.0
Turkey	−6.2	−6.4	−5.6	−11.9	−12.0	−8.7	−5.3	−1.5	−0.6	−1.6	−1.8	−5.4
South-East Asia												
Cambodia	−5.4	−3.8	−4.8	−6.3	−7.0	−6.1	−3.5	−2.2	−2.8	−2.2	−1.5	..
Indonesia	−1.7	−2.5	−1.1	−2.4	−1.5	−1.8	−1.0	−0.6	−0.9	−1.3	−0.1	−1.5
Lao People's Democratic Republic	−6.6	−2.5	−4.6	−4.5	−3.4	−5.7	−2.6	−4.5	−3.1	−2.6	−2.2	−7.8
Malaysia	−1.8	−3.2	−5.5	−5.2	−5.3	−5.0	−4.1	−3.6	−3.3	−3.2	−4.8	−7.7
Myanmar	0.8	−0.3	0.7	..	..	..	..	..	..	..	..	..
Philippines	−1.9	−3.8	−4.0	−4.0	−5.3	−4.6	−3.8	−2.7	−1.1	−0.2	−0.9	−3.9
Singapore	2.5	0.5	2.0	1.6	−1.1	−1.6	−1.1	−0.3	0.5	3.3	1.5	−1.1
Thailand	−2.8	−3.3	−2.2	−2.4	−1.4	0.4	0.1	−0.6	1.1	−1.7	−1.1	−4.4
Timor-Leste			2.0	1.0	4.0	14.0	46.0	102.0	174.0	284.0	384.0	178.0
Viet Nam	−2.5	−4.4	−5.0	−4.9	−4.8	−4.9	−4.9	−4.9	−5.0	−4.9	−4.5	−8.2

Note: Figures for 2009 are estimates.

Sources: ESCAP, based on national sources; ADB, *Key Indicators for Asia and the Pacific 2009* (Manila, 2009); International Monetary Fund, *International Monetary Fund Article IV Consultation,* various issues; and ESCAP estimates.

Table 6. Current account balance

(Percentage of GDP)

	1998	1999	2000	2001	2002	2003	2004	2005	2006	2007	2008	2009
East and North-East Asia												
China	3.0	1.9	1.7	1.3	2.4	2.8	3.6	7.2	9.5	11.0	9.8	6.6
Hong Kong, China	1.5	6.3	4.1	5.9	7.6	10.4	9.5	11.4	12.1	12.3	14.2	8.7
Japan	3.1	2.6	2.6	2.1	2.9	3.2	3.7	3.6	3.9	4.8	3.2	2.8
Macao, China	..	..	..	..	54.2	59.1	63.6	41.4	30.6	49.0	..	..
Mongolia	−6.8	−5.8	−5.0	−12.0	−8.6	−7.1	1.3	1.3	7.0	6.7	−13.1	−7.0
Republic of Korea	11.7	5.5	2.3	1.6	0.9	1.9	3.9	1.8	0.6	0.6	−0.7	4.6
Russian Federation	0.1	12.6	18.0	11.0	8.5	8.2	10.1	11.1	9.6	6.0	6.1	3.9
North and Central Asia												
Armenia	−22.1	−16.6	−14.6	−9.4	−6.2	−6.7	−0.5	−1.1	−1.8	−6.4	−11.6	−12.5
Azerbaijan	−30.7	−13.1	−3.2	−0.9	−12.3	−27.8	−29.8	1.3	17.7	30.7	35.5	16.0
Georgia	−12.8	−10.0	−7.9	−6.4	−6.4	−9.6	−6.9	−11.1	−15.1	−19.6	−22.7	−16.8
Kazakhstan	−5.8	−1.0	2.0	−6.5	−4.4	−0.9	0.8	−1.8	−2.5	−8.0	5.3	−1.9
Kyrgyzstan	−25.1	−20.1	−9.0	−3.4	−3.8	−3.2	0.2	−2.4	−10.6	−6.9	−13.4	−8.1
Russian Federation	0.1	12.6	18.0	11.0	8.5	8.2	10.1	11.1	9.6	6.0	6.1	3.9
Tajikistan	−7.3	−0.9	−1.6	−4.9	−3.5	−1.3	−3.9	−2.7	−2.8	−8.6	−7.9	−6.5
Turkmenistan	−32.7	−14.8	8.2	1.7	6.7	2.7	0.6	5.1	15.7	15.5	18.7	20.4
Uzbekistan	−0.7	−1.0	1.8	−1.0	1.2	5.8	7.2	7.7	9.1	7.3	12.8	7.2
Oceania												
Australia	−4.8	−5.3	−3.8	−2.0	−3.8	−5.4	−6.1	−5.8	−5.5	−6.3	−4.4	−3.8
Fiji	4.6	−1.1	−4.0	−6.7	2.6	−6.6	−12.9	−11.4	−19.0	−14.0	−18.6	−8.7
Kiribati	27.7	11.9	−0.8	16.1	7.6	−19.5	−11.1	−19.1	−2.9	−1.0	−0.9	−3.1
New Zealand	−3.8	−6.1	−5.1	−2.7	−3.9	−4.3	−6.3	−8.4	−8.6	−8.1	−8.9	−6.1
Papua New Guinea	0.9	3.9	10.1	8.8	−4.2	3.8	4.4	12.4	7.3	1.8	2.8	−6.7
Samoa	6.6	2.3	−3.3	−36.2	−22.2	−8.1	−6.9	−10.7	−16.8	−8.4	−12.4	−16.4
Solomon Islands	−1.3	3.0	−7.3	−6.4	−4.4	6.3	16.3	−6.9	−6.3	−12.4	−18.7	−11.1
Tonga	−11.9	−1.0	−6.7	−9.9	4.9	−2.9	3.8	−2.7	−8.0	−8.5	−9.0	−6.5
Vanuatu	2.5	−4.9	2.0	2.0	−5.4	−6.6	−5.0	−7.4	−4.1	−5.9	−7.4	−6.0
South and South-West Asia												
Bangladesh	−0.6	−0.9	0.0	−1.7	0.5	0.4	0.9	−0.6	1.2	1.4	0.9	1.0
Bhutan	10.6	2.2	5.4	−8.8	−14.9	−21.8	−17.0	−28.4	−4.5	14.4	−2.1	−10.1
India	−1.0	−1.0	−0.6	0.7	1.3	2.4	−0.4	−1.2	−1.0	−1.3	−2.4	−3.3
Iran (Islamic Republic of)	−2.2	6.3	13.0	5.2	3.1	0.6	0.6	8.8	9.2	11.9	6.0	−0.2
Maldives	−4.1	−13.4	−8.2	−9.8	−5.6	−4.5	−15.8	−36.4	−33.0	−41.5	−51.4	−25.1
Nepal	−0.9	4.0	2.9	4.5	4.2	2.4	2.7	2.0	2.2	−0.1	2.9	4.3
Pakistan	−2.2	−2.6	−0.3	0.4	3.9	4.9	1.8	−1.4	−3.9	−4.8	−8.4	−5.3
Sri Lanka	−1.4	−3.5	−6.3	−1.1	−1.4	−0.4	−3.1	−2.5	−5.3	−4.3	−9.0	−0.3
Turkey	0.7	−0.4	−3.7	1.9	−0.3	−2.5	−3.7	−4.6	−6.0	−5.8	−5.7	−2.1
South-East Asia												
Cambodia	−5.7	−5.0	−2.7	−1.1	−2.3	−3.6	−2.2	−3.6	0.4	−2.8	−7.3	−5.4
Indonesia	4.3	4.1	4.8	4.3	4.0	3.5	0.6	0.1	3.0	2.4	0.1	2.0
Lao People's Democratic Republic	−11.7	−8.3	−0.5	−4.7	0.3	−2.0	−7.7	−5.7	1.4	2.6	3.3	..
Malaysia	13.2	15.9	9.0	7.9	7.1	12.1	12.1	14.5	16.3	15.5	17.6	15.0
Myanmar	−0.2	−0.1	−0.1	−0.03	0.01	0.00	0.01	0.00	0.03	..	..	..
Philippines	2.4	−3.8	−2.9	−2.4	−0.4	0.4	1.9	2.0	4.5	4.9	2.5	3.6
Singapore	22.2	17.4	11.6	12.5	12.6	23.1	16.6	18.3	21.4	23.5	14.8	13.4
Thailand	12.7	10.1	7.6	4.4	3.7	3.3	1.7	−4.3	1.1	6.3	0.6	7.7
Timor-Leste			−7.1	−12.6	−15.9	−15.4	20.7	78.4	165.2	296.1	405.0	191.0
Viet Nam	−3.9	4.1	3.5	2.1	−1.7	−4.9	−3.5	−1.1	−0.3	−9.8	−11.9	−9.0

Note: Figures for 2009 are estimates.
Current account balance of Papua New Guinea for 2005-2008 is based on International Monetary Fund 2007 Article IV Consultation.
Current account balance of Samoa and Tonga for 2005-2008 is based on International Monetary Fund 2008 Article IV Consultation.

Sources: ESCAP, based on International Monetary Fund, *International Financial Statistcs* databases (Washington, D.C., September 2009) and *World Economic Outlook Databases* (Washington, D.C., October 2009) with updates and estimates from national sources.

Table 7. Change in money supply

(Percentages)

	1998	1999	2000	2001	2002	2003	2004	2005	2006	2007	2008	2009
East and North-East Asia												
China	14.9	14.7	12.3	15.0	13.1	19.2	14.9	16.7	22.1	16.7	17.8	29.6[a]
Hong Kong, China	11.1	8.3	9.3	−0.3	0.5	6.3	7.3	3.5	16.2	18.8	4.2	8.9[a]
Japan	3.1	2.8	1.3	−17.1	0.9	0.5	0.6	0.5	−0.7	0.7	0.8	3.3[a]
Macao, China					8.1	12.3	8.9	12.2	24.5	9.8	2.3	14.2[a]
Mongolia	−1.7	31.6	17.6	27.9	42.0	49.6	20.4	34.6	34.8	56.3	−5.5	26.9
Republic of Korea	27.0	27.4	25.4	13.2	11.0	6.7	−0.6	3.1	4.4	0.3	15.9	11.8[b]
Russian Federation	37.6	56.7	58.0	36.3	33.8	38.5	33.7	36.3	40.6	44.2	14.6	16.4
North and Central Asia												
Armenia	36.7	14.0	38.6	4.3	34.0	10.4	22.3	27.8	32.9	42.3	2.4	16.4
Azerbaijan	−15.2	20.1	73.4	−11.3	14.5	29.7	47.5	22.1	86.8	71.7	44.0	−0.3
Georgia	−0.8	20.6	39.2	17.6	17.9	22.8	42.4	26.5	39.7	49.7	6.9	8.2
Kazakhstan	−14.1	84.4	45.0	40.2	30.1	34.2	68.2	26.3	78.1	25.9	35.4	17.9
Kyrgyzstan	17.5	33.7	11.7	11.3	33.9	33.4	32.1	10.0	51.5	33.2	..	..
Russian Federation	37.6	56.7	58.0	36.3	33.8	38.5	33.7	36.3	40.6	44.2	14.6	16.4
Tajikistan	28.2	24.6	63.3	35.0	40.5	40.9	9.8	113.3	65.4	108.7	−3.6	−14.0[c]
Turkmenistan	67.7	75.7	83.3	23.8	1.5	40.9	13.4	27.2	17.7	..	..	..
Uzbekistan	27.5	32.7	37.1	54.3	29.7	27.1	47.8	54.3	36.8	46.1	32.4	..
Oceania												
Australia	8.4	11.7	3.7	13.2	5.7	12.8	11.4	8.6	15.0	29.9	14.3	0.5
Cook Islands	12.1	16.7	4.8	14.4	3.2	9.9	9.6	−5.2	22.4	−5.8	4.0	..
Fiji	−0.5	13.6	−1.5	−3.1	7.8	25.0	10.5	15.1	20.2	10.3	−6.7	3.7[a]
Kiribati	..	..	..	..	..	..	..	..	..	..	..	..
Micronesia (Federated States of)	0.7	3.4	−1.0	6.0	−12.0	−3.7	−0.1	1.6	−8.5	4.6	3.2	8.6[b]
New Zealand	0.3	7.1	1.5	−1.9	11.5	9.5	3.5	9.5	11.3	11.1	10.3	−0.6
Papua New Guinea	2.5	9.2	5.0	6.2	7.3	−4.4	14.8	29.5	38.9	27.8	11.2	19.3
Samoa	2.5	15.7	16.3	6.1	10.2	14.0	8.3	15.6	13.7	11.0	5.8	8.4[a]
Solomon Islands	..	..	..	..	6.4	23.8	17.7	37.1	25.3	24.0	6.9	14.5
Tonga	14.8	12.0	18.7	14.3	8.3	14.5	13.9	22.1	5.4	13.5	0.7	2.3[b]
Tuvalu	..	..	..	..	..	..	..	..	..	..	..	..
Vanuatu	12.6	−9.2	5.5	5.5	−1.6	−0.9	9.9	11.6	7.0	16.0	13.4	1.8[a]
South and South-West Asia												
Bangladesh	10.4	12.8	18.6	16.6	13.1	15.6	13.8	16.7	19.3	17.1	17.6	19.4
Bhutan	13.9	32.0	17.4	7.9	26.9	1.8	19.9	11.9	13.0	13.0	32.4	24.6[d]
India	18.2	17.1	15.2	14.3	16.8	13.0	16.7	15.6	21.6	22.3	20.5	18.1[a]
Iran (Islamic Republic of)	20.4	21.5	22.4	27.6	24.9	24.5	23.0	22.8	29.1	30.6	7.9	18.7[d]
Maldives	23.0	3.5	4.2	9.1	19.5	14.5	32.8	11.7	20.6	23.7	23.6	12.5
Nepal	21.9	20.8	21.8	15.2	4.4	9.8	12.8	8.3	15.6	13.8	20.9	27.1[b]
Pakistan	7.9	4.3	12.1	11.7	16.8	17.5	20.5	16.5	14.6	19.5	15.5[d]	..
Sri Lanka	13.2	13.4	12.9	13.6	13.4	15.5	19.6	19.0	17.9	16.5	8.4	..
Turkey	89.3	102.0	40.7	87.4	29.8	14.4	20.8	36.0	22.2	15.2	24.8	13.7[a]
South-East Asia												
Brunei Darussalam	..	..	38.0	−16.7	1.9	4.1	15.8	−4.5	2.1	6.7	9.6	17.4
Cambodia	15.7	17.3	26.9	20.4	31.1	15.4	28.3	15.8	40.5	61.8	5.4	35.6
Indonesia	62.3	11.9	15.6	13.0	4.7	8.1	8.2	16.3	14.9	19.3	14.9	13.0
Lao People's Democratic Republic	113.3	78.4	46.0	13.7	37.6	20.1	21.6	7.9	26.7	38.7	18.3	..
Malaysia	1.5	14.2	5.3	2.3	6.0	11.1	25.2	15.6	17.1	9.5	13.4	10.4[a]
Myanmar	34.2	29.5	42.5	43.9	34.7	1.4	32.4	27.3	27.2	30.0	14.8	27.3[e]
Philippines	8.6	16.9	8.1	3.6	10.4	3.6	9.9	6.4	19.6	5.4	2.9	..
Singapore	30.2	8.5	−2.0	5.9	−0.3	8.1	6.2	6.2	19.4	13.4	12.0	11.3
Thailand	9.4	1.8	4.0	5.8	1.3	6.2	5.8	6.1	8.2	6.3	9.2	6.5
Timor-Leste						41.1	6.9	18.3	28.2	43.9	34.1	29.6
Viet Nam	23.5	66.5	35.4	27.3	13.3	33.1	31.0	30.9	29.7	49.1	20.7	38.6[f]

Notes:
[a] November compared with the corresponding period of the previous year.
[b] October compared with the corresponding period of the previous year.
[c] March compared with the corresponding period of the previous year.
[d] June compared with the corresponding period of the previous year.
[e] September compared with the corresponding period of the previous year.
[f] August compared with the corresponding period of the previous year.

Sources: ESCAP, based on national sources; International Monetary Fund, *International Financial Statistics* databases (Washington, D.C., February 2010); and ADB, *Key Indicators for Asia and the Pacific 2009* (Manila, 2009) (for Cook Islands, Turkmenistan and Uzbekistan).

Table 8. Merchandise export growth rates

(Percentages)

	1998	1999	2000	2001	2002	2003	2004	2005	2006	2007	2008	2009
East and North-East Asia												
China	0.5	6.1	27.9	7.0	22.1	34.6	35.4	28.4	27.2	25.7	17.3	−15.9
Hong Kong, China	−7.5	0.0	16.1	−5.9	5.4	11.8	15.8	11.6	9.4	8.8	5.3	−12.2
Japan	−7.8	8.1	14.3	−15.9	3.4	13.1	19.9	5.2	8.7	10.4	9.5	−25.7
Macao, China	−0.8	2.8	16.3	−9.4	2.4	9.5	9.0	−11.9	3.3	−0.6	−21.4	−52.2ª
Mongolia	−23.5	3.8	30.1	11.9	0.5	17.5	41.2	22.4	44.5	26.3ᵇ	10.8ᶜ	..
Republic of Korea	−2.8	8.6	19.9	−12.7	8.0	19.3	31.0	12.0	14.4	14.1	13.6	−13.8
Russian Federation	..	2.2	41.4	−3.0	6.7	25.2	35.9	32.9	24.8	16.8	32.9	−39.2ᵈ
Taiwan Province of China	−9.3	9.9	22.8	−16.9	7.1	11.3	21.1	8.8	12.9	10.1	3.6	−20.3
North and Central Asia												
Armenia	−5.2	5.1	29.7	13.8	47.8	35.7	5.4	34.7	1.1	17.0	−8.3	−34.0
Azerbaijan	−16.1	51.3	81.3	11.9	10.9	13.9	42.6	104.4	70.1	63.4	43.8	−69.2
Georgia	−21.7	24.4	35.6	−1.6	8.9	33.4	40.2	33.8	8.2	31.6	21.4	−35.3ᵉ
Kazakhstan	..	−7.5	63.2	−5.2	12.3	33.5	55.0	38.6	37.3	24.8	49.1	−39.3
Kyrgyzstan	−15.2	−13.5	10.4	−6.1	3.8	18.5	24.2	−6.3	31.9	45.8	24.3	−22.4
Russian Federation	..	2.2	41.4	−3.0	6.7	25.2	35.9	32.9	24.8	16.8	32.9	−35.5
Tajikistan	..	..	..	−22.3	7.0	14.5	14.7	−0.7	54.0	4.9	−4.2	−28.3
Turkmenistan	−19.1	93.3	111.1	4.7	9.1	21.1	11.2	28.3	44.7	12.9	52.7	−46.6ᵇ
Uzbekistan	..	..	..	8.0	−20.8	29.1	31.6	11.6	18.0	42.9	29.2	−3.8ᵇ
Oceania												
Australia	−12.8	−0.5	13.3	1.2	1.9	9.6	20.9	21.3	18.9	14.1	29.9	−15.5ᶠ
Fiji	−11.6	19.4	−13.5	0.1	3.7	34.4	−0.6	−6.7	5.6	8.0	6.9	−38.6ᵉ
New Zealand	−15.4	3.7	6.6	3.2	4.8	14.9	23.1	6.8	3.2	18.7	14.9	−26.5ª
Papua New Guinea	−16.1	9.1	7.3	−13.7	−9.5	34.4	18.5	26.8	26.7	13.0	25.2	−35.5ᵉ
Samoaᵍ	30.5	..	..	9.7	−8.9	5.2	−18.4	−9.6	−17.0	7.7	10.5	−22.5
Solomon Islands	−27.6	4.4	−47.4	−5.0	−21.8	33.7	28.6	22.2	7.5	41.7	21.0	−28.0ʰ
Tongaᵍ	−17.8	12.6	−9.9	8.3	50.8	−1.1	−21.6	15.9	−4.0	−13.5	−7.4	−55.4
Vanuatu	−4.0	−24.2	5.8	−24.4	−6.3	43.1	39.9	1.2	−1.8	−19.8	40.6	..
South and South-West Asia												
Afghanistanᵍ	..	..	..	..	46.8	43.6	111.1	26.5	8.5	9.6	19.9	..
Bangladeshᵍ	16.8	2.9	8.3	12.4	−7.4	9.4	16.1	13.8	21.6	15.6	17.4	10.1ⁱ
Bhutanᵍ	12.1	−5.9	9.2	−12.9	4.5	8.7	39.7	34.5	47.2	83.7	−18.2	..
Indiaᵍ	−3.9	9.5	21.1	1.5	20.3	23.3	28.5	23.4	21.8	28.9	12.1	−19.1ᶠ
Iran (Islamic Republic of)ᵍ	−28.6	60.3	35.3	−16.0	18.1	20.4	29.0	47.2	18.1	28.2	3.0	−13.2ᵉ
Maldives	6.6	−4.3	18.8	1.4	20.1	14.8	19.1	−10.7	39.4	1.2	45.0	−30.7ᵉ
Nepalᵍ	12.7	17.4	37.6	4.6	−18.8	4.3	8.9	13.0	2.2	1.2	8.2	−4.1ᵇ
Pakistanᵍ	3.7	−9.8	10.1	7.4	−0.7	22.2	10.3	16.9	14.3	4.4	18.2	−6.4
Sri Lanka	1.9	−2.6	19.8	−12.8	−2.4	9.2	12.2	10.2	8.4	11.6	5.9	−12.9
Turkey	2.7	−1.4	4.5	12.8	15.1	31.0	33.7	16.3	16.4	25.4	23.1	−22.6
South-East Asia												
Brunei Darussalam	−50.2	28.9	23.9	5.5	3.1	29.2	1.5	24.9	26.0	0.9	43.4	−17.1ª
Cambodia	49.2	11.4	7.9	15.4	15.0	18.9	23.5	37.8	18.2	14.3	4.4	−7.2ª
Indonesia	−10.5	1.7	27.6	−12.3	3.1	8.4	12.6	19.5	18.3	16.8	16.9	−14.4
Lao People's Democratic Republic	93.0	24.7	−15.4	−4.0	2.7	13.4	22.3	30.2	69.1	12.4	21.3	−7.3ª
Malaysia	−6.9	15.5	16.1	−10.4	6.9	11.3	21.0	11.8	13.5	9.7	13.3	−21.1
Myanmar	0.6	22.4	42.1	32.6	4.8	0.5	14.1	17.4	20.9	7.0	38.3	−21.9ª
Philippines	16.9	18.8	8.7	−15.6	9.5	2.9	9.5	4.0	14.9	6.4	−2.8	−21.9
Singapore	−12.1	4.4	20.2	−11.7	2.8	27.8	24.2	15.6	18.4	10.1	13.0	−20.2
Thailand	−6.8	7.4	19.3	−6.6	4.6	17.4	20.6	15.0	16.9	18.6	15.5	−14.2
Timor-Leste	..	..	..	230.8	48.8	21.9	6.4	10.8	12.5	−22.2	100.0ᵇ	−28.6ᵇ
Viet Nam	1.9	23.3	25.5	3.8	11.2	19.0	30.8	24.0	22.9	22.2	29.5	−9.7

Notes: ᵃ Refers to the first 8 months.
ᵇ Estimate.
ᶜ Projection.
ᵈ Refers to the first 11 months.
ᵉ Refers to first 6 months.
ᶠ Refers to the first 10 months.
ᵍ Fiscal year.
ʰ Refers to the first 9 months.
ⁱ Provisional.

Sources: ESCAP, calculated from national sources; International Monetary Fund, *Direction of Trade Statistics Database*; and Country Reports Series; Economist Intelligence Unit, Country Reports; CEIC Data Company Limited; and the website of the Interstate Statistical Committee of the Commonwealth of Independent States (www.cisstat.com).

Table 9. Merchandise import growth rates

(Percentages)

	1998	1999	2000	2001	2002	2003	2004	2005	2006	2007	2008	2009
East and North-East Asia												
China	−1.5	18.2	35.8	8.2	21.2	39.9	35.8	17.7	19.9	20.8	18.4	−11.3
Hong Kong, China	−11.5	−2.7	18.6	−5.4	3.2	11.8	16.7	10.5	11.6	10.0	5.6	−10.6
Japan	−17.2	11.0	22.0	−8.0	−3.3	13.5	18.8	13.4	12.2	7.4	22.6	−27.8
Macao, China	−10.8	4.5	11.4	5.8	6.0	8.9	26.2	12.5	16.6	17.5	0.0	−11.2[a]
Mongolia	7.5	1.9	19.8	3.8	8.3	16.0	27.5	16.0	23.9	43.1[b]	38.3[c]	..
Republic of Korea	−35.5	28.4	34.0	−12.1	7.8	17.6	25.5	16.4	18.4	15.3	22.0	−25.8
Russian Federation	..	−30.5	11.9	23.6	10.2	24.2	31.8	30.6	39.6	45.0	33.7	−39.6[d]
Taiwan Province of China	−8.5	5.7	26.6	−23.3	4.9	13.0	31.8	8.2	11.0	8.2	9.7	−27.4
North and Central Asia												
Armenia	1.1	−10.1	9.1	−0.8	12.5	29.6	5.6	33.4	21.6	49.1	35.4	−25.3
Azerbaijan	..	−16.9	7.4	−4.8	24.5	49.3	31.5	21.4	21.1	14.7	25.3	−14.6
Georgia	−11.3	−21.9	2.9	6.2	5.6	43.4	61.7	34.9	47.7	41.8	20.9	−37.7
Kazakhstan	..	−52.4	37.0	26.0	2.0	29.3	52.3	35.8	36.4	38.3	15.7	−25.0
Kyrgyzstan	17.0	−27.1	−8.2	−11.3	27.2	26.6	25.0	22.3	62.0	55.6	46.1	−25.3
Russian Federation	..	−30.5	11.9	23.6	10.2	24.2	31.8	30.6	39.6	45.0	33.7	−37.3
Tajikistan	..	..	..	−20.0	0.0	28.2	56.0	−3.3	29.5	42.5	33.2	−21.5
Turkmenistan[f]	..	..	..	..	..	40.8	22.1	−6.4	−13.2	41.5	54.8	−28.8[b]
Uzbekistan[f]	..	..	..	28.5	−30.3	10.0	27.3	8.1	16.0	49.2	23.4	19.5[b]
Oceania												
Australia	−1.2	6.4	5.2	−9.6	11.3	25.4	20.7	14.5	12.0	19.3	18.9	−19.0[g]
Fiji	−19.7	25.3	−7.9	4.8	9.2	39.1	14.6	2.6	20.3	−0.8	9.6	−34.4[e]
New Zealand	−13.9	14.4	−2.7	−4.3	13.1	23.3	25.0	13.1	0.7	16.1	12.0	−33.5[a]
Papua New Guinea	−27.0	−0.1	−7.0	−6.4	14.6	10.3	22.4	4.6	30.5	32.2	22.3	−17.9[e]
Samoa[h]	1.9	..	..	30.9	12.9	−7.6	23.3	24.3	16.6	14.5	2.6	−5.8
Solomon Islands	−40.8	−13.7	−24.5	−13.0	−19.0	36.3	29.5	52.3	17.3	32.3	12.6	−21.3[i]
Tonga[f h]	18.6	−21.2	12.8	−2.9	0.8	21.0	11.6	27.6	15.8	−11.4	27.4	−5.7[f]
Vanuatu	−5.6	9.3	−7.2	0.7	−0.7	16.5	22.9	16.5	8.0	24.8	42.6	..
South and South-West Asia												
Afghanistan[h]	..	..	..	..	36.9	−8.8	1.5	14.9	11.1	10.1	5.7	..
Bangladesh[h]	5.1	6.5	4.6	11.5	−8.5	13.1	12.9	20.6	12.2	16.6	25.6	4.2[j]
Bhutan[h]	3.7	19.3	14.0	6.1	−5.2	2.2	29.2	75.5	−5.6	21.1	3.6	..
India[h]	−7.1	16.5	4.6	12.3	14.5	24.1	48.6	33.8	21.8	35.4	15.9	−22.9[g]
Iran (Islamic Republic of)[f h]	1.2	−6.0	12.3	20.2	21.6	34.1	31.1	11.9	15.2	16.5	17.7	22.5[e]
Maldives	1.5	13.6	−3.4	−0.3	1.1	20.2	36.3	16.1	24.4	18.3	26.6	−34.5[e]
Nepal[h]	−11.8	−11.0	22.1	−0.2	−10.6	13.6	10.6	13.8	15.8	15.0	23.6	8.4[b]
Pakistan[h]	−14.9	−6.8	9.3	4.1	−3.6	18.2	27.6	32.1	31.6	8.0	31.2	−10.3
Sri Lanka	0.4	1.5	17.4	−14.9	2.2	9.3	19.9	10.8	15.7	10.2	24.0	−29.5
Turkey	−5.4	−11.4	34.0	−24.0	24.5	34.5	40.7	19.7	19.5	21.8	18.8	−30.3
South-East Asia												
Brunei Darussalam	−26.0	−43.1	7.5	−7.9	23.9	−17.7	22.2	1.8	17.5	98.2	−32.6	1.8[a]
Cambodia[f]	1.1	10.1	14.5	2.2	15.2	3.4	19.7	22.9	17.2	118.8	25.6	−20.5[a]
Indonesia[f]	−31.2	−5.6	30.8	−13.9	2.1	10.3	29.9	26.7	14.6	15.4	37.7	−26.6
Lao People's Democratic Republic	57.8	25.5	−14.7	4.3	0.4	12.0	30.5	20.3	30.1	27.6	34.2	−10.4[a]
Malaysia	−26.2	12.2	25.3	−10.0	8.2	4.4	26.3	8.7	14.1	12.7	6.8	−21.1
Myanmar	−17.6	7.2	20.2	−12.4	11.5	8.7	7.1	3.5	7.3	43.9	25.9	−8.4[a]
Philippines[f]	−17.5	3.6	12.3	−4.2	18.7	3.1	8.8	7.7	9.2	7.2	2.2	−24.2
Singapore	−23.3	9.3	21.1	−13.8	0.4	17.0	27.4	15.2	19.3	10.2	21.5	−23.1
Thailand	−33.0	17.7	24.6	−0.7	4.0	16.8	25.3	25.7	9.0	8.7	27.7	−25.1
Timor-Leste	..	..	..	13.5	−16.8	−10.8	−16.1	−16.0	−9.8	74.3	100.6[b]	24.6[b]
Viet Nam	−0.8	2.1	33.2	3.7	21.7	26.7	26.1	17.0	20.4	37.0	32.7	−14.7

Notes: [a] Refers to the first 8 months.
   [b] Estimate.
   [c] Projection.
   [d] Refers to the first 11 months.
   [e] Refers to the first 6 months.
   [f] f.o.b. value.
   [g] Refers to the first 10 months.
   [h] Fiscal year.
   [i] Refers to the first 9 months.
   [j] Provisional.

Sources: ESCAP, calculated from national sources; International Monetary Fund, *Direction of Trade Statistics Database;* and Country Reports Series; Economist Intelligence Unit, Country Reports; CEIC Data Company Limited; and the website of Interstate Statistical Committee of the Commonwealth of Independent States (www.cisstat.com).

Table 10. Inward foreign direct investment

	FDI inward stock					FDI net inflows				
	Millions of US dollars	Percentage of GDP				Millions of US dollars	Percentage of GDP			
	2008	90-95	96-00	01-05	2008	2008	90-95	96-00	01-05	2008
East and North-East Asia										
China	378 083	9.7	16.0	13.5	8.7	108 312	3.6	4.1	3.3	2.5
Democratic People's Republic of Korea	1 435	6.4	9.4	10.6	10.8	44	0.1	0.6	0.7	0.3
Hong Kong, China	835 764	190.2	188.5	253.8	387.7	63 003	4.4	14.7	13.8	29.2
Japan	203 372	0.4	0.8	1.9	4.1	24 426	0.0	0.1	0.2	0.5
Macao, China	9 749	54.5	44.5	44.1	44.7	1 905	0.0	0.0	6.2	8.7
Mongolia	1 946	1.4	9.3	27.5	37.0	683	0.5	2.5	6.6	13.0
Republic of Korea	90 693	1.9	4.5	11.4	9.8	7 603	0.2	1.2	0.8	0.8
Russian Federation	213 734	0.3	5.6	21.4	12.7	70 320	0.2	1.1	1.7	4.2
North and Central Asia										
Armenia	3 521	2.3	18.4	30.2	29.5	1 132	0.7	5.8	5.0	9.5
Azerbaijan	6 612	1.1	62.9	102.3	14.3	11	0.6	13.9	24.4	0.0
Georgia	6 919	0.3	13.6	34.4	54.1	1 564	0.1	4.8	7.0	12.2
Kazakhstan	58 284	4.1	33.8	52.8	44.0	14 543	2.0	6.3	7.7	11.0
Kyrgyzstan	1 015	1.7	21.7	27.1	20.1	233	1.2	3.6	2.8	4.6
Russian Federation	213 734	0.3	5.6	21.4	12.7	70 320	0.2	1.1	1.7	4.2
Tajikistan	862	0.8	9.3	13.3	34.8	376	0.3	1.8	4.9	15.2
Turkmenistan	4 748	4.2	22.7	34.1	53.7	820	2.6	3.4	5.8	9.3
Uzbekistan	3 043	0.4	3.2	8.8	11.8	918	0.1	0.8	0.9	3.6
Oceania										
American Samoa										
Australia	272 174	25.5	27.1	33.8	26.8	46 774	2.0	1.8	1.4	4.6
Cook Islands	39	18.9	66.2	25.4		1	1.0	4.8	0.1	
Fiji	1 759	25.4	26.3	21.5	48.9	274	3.3	2.9	4.1	7.6
French Polynesia	324	3.8	4.8	5.4	6.9	32	0.4	0.3	0.4	0.7
Guam										
Kiribati	141	2.6	74.1	209.1	181.9	2	0.4	29.2	24.2	2.5
Marshall Islands						6	−1.2	37.0	−5.2	3.3
Micronesia (Federated States of)						6	0.0	−7.0	0.0	2.4
Nauru						0	−0.6	1.2	4.5	2.0
New Caledonia	2 239	2.8	2.7	6.2	24.1	467	0.3	−0.2	1.2	5.0
New Zealand	53 424	33.2	52.3	49.5	42.3	1 979	4.3	3.3	2.0	1.6
Niue	7					0				
Northern Mariana Islands										
Palau	124	0.0	57.4	87.3	69.3	2	0.6	17.0	3.3	1.0
Papua New Guinea	2 312	36.6	43.2	57.4	28.9	−30	5.7	6.0	1.3	−0.4
Samoa	74	13.4	20.9	16.7	13.8	6	3.1	2.1	0.0	1.0
Solomon Islands	700	121.6	101.8	108.2	106.8	76	4.0	1.3	0.5	11.5
Tonga	84	2.6	6.0	13.0	28.0	6	0.8	0.7	2.9	1.9
Tuvalu	32	0.8	1.0	106.7	99.2	2	0.4	−1.2	27.3	5.2
Vanuatu	1 019	135.0	167.0	182.7	182.4	34	12.7	9.3	5.7	6.0
South and South-West Asia										
Afghanistan	1 365	0.4	0.5	4.5	10.8	300	0.0	0.0	2.3	2.4
Bangladesh	4 817	1.6	3.8	5.5	6.1	1 086	0.1	1.1	0.9	1.4
Bhutan	131	1.0	1.0	1.7	9.8	30	0.1	0.1	0.5	2.2
India	123 288	0.9	3.0	5.2	9.8	41 554	0.2	0.7	0.9	3.3
Iran (Islamic Republic of)	20 811	2.1	2.2	6.8	6.0	1 492	0.0	0.1	1.8	0.4
Maldives	225	14.9	17.3	22.4	17.8	15	2.4	2.1	1.8	1.2
Nepal	127	0.3	1.1	1.6	1.0	1	0.0	0.2	0.1	0.0
Pakistan	31 059	4.5	9.8	7.5	17.4	5 438	0.6	0.6	1.0	3.0
Sri Lanka	4 283	9.3	11.5	10.1	10.5	752	1.0	1.4	1.1	1.8
Turkey	69 871	6.2	6.8	11.3	9.4	18 198	0.4	0.3	1.2	2.5
South-East Asia										
Brunei Darussalam	10 361	3.6	52.3	105.1	71.3	239	2.5	12.9	15.7	1.6
Cambodia	4 637	6.0	35.4	41.2	41.4	815	2.2	6.3	3.6	7.3
Indonesia	67 044	8.1	15.9	7.9	13.1	7 919	1.3	0.5	0.6	1.6
Lao People's Democratic Republic	1 408	6.1	29.9	29.5	26.4	228	2.7	4.5	1.1	4.3
Malaysia	73 262	28.2	49.0	35.3	33.1	8 053	7.0	5.2	2.6	3.6
Myanmar	5 546	11.4	41.4	44.8	19.3	283	3.0	7.2	2.3	1.0
Philippines	21 470	12.4	19.2	14.8	12.7	1 520	1.8	2.1	1.2	0.9
Singapore	326 142	77.1	104.0	152.3	179.3	22 725	10.9	14.3	13.6	12.5
Thailand	104 850	10.7	17.3	32.4	37.2	10 091	1.6	3.4	3.8	3.6
Timor-Leste	166	19.0	25.2	46.4	29.2	0	5.2	0.0	5.4	0.1
Viet Nam	48 325	29.8	56.1	66.5	53.3	8 050	7.7	6.4	3.7	8.9

Source: See Technical Notes at the end.

Table 11. Official development assistance and workers' remittances

	ODA received						Workers' remittances					
	Millions of US dollars			Percentage of GNI			Millions of US dollars			Percentage of GNI		
	1990	2000	2007	1990	2000	2007	1995	2000	2007	1995	2000	2007
East and North-East Asia												
China	2 030	1 728	1 439	0.5	0.1	0.0	350	556	10 680	0.0	0.0	0.3
Democratic People's Republic of Korea	8	73	98	0.0	0.7	0.7						
Hong Kong, China	38			0.1								
Japan								505	1 261		0.0	0.0
Macao, China	0			0.0								
Mongolia	13	217	228	1.0	20.1	5.8		12			1.1	
Republic of Korea	52			0.0			291	63	172	0.1	0.0	0.0
Russian Federation									852			0.1
North and Central Asia												
Armenia		216	352		11.4	4.0	12	9	94	1.0	0.5	1.1
Azerbaijan		139	225		2.7	0.8		57	1 192		1.1	4.2
Georgia		169	382		5.3	3.7		95	245		3.0	2.4
Kazakhstan		189	202		1.1	0.2		64	132		0.4	0.1
Kyrgyzstan		215	274		16.7	7.3	1	2	705	0.1	0.2	18.8
Russian Federation									852			0.1
Tajikistan		124	221		11.7	7.4			1 685			56.5
Turkmenistan		31	28		0.8	0.4						
Uzbekistan		186	166		1.4	0.7						
Oceania												
American Samoa												
Australia												
Cook Islands	12	4	9	20.7	5.3	4.4						
Fiji	50	29	57	3.7	1.7	1.9		26			1.5	
French Polynesia	260			11.2					14			0.3
Guam												
Kiribati	20	18	27	50.9	20.4	20.6						
Marshall Islands		57	52		42.8	27.1						
Micronesia (Federated States of)		102	115		43.0	44.9						
Nauru	0	4	26	0.4	14.8	77.0						
New Caledonia	302			12.0					3			0.0
New Zealand												
Niue	7	3	15									
Northern Mariana Islands	63											
Palau		39	22		31.2	13.0						
Papua New Guinea	412	275	321	15.5	8.7	6.3						
Samoa	48	27	37	28.9	11.8	7.1	39			20.3		
Solomon Islands	46	68	246	22.3	20.2	42.6						
Tonga	30	19	31	21.5	12.2	12.1			96			37.7
Tuvalu	5	4	12	53.1	32.9	39.1						
Vanuatu	50	46	57	26.8	19.8	11.8	6	11	1	2.5	4.7	0.3
South and South-West Asia												
Afghanistan	122	136	3 951	3.4	5.0	39.0						
Bangladesh	2 093	1 172	1 502	7.3	2.5	2.0	1 202	1 958	6 553	3.1	4.2	8.9
Bhutan	46	53	89	17.6	11.9	7.3						
India	1 399	1 463	1 298	0.4	0.3	0.1	6 139	12 745		1.7	2.8	
Iran (Islamic Republic of)	105	130	102	0.1	0.1	0.0						
Maldives	21	19	37	11.1	3.2	3.7						
Nepal	423	387	598	10.4	6.2	4.8	57	111	1 647	1.2	1.8	13.2
Pakistan	1 127	700	2 212	1.9	0.9	1.3	1 712	1 075	5 992	2.1	1.4	3.4
Sri Lanka	728	276	601	9.1	1.7	1.9	790	1 142	2 502	6.0	7.0	7.8
Turkey	1 202	327	795	0.6	0.1	0.1	3 327	4 560	1 209	1.4	1.7	0.2
South-East Asia												
Brunei Darussalam	4			0.1								
Cambodia	41	396	672	3.3	12.6	9.1	10	100	184	0.3	3.2	2.5
Indonesia	1 716	1 654	872	1.6	1.2	0.2	651	1 190	6 004	0.3	0.9	1.4
Lao People's Democratic Republic	149	282	396	17.2	17.8	10.6						
Malaysia	468	45	200	1.1	0.1	0.1						
Myanmar	161	106	197	3.1	1.5	1.1	81	77		1.0	1.1	
Philippines	1 271	575	634	2.9	0.7	0.4	432	5 161	13 266	0.6	6.4	8.4
Singapore	−3			0.0								
Thailand	796	698	−312	0.9	0.6	−0.1						
Timor-Leste	0	231	278	0.1	71.6	16.1						
Viet Nam	181	1 681	2 497	3.0	5.5	3.6						

Source: See Technical Notes at the end.

Table 12. International migration

	Stock of foreign population Thousands				Stock of foreign population as share of total population Percentages				Net migration rate Per 1,000 population			
	1990	1995	2000	2005	1990	1995	2000	2005	90-95	95-00	00-05	05-10
East and North-East Asia												
China	376	437	508	590	0.0	0.0	0.0	0.0	−0.1	−0.1	−0.3	−0.3
Democratic People's Republic of Korea	34	35	36	37	0.2	0.2	0.2	0.2				
Hong Kong, China	2 218	2 431	2 669	2 721	38.9	39.1	40.0	39.5	10.1	9.3	3.3	3.3
Japan	1 076	1 363	1 687	1 999	0.9	1.1	1.3	1.6	0.8	0.1	0.1	0.2
Macao, China	200	224	240	278	53.9	54.5	54.5	57.0	7.8	7.1	17.2	19.3
Mongolia	7	7	8	9	0.3	0.3	0.3	0.4	−15.4	−4.3	1.4	−0.8
Republic of Korea	572	584	568	551	1.3	1.3	1.2	1.2	−2.9	−0.3	−0.3	−0.1
Russian Federation	11 525	11 707	11 892	12 080	7.8	7.9	8.1	8.4	3.0	3.0	1.3	0.4
North and Central Asia												
Armenia	659	682	574	493	18.6	21.1	18.7	16.1	−29.6	−14.3	−6.5	−4.9
Azerbaijan	361	525	348	255	5.0	6.7	4.3	3.0	−3.1	−3.2	−2.4	−1.2
Georgia	338	250	219	191	6.2	4.9	4.6	4.3	−20.7	−15.9	−13.4	−11.5
Kazakhstan	3 619	3 295	2 871	2 974	21.9	20.7	19.2	19.6	−18.6	−17.1	−2.7	−1.3
Kyrgyzstan	623	482	373	288	14.2	10.5	7.5	5.5	−12.2	−1.1	−2.9	−2.8
Russian Federation	11 525	11 707	11 892	12 080	7.8	7.9	8.1	8.4	3.0	3.0	1.3	0.4
Tajikistan	426	305	330	306	8.0	5.3	5.4	4.7	−10.7	−11.2	−10.9	−5.9
Turkmenistan	307	260	241	224	8.4	6.2	5.4	4.6	2.5	−2.3	−1.1	−1.0
Uzbekistan	1 653	1 474	1 367	1 268	8.1	6.4	5.5	4.8	−3.1	−3.4	−3.1	−3.0
Oceania												
American Samoa	21	23	25	27	45.2	43.7	43.2	42.3				
Australia	3 581	3 854	4 027	4 336	21.0	21.3	21.0	21.3	4.2	5.0	6.5	4.8
Cook Islands	3	3	3	3	14.6	14.8	15.9	14.6				
Fiji	14	15	16	17	1.9	1.9	2.0	2.1	−9.3	−10.7	−10.3	−8.3
French Polynesia	26	28	30	32	13.2	13.1	12.9	12.7	−0.5	1.4	1.5	
Guam	70	72	74	76	52.1	49.4	47.8	45.4	−4.6	−6.4	1.0	
Kiribati	2	2	2	2	3.0	2.6	2.4	2.2				
Marshall Islands	2	2	2	2	3.3	3.1	3.1	2.9				
Micronesia (Federated States of)	4	3	3	3	3.8	3.1	2.9	2.6	−4.4	−25.4	−17.9	−16.3
Nauru	4	4	5	5	42.9	42.5	45.4	48.7				
New Caledonia	38	45	50	54	22.0	23.1	23.1	23.2	5.8	5.5	4.3	4.5
New Zealand	523	594	685	858	15.5	16.1	17.7	20.9	8.1	2.3	5.1	2.4
Niue	0	0	0	0	20.0	20.6	21.8	23.7				
Northern Mariana Islands	27	36	45	51	61.6	62.8	65.0	63.4				
Palau	3	5	6	6	19.2	27.3	32.7	30.0				
Papua New Guinea	33	31	26	25	0.8	0.7	0.5	0.4				
Samoa	3	5	6	7	2.0	2.7	3.2	4.0	−15.8	−16.3	−20.8	−18.4
Solomon Islands	5	5	6	6	1.5	1.5	1.4	1.4				
Tonga	3	2	2	1	3.2	2.3	1.6	1.1	−18.0	−19.5	−15.9	−17.5
Tuvalu	0	0	0	0	3.6	2.9	2.3	1.9				
Vanuatu	2	2	1	1	1.4	1.0	0.7	0.5	−1.1	−7.9		
South and South-West Asia												
Afghanistan	58	70	76	86	0.5	0.4	0.4	0.4	42.6	−3.8	7.2	7.5
Bangladesh	882	1 006	988	1 032	0.8	0.8	0.7	0.7	−0.8	−0.8	−1.0	−0.7
Bhutan	24	28	32	37	4.3	5.4	5.7	5.7	−38.2	0.1	11.6	2.9
India	7 493	7 022	6 411	5 887	0.9	0.7	0.6	0.5	−0.2	−0.3	−0.3	−0.2
Iran (Islamic Republic of)	4 292	3 016	2 804	2 062	7.6	4.8	4.2	2.9	−3.9	−0.2	−2.9	−1.4
Maldives	3	3	3	3	1.2	1.2	1.1	1.1				
Nepal	431	625	718	819	2.3	2.9	2.9	3.0	−1.0	−0.9	−0.8	−0.7
Pakistan	6 556	4 077	4 243	3 554	5.7	3.1	2.9	2.1	−4.2	−0.1	−1.6	−1.6
Sri Lanka	459	426	395	366	2.7	2.3	2.1	1.9	−2.9	−4.3	−4.6	−3.0
Turkey	1 150	1 212	1 263	1 334	2.1	2.0	1.9	1.9	−0.2	0.0	−0.2	−0.1
South-East Asia												
Brunei Darussalam	73	87	104	124	28.5	29.6	31.2	33.6	2.6	2.2	2.0	1.8
Cambodia	38	116	237	304	0.4	1.0	1.9	2.2	2.8	1.3	0.2	−0.1
Indonesia	466	219	292	136	0.3	0.1	0.1	0.1	−0.8	−0.9	−0.9	−0.6
Lao People's Democratic Republic	23	23	22	20	0.5	0.5	0.4	0.3	−1.3	−3.4	−4.1	−2.4
Malaysia	1 014	1 193	1 554	2 029	5.6	5.8	6.7	7.9	3.0	4.5	1.2	1.0
Myanmar	134	114	98	93	0.3	0.3	0.2	0.2	−0.6	0.0	−4.2	−2.0
Philippines	159	210	323	375	0.3	0.3	0.4	0.4	−2.7	−2.4	−2.2	−2.0
Singapore	727	992	1 352	1 494	24.1	28.5	33.6	35.0	15.4	19.6	6.7	22.0
Thailand	387	549	792	982	0.7	0.9	1.3	1.5	−0.1	−1.5	4.4	0.9
Timor-Leste	9	10	9	12	1.2	1.1	1.1	1.2		−40.9	9.1	1.8
Viet Nam	29	39	56	55	0.0	0.1	0.1	0.1	−2.4	−0.5	−0.5	−0.5

Source: See Technical Notes at the end.

Table 13. Primary, secondary and tertiary education

	Net enrolment ratio in primary education Percentage of primary school-aged children			Net enrolment ratio in secondary education Percentage of secondary school-aged children				Gross enrolment ratio in tertiary education Percentage of tertiary school-aged children			
	1991	2000	2007	1999	2002	2004	2007	1999	2002	2004	2007
East and North-East Asia											
China	98.0							6.4	12.7	17.8	22.9
Democratic People's Republic of Korea											
Hong Kong, China	92.4				74.3	76.0	78.6			31.0	33.8
Japan	99.7	100.0	99.8	99.4	99.7	99.9	98.2	45.1	50.5	54.0	58.1
Macao, China	81.1	85.5	92.9	62.1	71.7	76.1	77.6	27.7	64.6	68.0	57.0
Mongolia	90.1	89.9	88.8	55.5	71.7	81.4	81.1	25.7	34.0	39.0	47.7
Republic of Korea	99.7	96.9		94.5	87.3	90.4	96.9	72.6	86.8	89.9	94.7
Russian Federation	97.9									69.0	74.7
North and Central Asia											
Armenia			85.0		83.0	83.5	85.0	23.7	26.5	26.2	34.2
Azerbaijan	88.8	89.5	95.3	75.3	77.8	80.7	83.0	15.7	15.9	14.9	15.2
Georgia	97.1		93.7	76.4			81.9	35.9	40.9	41.5	37.3
Kazakhstan	88.0	87.2	90.2		87.9	90.6	86.2	24.5	38.8	47.1	51.2
Kyrgyzstan	92.3	86.7	84.5			82.1	80.5	29.0	42.9	39.6	42.8
Russian Federation	97.9									69.0	74.7
Tajikistan	76.7	95.9	97.2	62.8	76.2	79.6	81.3	13.6	14.0	16.4	19.8
Turkmenistan											
Uzbekistan	78.2		91.0				91.7	12.9	13.8	14.1	9.8
Oceania											
American Samoa											
Australia	99.4	94.7	97.1		87.8	85.9	87.9	65.4	76.5	72.4	75.1
Cook Islands		77.4	67.4	59.0			70.1				
Fiji			97.5	78.6	77.0	81.1				15.5	
French Polynesia											
Guam											
Kiribati						70.4					
Marshall Islands			66.3		74.4				16.9		
Micronesia (Federated States of)	98.2							14.1			
Nauru		72.3									
New Caledonia	95.4										
New Zealand	98.1	98.7	99.1		91.9			64.3	69.2	85.7	79.8
Niue				93.4							
Northern Mariana Islands											
Palau		96.4							40.2		
Papua New Guinea	66.0							2.0			
Samoa		90.0		71.5	65.6	66.0		11.5			
Solomon Islands	83.5			23.0	27.6						
Tonga	96.5			72.2		66.4		3.4	5.4	6.0	
Tuvalu											
Vanuatu	70.6	93.9	86.9	29.6	36.2	38.1		4.0	5.0	4.8	
South and South-West Asia											
Afghanistan	24.7						25.9			1.3	
Bangladesh	76.3			42.1	44.7	41.0	40.7	5.4	6.0	5.5	7.2
Bhutan	55.5	58.8		16.9	24.5			2.7			5.3
India		79.2							10.4	9.5	
Iran (Islamic Republic of)	92.4	80.2				78.5		18.9	19.4	22.6	31.4
Maldives	86.7	98.2	96.3	31.5	51.1		69.0			0.2	
Nepal	63.0	70.5	76.1				42.0		5.0	5.6	11.3
Pakistan	33.3			22.0		28.3	32.2		2.5	3.1	5.1
Sri Lanka	84.3										
Turkey	89.2		92.3				69.5	21.5	24.4	28.9	36.3
South-East Asia											
Brunei Darussalam	92.0		92.8				89.1	12.3	13.7	14.9	15.4
Cambodia	72.0	87.2	89.4	15.4	22.1	25.8	34.1		2.5	3.0	5.3
Indonesia	96.3	92.6	94.8			56.1	67.5		15.0	16.6	17.5
Lao People's Democratic Republic	62.1	77.2	86.3	26.3	30.5	35.3	35.9	2.4	4.3	5.8	11.6
Malaysia	93.0	96.8		65.1	65.4	72.0		23.0	28.0	30.6	
Myanmar	98.6										
Philippines	96.4		91.3	50.7	56.3	60.8	61.3	28.7	30.4	28.8	
Singapore											
Thailand	87.7		93.9				76.1	33.0	41.0	43.6	49.5
Timor-Leste			63.0						9.6		
Viet Nam	90.4	94.5		59.1				10.6			

Source: See Technical Notes at the end.

Table 14. Poverty and malnutrition

| | Population living below $1 (2005 PPP) a day | | | | Population undernourished | | Prevalence of underweight children | |
| | Percentage | | | | Percentages | | Percentage of children under 5 | |
	1990	1996	2002	2005	1991	2004	Earliest	Latest
East and North-East Asia								
China	60.2	36.4	28.4	15.9	15	9	19 (90)	7 (05)
Democratic People's Republic of Korea					21	32	60 (98)	23 (04)
Hong Kong, China								
Japan					5	5		
Macao, China								
Mongolia		18.8 (95)	15.5	22.4	30	29	12 (92)	6 (05)
Republic of Korea		2.0 (98)			5	5		
Russian Federation	2.8 (93)	3.5	2.0	2.0	5	5	3 (95)	
North and Central Asia								
Armenia		17.5	15.0	10.6 (03)	46	21	4 (98)	4 (05)
Azerbaijan		15.6 (95)	6.3 (01)	2.0	27	12	10 (96)	10 (06)
Georgia		4.5	15.1	13.4	47	13		2 (05)
Kazakhstan	4.2 (93)	5.0	5.2	3.1 (03)	5	5	8 (95)	4 (06)
Kyrgyzstan	18.6 (93)	15.5 (99)	34.0	21.8 (04)	17	5	11 (97)	3 (06)
Russian Federation	2.8 (93)	3.5	2.0	2.0	5	5	3 (95)	
Tajikistan		44.5 (99)		21.5 (04)	34	34		17 (05)
Turkmenistan	63.5 (93)	24.8 (98)			9	6		11 (05)
Uzbekistan		32.1 (98)	42.3	46.3 (03)	5	14	19 (96)	5 (06)
Oceania								
American Samoa								
Australia					5	5		
Cook Islands							10 (97)	
Fiji					8	5	8 (93)	
French Polynesia					5	5		
Guam								
Kiribati					8	5		13 (99)
Marshall Islands								
Micronesia (Federated States of)							15 (97)	
Nauru								
New Caledonia					8	9		
New Zealand					5	5		
Niue								
Northern Mariana Islands								
Palau								
Papua New Guinea		35.8						
Samoa					9	5		
Solomon Islands					25	9		
Tonga								
Tuvalu								
Vanuatu					10	7		
South and South-West Asia								
Afghanistan							48 (97)	39 (04)
Bangladesh	66.8 (92)	59.4	57.8 (00)	49.6	36	27	67 (92)	46 (07)
Bhutan				26.2 (03)				19 (99)
India		49.4 (94)		41.6	24	21	53 (93)	48 (05)
Iran (Islamic Republic of)	3.9	2.0 (98)		2.0	5	5	16 (95)	
Maldives					9	7	39 (94)	30 (01)
Nepal		68.4		55.1 (04)	21	15	49 (95)	45 (06)
Pakistan	64.7 (91)	48.1 (97)	35.9	22.6	22	23	40 (91)	38 (02)
Sri Lanka	15.0 (91)	16.3	14.0		27	21	38 (93)	29 (00)
Turkey		2.1 (94)	2.0	2.7	5	5	10 (93)	4 (03)
South-East Asia								
Brunei Darussalam					5	5		
Cambodia	48.6 (94)			40.2 (04)	38	26	40 (93)	36 (05)
Indonesia					19	17	34 (95)	28 (03)
Lao People's Democratic Republic	55.7 (92)	49.3 (97)	44.0		27	19	44 (93)	37 (06)
Malaysia	2.0 (92)	2.1 (95)		2.0 (04)	5	5	23 (93)	8 (05)
Myanmar					44	19	32 (90)	32 (03)
Philippines	30.7 (91)	28.1 (94)	22.0 (03)	22.6 (06)	21	16	34 (90)	28 (03)
Singapore								3 (00)
Thailand	5.5 (92)	2.0		2.0 (04)	29	17	19 (93)	9 (05)
Timor-Leste			52.9 (01)		18	22		49 (07)
Viet Nam	63.7 (93)	49.7 (98)	40.1	21.5 (06)	28	14	45 (94)	20 (06)

Source: See Technical Notes at the end.

Table 15. Unemployment rate by gender and age group

	Total Percentage of labour force			Female Percentage of female labour force			Male Percentage of male labour force			Youth unemployment rate Percentage of labour force aged 15-24		
	1991	2000	2007	1991	2000	2007	1991	2000	2007	1991	2000	2007
East and North-East Asia												
China	2.3	3.1	4.0									
Democratic People's Republic of Korea												
Hong Kong, China	1.8	4.9	4.0	1.6	4.0	3.4	1.9	5.6	4.5	4.2	11.2	9.0
Japan	2.1	4.8	3.9	2.2	4.5	3.7	1.9	5.0	4.0	4.5	9.2	7.7
Macao, China	3.0	6.7	3.0	3.7	4.6	2.7	2.5	8.6	3.4		9.9	6.2
Mongolia			2.8								22.8	
Republic of Korea	2.4	4.4	3.2	2.0	3.6	2.6	2.7	5.0	3.7	7.4	11.8	8.9
Russian Federation			6.1			5.8			6.4			14.5
North and Central Asia												
Armenia			28.4									
Azerbaijan			6.5			5.3			7.8			14.0
Georgia		10.8	13.3		10.5	12.6		11.1	13.9		21.1	31.5
Kazakhstan		12.8	7.3									
Kyrgyzstan			8.2									
Russian Federation			6.1			5.8			6.4			14.5
Tajikistan			2.5									
Turkmenistan												
Uzbekistan												
Oceania												
American Samoa		5.0			6.0			4.9				
Australia	9.6	6.3	4.4	9.2	6.1	4.8	9.9	6.5	4.0	17.5	12.1	9.4
Cook Islands	7.2			9.3			6.1			14.7		
Fiji	5.9											
French Polynesia												
Guam	3.5	11.5			11.5			11.5				
Kiribati												
Marshall Islands												
Micronesia (Federated States of)												
Nauru												
New Caledonia												
New Zealand	10.3	5.9	3.6	9.5	5.8	3.9	10.9	6.1	3.3	18.8	13.2	9.7
Niue												
Northern Mariana Islands												
Palau												
Papua New Guinea		2.8			1.3			4.3			5.3	
Samoa												
Solomon Islands												
Tonga												
Tuvalu												
Vanuatu												
South and South-West Asia												
Afghanistan												
Bangladesh		3.3			3.3			3.2			10.7	
Bhutan												
India		4.3			4.1			4.4			10.1	
Iran (Islamic Republic of)	11.1		10.5	24.4		15.7	9.5		9.3			22.3
Maldives		2.0			2.7			1.6			4.4	
Nepal												
Pakistan	5.9	7.2	5.1	16.3	15.8	8.6	4.2	5.5	4.2	10.1	13.3	7.5
Sri Lanka	14.7	7.7	6.0	21.2	11.3	9.0	10.0	5.9	4.3		23.6	21.2
Turkey	8.2	6.5	9.9	7.1	6.3	10.2	8.7	6.6	9.8	15.3	13.1	19.6
South-East Asia												
Brunei Darussalam	4.7			6.7			3.7					
Cambodia		2.5			2.8			2.1				
Indonesia			9.1			10.8			8.1		19.9	25.1
Lao People's Democratic Republic												
Malaysia		3.0	3.2		3.1	3.4		2.9	3.1		8.3	10.9
Myanmar												
Philippines	9.0	10.1	6.3	10.5	9.9	6.0	8.1	10.3	6.4	17.6	21.2	14.9
Singapore	1.9	6.0	4.0	1.8	6.6	4.3	2.0	5.6	3.7		8.8	8.9
Thailand	2.7	2.4	1.2	3.5	2.3	1.1	2.0	2.4	1.3		6.6	4.5
Timor-Leste												
Viet Nam		2.3			2.1			2.4			4.8	

Source: See Technical Notes at the end.

Technical notes

Table 1. Real gross domestic product growth rates

GDP growth rate at constant prices. The real annual percentage changes in GDP (at constant market prices) in national currencies are reported in this table. GDP is defined as the total cost of all finished goods and services produced within the country in a given year. Most countries use constant market price values. The growth rates of some countries are at factor cost, including Fiji, India, the Islamic Republic of Iran and Pakistan, while Nepal is at producers' prices. In the case of Timor-Leste, the data refer to real non-oil GDP. The table contains historical data from 1998 to 2008. Historical data are mainly based on IMF, *International Financial Statistics* databases and ADB, *Key Indicators for Asia and the Pacific 2009* with updates from national and local sources. The data for 2009 are generally ESCAP estimates and calculations, although some projections are in line with the economic programmes/projections of the Governments concerned.

Tables 2 and 3. Gross domestic savings and investment rates

Gross domestic savings and investment as a percentage of GDP. Gross domestic savings (GDS) are calculated as the difference between GDP and total consumption expenditure in the national accounts statistics. Gross domestic investment (GDI) is the sum of gross fixed capital formation and changes in inventories. Gross fixed capital formation is measured by the total value of a producer's acquisitions minus disposals of fixed assets in a given accounting period. Additions to the value of non-produced assets, such as land, form part of gross fixed capital formation. Inventories are stocks of goods held by institutional units to meet temporary or unexpected fluctuations in production and sales. The amounts computed in the table refer to GDS and GDI as a percentage of GDP at current prices. Historical data are mostly derived from ADB, *Key Indicators for Asia and the Pacific 2009* while data on some countries/areas (Georgia, Maldives, Russian Federation, Solomon Islands, Tajikistan, Turkey, Turkmenistan, Uzbekistan and Macao, China) are based on World Bank, *World Development Indicators*. The 2009 data are obtained from input supplied by national authorities and ESCAP calculations and estimates.

Table 4. Inflation rates

Inflation rates. Rates of inflation in this table refer to changes in the consumer price index (CPI) and reflect changes in the cost of acquiring a fixed basket of goods and services by an average consumer. Historical data are based on IMF, *International Financial Statistics* databases and *World Economic Outlook* databases, October 2009 while data on Brunei Darussalam, Cook Islands, Micronesia (Federated States of), Nauru, Palau and Tuvalu are based on ADB, *Key Indicators for Asia and the Pacific 2009*. The figures for 2009 are generally estimates and based on ESCAP calculations. The projections/estimates are also provided by country authorities. For India, data refer to the industrial workers index. Consumer price inflation are for a given city or group of consumers in respect of the following countries: Cambodia is for Phnom Penh; Sri Lanka is for Colombo; and Nepal is for national urban consumers.

Table 5. Budget balance

Government surplus or deficit, as percentage of GDP. The Government fiscal balance (surplus/deficit) is the difference between central government total revenues (including grants) and total expenditures as a percentage of GDP. This provides a picture of the changes in the Government's financial position each year. When the difference is positive, the fiscal position is in surplus; otherwise, it is in deficit. Government revenue is the sum of current and capital revenues. Current revenue is the revenue accruing from taxes, as well as all current non-tax revenues, except for transfers received from other (foreign or domestic) governments and international institutions. Major items of non-tax revenue include receipts from government enterprises, rents and royalties, fees and fines, forfeits, private donations and repayments of loans properly defined as components of net lending. Capital revenue is the proceeds from the sale of non-financial capital assets. As for government expenditure, it is the sum of current and capital expenditure. Current expenditure comprises purchases of goods and services by the central Government, transfers to non-central government units and to households, subsidies to producers and the interest on public debt. Capital expenditures, on the other hand, cover outlays for the acquisition or construction of capital assets and for the purchase of land and intangible assets, as well as capital transfers to domestic and foreign recipients. Loans and advances for capital purposes are also included. Grants are excluded in Bangladesh, Cambodia, China, Hong Kong (China), Indonesia, Iran (Islamic Republic of), Kiribati, Malaysia, Pakistan, the Republic of Korea, Singapore, Sri Lanka, Thailand, Turkmenistan, and developed ESCAP countries. In the case of Timor-Leste, the amounts are computed as a share of non-oil GDP. The budget surplus/deficit of Singapore was computed from government operating revenue minus government operating expenditure and minus government development expenditure; while the budget balance of Thailand refers to a government cash balance comprising the budgetary balance and non-budgetary balance.

Table 6. Current account balance

Current account balance, as a share of GDP. The current account balance refers to the sum of the balance on goods, services and income. It also includes current transfers crossing national borders. A positive balance shows that the foreign currencies flow into the domestic economy; likewise, a negative balance shows the opposite. The figures are reported as a percentage of GDP at current prices (national currency) to allow for cross-country comparisons. Historical data are mainly based on IMF, *International Financial Statistics* databases and *World Economic Outlook* database, October 2009, with updates and estimates from national, local and country sources. The 2009 data are derived from projections supplied by national authorities and ESCAP estimates. In the case of Timor-Leste, current account balance includes international assistance and the amount is computed as a percentage of non-oil GDP.

Table 7. Change in money supply

Growth of money supply. The annual growth rates of board money supply (at the end of a given period) as represented by M2. M2 is defined as the sum of currency in circulation plus demand deposits (M1) and quasi-money, which consists of time and savings deposits, including foreign currency deposits. Historical data for M2 are mainly obtained from IMF, *International Financial Statistics* databases with updates and estimates from national and local sources. In the case of Cook Islands, Turkmenistan and Uzbekistan, the data are based on ADB, *Key Indicators for Asia and the Pacific 2009*. The data for 2009 are computed by ESCAP on the basis of IMF data and estimates based on national sources.

Tables 8 and 9. Growth rates of merchandise exports and imports

Growth rates of exports and imports. The annual growth rates of exports and imports, in terms of merchandise goods only, are shown in these tables. Data are in millions of United States dollars primarily obtained from the balance-of-payments accounts of each country. Exports in general are reported on a free-on-board (f.o.b.) basis. In this case, exports are valued at the customs frontier of the exporting country plus export duties and the costs of loading the goods onto the carriers unless the latter is borne by the carrier. It excludes the cost of freight and insurance beyond the customs frontier. As for imports, data are reported either on an f.o.b. or c.i.f. (cost, insurance, freight) basis. On a c.i.f. basis, the value of imports includes the cost of international freight and insurance up to the customs frontier of the importing country. It excludes the cost of unloading the goods from the carrier unless it is borne by the carrier.

Historical data on exports and imports are mainly obtained from country sources, statistical publications, and secondary publications. The figures for 2009 are generally estimates based on country sources and calculations by ESCAP, and are also provided by national consultants.

Table 10. Inward foreign direct investment

Foreign direct investment (FDI) inward stock. Represents the value of the share of capital and reserves (including retained profits) attributable to the parent enterprise, plus the net indebtedness of affiliates to the parent enterprise. *Inward stock* is the value of the capital and reserves in the economy attributable to a parent enterprise resident in a different economy. Expressed in millions of United States dollars and as a percentage of GDP. **Source:** Calculated by ESCAP using data from United Nations Conference on Trade and Development, Foreign Direct Investment and National Accounts Main Aggregates database (online database accessed on 21 September 2009 and 22 October 2009).

Foreign direct investment (FDI) inflows. Comprise capital provided (either directly or through other related enterprises) by a foreign direct investor to an FDI enterprise, or capital received by a foreign direct investor from an FDI enterprise. FDI *inflows* comprise capital provided (either directly or through other related enterprises) by a foreign direct investor to an FDI enterprise in the reporting economy. Expressed in millions of United States dollars and as a percentage of GDP. **Source:** Calculated by ESCAP using data from United Nations Conference on Trade and Development, Foreign Direct Investment and National Accounts Main Aggregates database (online database accessed on 21 September 2009 and 22 October 2009).

Table 11. Official development assistance and workers' remittances

Official development assistance received. The amount of official development assistance (ODA) received in grants and loans during the reporting period, expressed in millions of United States dollars and as a percentage of the gross national income (GNI). **Source:** Calculated by ESCAP using data from Organization for Economic Co-operation and Development, Development Database on Aid from DAC Members and National Accounts Main Aggregates database (online database accessed on 2 October 2009 and 5 November 2009).

Workers' remittances received. Current transfers from abroad by migrants who are employed or intend to remain employed for more than a year in another economy in which they are considered residents, expressed in millions of United States dollars and as a percentage of gross national income (GNI). **Source:** Calculated by ESCAP using data from International Monetary Fund, Balance of Payment Statistics (CD-ROM, August 2009) and National Accounts Main Aggregates Database (online database accessed on 5 November 2009).

Table 12. International migration

Stock of foreign population. Estimated number of international immigrants, male and female, in the middle of the indicated year, expressed in thousands. Generally, this represents the number of persons born in a country other than where they live. **Source:** *World Migrant Stock: The 2008 Revision* population database (online database accessed on 25 August 2009).

Stock of foreign population as share of total population. The number of international immigrants divided by the total population. Expressed as a percentage in the middle of the indicated year. Where data on the place of birth was unavailable, the number of non-citizens was used as a proxy for the number of international immigrants. In either case, the migrant stock includes refugees, some of whom may not be foreign-born. **Source:** *World Migrant Stock: The 2008 Revision* population database (online database accessed on 25 August 2009).

Net migration rate. The number of international immigrants minus the number of emigrants over a period, divided by the average population of the receiving country over that period. Expressed as the net number of migrants per 1,000 population. **Source:** *World Population Prospects: The 2008 Revision* population database (online database accessed on 28 April 2009).

Table 13. Primary, secondary and tertiary education

Net enrolment ratio in primary education. The number of pupils of the theoretical school-age group for primary education, expressed as a percentage of the total population in that age group. **Source:** UNESCO Institute for Statistics, Data Centre (online database accessed on 17 November 2009).

Net enrolment ratio in secondary education. The number of pupils of the theoretical school-age group for secondary education, expressed as a percentage of the total population in that age group. **Source:** UNESCO Institute for Statistics, Data Centre (online database accessed on 28 August 2009).

Gross enrolment ratio in tertiary education. The number of pupils enrolled in the tertiary level of education, regardless of age, expressed as a percentage of the population in the theoretical age group for the same level of education. For the tertiary level, the population used is the five-year age group following on from the secondary school leaving age. **Source:** UNESCO Institute for Statistics, Data Centre (online database accessed on 10 August 2009).

Table 14. Poverty and malnutrition

Population living below $1.25 (2005 PPP) a day. The poverty rate at $1.25 a day is the proportion of the population living on less than $1.25 a day, measured at 2005 international prices, adjusted for purchasing power parity (PPP). The purchasing power parity conversion factor is the number of units of a country's currency required to buy the same amounts of goods and services in the domestic market as the United States dollar would buy in the United States. **Source:** United Nations Millennium Development Goals Indicators (online database accessed on 3 September 2009).

Population undernourished. The prevalence of (severely) underweight children, expressed as the percentage of children aged 0-59 months whose weight for age is less than minus 3 standard deviations from the median for the international reference population ages 0-59 months. **Source:** United Nations Millennium Development Goals Indicators (online database accessed on 3 September 2009).

Prevalence of underweight children. The percentage of children aged 0-59 months who fall below minus 2 standard deviations from the median weight for age of the international reference population. The international reference population, often referred to as the NCHS/WHO reference population, was formulated by the National Center for Health Statistics (NCHS) as a reference for the United States and later adopted by the World Health Organization (WHO). **Source:** United Nations Millennium Development Goals Indicators (online database accessed on 4 August 2009).

Table 15. Unemployment rate by gender and age group

Unemployment rate: total, female, male. The number of persons of working age who, during the reference period, were without work, currently available for work and seeking work, divided by the total labour force. National definitions and coverage of unemployment may vary. Data are disaggregated by sex. **Source:** Calculated by ESCAP using data from International Labour Organization, *Key Indicators of the Labour Market,* Sixth Edition (online database accessed on 14 September 2009).

Youth unemployment rate: total. The number of young persons aged 15-24 who are without work, currently available for work and seeking work, divided by the total labour force of that age group. **Source:** United Nations Millennium Development Goals Indicators (online database accessed on 27 July 2009).

Since the 1957 issue, the *Economic and Social Survey of Asia and the Pacific* has, in addition to a review of the current situation of the region, contained a study or studies of some major aspect or problem of the economies of the Asian and Pacific region, as specified below:

1957: Postwar problems of economic development

1958: Review of postwar industrialization

1959: Foreign trade of ECAFE primary exporting countries

1960: Public finance in the postwar period

1961: Economic growth of ECAFE countries

1962: Asia's trade with western Europe

1963: Imports substitution and export diversification

1964: Economic development and the role of the agricultural sector

1965: Economic development and human resources

1966: Aspects of the finance of development

1967: Policies and planning for export

1968: Economic problems of export-dependent countries. Implications of economic controls and liberalization

1969: Strategies for agricultural development. Intraregional trade as a growth strategy

1970: The role of foreign private investment in economic development and cooperation in the ECAFE region. Problems and prospects of the ECAFE region in the Second Development Decade

1971: Economic growth and social justice. Economic growth and employment. Economic growth and income distribution

1972: First biennial review of social and economic developments in ECAFE developing countries during the Second United Nations Development Decade

1973: Education and employment

1974: Mid-term review and appraisal of the International Development Strategy for the Second United Nations Development Decade in the ESCAP region, 1974

1975: Rural development, the small farmer and institutional reform

1976: Biennial review and appraisal of the International Development Strategy at the regional level for the Second United Nations Development Decade in the ESCAP region, 1976

1977: The international economic crises and developing Asia and the Pacific

1978: Biennial review and appraisal at the regional level of the International Development Strategy for the Second United Nations Development Decade

1979: Regional development strategy for the 1980s

1980: Short-term economic policy aspects of the energy situation in the ESCAP region

1981: Recent economic developments in major subregions of the ESCAP region

1982: Fiscal policy for development in the ESCAP region

1983: Implementing the International Development Strategy: major issues facing the developing ESCAP region

1984: Financing development

1985: Trade, trade policies and development

1986: Human resources development in Asia and the Pacific: problems, policies and perspectives

1987: International trade in primary commodities

1988: Recent economic and social developments

1989: Patterns of economic growth and structural transformation in the least developed and Pacific island countries of the ESCAP region: implications for development policy and planning for the 1990s

1990: Infrastructure development in the developing ESCAP region: needs, issues and policy options

1991: Challenges of macroeconomic management in the developing ESCAP region

1992: Expansion of investment and intraregional trade as a vehicle for enhancing regional economic cooperation and development in Asia and the Pacific

1993: Fiscal reform. Economic transformation and social development. Population dynamics: implications for development

1995: Reform and liberalization of the financial sector. Social security

1996: Enhancing the role of the private sector in development. The role of public expenditure in the provision of social services

1997: External financial and investment flows. Transport and communications

1998: Managing the external sector. Growth and equity

1999: Social impact of the economic crisis. Information technology, globalization, economic security and development

2000: Social security and safety nets. Economic and financial monitoring and surveillance

2001: Socio-economic implications of demographic dynamics. Financing for development

2002: The feasibility of achieving the Millennium Development Goals in Asia and the Pacific. Regional development cooperation in Asia and the Pacific

2003: The role of public expenditure in the provision of education and health. Environment-poverty nexus revisited: linkages and policy options

2004: Poverty reduction strategies: tackling the multidimensional nature of poverty

2005: Dynamics of population ageing: how can Asia and the Pacific respond?

2006: Emerging unemployment issues in Asia and the Pacific: rising to the challenges

2007: Gender inequality continues – at great cost

2008: Unequal benefits of growth – agriculture left behind

2009: Triple threats to development: food, fuel and climate change policy challenges

This publication may be obtained from bookstores and distributors throughout the world. Please consult your bookstore or write to any of the following:

Sales Section
Room DC2-0853
United Nations Secretariat
New York, NY 10017
USA

Tel: (1) (212) 963-8302
Fax: (1) (212) 963-4116
E-mail: publications@un.org

Sales Section
United Nations Office at Geneva
Palais des Nations
CH-1211 Geneva 10
Switzerland

Tel: (41) (22) 917-1234
Fax: (41) (22) 917-0123
E-mail: unpubli@unog.ch

Chief
Conference Management Unit
Conference Services Section
Administrative Services Division
Economic and Social Commission for
  Asia and the Pacific (ESCAP)
United Nations Building
Rajadamnern Nok Avenue
Bangkok 10200, Thailand

Tel: (662) 288-1234
Fax: (662) 288-1000
E-mail: yafei.unescap@un.org

For further information on publications in this series, please address your enquiries to:

Director
Macroeconomic Policy and Development Division
Economic and Social Commission for
  Asia and the Pacific (ESCAP)
United Nations Building
Rajadamnern Nok Avenue
Bangkok 10200, Thailand

Tel: (662) 288-1430
Fax: (662) 288-1000, 288-3007
E-mail: escap-mpdd@un.org

READERSHIP SURVEY

The Macroeconomic Policy and Development Division of ESCAP is undertaking an evaluation of this publication, **Economic and Social Survey of Asia and the Pacific 2010,** with a view to making future issues more useful for our readers. We would appreciate it if you could complete this questionnaire and return it, at your earliest convenience, to:

Director
Macroeconomic Policy and Development Division
ESCAP, United Nations Building
Rajadamnern Nok Avenue
Bangkok 10200, THAILAND

QUESTIONNAIRE

	Excellent	Very good	Average	Poor
1. Please indicate your assessment of the *quality* of the publication on:				
• Presentation/format	4	3	2	1
• Readability	4	3	2	1
• Timeliness of information	4	3	2	1
• Coverage of subject matter	4	3	2	1
• Analytical rigour	4	3	2	1
• Overall quality	4	3	2	1
2. How *useful* is the publication for your work?				
• Provision of information	4	3	2	1
• Clarification of issues	4	3	2	1
• Its findings	4	3	2	1
• Policy suggestions	4	3	2	1
• Overall usefulness	4	3	2	1

---

3. **Please give examples of how this publication has contributed to your work:**

....

....

....

....

4. **Suggestions for improving the publication:**

    ....

    ....

    ....

    ....

5. **Your background information, please:**

    Name: ....

    Title/position: ....

    Institution: ....

    Office address: ....

    ....

DATE DUE

Please use ad..er the questions.
Thank you f..questionnaire.

WITHDRAWN